D0250210

The Republic of
Mass Culture

DATE DUE

DEMCO 38-296

THE AMERICAN MOMENT
Stanley I. Kutler, Series Editor

THE REPUBLIC OF MASS CULTURE

Journalism, Filmmaking, and Broadcasting in America since 1941

Second Edition

James L. Baughman

The Johns Hopkins University Press

BALTIMORE AND LONDON

Riverside Community College
Library
'03
APR 4800 Magnolia Avenue
Riverside, CA 92506

P92.U5 B345 1997
Baughman, James L., 1952–
The republic of mass cultur
: journalism, filmmaking,
and broadcasting in America
since 1941

© 1992, 1997 The Johns Hopkins University Press
All rights reserved. First edition, 1992
Second edition, 1997
Printed in the United States of America on acid-free paper
06 05 04 03 02 01 00 99 98 97   5 4 3 2 1

The Johns Hopkins University Press
2715 North Charles Street
Baltimore, Maryland 21218-4319
The Johns Hopkins Press Ltd., London

"Ladies Who Lunch" by Stephen Sondheim,
© Copyright 1970 Range Road Music Inc.,
Quartet Music Inc., and Rilting Music Inc.
Used by permission. All rights reserved.
To quote from the oral history of Louis Cowan,
permission is granted by the Trustees of
Columbia University in the City of New York.

Library of Congress Cataloging-in-Publication Data
will be found at the end of this book.

A catalog record for this book is available from the British Library.

ISBN 0-8018-5520-9
ISBN 0-8018-5521-7 (pbk.)

For Bill Leuchtenburg

Contents

Series Editor's Foreword

"The Media" is a pervasive force in American life, influencing our politics, culture, families, work, and leisure. When World War II ended in 1945, Americans relied on their newspapers and radio for information; radio drama and comedy, as well as the movies, fulfilled entertainment needs. But a decade later, television had transformed the nature of the media and the habits of the audience. The changes have been nothing short of revolutionary, for both the media and the society.

Television is the dominant media force, whether measured by audience numbers, commercial success, or cultural influence. Print media, radio, and movies are fragmented in their audience appeal, although each component has carved out its own niche and measure of success. But television's visual images, readily available and easy to understand, give it a decided edge over its media rivals. Its immediacy and intimacy seem especially matched to American tastes.

In *The Republic of Mass Culture*, James L. Baughman offers the raw material for a critical analysis of the phenomenon. Do the media, particularly television, threaten or enhance our cultural diversity? Has the impact of the mass media led to a homogenization of politics and culture, reducing ideas and entertainment to a mass common denominator? Do media have a biased political stance? Do media unduly project what the historian Daniel Boorstin has called "pseudo-events," that is unimportant, trivial, often artificially contrived matters that demand our intense attention for the moment? Media analyst Marshall McLuhan once said that the "medium is the message." Have we lost contact with the reality of substance?

Yet Baughman signals a cautionary warning that we not magnify the media's influence. Were the media the primary animating force in turning the nation against the Vietnam War, for example? Should the media receive the lion's share of credit for uncovering the crimes of Watergate and bringing Richard Nixon to account? Too often, as Baughman notes, media celebrants and critics alike exaggerate their role.

Still, historians of modern America must acknowledge, analyze, and incorporate the workings of the media into their narratives of society. Baughman has sifted this immense history with care and has thoughtfully charted some guidelines for such understanding. His account is more than a mere catalogue of media history; instead, he has deftly woven that record of events, achievements, and failings into the backdrop of the larger societal picture. In sum, Baughman has enriched our knowledge of that record, and his work vitally informs other segments of American life, including our politics, economy, culture, and values.

Stanley I. Kutler
The University of Wisconsin

Acknowledgments

Friends, family, and students, not all of them listed here, helped me complete this book. Some assisted me directly with insights, citations, and copies of materials. Others suffered through some of my tentative conclusions about the American mass media in our time and tried or succeeded in changing my mind.

Of my colleagues at the School of Journalism and Mass Communication, I am especially grateful to William B. Blankenburg, Robert Drechsel, Tom Grimes, Robert Hawkins, Arthur Hove, James L. Hoyt, Robert W. McChesney, Diana Mutz, Charles T. Salmon, and Stephen Vaughn. Andrew Feldman, Betsy Krueger, Karen Miller, and Todd Wixson gathered some materials for me, while Brian Deith saved my computer from abuse on numerous occasions. Students in my Cold War and the Press seminar confirmed and upset some assumptions, while Jeff Hart, for another class, alerted me to the literature on the press and the Japanese-American internment. However, no one is to be praised more than Cindy Schkirkie, who ably prepared the first half of the manuscript in addition to performing other related tasks. Cindy never lost her sense of humor, despite dealing with some seemingly deranged faculty.

Many friends aided me as well, including Tino Balio, Andre T. Baughman, Harvey Black, James Danky, Diane Levesque, Paul Moskowitz, Jay Rath, Nora Schaeffer, Lucinda Tiajoloff, and Kate Wittenberg. Paul DiMaggio and Vera Zolberg provided me with important citations on the sociology of popular music. Gregory Black sent me copies of two excellent papers he had prepared on the Production Code Administration; I also drew upon a fine unpublished study by Giacomo

L. Ortizano on music censorship in the 1950s. Back home, John McDonald, hosting a local rock 'n' roll radio program, provided weekly instruction. Also to be thanked are Phyllis and Ness Flores, who rented me their cottage on Green Bay, where I began composing the manuscript. Peet's Coffee and Tea and, during baseball season, Doug Jones, relief ace of the Cleveland Indians, greatly inspired me.

Phil Ranlet read and commented on the entire manuscript, while Steven H. Chaffee, John M. Cooper, Jr., and David P. Schuyler reviewed parts of the work. Joanne Allen skillfully copy-edited everything. All offered valuable counsel, for which I thank them.

I am grateful to Stanley Kutler and Henry Tom for their faith in me and this enterprise. I hope that the end product is worth their confidence and that the dedication to the greatest historian I have ever known is no discredit.

Many of those who helped me with the first edition of this book continued to be of assistance. For this edition, I need to thank still more colleagues, students and friends, including Carla B. Baughman, Joseph Champ, Lewis Friedland, William A. Hachten, Steven Frye, Roger Rathke, Julie Reckamp, Phil Rosenthal, Sheila Webb, and Bob Wolfley. I am especially grateful to David MacLaren McDonald for reading chapter ten, and to Celestia Ward of the Johns Hopkins University Press for overseeing this edition's preparation. Finally, no one has been more important and supportive in the second edition of my life than Michele M. Michuda.

Introduction

During the second half of the twentieth century, the American mass media underwent an extraordinary transformation. A new mass medium, television, quickly proved the most popular of the public arts. Americans who had once spent their evenings using a variety of mass media—films, newspapers, periodicals, and radio—were likely by the mid and late 1950s to watch television. People still went to the movie house, read a daily paper or a magazine, and listened to a radio program, but the amount of time they devoted to each activity declined, in some cases dramatically.

Although the established mass media's managers had anticipated television's arrival, the rapidity with which TV came to dominate what might be called the "republic" of mass culture presented them with a severe challenge. Before the late 1940s, when regular network telecasts and a boom in TV set sales began, radio, motion pictures, newspapers, and magazines had enjoyed a rough equality. Americans might prefer, surveys suggested, radio to the printed page or a feature film, yet they subscribed to one or two dailies and continued to patronize, often twice a week or more, the neighborhood or downtown theater. This equilibrium was forever upset by TV's advent. Most American homes had television sets by the late 1950s, and to the surprise of some competitors for consumers' spare time, the newest medium did not lose its hold. Television proved to be no novelty: in most households, TV viewing continued to be a nightly experience long past the first year or two of set ownership. This permanence in effect transformed the established mass media into secondary activities for most Americans. And after much trial and error, each medium eventually ceased competing with television for the largest audience. Each developed strategies that would allow it to prosper in an age dominated by the "home screen."

In describing this transformation, this work emphasizes the institutions that collectively constituted the major mass media in the second half of the twentieth century: newspapers, magazines, radio, television, and motion pictures. Their "products," broadcast programming, filmmaking, popular music, and journalism, receive less consideration. Such an organizational bias has its logic. Although audience demand, to be sure, plays a major role in determining what the producer presents, various other factors, often involving competition and its effects on demand, influence the mass communicator.

One justification for an emphasis on the communicator comes from sociologists studying the emergence of rock 'n' roll in the 1950s. As television robbed radio of much of the adult audience, desperate station managers began airing music that appealed to a smaller body of adolescent listeners. Before TV, the teenage market had been deemed too small to warrant substantial airtime. Thus, the historian of popular music should attribute only so much of the new sound's success to the skills of singer Elvis Presley and his songwriters. There were undoubtedly other Presleys a decade or two earlier who, because of the attitudes of music publishers and radio's operators, were denied access to the airwaves. Television had forced radio to attend to audience "subgroups."

TV's effects on the motion picture industry similarly shaped the content of films. The biblical epics Hollywood made with enthusiasm in the 1950s might reflect the new religiosity of the American middle class; it is more probable, however, that the movie colony produced such films because their scale—elaborate sets, costumes, and special effects, including the parting of the Red Sea in one picture—dwarfed anything then being offered on television. Two decades later, the filmmakers' abandonment of codes that had forbidden the use of certain words or portrayal of nudity could be related to Hollywood's perception that Americans had adopted a new, less repressed attitude toward sexual relations. More likely, moviemakers regarded the new realism as a competitive advantage over television, which because of its far larger and more diverse audience, had to honor the older morality by having characters fully clothed and obscenity-free.

Any extended discussion of mass culture must also come to terms with its influence. At no time in their history have Americans taken the mass media and their "stars" so seriously. Politicians in particular behave as if Americans do nothing but watch television and derive every opinion from a TV advertisement or news program. Television's very presence in virtually all American households, as well as advertising's invasion of practically every sphere, reinforces an image of omnipotence.

Almost all formal investigations acknowledge that some subgroups can be swayed by certain mass-produced images. Those who watch a great deal of television, so-called "heavy viewers," are often left feeling passive, less mentally alert. Many viewers ascribe more significance to social or political crises that are highlighted on TV news and judge political leaders by their ability to deal with such problems. Carefully crafted commercial messages can affect large numbers of consumers. A well-produced advertisement can cause many to try a product (or can reinforce their loyalty to a brand) or regard a candidate for public office more sympathetically. More sensitive treatments of minority groups, on television or in films, can alter the attitudes of *some* viewers.

Yet the numbers of consumers and the ease with which they can be manipulated by the mass media should not be overstated. On command, TV cannot drive millions to extreme antisocial behavior, nor can advertising hypnotize legions of consumers and voters. The great majority carry in their heads different individual filters—fashioned by class, race or ethnicity, family upbringing, formal education—that limit the effectiveness of mass communication. A child being raised in a stable and loving environment is not about to mimic the villain in an especially violent TV program. If another child, in a very different family setting, does turn sadistic, he or she is likely to suffer from a psychological imbalance, which the television episode only untapped. An ardent, third-generation Democrat will probably jeer rather than be converted by a slick ad for a Republican presidential candidate. The audience, Raymond A. Bauer wrote, "selects what it will attend to. Since people generally listen to and read things they are interested in, these usually are topics on which they have a good deal of information and fixed opinions. Hence, the very people most likely to attend to a message are those most difficult to change; those who can be converted do not look or listen." "Sometimes, it is true," remarked sociologist W. Phillips Davison. "the manipulator is able to lead his audience into a bad bargain by emphasizing one need at the expense of another or by representing a change in the significant environment as greater than it actually has been. But audiences, too, can drive a hard bargain. Many communicators who have been widely disregarded or misunderstood know that to their cost."

Alas, many who comment on the mass media in modern America give the audience little credit. In some cases, ideological needs take precedence. A loser's bitterness, a groping for a larger, invidious cause, distorts analyses. Conservatives and evangelical Protestants, despite many political and cultural triumphs in the 1980s, failed to restore an older morality regarding sex, the family, and "lifestyle." And they blame mass entertainment for what they construe to be looser moral codes. President Ronald Reagan, once a film star, accused his previous employers of having glamorized casual drug use. Liberals, in contrast, fault the mass media and especially political advertising for their electoral setbacks. Some go further: American journalism, they aver, consciously avoids subjects and solutions hazardous to "late capitalism." According to these critics, the mainstream news media uphold existing power structures by ignoring or trivializing certain issues. Even the popular arts could be attacked for their "escapism" or proclivity, as Todd Gitlin has observed in his essay on the TV movie, for treating crises as the result of individual decisions and not social inequalities. In such speculations, the power of the mass media is implied, and beyond proof. The mass media need only cover or deal seriously with given issues and citizens will follow their lead to a new and better world. The possibility that most consumers essentially prefer existing arrangements or would ignore a didactic social realism in entertainment and information is not broached.

More ideologically neutral observers have decried the mass media's effects on democracy. Upset by the declining percentage of Americans who vote, political scientists have accused TV news of undermining self-government by limiting its coverage of political campaigns to short "sound bites." Because it stresses "who's ahead" rather than who will do what about a problem, broadcast news has been charged with causing citizens to feel like spectators, watching rather than participating in democracy's rituals.

Such attributions of influence do not inform this study. By definition, mass media–centered explanations for political apathy or moral laxity fail to give other possibilities sufficient weight. Nor should the audience be denied its ultimate sovereignty. What people actually watched, and why, must be considered. Before investing great power in network TV news, for example, the relatively small numbers of Americans who regularly view such programming should be noted. Moreover, recent studies, suggesting that people who watch TV news are often inattentive or distracted, must be taken into account. Before being too scornful of popular preferences for melodrama or certain rock musicians, the critic must realize that individuals bring to encounters with mass culture very personal needs or associations. The consumers' reasons for admiring or hissing a performance can differ sharply. Observing the television viewing habits of Italian-Americans in Boston's West

End in 1957–58, sociologist Herbert Gans was among the first to make this point. "West Enders accept themes that mirror their own values, and reject others as illustrating the immorality and dishonesty of the outside world." Thirty years later, ethnographers interviewing consumers of mass culture offer a similar appreciation of the audience's diversity. Ethnographic studies, John Fiske writes, "trace differences amongst viewers, modes of viewing, and the meaning or pleasures produced." Ethnography "acknowledges the differences between people despite their social construction, and pluralizes the meanings and pleasures that they find in television."

Although television's influence on American society will long be debated, the nation's popular cultural institutions can be said to have changed significantly in response to television. Indeed, the effects that can be demonstrated are institutional, not social. Some of TV's rivals adjusted quickly to the challenge of the home screen; others showed what in retrospect appears to have been an almost self-destructive indifference. But nearly all came to adopt a common anti-TV strategy. Recognizing television's capture of the mass audience, most began cultivating the subgroup, segments of the audience denoted by such factors as class, education, or age. In time, even cable television drew upon this tactic to reduce network TV's power.

Describing American mass culture before the advent of television is this work's first purpose. In chapter 1, the mass media's role in World War II is briefly noted to convey its self-conscious place in American society and to understand the news media's supportive role in the selling of the cold war with the Soviet Union after 1945. Chapter 2 carries forward these themes, outlining the rough equality of film, radio, and the printed page, while describing in greater detail the ways Americans used their mass media. Chapter 3 continues the history of the mass media in the late 1940s and early 1950s, ending with the coming of television. The differing responses of sectors of the mass media through the 1950s and Hollywood's partial capture of TV production are reviewed in chapter 4. Network television's dominance of American mass culture in the 1960s and 1970s is discussed in chapters 5 and 7, while chapters 6 and 8 deal with TV's rivals between 1960 and 1990. Chapter 9 is primarily concerned with the decline of network television, and the possibility that everything will change again.

The Republic of
Mass Culture

THE VOLUNTARY PROPAGANDISTS 1

WORLD WAR II, despite its inconveniences for many and heartaches for some, was good for the businesses that constituted the American mass media. Between the attack on Pearl Harbor in 1941 and V-J Day nearly four years later, people found themselves unusually dependent on mass-produced diversion and information. They bought more newspapers and magazines, listened to more radio broadcasts, and attended more films. And their use of a variety of mass media suggested their rough equality; Americans did not rely disproportionately or exclusively on one medium over another.

Such popularity carried its price. In 1940s America, all of the mass media were self-conscious instruments. With ready access to what critic Gilbert Seldes called "the great audience," they were loath to offend any well-organized subgroup of the population. The mass media were, after all, producing culture for everyone: people of all ages, many deeply committed to traditional moral values, regularly listened to popular music on the radio or attended a film. Most mass communicators similarly proved unusually mindful of the federal government. Indeed, during the war the mass media made common cause with the government and became voluntary propagandists. In some cases, what the government could not achieve freely came after a threat, sometimes implied, sometimes explicit. Few in the communication industries complained; the war was broadly backed, and neither the press nor any other mass medium had pretensions to being a true fourth branch of government or an independent force in America's political culture.

The war itself upset peacetime advertising and production patterns within the information media. Manpower shortages forced newspapers to follow other industries in hiring more women. Paper rationing compelled dailies to reduce their size and refuse some advertising. Many companies, permitted to deduct advertising expenses from their corporate income taxes, expanded their purchases of airtime on network radio, which allowed it to recover the costs of expanded news programming.

With millions of Americans in uniform, many felt obligated to follow the war's course. The circulations of newspapers and newsmagazines rose. Two New York women told sociologist Bernard Berelson in 1945 that "they forced themselves to read the war news, as the least they could do in prosecuting the war." Radio news was the major beneficiary of this new conscientiousness. Regarded primarily as cheap and convenient entertainment in the mid thirties, radio assumed a new role on the eve of the Second World War. More and more turned to radio for the latest bulletins on the crisis in Europe; some began to buy second, "portable" receivers for their kitchens and bedrooms.

Although radio continued to devote most hours to entertainment, it did become relatively more serious. According to Mitchell V. Charnley, the percentage of network evening programming given to news and informational programming rose from 6 percent in the winter of 1938–39 to 18 percent the winter of 1943–44. There were special war-related initiatives as well. For eighteen hours on the Columbia Broadcasting System (CBS) network on September 21, 1943, the popular singer and radio star Kate Smith urged Americans to buy war bonds. Smith's pleas resulted in some $39 million worth of pledges. Entertainment shows played their part by flavoring scripts with bits of prowar commentary and by reminding listeners that the sacrifices of some were not unique but widely shared. The war became a constant reference or a serious aside in comedians' monologues; in daytime serials it was a cause for a loved one's absence. The husband of Mary Noble of "Backstage Wife" enlisted in the Coast Guard; the son of Ma Perkins joined the infantry and died in battle.

The war also appeared to confirm radio's advantages as an information medium. Newspapers could not compete with radio in providing up-to-the-minute bulletins. Nor did daily papers in many communities appear to be trustworthy messengers. By the late 1930s, most newspapers had become sharp editorial critics of, if not crusaders against, the liberal reform measures of President Franklin D. Roosevelt. Especially among the working classes, newspapers had become suspect mediators. More well-to-do but progressive readers were no more trusting. Living in a community served by the ferociously anti-Roosevelt *Chicago Tribune*, Chancellor of the University of Chicago Robert M. Hutchins concluded, "Newspapers cannot be relied on to present an unbiased account of events." Radio, in contrast, offered the voice of the president and his supporters and the unfiltered sensation of "being there," of hearing the Ohio River floodwaters or the explosion of the airship *Hindenburg* in 1937. Thus for many Americans, memories of the German air force's fierce attacks on London in 1940 were not of newspaper photographs or a correspondent's written account of a given raid but of radio reporter Edward R. Murrow's deep and halting voice, live from Britain, speaking as the bombs fell. Murrow, Librarian of Congress Archibald MacLeish declared, "burned the city of London in our houses and we felt the flames that burned it." He "laid the dead of London at our doors and we knew the dead were our dead—were all men's dead." Murrow's broadcasts "destroyed the superstition of distance."

Radio benefited from such a pseudo-intimacy. News commentaries lacked the intelligence or depth of the best newspaper columns. But for many, the fact that one could hear the voice of an H. V. Kaltenborn gave him more authority than a Raymond Clapper, whose words one could only read. No newspaper account of Roosevelt's funeral in April 1945 had the emotional power of the broadcast by CBS's Arthur Godfrey, who lost control and began to weep on the air as the president's body passed him on Pennsylvania Avenue. Many of those tuning to Kate Smith's radio bond drive were sure that the singer was speaking directly to them. Smith's folksiness, sociologist Robert K. Merton suggested, created an electronic "community" or "pseudo-Gemeinschaft," the modern-day equivalent of a barn raising or quilting bee.

All in all, the war encouraged an overestimation of network radio's impact. For example, only 2–4 percent of Kate Smith's audience, Raymond A. Bauer noted, actually pledged to donate to her bond drive. Nevertheless, many working in radio, especially radio news, became immodest about their hold on the public. On the eve of Germany's surrender in 1945, Murrow cried to his colleagues, "We've seen what radio can do for the nation in war. Now let's go back to show what we can do in peace!" Yet even during the war, most listeners preferred local newscasts to the network reports of Murrow and others. And Murrow's medium had not, after all, prevented global conflict. In 1941, the *Minneapolis Tribune* had mournfully observed that radio, "crowning so many other advances in the field of improved communications . . . should have ushered in the era when, with distance annihilated, the world was just one happy family. It will take more than scientific advance to achieve that idyllic state."

Nor did radio's supposed dominance in the republic of mass culture go unchallenged. On a given day, more Americans looked at a newspaper than listened to a radio newscast. How many and how thoroughly they read their papers varied by class, region, and political affiliation. Some, as before, merely scanned the headlines of national and international stories, devoting most of their attention to the paper's "features," the comic pages, local news items, and the latest baseball box scores. A readership study of the *Canton* (Ohio) *Repository* conducted by the Advertising Research Foundation in 1940 suggested that three times as many people looked at the comic strip "Popeye" as read the syndicated columnist Walter Lippmann. Still another wartime diversion was the movie house. Because gas rationing and lower speed limits restricted much traveling, the simplest escape from work and home often was two or three visits a week to the neighborhood or downtown theater.

Hollywood and other cultural industries did not merely entertain. Collectively they sought to inculcate into Americans a voluntary totalitarianism, that dedication which Pericles had instilled in Athenians during the Peloponnesian War and which made modern democracies so much more difficult to overcome than their adversaries had anticipated. "The reason you won and we lost," an aide to Hitler remarked, "was that you made total war and we did not." American popular magazines, in cooperation with the Magazine Bureau of the government's Office of War Information (OWI), ran short stories encouraging women to heed government appeals for rationing and to replace men in factories. Such work, writers cautioned readers, should be regarded as temporary, necessitated by manpower shortages. With peace near, the same periodicals promoted household engineering and childrearing. Morale was a primary mission as well. For many a postadolescent male in uniform, a *Life* magazine cover of an attractive young actress or model did wonders for the soul. Some five million GIs carried or posted pin-ups of film star Betty Grable, thought to have the best legs in the movie colony. On various fronts American soldiers and sailors viewed films and listened to American songs on Armed Forces Radio. Occasionally, an actor or radio comedian like Bob Hope showed up with a USO troupe. Hope had no trouble drawing an audience: during a 1945 tour, six hundred soldiers marched ten miles to see one of his shows. Hope and others, like their predecessors a generation earlier, actively encouraged Americans to buy war bonds. Film actress Carole Lombard died in an air crash following a successful 1942 rally; her agent had begged her to take the train. Others in their enthusiasm only jeopardized their reputation. Film actor and director Charlie Chaplin gave speeches on behalf of America's ally, the Soviet Union, addresses that contributed to his going into voluntary exile in 1952. By then, the Soviet Union had become the enemy Hitler's Germany had been.

Younger and overwhelmingly male stars, together with many more industry employees, by comparison mere credit lines at the end of a feature, joined the armed forces. Wartime service permanently disrupted some careers carefully nurtured by the studios in the years just before Pearl Harbor. In their places actors with physical deferments such as Hope and John Wayne had their names on a thousand more marquees. Most stars in the armed forces never saw action. The War Department considered even such a relatively minor player as Ronald Reagan more valuable featured in Signal Corps films than as cannon fodder. Some, such as Jimmy Stewart, Clark Gable, and Robert Montgomery, did force themselves in harm's way, as did directors John Ford and John Huston, photographing documentaries for the services. The relatively anonymous writers and technicians were most likely to meet the enemy. A screenwriter died leading a group of Army Rangers assaulting a German fortress at Brest. His baby daughter was christened Jo Victory. Stateside, some suffered unexpected risks. Actress Gene Tierney contracted German measles while doing volunteer work at the Hollywood canteen for soldiers and sailors and gave birth to a deformed baby.

The stars of the information media, on the other hand, were paid to face such dangers. Perhaps none risked more than photographers, whose determination to be at the scene of battle made World War II the first "living room war." Radio broadcasters, too, took their chances, flying with the U.S. Air Force on bomber missions. Thirty-four correspondents—thirty-three men and one woman—died covering the war. Airborne in the Pacific, Raymond Clapper, perhaps the nation's most widely read columnist, never returned; resting in his typewriter as he departed was the journalist's line of continuation, "MORE TO COME." Elsewhere in the Pacific, a Japanese sniper took the life of correspondent Ernie Pyle, whose plain, unpretentious dispatches, in which he always listed the hometowns of the servicemen he featured, had personalized the conflict for millions.

Cooperation, if sometimes strained, usually characterized relations between the government and the press. In the first months of war, with the Allies losing on most fronts, the federal government imposed restrictions on coverage of the conflict and contemplated actions against some critics of the Roosevelt administration. Photographs and newsreel shots of American dead were initially forbidden so as not to hurt morale. The Navy seized unusually graphic Fox Movietone newsreel footage of the attack on Pearl Harbor and delayed its release for a year, when it was heavily censored. When the *Chicago Tribune's* coverage of the Battle of Midway in 1942 indicated that America had broken the Japanese secret code, the Department of Justice tried to prosecute the Midwest's largest daily, which was, not coincidentally, Roosevelt's most prominent editorial critic. FBI agents that year attempted to intimidate black newspaper publishers angry over the government's laggard civil rights policy. Yet most of the American news media escaped such confrontations. Fully supportive of the war, they regarded government controls as more of a nuisance than a threat and took it upon themselves to police their ranks. Early in 1942, with Germany and Japan seemingly winning everywhere, the National Association of Broadcasters urged the newscasters of member stations not to use the transitional sentence "Now for some good news." With more than 11 million men and women in uniform by 1945, few in the fourth estate challenged a request to kill, or "spike," stories considered dangerous to national security. The press voluntarily agreed not to report the detonation of Japanese balloon bombs in the western United States or research on atomic weaponry in Tennessee.

Newspapers uniformly endorsed the government's internment of one hundred ten thousand Japanese-Americans living on the West Coast in 1942. Immediately after the attack on Pearl Harbor, few dailies had questioned the loyalty of Japanese-Americans; editorials had dismissed fears that they might constitute a fifth column. Even in California, with its legacy of racism toward those of Asian descent, editorial writers had defended the patriotism of Japanese-Americans. But after an orchestrated campaign by some in the Roosevelt administration, journalists, led by nationally syndicated columnists Drew Pearson and Walter Lippmann, favored placing Japanese-Americans into what President Roosevelt himself dubbed "concentration camps." "In this fight we cannot pussyfoot," the *San Francisco Chronicle*, perhaps the state's most prominent liberal daily, declared in February 1942. "We have to be tough, even if civil rights do take a beating for a time."

From the beginning of hostilities, most combat reporters found themselves being treated as virtual junior partners of the military and naval commands. "This disposition to take American newspapermen into full confidence was typical throughout the armed services during the war," recalled Turner Catledge of the *New York Times*. Indeed, Army units, anxious for publicity, competed for the attentions of correspondents and photographers. To the U.S. commander in Italy, cracked one wag, "war was the pursuit of publicity by other means." Back home, Americans began occasionally to see pictures of their dead, though regulations, out of respect for loved ones, still forbade showing their faces.

Early in 1945 *Life* ran a series of pictures by Robert Capa showing an American soldier, his face covered by a black insert, being shot and killed by a German sniper. The caption read, "Blood starts flowing from the soldier's forehead forming pool on floor. He died instantaneously."

For all their attempts at realism, however, *Life* and other publications did not begin to capture the deeply disquieting realities of the conflict. Death was ennobled and neat. Readers did not see the disfigured corpses of American servicemen or learn of soldiers' being struck by the body parts of platoon buddies. Such aspects of modern warfare went unreported. "The letterpress correspondents, radio broadcasters, and film people who perceived these horrors kept quiet about them on behalf of the War Effort," Paul Fussell, himself a combat veteran, observed years later. The fourth estate chose to ignore or explain away incompetently led or executed offensives. "Most military operations are examples of 'organized insanity,'" Fussell wrote, "but the morale of the home front must not be jeopardized by an eye-witness saying so." When U.S. bombers mistakenly killed 136 American troops near Saint-Lô in 1944, Pyle argued, "Anybody makes mistakes." "'Precision bombing,'" Fussell noted, "became a comical oxymoron relished by bomber crews with a sense of black humor. It became obvious to everyone except the home folks reading *Life* and the *Saturday Evening Post* that although you could destroy lots of things with bombs, they weren't necessarily the things you had in mind."

Hollywood, too, joined hands with the government. Even before America's participation in the war, the movie industry had begun to produce films like *Watch on the Rhine*, criticizing Germany, and *Sergeant York*, celebrating preparedness. The war itself inspired various combat features. Newsreels treated the Allied cause and conduct of the fighting uncritically. None challenged war as national policy. The enemy became a stereotype. Warner Brothers's popular cartoon rabbit accepted the charge in "Bugs Bunny Nips the Nips." To explain the rise of the fascist dictators, director Frank Capra modeled his documentary *Prelude to War* after the 1930s gangster films. "*Prelude* was, in essence, a morality play," historian Richard W. Steele wrote. It "reinforced the simplistic dichotomies Americans were prone to make about international affairs, and left Americans fundamentally naive on the issues of war and peace, and the nature of the American way."

In most instances, the movie colony's manufacture of such images was spontaneous. The five major newsreel companies proved unusually cooperative. Hollywood mirrored the nation in its support for the war. Yet public relations mattered as well: self-conscious about their place in a society dominated by cultural "guardians" suspicious of show-business types, filmmakers sought to appear as committed as the rest of America. That imperative to conform notwithstanding, occasionally the government involved itself in wartime filmmaking. Hollywood did not suffer from censorship per se as much as from the power of suggestion. If not formally subject to federal oversight, the motion picture industry did take with a deadly seriousness "recommendations" from Washington. Some were defensible, such as when government officials endorsed the National Association for the Advancement of Colored People's demand that blacks be treated in a more favorable light. The image of the comic, shiftless male was dropped or softened. Other government-supported projects proved embarrassing, such as when the movie colony offered features hailing the Soviet Union. Perhaps the most notorious of these efforts, *Mission to Moscow*, justified almost every excess of Russia under Joseph Stalin. To philosopher John Dewey, the film represented "the first instance in our country of totalitarian propaganda for mass consumption—a propaganda which falsifies history through distortion, omission or pure invention of facts."

Finally, the war allowed the federal government to postpone the introduction of what promised to be the most popular of new communication technologies. In the 1930s the nation's largest producer of radio receivers, the Radio Corporation of America (RCA), had invested heavily in developing "radio with eyes," the transmitting through radio waves of pictures that could be received by sets in the home much as radios picked up aural signals. Beginning in 1939, RCA began to promote its "television" system over those of smaller rivals. In a vigorous campaign, RCA promoted TV at the 1939 World's Fair in New York and experimented with telecasts of baseball games from New York and portions of the 1940 Republican National Convention from Philadelphia. The ultimate success of RCA's process, however, rested with the nation's broadcast authority, the Federal Communications Commission (FCC), which established transmittal standards and allocated space on the radio spectrum. Chairman James Lawrence Fly refused to bend to RCA's pressures. Fly insisted that with America at war, TV's advocates should return to their laboratories. Those few, including President Roosevelt, who had RCA sets, had to view civil defense programs.

Peace promised an end to such foot-dragging, suggestions, and demands by the federal government. The American mass media, less regulated than those in any other democratic nation, could return to prewar patterns and, in the case of those gambling on television, hope for a new and financially lucrative communication technology.

AMERICANS AND THEIR   2
MASS MEDIA IN 1945

As HOSTILITIES with Germany and Japan ended in 1945, the production and consumption of the mass media in America assumed definite forms, many of which predated the war. Demand possessed a predictability that cheered the film producer, the radio station owner, and the editor of a daily paper or magazine. Although to varying degrees operators of mass media faced challenges, each had cause for confidence. People took in fewer movies, listened to less news as opposed to entertainment on the radio, and were more likely to skip those parts of a daily paper that dealt with national and international events. Yet a rough equality among the mass media remained. Most adult Americans continued to read newspapers regularly, and at least once a week they went to a movie house. Nightly, the radio created vast communities of listeners.

Daily Rituals

Daily newspapers constituted the oldest and most widely consumed mass medium. Publishers in the late nineteenth century had greatly broadened "news" to encompass the nonpolitical—human interest stories, sports, gossip, fashion, comics. This extended agenda, along with sharp cuts in newspaper prices, had created for most Americans the habit of taking one or more dailies. Editors also fostered an identity with place, which made their paper appear to be a necessity for the many who sought an association with their community or an awareness of local happenings. Heavily laden with area news, most dailies gave residents the sensation, sometimes illusionary, that they knew all that

9

mattered about their town. In the larger cities, newspaper reading, aside from easing commutes in crowded trolleys, played to the fascination with the bizarre goings on of a great metropolis. In smaller towns, newspapers cultivated the localistic by formalizing gossip. Births and deaths enjoyed the dignity of published announcement.

A community's size and location closely related to a newspaper's circulation. Fewer southerners than midwesterners, for example, read newspapers. The size of the village, town, or city similarly affected circulation. In the mid 1940s just under one-third of the population lived in cities of 100,000 or more residents; another third lived in towns of 2,500 to 100,000, and still another third lived in villages of fewer than 2,500 people. Country weeklies or dailies published in a nearby town served farmers and villagers, who were for various reasons, including lower literacy rates, among the least likely to read a newspaper regularly. Many residents of big cities, whether because of illiteracy or poverty, similarly did not buy dailies. Some were shared or retrieved from trash bins. Paper carriers were busiest in such medium-sized locales as Wichita, Kansas. In Paducah, Kentucky, in early 1947, with a population of about 40,000, 97 percent of all households took the local daily, the *Sun Democrat*.

Location set the filling of the paper's columns or "news hole." The smallest papers found it wise to get every resident's name in the paper, listing such passing occurrences as cookie bakes and visiting cousins. In contrast, big-city patrons of the lavishly illustrated tabloids were treated to the weird murders and stunts more likely to occur in densely populated centers. In the "tabs," serious political news received relatively little attention compared with that paid to sensational crimes; entertainment value largely defined news.

Most dailies emphasized breaking stories, that is, ones about something that had just happened, reconstructed in a rigid structure developed by the national wire services, led by the Associated Press (AP). Reporters composed stories in accord with a formula news syndication services had developed over the decades, with the most important facts given in the first paragraph, or "lead." Usually jammed with qualification, leads could be hard to read and were almost invariably inelegant. Russell Baker remembered a colleague at the *Baltimore Sun* in the late 1940s who "wrote in blunt, graceless sentences and paragraphs that made no music but seemed to be written with a sledgehammer."

Despite surveys suggesting that consumers wanted more readable copy, publishers avoided change. Many papers did introduce analyses of news in the form of weekly reviews and daily commentaries, but only after the success of the newsweekly *Time* indicated a large middle-class audience for synthesis. On the whole, newspapers resisted innovation. They retained the eight-column-per-page layout developed in the late nineteenth century; and status-conscious editors, who associated photographs with the tabloids and their working-class readers, still greatly preferred the word over the illustration.

All in all, newspaper publishers in the mid and late 1940s conveyed a complacency that owed the most to the condition of the market. In most medium-sized and small cities and towns, the typical newspaper publisher no longer had a competitor or even the prospect of one. The high cost of new presses and paper made starting a daily, even in the largest market, a relatively poor investment. Instead, newspapers had begun to amalgamate into hyphenated entities. Big cities usually had two or more dailies, one coming out in the evening and one in the morning, with publishers able to carve the market by class. The Brahmin at South Station in Boston read the blue-blood Republican *Herald Traveler* as a bootblack shined his wingtips, a copy of the *Boston Post* holed under the chair. In New York, Chicago, Boston, Philadelphia, and Washington, demand proved sufficient to sustain two papers serving similar classes of different parties. Republican civil servants in Washington could read the *Star*, while their Democratic counterparts pored over the *Post*.

Papers were closely read in the late 1940s. Subscribers devoted about twenty minutes to reading their dailies. Most Americans took an evening paper, and before or after supper, in a favored seat, gave their daily a thorough examination. Although the radio might provide background noise, the paper was the major object of attention. Many carefully folded and refolded the paper to check across and down each page. Not all readers read every section or story, and relatively few looked at those with an international dateline. The war's end had quieted much of the interest in foreign news. Then, too, men were three times as likely as women to read the sports section; the self-conscious maleness of sports reporting discouraged the female reader.

The relative provincialism of readers proved an even more powerful predictor of what they read in a paper. Perhaps three-fourths of America's newspaper readers, dubbed "metropolitans" by sociologist Robert K. Merton, preferred local news. A smaller class of readers, "cosmopolitans," read national and international stories, as well as the analytical columns of such commentators as Walter Lippmann and David Lawrence. During the war, cosmopolitans not only followed overseas news but might post a map in their studies and attach flags tracing the advance of Allied armies. Cosmopolitans included business men and women with a direct financial stake in national and world developments, as well as better-educated professionals, high-school civics teachers, and town librarians, who were regarded as (or considered themselves to be) "opinion leaders" to friends and neighbors.

Cosmopolitans often took a second newspaper, as well as magazines covering and analyzing politics and government. In small towns, a cosmopolitan read the local daily as well as the most "respected" newspaper in the nearest large city. A Republican cosmopolitan in northeastern Wisconsin's Fox River Valley subscribed to his local paper and the conservative *Chicago Tribune*. A then overdeveloped railroad network made same-day delivery of a big-city daily possible for a large section of the country. In 1945, eastern Montanans could get the *Minneapolis Tribune*; and although they were more than five hundred miles from Gotham, Ohioans could buy the daily *New York Times* and *Herald Tribune*.

Because America, unlike other developed nations, lacked national newspapers–the nation was too vast and technology was too primitive to permit the publication and delivery of a single daily nationwide— the cosmopolitan had to settle for a big-city daily. Only a relative few— the *New York Times*, the *New York Herald Tribune*, and the *Chicago Daily News*—provided substantial national and international coverage. Other metropolitan papers, such as the *Milwaukee Journal*, the *Philadelphia Bulletin*, and the *Los Angeles Times*, were chronically provincial. "Measured against the best newspapers of the East and Midwest," Marshall Berges wrote, the *Los Angeles Times* "was arguably a narrow, parochial paper, boosting its friends and denouncing its enemies. There was no fine-arts section, no Sunday opinion or business section, no wide-open window on Washington or the world. The best items were wire service stories and canned features bought from syndicates."

The *Chicago Tribune* and dailies owned by William Randolph Hearst combined provincialism and prejudice. Hearst was one of the last big-city publishers to regard his newspapers as forums for his personal opinions and eccentricities. And he had come to be the most hated figure in American journalism. "As a stimulator of mob passions and a perverter of plain facts for the purposes of fomenting murder," wrote one left-wing critic in 1935, Hearst "has had no superior since Caligula." In Chicago, Colonel Robert R. McCormick, publisher of the *Tribune*, inspired a similar rancor, and dread. Reporters at the *Tribune* understood that their stories should not contradict the views of the paper's owner. "A single phrase from the Colonel," Lloyd Wendt wrote in his history of the *Tribune*, "could generate not only an editorial pleasing to him but a campaign of months' duration." McCormick's cousin Cissy Patterson, publisher of the *Washington Times-Herald* during World

War II, frequently arrived late in the evening, when the editors were preparing to go to press. In a sable coat, smoking a cigarette in a diamond-studded holder, Patterson often ordered that page 1 be reset to launch, David Brinkley recalled, "a personal attack on whatever public figure displeased her at the moment."

Other owners had been gradually (and, for some, grudgingly) relinquishing opinion leadership. A study by Frank Luther Mott of ten prominent dailies between 1910 and 1940 found that the percentage of nonadvertising space given to the papers' own portion of the opinion page had fallen by 50 percent. Instead of a feisty, opinionated molder of minds, many a big-city publisher had become a mere signer of checks and host of Christmas parties. Such second- and third-generation newspaper owners, busy spending their inheritance, never mastered the details of newspaper publishing. "The number of big newspaper owners today who could perform any operation on the paper except sweeping the floor," commented one New York editor in the late 1940s, "could, I think, be numbered on the fingers of both hands."

In covering national and international news, most large and small dailies relied on wire-service copy composed for both Democratic and Republican editors. Strenuously "objective," it refrained from any manifest interpretation of an episode or newsmaker. In smaller, one-newspaper towns, publishers and their operatives found an economic rationale for evenhandedness: a dread of offending large blocs of readers. "Monopoly is more difficult than competition," a publisher in a one-newspaper town admitted in 1944. "You don't shoot quite so fast and throw things around so vigorously." "For business reasons," Robert Hutchins complained, "many owners suppress their convictions." At journalism schools, which trained about one-fourth of the nation's reporters and editors in the mid forties, the hard-nosed neutrality of the AP had already been transformed into a sacred obligation of the would-be scribe.

Still, bias could be located with some ease. Rarely were extreme political groups handled with the same evenhandedness extended to centrist ones. Objective reporters, by merely announcing a government or business action, in effect publicized rather than analyzed or criticized the behavior of established institutions. Various subtle controls constrained those reporters challenging the views of an editor, who normally owed his position to owner fealty. Promotions and choice story assignments did not go to those taking positions inimical to the editor or publisher.

Low self-esteem, eased occasionally by too much alcohol, more often by an easy cynicism, kept most of the ranks quiet. Few entering jour-

nalism had any illusions about their calling. Salaries, despite unioniza-
tion at many dailies a decade earlier, remained modest. "Newspaper
work was for life's losers," Russell Baker wrote. Journalists "occupied
the social pit. Respectable folks did not want their daughters to marry
one. They were thought to be a vagabond crowd addicted to booze, vul-
gar language, bad manners, smelly wardrobes, heavy debt, and low
company." Relatively few regarded themselves as more than notetak-
ers. Correspondents at the best dailies had begun to "mediate" rather
than merely paraphrase an important speech; however, they remained
in the minority. Reporters rarely identified with the power brokers of a
town or country. From relatively modest middle-class families, many
journalists had never finished college; most of those who did had attended the less prestigious state universities. For the ambitious, the
newsroom was only a way station before entering politics, completing
that first novel, or becoming a firm's vice president for public relations.

Journalists as a group shared certain characteristics common to those
in the middle-class professions. Nearly all were white. Blacks who
wished to join the fourth estate had to work for African-American
newspapers; those who broke the color line found the going rough, if
not impossible. The *Washington Post* tried to desegregate its newsroom
in 1952, hiring Simeon Booker to cover city news in what was then a
very southern community. Booker had to contend with hostility at the
paper, which had segregated washrooms, and in dealing with city authorities, angry when he covered fires in white neighborhoods. After
two years, he left the *Post* for an African-American newspaper. "It was
a real tense situation," Booker remarked, "and had made me neurotic."

Would-be female reporters suffered a different segregation. Editors
hired women to cover fashion or homemaking. Those who sought to be
political reporters or war correspondents had to overcome male resistance and resentment. During the war, when a female reporter or pho-
tographer got a "scoop," her male rivals assumed that it was because
she had provided the newsmaker with her sexual favors. In Washington, women were barred from the National Press Club. Female reporters sent to cover a speech at a National Press Club dinner had to wait
until the meal had been served before entering the hall.

Periodical Pleasures

If newspapers and newspeople aimed for the mass audience, magazines and books played to more specialized ones. Differences in sex,
class, age, and income were easily served by book and magazine publishers. Nervous book buyers could join a club that each month cau-

tiously designated a few new works appropriate for middle-class shelves. For others, the relatively high cost of books in the mid 1940s encouraged frequent trips to public libraries and department stores that lent titles. They could also subscribe to magazines that carried short stories, such as the *Saturday Evening Post* or *Collier's*. To varying degrees, all offered an affordable escape. For many women, reading *True Confessions* or *True Romance* provided time away from husbands and household tasks. Children, too, by reading comic books, escaped by entering a world of fantasy. Especially in more densely populated urban centers, men who were unfulfilled by the sensationalism of the tabloids could read gory detective magazines. Men from smaller towns, such as General Dwight D. Eisenhower, commander of Allied forces in Western Europe, preferred Westerns. Those in need of sexual gratification secreted copies of *Esquire* into the house.

Magazine reading, even more than newspaper consumption, varied by income and locale. City dwellers in the northeast appear to have had less time for periodicals than those in midwestern and western towns. Perhaps in part because most magazines were produced by Yankees, periodicals were less likely to be found in southern homes. Class was the most powerful predictor of magazine reading. Despite sharp reductions in newsstand and subscription prices in the 1890s, the middle class dominated the audience for periodicals. Subscribers to the nation's two most popular magazines, the *Saturday Evening Post* and *Life*, were likely to own their residence and to drive a car to work rather than take a bus. For much of the country, magazines were consumed in the library, barber shop, or beauty parlor.

Cosmopolitans were heavy magazine readers. Prominent business executives took *Fortune*, many middle managers *Business Week*. They and others prized newsmagazines such as *Time*, which neatly organized outside events and trends each week. A much smaller number took opinion magazines, mostly liberal ones, such as the *New Republic* and the *Nation*.

The content of magazines came from various sources. Many were mere conduits for outside contributors. Others, such as *Collier's* and *Time*, produced much or all of their copy and had substantial, full-time staffs. These periodicals tended to resemble larger dailies in their organization of work and routine. Writers had relatively little autonomy, and at the newsmagazines, no names or "by-lines" were attached to entries. Still, the extent to which reporters merely echoed the whims of their editors or publishers can be overstated; cues as to the importance or appropriate interpretation of individual stories were often taken from fellow reporters or the *New York Times*. One increasingly apparent exception was at Time Inc., where owner and editor-in-chief Henry R. Luce had begun to demand that his staff conform to his views on American foreign policy.

"We have got so we need the noise"

Most Americans in 1945 who read in the evening had the radio on. "We have got so we need the noise," Robert M. Hutchins observed. A decade earlier, radio had become the most popular mass medium, overtaking both newspapers and films. By 1945 an American home or apartment was more likely to have a radio than indoor plumbing or a telephone. Two polls found Americans to be more satisfied with radio than with religion.

The typical home had a large receiver in the room where the family congregated in the evening, with a second, smaller set in the kitchen. "If you're a Republican and your wife's a Democrat," an RCA ad declared in 1940, "keep peace in the family with a radio in every room!" About one-fourth of all cars included the then expensive option of a radio. Such convenience gave radio a competitive edge over rival mass media. The presence of radios in the home made turning one on a far simpler task than traveling to a newsstand for the late edition or going to the picture show. Indeed, 84 percent of those polled in a November 1945 survey by Paul F. Lazarsfeld and Harry Field indicated that if they had to choose between listening to the radio and going to the movies, they would prefer to give up the latter, while only 11 percent reported that they would forgo listening to the radio. Those polled were twice as likely (62 percent to 30 percent) to surrender their newspapers as they were to give up their radios.

Radio's great popularity had little to do with its uniqueness as a cultural form. The medium's first stars had been vaudevillians; popular performers in the mid forties, stars such as Bob Hope and Jack Benny had begun their careers in music halls. Most radio newscasters aimed for the language and style of newspaper reporters and relied heavily on the wire services for their broadcast "copy." In the late 1930s, entertainment programs began to originate from the movie colony. Hollywood gossip columnist Louella Parsons and director Cecil De Mille hosted programs with film stars as their guests. "When De Mille said good night 'from Hollywood,' " one listener recalled, "the word rolled off his tongue, with a rising inflection on the second syllable that sent shivers down his young listener's spine."

Radio's enormous following marked another step in the nationalization of culture. At night, when most people used their radios, they normally tuned in a program aired on one of the four radio networks—the National Broadcasting Company (NBC), the Columbia Broadcasting System (CBS), the Mutual Broadcasting System, and the American Broadcasting Company (ABC). Critics called them "chains." NBC had operated two networks, but it was considered so powerful that in 1941 the federal government ruled that NBC's parent corporation, RCA, must sell one of its chains, which became ABC.

Despite the opportunity radio provided for increasing the number of "voices" in a given town, stations often were owned by the local newspaper publisher or belonged to a regional chain of stations. More than half of all stations were "affiliated" with one of the networks; the networks had affiliates in every large city. (The government restricted the number of stations a network could own and operate, called "O & Os.") In order for a station to become an affiliate, the station manager signed an "option time" agreement, which awarded most hours of the day and evening to the network in exchange for programming and compensation. Because they spared the local stations the cost of producing their own programs, such deals made eminent sense for them. And most consumers since the late 1920s had preferred shows originating from New York and Hollywood to the usually less sophisticated local efforts. Nevertheless, not every observer accepted the networks' hegemony. Affiliated stations were "sleeping partners," complained one critic, "tollkeepers on a bridge that others built."

Radio programming fell into different "genres." The most common at the war's end, constituting just under half of the typical station's schedule, was musical. Such shows were normally aired live and took several forms. Some, such as the "Lucky Strike Hit Parade" or the "Carnation Contented Hour," originated from network or station studios with an orchestra playing current favorites. The most popular had well-known singers such as Kate Smith and Bing Crosby as hosts. With the "big band" sound popular, stations broadcast performances from distant night spots or hotel ballrooms. ("And now," the announcer intoned to unseen millions, "enjoy the music of Little Jack Little and His Orchestra, performing in the Green Room of the Hotel Edison, near New York's Times Square.") For those more upper- or middle-brow sensibilities, individual companies underwrote shows like the "Voice of Firestone" and "The Telephone Hour." On Saturday afternoons, Texaco sponsored New York's Metropolitan Opera on NBC.

The second most common program type was dramatic. These programs included daytime serials, which, intended for the homemaker, told never-ending and usually humorless stories of women and their families. At a time when women were being actively discouraged from such aspirations, the lead roles in many soap operas were female law-yers, entrepreneurs, and politicians. More conventional was the day-time serial's handling of sex: expressions of romantic attachment never led to explicit physical contact; instead, verbal encounters ended with organ music, followed by the narrator asking whether the patient, suf-fering heroine would indeed find happiness. In the evening, serials sought the male or child listener. "Action-adventure" dramas had a reg-ular cast of heroes—detectives, policemen, cowboys, space warriors—who battled the foes of order in the nation, the Old West, or the universe.

There were other genres. Quiz programs tested in-studio partici-pants and sometimes listeners on the trivial and the substantial. Situ-ation comedies involved the weekly "adventures" of a regular cast of players, such as the two blacks in Harlem ("Amos 'n' Andy") or rural southerners ("Lum and Abner"). The Great Gildersleeve's daily routine always proved more humorous than the typical listener's. In many com-edies, performers like Gracie Allen and Jane Ace played charming scat-terbrains whose nonsensical "crises" were resolved at each episode's end. As Jane Ace remarked, "Time wounds all heels."

Such regular series standardized radio entertainment and audience expectations. Advertisers paid for a fifteen- or thirty-minute time slot, then contracted the "labor" for the program. "Specials" required that these steps be taken with each broadcast. The network could air a series like "Fibber McGee and Molly" over the years and build an audience for the program and time slot. Like readers of comic strips, which had inspired some of the first radio serials, listeners grew to recognize char-acters, anticipating witticisms from the more comic ones and certain gags, for example, the crash that invariably accompanied McGee's opening his closet door, and the line: "By George, one of these days I gotta straighten out that closet!" Fans of Jack Benny knew his vanities and tight-fisted ways and laughed at the slightest reference to the fully depreciated Maxwell automobile that he was too cheap to replace.

The networks in some ways served as mere brokers between affil-iates and advertisers. Individual companies and their advertising agen-cies produced series, overseeing every aspect of production. The adver-tiser was sovereign; before airtime, writers of radio comedies made in Hollywood had to teletype their guest star list, story suggestions, and individual scripts to New York agencies for approval. "The teletype," observed former ad agent Frederic Wakeman in his novel *The Hucksters*, "had created perhaps more occupational ulcers than straight whiskey or hastily eaten ham sandwiches." News commentators, most of them employees of the networks, signed second contracts with companies who paid for their nightly five and fifteen minutes of news analysis.

Advertisers delighted in a buyer's market. About a third of all radio air time was unsold in the mid 1940s. That condition and the competition between the two strongest networks, NBC and CBS, gave advertisers great leverage. Some resembled the tyrannical Evan Llewelyn Evans, owner of Beautee Soap in Wakeman's *The Hucksters*. Most insisted on the largest possible audience and offered a network programming that made few concessions to intelligence or wit. Hutchins complained that sponsors had convinced the fifth estate that "a mass audience is the only audience." With their products so closely associated with individual programs or commentators, advertisers abhorred artistic or political controversy. The biggest buyer of airtime, Procter & Gamble, noted *Broadcasting* magazine, "has a policy never to offend a single listener." Thus sponsors actively discouraged more experimental attempts at radio drama or comedy as well as extreme political commentaries. FCC Commissioner Clifford J. Durr wondered, "Never to offend anyone may be good salesmanship. But is it good radio?"

Yet the programming philosophy of some sponsors encouraged diversity. A few companies eyed influential, as opposed to large, audiences. By sponsoring the opera, an oil company hoped to create goodwill among the better educated. Or a stubborn corporate executive might simply wish to impose his taste—or, in the case of Harvey Firestone, his wife's—for classical music on the radio audience. And Italian-Americans in Buffalo and Brooklyn could savor the opera, while many in smaller towns heard their first symphonies.

Unwanted airtime boosted program variety. With a third or more of the broadcast day unsold, networks, as part of their station agreements, had to offer affiliates "sustaining" or unsponsored programming, usually news shows; this obligation partly explains CBS's creation of a strong news service in the late 1930s. Since NBC was the more popular network, fewer advertisers offered entertainment series to Columbia. Having an excess of unsold airtime, CBS began producing news shows, which placated affiliates who expected programming while not coincidentally creating goodwill for the network. Vacant hours or half-hours also encouraged the broadcast of town meetings, debates between prominent citizens on great public issues. The major figures of both parties as well as Socialist party leader Norman Thomas could, on request, receive time to deliver radio talks. Thus the laws of supply and demand not only largely determined what Americans heard over the radio in 1945 but enriched the political discourse.

Government interference was decidedly indirect and infrequent. From the beginning of regular broadcasts in the 1920s, the "American system" of broadcasting, in contrast to the ones emerging abroad, emphasized private ownership and operation. The government directed "traffic," that is, awarded space on the radio spectrum, and only acted against the worst offenders of public decency. Although empowered to revoke station licenses, the FCC had not pronounced the "death sentence" on any operator since its creation in 1934.

That is not to dub federal oversight of radio in the 1940s irrelevant. The FCC did require that all license holders air some "minority interest" programming (usually less than 5 percent of its weekly schedule)—news or religious—some of which should originate with the station and not be a mere network "feed." With licenses up for renewal every three years, station managers normally met such expectations. Then, too, the FCC limited the number of licenses any one person or corporation could own. In 1941 the commission had ordered NBC to sell off its second, or "Blue," network. That year as well, the FCC had issued a ban on station editorials. Too many license holders, the commission majority argued, were using a public resource for personal propagandizing.

The FCC emerged from the war determined to increase its regulation of stations. Although James Lawrence Fly, whose chairmanship had brought a new activism at the agency, had stepped down in 1944, his replacement, Paul Porter, appeared to be even more enthusiastic about new government edicts and forms. Companies such as CBS, almost wholly dependent on their broadcast properties for revenues, viewed the commission warily.

Porter could only do so much. He was but one of seven commissioners, and several of his colleagues preferred doing nothing. Some members of Congress, wary of too "independent" an agency, prepared to check an overly vigorous, Porter-led majority. Congressional allies of the industry had public opinion on their side. Although most Americans were unhappy about some advertiser practices, they showed little sympathy for those who were inclined to increase federal regulation of broadcasting. "Majority radio," that is, the deliberate programming for large audiences, had all but guaranteed the absence of the kind of mass revolt that the state-run British Broadcasting Corporation faced a decade later. Critics of radio's commercial, oligopolistic foundations were few and far between. National broadcast leaders carefully nurtured congressional goodwill, while individual station owners usually belonged to local political elites with which many congressmen identified.

Radio news personnel were even more restricted in their freedoms than colleagues at the larger dailies and newsweeklies. Some who worked for stations, like those toiling at the *Chicago Tribune* and Hearst papers, had to fit the news to the specifications of the license holder. More often, restraints came from outside the studio. Radio news reporters and analysts had to respect the sensitivities of advertisers as well as congressmen and regulators. Rarely did sponsors actually make changes in copy. Instead, they rewarded with renewed contracts those commentators who observed the obvious. Government leaders similarly protested discreetly with late night phone calls or personal letters to the network's chief lobbyist or president.

Radio news people rarely complained about such restraints. Most shared the distaste of regulators over the extreme commentaries of the 1930s of news analysts such as Boake Carter. The pro-administration tilt of prominent radio analysts in 1940 and 1941 had invited nothing but gratitude from the White House and the Roosevelt-appointed FCC chairman. Younger radio news stars such as Murrow considered themselves "objective" journalists, respectful of those in power. Most who worked in radio had previously worked for newspapers or attended journalism schools that ennobled wire-service practices. Radio reporters, moreover, identified being "objective" with the new professionalism of the nation's best newspapers and major wire services. When his contract with CBS was renewed in 1947, Edward R. Murrow insisted that it restrict his right to inject opinion into his copy.

The Movie Colony

In 1945 the heads of the radio networks based themselves and their operations in New York, America's largest city and the seat of the nation's major financial institutions and the greatest number of large corporations. In New York, too, were found the country's most important advertising agencies, magazine publishers, legitimate theater, and the two best daily newspapers. Broadcast executives mingled with the nation's cultural and corporate leaders, belonged to their private clubs, attended their exclusive parties, and served on the same museum boards. At Long Island estates on weekends, they danced with each other's wives and drank each other's liquor.

A continent removed from such gatherings were the governors of America's movie colony, the heads of the motion picture companies. If isolated from much of the nation's corporate elite, the film executives rivaled broadcasters and the editors of big-city tabloids in the competition for the mass audience. In 1945 some eighteen thousand theaters in

America showed American films, virtually all of them created in large studios in or around Hollywood, California.

Five companies dominated not only the production but the distribution and exhibition of celluloid fantasies. "The Big Five"—Metro-Goldwyn-Mayer, Paramount, Warner Brothers, RKO, and Twentieth Century Fox—each had an army of indentured servants: actors, directors, writers, technicians, and carpenters. In her study of Hollywood, anthropologist Hortense Powdermaker used words like *medieval* and *totalitarian* to describe the film studios' hold over employees. Stars were well-paid serfs, but still serfs, compelled in most instances to sign seven-year contracts and subject to being "loaned" to another studio at the governor's whim. The movie executives designated the films actors appeared in and were expected to promote on nationwide publicity tours. Intransigent players were suspended without pay, with the time lost added to the life of their contract. An especially exasperated studio head could use a broadly defined "morals" clause present in most agreements to dismiss an actor outright. Although Warners's Olivia de Havilland had successfully challenged the contract system in court in 1944, her colleagues continued a year later to consider themselves convict labor.

The governors' imperial reach extended into cities and towns across the country. Local theater operators had to reckon with the sales representatives of the Big Five, who offered them packages of films. Larger theaters wanted the new "A"-pictures, those with the studios' biggest stars and highest production values, which in 1945 were films like *The Bells of St. Mary's,* starring Bing Crosby and Ingrid Bergman. Smaller, neighborhood houses took A-pictures after their first run or "B"-pictures, often Western action serials, which had less prominent players and a relatively shoddy look. A B-picture, it has been said, "is a movie in which the sets shake when an actor slams the door."

In many cases the studios did not have to barter with individual theater operators. In 1945 the Big Five enjoyed a vertical control over the creation and distribution of their products that was the envy of any large-scale capitalist. The Big Five not only produced films but through their ownership of large theaters in the country's best markets were all but assured that their movies would reach the largest possible audience. Although the Big Five owned only a sixth of the nation's theaters, Tino Balio noted in *The American Film Industry,* their houses tended to be the large, fourteen-hundred-seat "palaces" in the big cities, where moviegoing was most frequent. In 1945, Big Five–owned theaters accrued 70 percent of the nation's box-office receipts.

Film industry leaders had ample reason to be delighted over their hold on the American consumer of mass entertainment. Domestic gross box-office receipts had nearly trebled during the war. "Every night is Saturday night," cried *Variety*, the show-business periodical. Even more encouraging was the rise in the percentage of potential moviegoers who patronized theaters, which, according to one study cited by Robert Sklar, increased from 31 percent of the population in 1935 to 73.6 percent in 1945. At least twice a week the typical American visited a theater. Soldiers and sailors still overseas eagerly awaited the arrival of the latest film or movie stars in a USO troupe. A film producer Powdermaker interviewed compared himself to a god, able to make the masses laugh or cry at will. In his novel *The Last Tycoon* (1940), F. Scott Fitzgerald likened his protagonist, the head of a large studio, to Lincoln.

Yet the movie colony was a colony, not the mother country. Although the heads of the studios bullied actors, directors, and writers, none were truly titans. Their authority was in fact more tenuous than the casual observer might have guessed. Since the early 1930s the studios had been blackmailed by the theater projectionists' arm of the International Alliance of Theatrical Stage Employees, or "IA." With the projectionists' representatives able to shut down or sabotage the operations of most of the major theaters, the studio heads periodically and personally paid "protection money" in cash to the IA's chief saboteur, Willie Bioff. Jailed in 1941, Bioff eventually informed on some old Chicago business associates, who much later arranged for Bioff's Ford pickup to explode when he started the engine, killing him. Even with Bioff absent, the IA enjoyed extraordinary influence in the movie colony in 1945. Most of those who were involved in constructing movie sets (virtually all films were shot on sets and not on location) belonged to the IA. When craftsmen sought to organize a union independent of the IA, the studios accepted the IA's dismissal of the new union as Communist-led and refused to bargain with it. In October 1945, picketing by the insurgent craftsmen at the Warner Brothers lot ended in violence.

Another challenge to the Big Five's control over the exhibition of films came from the Justice Department. During Roosevelt's second term, Assistant Attorney General for Anti-Trust Thurman Arnold had begun a long inquiry into the studios' distribution and exhibition practices. Independent theater operators had complained to the Justice Department and the Federal Trade Commission that they were being denied access to certain A-pictures. The Big Five favored their own or other exhibitors, the independents cried, or compelled them to accept new releases without previews ("blind booking") or only if they accepted a long series of features, not all of them thought to have much box-office appeal ("block booking"). Although the studios voluntarily agreed to stop block booking and blind booking in 1940, the Antitrust Division contemplated seeking a court order forcing the Big Five to divest themselves of their theaters. The governors faced the loss of what had been a guaranteed outlet for their investments. Not surprisingly, the industry cooperated when government officials during the war suggested changes in the portrayal of minority groups or of America's allies. Asked to produce films to honor the Soviet Union, the studios responded with the obedience of a well-trained retriever. Pleasing the OWI might quiet the Justice Department.

Calls from New York and San Francisco, and not just Washington, gave studio executives cause for worry. The governors of the film colony had received their commissions from major shareholders and financiers; MGM's Louis B. Mayer actually worked for a theater chain, Loew's Inc. Warner Brothers and other studios were in debt to insurance companies and such major lenders as the Bank of America. A bad year at the box office might end a governor's tenure. In the opening of *The Last Tycoon*, Fitzgerald describes the pathetic Manny Schwartz. Once the head of a major studio—"I used to be a regular man of decision," he declares—Schwartz has lost everything and commits suicide. "No one wanted him further," Fitzgerald's narrator observes. In his 1941 short story "Somebody Has To Be Nobody," Budd Schulberg, himself the son of a film executive, describes a day in the life of studio mogul A. D. Nathan. He is busy overseeing new projects while planning an affair with a starlet. Everyone respects his power and seeks his approval. At an exclusive restaurant for dinner, with his wife and the starlet, among others, his guests, Nathan receives a long-awaited call from New York. Hoping for a screen test, the restaurant's telephone operator, "suffering from delusions of looking like Bette Davis," eyes him longingly. But the news from New York is bad: Nathan has been dethroned. Realizing that he has joined the list of toppled chieftains, Nathan thinks, "Make room for another ghost."

Even the most entrenched studio heads had to consider their industry's public image. Personal history caused some disquiet. Most film executives were first- or second-generation Jewish immigrants prospering in a society where old-line Protestants dominated the commercial elite and Jews were a distinct and, in many neighborhoods, hated minority. Geographical isolation also added to this discomfort. California could still be dismissed, as it was by one sociologist in 1935, as a place people retired to. More brutally four years later, Nathanael West said it was where people came to die. Its economy and population had boomed with the war and construction of aircraft plants near Los Angeles. Yet it remained a long plane ride from Manhattan. Relatively cut off from the national elite, studio executives shared the inferiority complex common among midwesterners and westerners. Cues about dress and interior decoration originated from New York.

Show business itself had historically invited negative images. Every entertainer, it seemed, suffered for the legacy of the seedy road shows, the nineteenth-century conmen that Twain portrayed in *Huckleberry Finn*. Backstage was considered barren of virtue. The best film executives fought such impressions head-on. Louis B. Mayer of MGM always called before visiting a whorehouse, demanding that other customers leave. It would not have been good public relations for the head of the world's largest studio to be seen fumbling with a prostitute. Actors were a far greater problem: gossips wagged that their wild parties became orgies and drug addiction was commonplace. Thus the studios insisted on a morals clause and certain expectations. Actors could not live with a lover but had to marry. Homosexuals had to adhere publicly to the era's rigid adherence to heterosexuality. And an army of publicity agents fought to create the image that actors were typical Americans, with spouses and children: loving husbands and wives, attentive parents, regular churchgoers.

Film industry publicists found easy conduits for their fictions in the nation's show-business reporters. Led by syndicated columnists Hedda Hopper and Louella Parsons, the Hollywood reporters actively watched over the movie colony's public and private existences. On his Sunday evening program from Hollywood, Jimmy Fidler decried divorce and admonished unfaithful spouses to save their marriages. "Mr. Fidler's moral purposes," wrote radio critic John Crosby in 1946, "are as intense as those of a small-town spinster." In the case of Parsons and Hopper, there was no little irony in their ostentatious championing of traditional relationships; both were divorced, Parsons twice. Nonetheless, they became the confidantes to many players, even suggesting marriage partners and film roles. Those who deferred to them were invariably rewarded with friendly copy. When, twenty years later, Ronald Reagan, one of the actors who had played by the Hollywood press's rules, entered public life, his wife was baffled and hurt by the relatively more searching and critical approach of political reporters. Nancy Reagan had thought Parsons was something other than a pamphleteer for the movie colony.

Parsons and Hopper could, on occasion, turn on their subjects. "In the 1940s," Otto Friedrich wrote in *City of Nets*, "these two vain and ignorant women tyrannized Hollywood." When, in 1941, Orson Welles completed for RKO a film whose hypocritical and egomaniac protagonist was clearly modeled after Parsons's employer, William Randolph

Hearst, Louella tried to prevent *Citizen Kane*'s release. Louis Mayer, on behalf of the industry, offered RKO $842,000, more than the film cost to produce, to destroy the original print and all copies of the motion picture. Although RKO's president turned down the offer, he could not salvage Welles's standing in the colony. At the 1941 Academy Awards, Parsons's many allies in the audience hissed each time a speaker announced Welles's nomination for a prize.

Outside southern California, show-business journalism had a limited if, to the studios, significant audience. Studies of newspaper reading found that only a minority turned to the fatuities of Parsons, Hopper, and others. A 1951 compilation by the Advertising Research Foundation estimated that 10 percent of male readers and 25 percent of female readers regularly read Hollywood columns. Although movie "fan" magazines could be located at every drugstore and train depot in America, other periodicals drew far more readers, and many neglected Hollywood. *Time* rarely placed a film (or radio) star on its cover; in the view of such magazines, political figures were still celebrities. Luce's more popular weekly, *Life*, did take Hollywood more seriously. And studio publicists rejoiced when *Life*'s "Goes to the Movies" weekly feature highlighted their films. Those who consumed the journalism of Lotusland were likely to be among the most frequent moviegoers, the ones who went to a film regardless of the story or the reviews.

Good public relations also lessened the likelihood of censorship. The federal government did not license or censor films, although the Supreme Court, in *Mutual Film Corporation v. Ohio* (1915), had refused to place films in the category of "protected speech" guaranteed by the First Amendment. The *Mutual* case, then, allowed state boards to regulate films and left open the possibility of federal oversight.

Nongovernmental bodies most unsettled the film industry. Women's clubs, led by the conservative Daughters of the American Revolution, monitored the movies and their moral and political "messages." Major religious denominations had long concerned themselves with the content of films, which were assumed to be powerful messengers, capable of leading whole audiences into wickedness. That many were produced by non-Christians only added to this anxiety.

No nongovernmental group watched over the film industry more actively than the Catholic church. None more unnerved the movie colony. Studio heads understood that any film offensive to the church might antagonize as much as a fifth of the national audience. Church and lay leaders, in turn, knew their power. Diocese newspapers previewed films, and a Catholic lay group, the Legion of Decency, devised a rating system that ranked films A, B, or C. A rating of C meant that the feature was "condemned," and church members were instructed not to see the picture. Needless to say, the governors dreaded the prospect of a C rating, and they willingly reedited films to which the Legion objected. More often, the studios tried to anticipate Legion objections and "precensor" their movies during story conferences and production.

Film executives had tried to placate the industry's self-appointed guardians with self-regulation. Since 1922 the studios had funded the Motion Picture Producers and Distributors of America, with former Postmaster General Will H. Hays as president. A devout Presbyterian, Hays as chairman of the Republican National Committee had begun committee meetings with a prayer. Although outsiders expected Hays to cleanse the industry of impurities, he initially had little power. The "Hays Office" took on new authority, however, with heightened complaints about the violence and sex in films in the early 1930s. Catholic lay and church leaders joined with major lenders to the studios to force the creation of a new self-regulatory authority. Nominally under the control of the Hays Office, the Production Code Administration (PCA) dutifully reviewed all scripts and completed films. Producers who ignored a PCA request for alterations would be denied the PCA's seal of approval and consequently would find few, if any, theater operators willing to exhibit their features. Although some moviemakers at first disdained the PCA, the industry as a whole found it to be in their best interest to follow the PCA's recommendations. Unconventional treatments of morality would likely offend many moviegoers, and Hollywood coveted *all* potential ticket buyers, not just the smaller audiences that enjoyed or winked at having social norms upset. With this mandate, the PCA struck at any nontraditional portrayals of morality. Criminal activity in films could no longer go unpunished; gentle kisses defined sexual contact. Prostitutes were "hostesses." Profanity, even belching, was prohibited. Only after the most protracted negotiations did the PCA allow Clark Gable to declare at the end of Gone With the Wind, "Frankly, my dear, I don't give a damn." Under pressure from some of the studios, the PCA acknowledged the less inhibited morality of the war years and relaxed its grip slightly. Nevertheless, the great majority of films in the 1940s were black and white both literally and figuratively. "Man, according to Hollywood, is either completely good, or bad," Powdermaker complained. "His personality is static, rarely showing any development either in growth or regression. The villain is a blackened sinner who can do no good and who cannot be saved; while the hero is a glamorous being, who can do no wrong."

The PCA also carefully kept the ideology of films in the mainstream. Scripts that upset the political and economic status quo were rewritten or, in the case of the adaptation of Sinclair Lewis's novel *It Can't Happen Here*, which described the coming of fascism to America, were never produced. *For Whom the Bell Tolls* (1943) managed to retain much of the sex of Hemingway's novel about the Spanish Civil War but not the author's infatuation with the politics of the Popular Front. "The censorship of Hollywood films," film historian Gregory D. Black writes, "was primarily a censorship of ideas."

Another form of pressure, from stockholders and moneylenders, inhibited innovation. Early in its history, the movie colony had settled on various genres that worked at the box office. Westerns had always fared well, as had detective dramas. As with radio, the safest course was the last one to pay off. Nor did Hollywood depart from a national cultural machinery—periodicals, newspapers, radio—that portrayed blacks as servile and lazy (though this imagery had been modified because of war-related protests), characterized women as "the weaker" sex, whose lives should exclusively involve husbands and families, and depicted Indians as duplicitous. War films utilized a viciously anti-Indian imagery in portraying the Japanese, with references to the enemy as "Japs," "beasts," "yellow monkeys," "nips," and "slant-eyed rats."

Stereotyping extended to actors. Stars, even many bit players, normally found themselves repeating the same roles. Film executives actively discouraged them from being actors, that is, from playing against their studio-fashioned "type." Those like Bette Davis, who protested, could only complain or, in the case of Warners's Humphrey Bogart, accidentally land a role that transformed him from a villain into a romantic lead. Bogart never did realize his most private ambition, to appear in a musical; his private dancing lessons went for naught. Other stars, such as Gary Cooper, were counseled by Hopper and others to maintain their image, departure from which might risk losing some of their fans. Americans, director Michael Curtiz explained, "pay their money to see Gary Cooper being Gary Cooper, not the hunchback of Notre Dame."

The studios were capable of producing art. Two generations of skilled directors and screenwriters numbered among the colony's citizenry. The system usually tolerated talented émigré directors, such as Fritz Lang, Otto Preminger, and Billy Wilder. Wilder's *Lost Weekend* (1945), the story of an alcoholic, in which he had cast a romantic lead, Ray Milland, in the role of the problem drinker, had broken many of the rules. Nor was the matter of alcoholism the sort Hollywood had in the past rushed to capture on film. Yet *The Lost Weekend* proved a hit and won the Best Picture citation from the Motion Picture Academy; and both Milland and Wilder took home Academy "Oscars."

Chance, too, often affected the artistic and popular success of a film. Warners's *Casablanca* had not been expected to cause lines to form outside ticket windows. Indeed, the movie's stars, led by Bogart, had finished the shooting downcast or confused about the picture and its potential. But the film's premiere coincided with a meeting of Allied war leaders in the Moroccan city, and headlines across America suddenly gave Warners's feature an unexpected currency. The last-minute reediting of Preminger's *Laura* (1944) and the addition of a haunting song about the film's policeman hero falling in love with the portrait of a murder victim brought what had been expected to be a routine detective movie the popular and critical success normally accorded "prestige" films, those that were expected to win awards, such as *Mrs. Miniver* (1942) or *Wilson* (1944).

Whether to *Wilson* or *Laura*, moviegoing was, compared with other forms of mass media consumption, a group activity. The typical film patron had a friend or neighbor or relation in tow. Gasoline rationing made seeing a movie an inexpensive date, and some theaters had special love seats. With the war ending, however, the lives of many couples for whom attending a film had been a courtship ritual would change dramatically. Marriage and the responsibilities and constraints of having children awaited them. There would, in effect, soon be less time for the consumption of certain mass amusements. And many of the discretionary hours that remained would be absorbed by a new mass medium. The rough equality of film, radio, and the printed page, each with a comparable share of Americans' spare moments, was about to end.

TEST PATTERNS   3
Television Comes to America, 1945–1955

In 1950, AS LATER, celebrities with a passion for baseball attended a game aware that the pleasure of watching the contest might be disrupted. Fans, impervious to what was transpiring on the field, insisted on an autograph. The radio and film star who tried to keep score had his patience sorely tested. Still, virtually all were used to such impositions; indeed, they constituted a reassurance of their standing.

One ballpark episode, by indicating a radically new preference among consumers of the public arts, gave established performers cause for concern. At a Pacific Coast League game in the late 1940s radio and film stars Groucho Marx, George Burns, and Jack Benny sat together. With them was Milton Berle, a far less successful night club and theater comic. A notorious thief of other comedians' material, he added insult to injury by using the purloined goods on his television program. With TV little watched, most of Berle's rivals refused to take him or his medium seriously. Who watched Berle? He was *awful*, they cried. Berle, comedian Joe Lewis cracked, "is responsible for more television sets being sold than anyone else. I sold mine, my father sold his. . . . " Yet at the baseball game, people all but ignored Benny, Burns, and Groucho. They sought out instead "Uncle Miltie." "The fans, all the people at the park, clustered around him for an autograph, and brushed by all of these men who in his opinion were the great giants of comedy," recalled a CBS executive. "This is what television had done."

At increasingly dramatic rates beginning in 1948, Americans were buying their first TV sets. In 1956, Americans were purchasing twenty thousand TVs a day. And by the end of the fifties, nine out of every ten American homes had a "home screen." It was an unprecedented acceptance of a new household technology. "By comparison," John Kittross wrote, "it took the telephone eighty years, the automobile forty-nine years, and sound radio twenty-five years to reach only three out of four homes in this country." Evenings that once went to radio listening, or reading, or moviegoing were lost to television. People even seemed to talk to each other less. TV, Goodman Ace complained, "has already revolutionized social grace by cutting down parlor conversation to two sentences: 'What's on television?' and 'Good night.' "

Reconversion, 1945–1948

Between 1945 and 1948 the established mass media paid relatively little attention to television. Most of those running newspapers, radio stations and networks, and film companies considered only their own recent histories. They had found the war a stimulating diversion, for some a profitable one. Peace seemed only to promise better days.

Reconversion least affected newspapers, the oldest and most tradition-bound of the mass media. Waves of discharged soldiers and sailors, looking for work, poured into editorial offices across the country and had jobs, some ill-defined, created for them. Ex-employees were treated best, though more than one editor had to struggle to find a slot for the worker who had left as an office boy in 1941 and showed up four years later in an Army major's uniform. Although the total number of editorial positions increased, female writers who had been hired because of the manpower shortage were encouraged to leave to marry and join in the postwar baby boom. The advent of the veterans little altered the content of most papers. Some dailies did boost their coverage of film and radio and carried more photographs. Editors, having been forced because of wartime newsprint rationing to reduce story length, had sought more condensed or concise newswriting. On the whole, however, the typical daily resembled its prewar self.

Smugness became loudly defensive in March 1947. During the war, Henry Luce of Time Inc. had sponsored a Commission on Freedom of the Press, chaired by Chancellor Robert M. Hutchins of the University of Chicago. Although Luce himself had been partly motivated by his concern over government interference with the press, the Hutchins Commission stressed the shortcomings of journalism. With a vital role to play in a democratic society and powers over the masses unimagined by the Founding Fathers, the commission determined, newspapers were failing the people. Too many publishers, like Robert R. McCormick in Hutchins's Chicago, were guilty of prejudiced reportage. Newspapers had to be "socially responsible" and present a more balanced picture of the world. Not surprisingly, reaction within the fourth estate was swift and severe. No journalists, critics noted, had served on Hutchins's distinguished panel. Even Luce disassociated himself from its recommendations. He and others took particular exception to one of the commission's prescriptions. The Hutchins Commission vaguely encouraged the government to play a more "positive" role by actually "participating in mass communications: to state its own case, to supplement private sources of information, and to propose standards for private emulation." Such was liberal opinion leaders' dismay with the press in 1947 that they would prefer a government spokesperson to a reporter for a major metropolitan daily.

Radio already faced the prospect of greater government regulation. A year before the release of the Hutchins recommendations, the Federal Communications Commission had issued a report critical of radio stations. Dubbed the "blue book" for its powder-blue cover, the *Public Service Responsibility of Broadcast Licenses* compared the programming of six stations with their promises of nonprofit, "public service" programs made to the FCC at the time their licenses were issued or renewed. Repeatedly, the FCC found that stations failed to fulfill their pledges. And despite much criticism from the industry, and with many of those pleased by Hutchins's attacks on newspapers applauding, the FCC announced that it would begin to enforce its public-service strictures.

There was to be no second act. The enthusiasm for regulation so evident at the FCC, as at other independent agencies during the New Deal, all but ended under President Truman. Roosevelt's successor made little effort to appoint liberal activists to vacancies at the FCC. Congress, too, discouraged bureaucratic purposefulness by budget cuts and hostile hearings. Then, too, the Administrative Procedure Act of 1946 and amendments to the Communications Act in 1951 provided new guarantees to license holders, thus making regulatory policework more cumbersome. One commissioner complained in 1958 that broadcast license holders enjoyed more due process than someone charged with murder. The FCC, as in the 1930s, became preoccupied with the technical, engineering questions of broadcasting. A broadcast franchise, as Canada's Lord Thomson had declared, again became a license to print money.

In one sense, government oversight of the news media was superfluous. Reporters routinely reported uncritically the statements of government officials. Wire service reporters in particular were stenographers with press credentials. In that regard, the war continued. The trust bred between the government and the fourth estate continued past V-J Day. Columnists might on the editorial page attack a policy, but news stories on page 1 and elsewhere publicized rather than scrutinized government actions. In March 1948 the normally skeptical *Louisville Courier-Journal* began a story on a congressional committee report with the lead "The Communists and Russian Government have but one goal—world revolution—and it cannot be accepted that they are friends of democracy." Dedicating the new *Washington Post* building three years later, Secretary of Defense George C. Marshall called the *Post* "one of the most delicate instruments in America's arsenal of freedom."

This virtual partnership had major consequences for the coverage of postwar diplomacy. With conflict the most powerful way of "framing" news, the fourth estate played up every confrontation between the Soviet Union and the United States. Indeed, it became the "big story." Some news people and news organizations—McCormick's *Tribune, Reader's Digest*, the Hearst papers, and Luce's *Life*—were more Russophobic than others. But all came to view Soviet boorishness in the new United Nations and the brutal subjugation of Eastern Europe through an American prism. The United States had just waged at great cost a widely supported war against one dictator. Suddenly history seemed to be repeating itself, American officials warned. Their imagery proved too fresh, too neat a way of organizing an otherwise complex set of overseas events, for the fourth estate to ignore. Joseph Stalin became Hitler, Communism "Red Fascism." The *Courier-Journal* in March 1948 ran a cartoon showing Stalin reshaping Hitler's swastika into the Communist hammer and sickle.

Although journalists divided over President Harry Truman's liberal domestic agenda, the administration had little difficulty selling a more confrontational foreign policy. The "interpretive press"—newspaper columnists, newsmagazines, and magazines of opinion such as the *Atlantic* and the *New Republic*—initially proved to be more suspicious onlookers, yet by the late 1940s the doubters had become true believers. And most joined the government's church voluntarily, though intimidation worked in a few cases. At least one prominent daily, the *New York Herald Tribune*, hardened its coverage of the cold war after some fervent anti-Communists accused it of being excessively detached about the new national-security state.

Radio news people underwent a similar cold war conversion. H. V. Kaltenborn, NBC Radio's popular news commentator, was among those who led the charge; by 1948 he was being joined, somewhat cautiously, by Edward R. Murrow, CBS News's most prominent reporter and analyst. For Murrow and most of those he had recruited to work for CBS in the late 1930s, the swallowing of Eastern Europe by Russia too painfully resembled Hitler's absorption of Central Europe a decade earlier. Then, too, Murrow and others feared a revival of the isolationism that had, they believed, crippled American foreign policy after World War I. Querulous reporting might play into the hands of internationalism's critics. Whatever misgivings he and others had about some of the anti-Communist regimes that the United States sought to help in the late 1940s, there could be no turning back. "It was customary during the war to say that democracy was on trial, as indeed it was," Murrow told listeners in 1946. Democracy "survived but the trial is not yet ended." Americans "have, whether we like it or not, come into our full inheritance, our full strength. The rest of the world knows it, if we do not."

Murrow and other network news people faced another postwar dilemma, a decline in the demand for overseas reporting and analysis. Station managers preferred to carry more local news. A 1946 *Broadcasting* survey indicated that more than three-fourths of stations had boosted their local news programming, largely at the expense of network news feeds. "A fire on Main Street has become important again," commented a radio news veteran in 1947. Networks in turn sharply cut their news and informational programming in the months following V-J Day. The cold war remained just that, a series of verbal duels between the two great survivors of the last conflict. With peace, advertisers and audiences preferred diversion. William L. Shirer's news show lost listeners and its sponsor; Murrow, temporarily in charge of CBS News, had to order the program's cancellation. Shirer never forgave Murrow or accepted his radio career's end as a consequence of the dwindling audience for international news. Because he had been less Russophobic than other commentators, Shirer preferred to believe that he was being silenced for his views.

In the realm of entertainment, Murrow's employer, CBS, took a major step toward equal footing with its great rival, NBC. In the postwar years, chain broadcasting remained in effect a duopoly. ABC and the Mutual Broadcasting System had far fewer affiliated stations and popular programs than either NBC or the Columbia Broadcasting System. Of the two, NBC had forever been the more popular network. One frustrated CBS vice president had even suggested to network owner William S. Paley in May 1945 that Columbia in effect surrender the mass audience to NBC and deliberately appeal to the smaller number of better-educated listeners. Paley refused. Unlike NBC, a division of RCA, CBS had to make money broadcasting. "To survive," Paley recalled later, "CBS had to give the majority of people the kind of programs it wanted to hear." Paley declared war.

His offensive took two forms. The network would wrestle from advertisers control of programming by producing its own shows. And Columbia would snare from NBC that chain's more popular stars. Although creating successful programs proved initially difficult, Columbia had greater luck raiding NBC's stable of talent. In 1948, Paley began offering NBC stars stock-option contracts. Under the agreement, presented to Paley by the Music Corporation of America (MCA), the largest actors' agency, prominent NBC performers set up corporations with themselves and their programs as assets; these companies were then sold to CBS. The Internal Revenue Service provided the crucial incentive: a high-salaried star had to suffer a 77 percent individual tax rate; proceeds from the sale of his "corporation," however, were subject to a more reasonable 25 percent capital gains assessment. The revolving doors began to spin, with the stars of "Amos 'n' Andy" and "Fibber McGee and Molly," as well as Jack Benny, Edgar Bergen, Phil Harris, and Red Skelton, quitting NBC for Columbia. The deal allowed Benny alone to squirrel away $1.35 million. Although the IRS eventually ruled against some of the arrangements, including Benny's, it was too late for any of the players to return home. Paley used the popularity of each, cultivated over the years by his nemesis, to create a built-in audience for other CBS offerings. An "audience flow" of listeners who selected Benny and others then stayed tuned to a home-grown CBS product. For the first time, Columbia led NBC in the ratings, with a majority of the most popular programs of 1949, according to the two major ratings services, broadcast on CBS.

Similar stock-option deals were being fashioned in Hollywood as the studios saw their control over their most popular stars weaken. Olivia de Havilland had successfully challenged in court the restrictiveness of her Warner Brothers contract. Soon after the war, some stars and directors began to form companies that produced films and handled their services. "If you talk to actors and directors and writers," a longtime Hollywood observer noted in *Harper's* in 1946, "you hear a new lilt in their conversation. They are machiavellian idealists who have discovered that they are finally edging over into the driver's seat."

Operating expenses posed a different dilemma for the studio executives. During the war, production costs had risen 70 percent. When filmmakers boosted admission prices to recover some of these expenditures, moviegoers resisted. In contrast to earlier years, the demand for films had turned elastic. Between 1946 and 1949, weekly individual admissions sales fell by 14.2 percent. Americans, Gilbert Seldes noted, spent a smaller share of their total income on movies in 1949 than at any time in the past two decades.

More and more executives in the late 1940s began to worry about "the Lost Audience." Television's advent did not explain the drop in attendance; revenues fell or became flat throughout the country and not just in those large cities with a TV station. Nor were export opportunities promising: foreign governments, led by Britain, imposed a variety of restrictions on the import of American-made films.

Concomitantly, the returning veterans were leaving the great cities, where moviegoing had been the most common distraction, to take up residence in new suburban developments. Going to a theater became less convenient and more of a luxury. Starting families, as the newly married did with unprecedented enthusiasm, further hurt Hollywood. Raising children ate into discretionary income, as did buying and maintaining a home. Suburban parents who did want to see a picture had to find babysitters, which in many neighborhoods were proving to be almost as scarce as fresh meat had been right after the war. Exhibitors compounded the problem by being slow to expand into the suburbs. The film consumer often had to travel downtown. A young husband told the *Saturday Evening Post* early in 1952 that going to the movies in postwar Los Angeles had become a logistical nightmare. "First I have to change my clothes," he said. "Then I have to hire a babysitter. I drive downtown in heavy traffic, fork up fifty cents at a parking lot, and walk seven blocks to pay about two dollars for two tickets. It's too much trouble and it costs too much."

Understating such demographic explanations, a March 1949 *Fortune* magazine survey suggested that Hollywood had simply lost its touch. Many of those questioned, like the harried Angeleno husband, complained that they no longer had time to see a picture. But some, including the once regular moviegoer who seemingly had bought tickets for anything on celluloid, expressed dismay over the postwar film. Asked to compare movies with radio, books, and magazines, those polled were the most unhappy with the late 1940s film.

To these and other challenges the rulers of the film colony reacted with extraordinary denseness. Most of the men who had risen to the top of the major studios were dimly educated; their success had far more to do with show-business acumen than with intelligence. Many film historians later presented movie executives as rational managers, shrewdly aware of television's consequences for the movie colony. Most in fact behaved like the heads of other industries in the history of business, such as British manufacturers in the late nineteenth century or American automakers in the 1970s: they were unable or slow to adjust to sudden shifts in consumer demand. Despite elaborate market research, the moguls in the late forties acted as if more of the same would do; there was nothing wrong with the film industry that a good movie would not fix. MGM's audience research chief observed, "Hollywood, by and large, resisted the development of high-level research. In the race between intuition and the IBM machine the latter came in a poor second."

Political and Sexual Sacrifices

Hollywood was also burdened, as earlier, by feelings of vulnerability. In 1947 the Un-American Activities Committee of the House of Representatives (HUAC) had held hearings on charges of Communist influence in the film industry. HUAC had been told that actors, directors, and screenwriters who were Communist party members had attempted to infuse party propaganda, or agitprop, into the movies. The prospect of the corner movie house as brainwashing center was preposterous. Although some of those charged had indeed tried to sell party wares, their films rarely, if ever, challenged the fundamental nature of capitalism and democracy. Journalist Murray Kempton noted that the Daughters of the American Revolution had praised features by those hostile witnesses first interrogated by HUAC. "Whatever their ideas," Kempton wrote, "the Hollywood Communists had written for Hollywood and not for Moscow." But the first ten suspected of Communist affiliations and called to testify in October 1947 overplayed their hand. None would answer any of the committee's questions about their politics; several boorishly attempted to lecture HUAC on their right of association. Instead of a pose on behalf of civil liberties, however, the Hollywood Ten's confrontational tactic suggested that they were dedicated Stalinists, as dangerous to the American filmgoer as poisoned popcorn. Liberals deserted them, and the industry panicked. Moviemakers needed no more public-relations problems. The solution seemed obvious. The industry blacklisted the Ten. No studio would employ them until they agreed to assist HUAC, and all ten went to jail for contempt of Congress.

The blacklist grew dramatically in the early 1950s. Many in Hollywood had joined left-wing groups in the late 1930s and during World War II, and some had been loyal party members. Others had been striving only to be politically correct. Regardless, all found themselves under tremendous pressure to repudiate their radical histories. As the cold war became a stalemate, Stephen J. Whitfield observes, many Americans vented their frustrations on real or imagined domestic enemies. "Since Stalin and his successors were out of reach," Whitfield writes, "making life difficult for Americans who admired them was more practicable." An informal anti-Communist coalition encouraged the blacklist and the "degradation ceremonies" endured by those who wished to escape it. Right-wing actors Adolph Menjou and Ward Bond, among others, urged the studios to cease employing individuals suspected of a Red past; conservative columnists Victor Riesel and George Sokolsky publicized such allegations. J. Edgar Hoover, director of the Federal Bureau of Investigation (FBI), used gossip columnists Louella Parsons and Hedda Hopper as informants. The affected player then faced a painful choice: leave the movie colony, hoping for work on Broadway or abroad, or tell HUAC of his past associations and "name names," that is, list others involved in party activities or fronts. Some, with the cold war suddenly bloody in Korea, spoke freely; others wallowed in self-hatred. Praised for his testimony, actor Sterling Hayden wrote, "Not often does a man find himself eulogized for having behaved in a manner that he himself despises."

In 1951, as HUAC expanded its Hollywood inquisition, the blacklist came to radio and the newest mass medium, television. A right-wing group newsletter, *Red Channels*, accused various broadcast employees of radical inclinations. Anxious advertisers insisted on their removal. In one case, an advertising agency buying a program from producer David Susskind removed an eight-year-old girl from the cast; her parents had apparently belonged to the wrong clubs. There was little or no due process from agency or network in-house internal security departments. Anxious to sell time, no network would stand up to a major sponsor or what attorney Louis Nizer later called the "private vigilantism" of *Red Channels*.

The victims tended to be the younger or supporting players or second- and third-rate writers and directors, who were easily sacrificed to public opinion. Only one of the seventeen highest paid screenwriters listed in 1938 was later "named" a Communist. More prominent victims, notably Charlie Chaplin, had lost most of their box-office appeal. Charges against a Murrow or Lucille Ball made executives sweat but not prepare pink slips.

Although to later generations the blacklist seemed both incomprehensible and morally repugnant, in truth it was only the latter. During World War II, fierce ideological schisms and labor factionalism—Communists had been effective union organizers—had left the film colony a bitter place. Cries of "Communist" and "Fascist" had been bandied about freely in southern California. With the deterioration of Soviet-American relations after 1945, the former charge gained enormous resonance. The American Communist party had routinely followed directives from Moscow and, in turn, obtained a similar fealty from its members in America in the 1930s and 1940s. Obedience defined party participation. Screenwriters in the party had their own degradation ceremonies, during which members apologized for writings that had violated Party guidelines on literature. American party members and "fellow travelers" were assumed, then, to be Moscow-manufactured automatons and had to be exposed. "The Committee," the politically centrist Eric Sevareid, of CBS, told listeners, "had a perfect right to seek those names, indeed, a duty." With the possibility of war between the Soviet Union and America, Communists and fellow travelers appeared to pose a potential threat to national security. Such reasoning explains why the worst excesses of the blacklist came during the Korean conflict: American troops faced Russian allies in combat. Reporters asked President Truman whether, given the imminence of a third world war, he was discouraging his daughter from traveling to Europe. An editor of the *Saturday Evening Post* late in 1951 predicted Russo-American fighting by 1953.

The plots and characterizations of movies conveyed the new dichotomy. At the insistence of Menjou and others, Hollywood produced films such as *Red Danube* (1949), on the fall of Eastern Europe; Menjou's forecasts notwithstanding, they were no more successful than the wartime pro-Russian features. More movies, for example, *My Son, John* (1952), concerned internal subversives. *Big Jim McLain* (1952), starring one of the colony's more avid Red hunters, John Wayne, paid tribute to a HUAC investigator. Director Elia Kazan, who had barely eluded the blacklist, drained *Viva Zapata!* (1952) of its revolutionary message and in *On the Waterfront* (1954) paid tribute to informing (Kazan and screenwriter Budd Schulberg themselves had been informers).

More often, anti-Communism had an indirect influence on filmmaking. Movies like *Diplomatic Courier* (1952) and *Night People* (1954), although ostensibly diversions, centered on East-West tensions and left audiences with no doubt as to the correctness of the heroes (Americans) and the evil of the villains (Russians). The detachment missing from newspapers and radio news had been abandoned in Hollywood as well. There could be no peace. Westerns in the 1950s, Michael Wood contended later, in *America in the Movies*, justified the postwar military buildup by portraying protagonists as nice guys who, possibly after some soul-searching, killed their adversaries. The casts of science fiction films in the fifties routinely included a weak, bespectacled scientist who tried to negotiate with the Thing, only to be destroyed by it. The Thing had to be annihilated.

The movie colony's keen sensitivity to prevailing sentiments might even jeopardize a star's career. Since coming to California in 1940,

Swedish actress Ingrid Bergman had been a publicist's dream. She had starred in such wartime hits as *Casablanca*, *For Whom the Bell Tolls*, and *Gaslight*, all the while maintaining the outward appearances of being happily married to a neurosurgeon, Petter Lindstrom. The Lindstroms had a daughter and lovely home. This image, however, shattered in 1949 and 1950 amid press reports that Bergman had fallen in love with another man, Italian director Roberto Rossellini. The two had been filming *Stromboli* on an island in the Tyrrhenian Sea. Bergman's friend Ernest Hemingway assured her, "Great actresses always have great troubles sooner or later. If they did not they would not be worth a shit." But Hemingway had not anticipated the extensive and critical coverage that ensued. Before either Bergman's or Rossellini's divorce could be finalized, Hearst columnist Louella Parsons announced that Bergman was carrying Rossellini's child. So many reporters and photographers rushed to the Rome hospital where Bergman gave birth to a son in February 1950 that the hospital administrator had to call in the police. Colorado Senator Edwin C. Johnson denounced Rossellini as "a swine inspired by the devil . . . a bedroom prowler." And Bergman, who had led all other actresses in box-office power in the forties, found herself ostracized by the film colony.

Bergman's fate, like that of countless leftists blacklisted by the studios, demonstrated what film critic Richard Schickel termed the industry's "accommodationist ethic." The movie colony still regarded itself as peculiarly vulnerable to the vicissitudes of public opinion. Hollywood would not ignore the American Legion's or a columnist's complaint about an actor's financial contribution to the losing side of the Spanish Civil War in the 1930s. The governors similarly paid heed to moral appearances. Actors had their dalliances, but away from the fourth estate, in remote and fancy motels. *Life* had shown Bergman and Rossellini holding hands! One of the screen's greatest actresses was warned to keep her hands to herself and not leave her husband. Too much had been invested in her wholesomeness to allow passion to intervene. Having disregarded her publicists, Bergman had to wait six years before a major studio starred her in a film. It was seven years before she returned to America for a brief visit.

Bergman's humiliation came too late to save the film industry from the U.S. Justice Department. Antitrust Division attorneys cared little about images; since the late thirties they had been collecting evidence of the movie colony's economic as opposed to moral improprieties. Taking the Big Five to court, the Justice Department sought to end their ownership of theaters. Department attorneys maintained that the control Paramount, MGM, RKO, Warners, and Twentieth Century exercised over the exhibition of films adversely affected the independent operators, many of whom traditionally had been forced to accept less promising features. In *United States v. Paramount* (1948), the Supreme Court upheld a lower court decision, finding for the Justice Department, that ordered the studios to divest themselves of their theaters in the next six years.

Although the industry came to adjust successfully to the court-imposed restructuring, the timing of the decision could not have been worse. The theaters had been the Big Five's most profitable divisions; Warners accrued just over 60 percent of its revenues from exhibition. A year after the *Paramount* decision, a screenwriter cracked, "The swimming pools are drying up all over Hollywood. I do not think I shall see them filled in my generation."

The Coming of the Home Screen

For Hollywood, the worst news came slowly. Across the continent, four different companies, three of them radio networks, had begun regularly scheduled TV broadcasts in 1947. What they "telecast" often seemed alternately laughable or dreary: live sessions of the United Nations, roller derbys, and wrestling matches. Each network aired live dramas, and though some Hollywood performers participated (originally only for the experience), even these efforts at art could not be taken too seriously. Reports that filtered back to the studios all but dismissed even the dramatic productions. Compared with those of a middling B-picture, the production values—the sets, lighting, make-up—were terrible. Viewers could *often* see the microphone boom, the sets rattled if a door was shut too vigorously. Filmmakers thus at first refused to regard television with alarm; after all, it showcased a second-rate night club comedian named Berle ("I've got a joke that could close this network") on Tuesday nights. "A smart telecaster," observed a critic for the *Chicago Sun-Times* in November 1948, "would have himself some sure-fire entertainment by crossing Milton Berle with a wrestling match."

Yet Americans in unanticipated numbers were buying sets to watch Berle and others. And the movie colony was suddenly speechless. "The very mention of television, in many important industry quarters, evokes only icy silence," the *New York Times* reported in April 1949. "Formal inquiries to official spokesmen ordinarily garrulous about activities, plans and opinions, now often elicit the almost unheard-of response in Hollywood: 'No comment.' " Filmmakers and their publicists had good reason to be stunned. The percentage of homes with TV sets shot up from 0.4 percent in 1948 to 9.0 percent in 1950, 23.5 percent in

1951, and 34.2 percent in 1952. By 1956 just under two-thirds of all homes (64.5 percent) had one or more TV receivers. Some consumers were tempted while visiting department stores, which promoted sets prominently in their electronics departments and street window displays. Bars and taverns were among the first to have sets, almost invariably tuned to sporting events. Teetotalers wandered in to see what was on the black and white screen. Manufacturers had to scramble to establish more distribution centers; in some parts of the country, beauty parlors, gasoline stations, and dry cleaners sold TV sets.

The diffusion of television only initially had a significant class bias. The first purchasers of sets were usually among the wealthiest members of a community or neighborhood. Many hosted "TV parties" for friends without sets. By the early 1950s, income lessened as a predictor of set ownership as more and more of the middle and working classes bought TV sets. Almost regardless of income, families with children were likely to secure a receiver. TV afforded cheaper entertainment for parents, who were spared the cost of hiring a babysitter in order to visit the local movie house. During the day, television kept youngsters occupied, often in a separate "family room," and out of mischief; this practice drew the approval of childcare expert Benjamin Spock. More than one mother shared the experience of a Washington, D.C., parent who discovered in 1948 that her nine-month-old ceased crying whenever she turned on the television, no matter what was on. One psychologist found that children were "less fussy" when they took their meals before the TV set.

There were regional distortions as well. The first TV stations were most likely to be in the larger cities, where the potential audience justified the high start-up cost of operating a station. Thus those in rural communities distant from the greatest metropolitan areas were among the last to buy sets. Without a station nearby, the TV receiver was an expensive and useless piece of furniture. NBC newscaster Tom Brokaw recalled that the South Dakota town where he grew up could not receive a TV signal until 1955. "Until then," he wrote, "*Life* magazine and the Sunday edition of the *Minneapolis Tribune* had been my windows on the world beyond the prairies."

Some farm families took up broadcast engineering by building tall antennas to receive faraway stations. A few bought sets to watch the "white noise" of a channel that could be heard but barely seen. Even those who were mechanically inclined had their frustrations. A Louisiana appliance dealer used a Baptist college's hilltop chapel to mount his antenna and laid a cable to his home; when he turned on his set, he could not tell whether he had picked up a Texas League baseball game or the Shreveport Symphony Orchestra.

Stations in larger cities such as Shreveport and New Orleans at first lacked direct connection to the networks. A hookup then required that individual stations be connected by a special coaxial cable laid by American Telephone & Telegraph (AT&T). When regular network broadcasts commenced in 1947 and 1948, the coaxial cable reached only the largest northeastern cities. Until AT&T completed laying the cable in 1952, station managers in many southern, western, and smaller cities scrambled to fill air time. Most channels aired just about any film footage they could find. Starting his station in 1949, an Omaha manager admitted later, "Some of the old movies at that time, which we had to resort to, were very pathetic, they were old stuff . . . almost ready to be thrown away, but the public was tolerant." Stations drafted local talent. Nearly all created their own children's programs with an actor playing a clown, train engineer, or sheriff as host (Atlanta's WAGA featured Morgus, the Crazy Weatherman). Regional diversity enjoyed a new life as southern and western stations produced programs featuring the country music normally spurned by the national networks. The ethnic pluralism of Milwaukee and Cleveland encouraged stations there to offer polka shows.

Chicago, cut off from network connection until 1949, proved to be the most creative source of local programming. Then the nation's second largest city, Chicago already had a pool of talent working in radio. These and others in "the second city" created what came to be known as the "Chicago style" of television. It possessed a detachment absent in the easily excited comedians and variety show hosts that the networks offered from New York. Chicago TV performers were also less taken by the glitz that affected those working in Hollywood. No one better exemplified the Chicago touch than Dave Garroway, who had hosted a popular radio music program prior to starring in "Garroway at Large" on TV. Unlike Berle, Garroway never mugged; eyebrows, not arm waving, denoted reactions. And he spoke wryly to the camera, not loudly to the crowd. The Chicago stations created children's programs like "Mr. Wizard" and "Kukla, Fran and Ollie." The latter, a puppet show, quickly enjoyed an adult following and eventually joined NBC's schedule. New York actress Tallulah Bankhead, it was said, never left for dinner until she had viewed the program. All in all, the Chicago school impressed critics. Harriet Van Horne wrote, "People in the trade say the Chicago touch is to television what the French touch is to cooking."

In time, most forms of local programming disappeared. Virtually all stations in the 1950s had a network affiliation, and in the evening, when the vast majority used their sets, the typical station carried only network programs. Local initiatives typically appeared during hours when relatively few watched TV, Sunday mornings and late Saturday afternoons. Although champions of "local expression" bemoaned the dumping of local programming on the schedule, most viewers and advertisers preferred to see old network programs telecast as "reruns" and "syndicated" series, like "Sea Hunt" and "Highway Patrol," produced by independent companies for stations. In time, network or syndicated cartoon programs displaced even local children's programs. By the late 1960s, station-produced programming consisted of evening newscasts, state basketball tournaments, and local Sunday morning religious services.

By the mid fifties, Chicago, too, no longer served as a center of national program production, though three networks owned stations in the city. More and more, Chicagoans viewed fare produced in New York or California. Actors and writers who had come to Chicago in the late 1940s to work in the new medium had left a decade later. Each network-owned Chicago station cut its production staff; at NBC's WNBQ, the number of engineers fell from 130 in 1957 to 8 in 1962. That year an attorney for the Writers Guild protested, "We are very much like tenants ruled by absentee landlords."

Both advertisers and the networks could be blamed for the centralization of program production. In the 1950s, advertisers heavily involved themselves in overseeing the production of series they sponsored; with most agencies based in New York, ad executives preferred to have shows produced near their headquarters. "Clients advertise to make money, not out of possible regional chauvinism," wrote Ted Mills, a Chicago TV pioneer, in 1962. The networks, too, proved regionally unsentimental. In the late fifties, NBC rejected several requests from TV comedians who wished to originate their series from Chicago. Asked to name television's "most disheartening trend" in late 1954, *Chicago American* TV critic Janet Kern replied, "The tendency toward totalitarian network control over public taste."

With program production bicoastal, viewers in the Midwest, the South, the Pacific Northwest, and the Rocky Mountain states had to suffer borscht belt comedians' jokes about Brooklyn and, in time, about car dealers in Pasadena. Series produced in California rarely showed snow and never a steel mill. Although many situation comedies claimed to be situated in the Midwest, the actors and plots were, in assembly-line fashion, interchangeable with ones based elsewhere. In

1962 Ted Mills complained, "The Hollywoodization of the medium and its viewers will continue its growing stranglehold."

The relatively high costs of programming largely explained the inability of the medium to nurture much regional production. Compared with radio fare, television series proved to be expensive propositions. Actors had to appear before a camera as well as a microphone; they had to be costumed and made-up. Sets had to be created, lighting designed. With radio personnel doing most of the early programming, mistakes occurred, so many, in fact, that some in the movie colony momentarily thought that Americans would forsake the newest medium. But the four networks—NBC, CBS, ABC, and Du Mont—pressed on. CBS and NBC had the resources to lose money (which they did) until the entire nation took up the TV habit.

Networks had to discover audiences before most potential sponsors bought airtime. Few advertisers would help to subsidize early TV programming until the medium's potential as a marketing device had been demonstrated. Evidence of television's possibilities, however, came quickly. Some early buyers of TV time were rewarded—even overwhelmed. Admiral had to cancel "Admiral Broadway Revue" on NBC in 1949 because the company could not produce enough of the TV sets promoted on the program. Four years later, Dow Chemical, stuck with an excess of Saran Wrap, began to advertise the product on television and saw sales increase thirtyfold. Sponsors became easier to secure.

Advertising carried a price. Most companies bought time to sponsor all of a program and accordingly insisted that the network follow their wishes. Soap operas sponsored by Procter & Gamble followed that company's rules for employees and did not show characters smoking or drinking coffee. Schick forbade the producers of a historical drama from showing a character in 1860 using a straight razor. A tobacco company that sponsored another program did not want Russians to be seen smoking too many cigarettes. Still, such sponsor intervention can be exaggerated. For example, Alcoa never interfered with Murrow's "See It Now." Some of early television's best programming was possible only because certain sponsors, in exchange for compromises about straight razors and Communist tobacco consumption, gave producers wide leeway in what they presented. "Kraft, U.S. Steel, Goodyear, the Bell System, Philco and many other companies sponsored programs of such quality," advertising agent John O'Toole wrote in 1978, "that they still stand out to those of us with long memories."

Increasing advertiser interest made TV profitable for most early investors. In 1951, the FCC reported, only 5 of 108 stations showed a profit. Within the next two years, however, most stations began to earn money on their original investment in equipment and programming. Within six years of its founding, the *Analysts Journal* reported in 1954, a network-affiliated station in a larger market might enjoy annual returns of 35 percent. Although CBS and NBC continued to lose money because of high programming costs, earnings from their owned and operated stations more than justified the expense.

New station operators coveted an affiliation with NBC or CBS, and FCC policies unintentionally encouraged this duopoly. Television frequencies were the hungriest consumer of the radio spectrum. A TV channel required three times as much space as a radio frequency. Then, too, all available allocations were initially restricted to the Very High Frequency (VHF) portion of the radio band, channels 2 through 13. Thus, only a limited number of stations could serve individual communities; allocating too many channels in the more densely populated parts of the Northeast and Midwest caused interference. At first, with demand for channels limited, the FCC awarded them on a first-come, first-serve basis. When the number of would-be telecasters rose sharply in the late 1940s, the commission developed a cumbersome "comparative license" procedure for awarding individual TV frequencies, which often greatly delayed the granting of licenses. As a result, viewers in many cities (or TV "markets") had to wait years for second, third, or fourth channels. The pioneer in a given market was likely to affiliate with NBC or CBS.

The FCC labored to create a more equitable distribution of channels. In 1948 it ceased issuing new licenses pending the formulation of a master allocation of station frequencies. Over the next four years, the FCC developed a plan that it believed would not only provide all Americans with television service—the commission's first concern—but also create opportunities for the two struggling chains, ABC and Du Mont, as well as potential new networks. The FCC banked heavily on an experimental portion of the spectrum, the Ultra High Frequency (UHF) channels 14–83. UHF, the FCC majority argued, allowed for the allocation of third, fourth, or fifth stations in most communities. Moreover, nonprofit or educational systems could use the UHF channels. Small towns, including Worland, Wyoming, with a population of four thousand, received station allocations.

The FCC's gamble on UHF proved to be characteristically ineffective, demonstrating again its Candide-like sense of network economics and broadcast technology. The freeze itself had aided NBC and CBS. In all but twelve of the sixty-three markets that had television service before the freeze, Du Mont and ABC had no affiliates or had to share access with CBS or NBC. The end of the freeze and establishment of UHF stations did not increase network competition as hoped. UHF reception compared poorly with that of VHF and required a special converter priced at thirty-five dollars, which few consumers bought. Du Mont and ABC were hit the hardest. In the three years after the freeze, the majority of their affiliates in the one hundred largest markets were UHF outlets. Competing against NBC- and CBS-affiliated stations on VHF, the Du Mont and ABC UHF channels could not reach the same number of homes; most UHF outlets left the air by 1956. Advertisers frustrated the FCC as well. Although more and more companies bought TV air time, the total demand among underwriters for television would initially support only two networks and only those stations located in the larger cities. Advertisers prized audiences, not diversity.

Filling the Air

To create programming, anxious broadcast executives borrowed from every established cultural form. Variety programs initially emphasized acts—jugglers, acrobats, trained seals—and the masters of ceremonies often were veterans of the vaudeville stage. "Show people generally see television as a great boon to vaudeville," *San Francisco Chronicle* TV critic Terrence O'Flaherty observed in August 1949. "At least 20, probably more, weekly programs on the national TV networks use a vaudeville format. They use up at least 60 vaudeville acts a week." Not everyone delighted in vaudeville's new life. TV, Goodman Ace complained, stood for "Terrible Vaudeville."

Situation comedies like "The Life of Riley" and "My Friend Irma," action dramas like "Sky King" and "The Lone Ranger," and quiz programs like "Truth or Consequences" and "Queen for a Day" had all originated on radio. Although two of the medium's earliest stars, Milton Berle and Lucille Ball, enjoyed successes on TV that dwarfed any success they had had previously, both had worked in radio and the movie colony. NBC's Dave Garroway had hosted a jazz music program on a Chicago radio station; CBS's highest-paid variety show host, Arthur Godfrey, had already starred in his own radio program. Groucho Marx had perfected his game show, "You Bet Your Life," on NBC radio, and it ran on NBC TV from 1950 to 1961. NBC stars whom Paley had lured to his stable similarly changed frequencies; Jack Benny was a fixture on CBS TV for fourteen years. Fred Allen, with whom Benny frequently feuded on their respective programs, was far less successful in making the shift to television and found sarcasm toward the medium to be the best revenge. "They call television a medium," Allen cracked, "because nothing on it is ever well done." Although almost as disdainful toward television, most network radio newscasters tried to make the transition to the home screen. Murrow had the looks to succeed on TV, though he waited until 1951 to show them off. Others struggled with being seen. By vainly disguising his baldness with a large fedora, Walter Winchell upset millions: TV affected to be a guest in the living room, and no respectable male visitor wore a hat in the house.

Like radio, television relied on certain established "genres," with none more particular to TV's early years than the live variety shows hosted by Berle, Ed Wynn, Jackie Gleason, and Arthur Godfrey. Some, like Paul Whiteman's "TV Teen Club," stressed music; others, like Berle's Texaco program, emphasized comedy. Berle and Godfrey triumphed in ways that almost matched their enormous egos. Berle was "Mr. Television." In late 1948 a higher percentage of homes watched Berle than had listened to President Roosevelt's address asking Congress to declare war on Japan in 1941. And on Election Day in 1948, NBC delayed reporting the voting until after Berle's show had aired. Not until the Du Mont network scheduled Bishop Fulton J. Sheen's program, "Life Is Worth Living," against him in 1953–54 did Berle have a serious rival. And Sheen, Berle liked to note, had better writers. Godfrey's relatively low-key manner made him CBS's premiere player; in 1954, advertising bought for his TV and radio programs accounted for 12 percent of CBS's total revenues. The news media treated Godfrey's hospital stays as major events, and Godfrey himself immodestly disagreed in public with President Eisenhower's efforts to contain military spending. The most curious casting of a variety program emcee proved the most lasting. For more than twenty years, New York City gossip columnist Ed Sullivan hosted a Sunday evening variety hour on CBS. No entertainer, Sullivan could not tell a joke or sing a song. Indeed, his awkward posture and slurred speech inspired two generations of mimics. Sullivan succeeded instead by assiduously securing the hottest acts for his program. "Ed Sullivan will be a success," Fred Allen wrote, "as long as other people have talent."

After 1951, the half-hour situation comedy, or "sitcom," became a permanent part of each network's evening schedule. Modeled after the radio series, the TV situation comedy featured a set lineup of characters humorously reckoning with usually trivial crises. Effective casting made many situation comedies memorable. Two programs about teachers, "Mr. Peepers" and "Our Miss Brooks," worked in part because both the stars and their supporting players were perfectly suited to their roles. Character actor Gale Gordon played Miss Brooks's pompous and tyrannical principal with a vigor only occasionally seen in later series. Nor did the commander of Fort Baxter, played by Paul Ford on

"The Phil Silvers Show" (CBS, 1955–59), convey authority any less comically, and at a time when American opinion leaders promoted military preparedness with the utmost seriousness.

Most situation comedies lacked such resonance. The majority left the air after one or two seasons; others owed their durability to the established popularity of their stars. The humor of "The Jack Benny Show" and "Burns and Allen" depended almost entirely on the viewer's recognition of the characters' comic peculiarities. Burns and Allen, a *Saturday Evening Post* writer observed in 1952, were "better known to American audiences than most United States Senators." Other series, starring the Nelson family, Ann Sothern, and Gale Storm, were similarly mere vehicles for performers whose comic gifts never approached those of Lucille Ball or Eve Arden of "Our Miss Brooks." Scripts were usually uninspired when not insipid.

Dramatic series, another network staple, similarly varied in quality. The earliest ones had been radio programs, and as with sitcoms, the majority had relatively short lives. Most frequently aired were ones about crime fighters. "Dragnet," concerning the adventures of Sergeant Joe Friday of the Los Angeles Police Department, was the most popular, drawing ten times as many viewers as any telecast of the 1954 hearings on Senator Joseph McCarthy's charges of Communism in the Army. Critics praised "Dragnet" star and producer Jack Webb for his deglamorization of police work. Preparing for the series, Webb had observed firsthand the workings of the Los Angeles Police Department. Hailed, too, was "Dragnet"'s spare dialog; over and over again, "Dragnet"'s Sergeant Friday declared, "All we want are the facts, ma'am."

Westerns, too, came to the home screen. Until the late 1950s, series about cowboys and lawmen appeared during the day. After a brief network run in 1948–51, "Hopalong Cassidy" continued as syndicated fare, transforming an obscure B-movie actor, William Boyd, into a childhood idol. Dairy companies ran endorsements by "Hoppy"; cowboys drank milk. Two other stars of old "B" Westerns, Roy Rogers and Gene Autry, attracted a new generation of fans. Although Rogers, unlike Boyd, did not own the rights to telecast his pictures, he did successfully promote an array of Roy Rogers paraphernalia. Girls, too, had their role model, in Rogers's costar and wife, Dale Evans. More conventional in its exclusively male casting was "The Lone Ranger." Originally a children's radio serial, this series about a lone vigilante and his Indian companion, Tonto, involved weekly confrontations against evil. At the end of each episode, the Ranger delivered a short lecture on goodness and, before being thanked, rode off on his horse, Silver. "The Lone Ranger" ran on ABC for eight years, until 1957, and lived on in syndication, leaving millions of American children baffled as to what Tonto meant when he called the Ranger "Kemo Sabe."

In California, the moguls were amazed. Although many of TV's stars, including Berle and Ball, had appeared in films, most had appeared in B-pictures. And the B-picture itself seemed to constitute TV's filmed product. Indeed, "Hopalong Cassidy" consisted of little more than edited Western serials Boyd had made for Republic studios. Meanwhile, Hollywood in the fifties produced perhaps its best "A" Westerns: *High Noon, Shane, The Searchers,* none of which played to the child-like sensibilities so cultivated by "Hoppy" or Tonto's faithful friend.

Not everything TV offered had been borrowed from the studios. One of the earliest and most convenient fillers of time was the live sporting event. From New York came roller derbys and wrestling matches. Boxing filled several evening slots. Baseball, football, and basketball games, all of which had been radio fare, were telecast as well. Not all sports gained from TV's arrival. Many National Football League teams had difficulty selling their product to stations; technology partly explained their dilemma. Normally only one or two large TV cameras could be used for a game. There could be no instant replay until the introduction of videotaping in the 1960s. The immobility of the camera made baseball games boring to all but the most devoted fan. One camera behind home plate tried to capture all the action. Adding to the tediousness, news crews handled baseball, Ron Powers wrote, giving them "the same, formalistic look and feel as a presidential ceremony." TV's shortcomings notwithstanding, baseball team owners grumbled that telecasts cut into their attendance. Minor league operators claimed that telecasts of major league contests all but doomed their franchises. They were only partly right. The minors had overexpanded after World War II, and that excess growth, and not televised games, largely accounted for the minors' woes. Some major league owners worried all the way to the bank as lucrative TV contracts encouraged franchises to move for the first time since 1902. Early in 1953 the Boston Braves, quitting for Milwaukee, began the migration; Milwaukee brewers had promised to sponsor statewide telecasts.

The networks aired sporting events inconsistently in the 1950s. In search of a network, the NFL had to settle for Du Mont, at that point about as lucrative as a Packard automobile dealership. Individual teams struck deals with independent stations and formed their own networks. On Sunday afternoons, which eventually came to be the most common time to air sports contests, NBC and CBS offered high cultural programming like the Ford Foundation's "Omnibus" and news shows. CBS's "See It Now" and NBC's "Victory at Sea" originally appeared on

Sunday afternoons. Not all critics approved. "Sunday is the day to be outdoors," Marya Mannes wrote in *Who Owns the Air?*, "to drive, to mow the lawn, to swim, to play golf, to sail . . . to nap. On Sunday, the time when most people turn on their sets is after seven." "It's always a mystery to me why a person, any civilized person, would be sitting at home on a Sunday afternoon watching television," Murrow told *Newsweek* in 1952. Yet a minority of viewers in search of culture found the Sunday "ghetto" better than nothing at all. "Sunday on television," actor Rod Steiger remarked, "makes up for everything during the week that you didn't like."

With much time unsold in TV's first years, all of the networks filled the hours by telecasting live various news events. The earliest were sessions of the United Nations at its temporary headquarters at Lake Success, New York. Although the Supreme Court and Congress refused to allow the televising of their proceedings, the networks did air some congressional committees at work. Both the 1948 and 1952 national party conventions were covered gavel to gavel.

The telecasting of the conventions offered one indication of TV's influence on American politics. The Democratic National Convention selected Philadelphia as its 1948 convention site in part because the coaxial cable to the city made possible network telecasting. Speakers at both conventions shortened speeches that before radio might have run three hours. On the convention floor, delegates similarly proved willing to cooperate with the new technology. In 1948, southern Democrats angry over the party's civil rights plank tossed down their badges before the NBC camera, only to retrieve them and resume their seats after the network eye had turned away. Four years later, the managers of General Dwight D. Eisenhower's campaign for the Republican presidential nomination cleverly insisted that TV cameras cover a convention committee meeting they had insisted upon as part of their effort to "open up" the nomination process. When those laboring for Eisenhower's opponent, Senator Robert A. Taft, objected to TV's presence, they unintentionally fueled the impression that they sought to "steal" the nomination from the general.

Except for the conventions and presidential addresses, CBS and NBC sharply reduced their telecasts of live news events in the early 1950s. No longer did each suffer the headache of filling unsold time. Unlike ABC and Du Mont, both CBS and NBC had daytime schedules of soap operas and talk programs; none would be sacrificed on the altar of "public service." As a result, live news events broadcast in the early fifties were most likely to be available on an ABC or Du Mont affiliate. Both ABC and Du Mont aired proceedings of two controversial congressional committees in 1951 and 1954. The first, chaired by Senator Estes Kefauver, of Tennessee, investigated organized crime and political corruption and transformed its chairman into a contender for the 1952 Democratic presidential nomination. In the suburbs, John Crosby wrote, "the well-heeled matrons have picked Sen. Kefauver as their matinee idol, a sort of Laurence Olivier with a briefcase." (The Kefauver sessions caused Murrow, who had refused to take TV seriously, to undergo a change of heart. "The midgets in the box have been real," he wrote.) Three years later, ABC and Du Mont aired a Senate inquiry into Joseph McCarthy's charges that the Army had Communist sympathizers. McCarthy, the foremost crusader against Communism in the federal bureaucracy, was widely considered one of the most powerful and most dangerous men in America. Yet few came away from viewing the hearings likening him to Laurence Olivier; if anything, television made McCarthy suffer a role reversal. On TV, he seemed to be, not a righteous avenger, but a cruel, at times fumbling, plugugly. A friend told John Steinbeck that McCarthy too closely resembled "the Bad Guy" on the TV Western. "He sneers. He bullies, he has a nasty laugh and he always looks as though he needs a shave. The only thing he lacks is a black hat." McCarthy's public-approval ratings fell, and in December the Senate overwhelmingly passed a resolution condemning the senator.

Too much can be made of television's role in McCarthy's fall. The senator's attack on the Army had already caused many of his allies in the fourth estate to abandon him. Then, too, relatively few Americans more than sampled one or two of the McCarthy sessions. Most TV stations, unaffiliated with ABC and Du Mont, did not carry the proceedings; those that did pick up the ABC feed saw their ratings drop sharply. The effect of Edward R. Murrow's attack on the senator on his evening news program, "See It Now," was also greatly overestimated. Although television's first historian, Leo Bogart, likened Murrow to Emile Zola, a third of CBS's affiliates did not even carry "See It Now." In cities where it could be viewed, the telecast apparently only reinforced the views of those already hostile to the senator. And in Washington, relatively few of those who were involved directly in the struggle with McCarthy saw the program. Thirteen years after the broadcast, former President Eisenhower could not recall Murrow's anti-McCarthy telecast.

The efforts of Murrow, ABC, and Du Mont did move critics, who believed that Murrow's program and the telecasting of congressional proceedings were creating a new electronic forum. Citizens enjoyed an access to their government unknown since Athens in the age of Pericles. All could monitor the workings of their government.

There were cultural opportunities as well. From the beginning, CBS and NBC aired live dramas from New York. Scrambling to locate adequate facilities, the networks converted old theaters, hotel dining rooms, empty stores, abandoned churches, and car barns into studios. Shows like "Studio One" (CBS) weekly offered original "teleplays." For NBC, Delbert Mann directed 100 one-hour dramas between 1949 and 1955. Although some established film stars participated initially, in time the live anthology dramas relied on New York–based talent. One recruit, novelist Gore Vidal, wrote in 1956, "The Golden Age for the dramatist is at hand. There is so much air to be illustrated, so many eyes watching, so much money to be spent, so many fine technicians and interpreters at one's command, that the playwright cannot but thrive."

Cramped quarters, tight time, and budget restraints gave most original TV dramas a minimalist quality. "Early television presented 'intimate' dramas because there was no room to do otherwise," one TV critic wrote later. Touched by the realism of Arthur Miller, William Inge, and Tennessee Williams, stories usually involved everyday characters, often alienated or lonely. *Marty* (1953) described the struggles of a plump and unmarried butcher, yearning to escape solitude. A couple struggles against alcoholism in *The Days of Wine and Roses* (1958). A lone juror convinces his peers of a man's innocence in *Twelve Angry Men* (1954). Only in the late fifties did anthologies take on the higher production values associated with Hollywood films. By then, anthologies sank the *Titanic* (in *A Night to Remember*) and refought the Spanish Civil War (in *For Whom the Bell Tolls*).

Most anthologies were telecast live. Since the early days of radio, broadcasters had assumed that consumers preferred live over transcribed performances. Indeed, one of the original justifications for networks in the late 1920s had been that they afforded Americans the simultaneous, live performance. And in the early fifties, most network broadcasts—virtually all variety shows and original dramas—in the Eastern and Central time zones were live; Pacific and Mountain state viewers more often saw programs on cheap "kinescope" film. In June 1953, 81.5 percent of the networks' programming was live. A would-be buyer of ABC had told the FCC a year earlier that "the real vitality in the future of television is in live broadcasting."

Viewers of TV dramas had the sensation of seeing a play as opposed to a movie. Most understood when Paul Newman blew a line at the end of *Bang the Drum Slowly*. Some could be misled, as when film veteran

James Cagney momentarily forgot several lines during his TV debut; critics, praising Cagney, assumed that he had been pausing for dramatic effect. Rehearsing *The Petrified Forest* for telecast in 1955, film star Lauren Bacall remembered being "totally terrified." David Selznick had warned her, "If you make a mistake, you make it in front of three million people."

Live telecasts did, in fact, involve risks. A nervous sportscaster doing a tobacco commercial lighted the filter end of his cigarette. Unaware that the camera remained on him, an actor who had just "died" rose and left the set. "Every night was opening night," recalled Bill Jobe, a costume designer, "with fluffed lines, ties askew, flys open, and overstuffed merry widows." Cleavage was a special worry of network censors. "The network didn't seem to care what anyone wore as long as there was no cleavage," Jobe wrote. "We always had flowers and bits of lace standing by to add to the fronts of lady performers."

The shortcomings of live television caused some to miss the mass medium's creativity. NBC was especially innovative. Under the presidency of Pat Weaver, NBC TV, if anything, stressed the irregular. NBC variety shows had rotating hosts. The network also invested heavily in "spectaculars," one-time specials of 90 to 120 minutes. The most popular, *Peter Pan*, aired in March 1955, cost an unprecedented $400,000 yet drew incredible ratings, with one out of every two Americans viewing the musical based on Sir James Barrie's fairy tale.

Various factors explained Weaver's programming philosophy. Paley's raid had left him with scant choice. With many of NBC's biggest stars lost to CBS in the late 1940s, NBC had to rely less on the regular weekly comedy series with an established radio performer. Then, too, RCA, heavily promoting new color television sets, expected NBC to schedule programs in color that would draw large audiences. Weaver could, then, spare no expense compared with his counterparts at CBS, whose own color TV set manufacturing process was proving to be a failure. Weaver had his own reasons for special programs: like many observers, Weaver feared that people would tire of television, that once the novelty factor wore off, Americans would reduce their viewing. "We program," he said in June 1953, "so that there is no falling off in attendance at the set as the years go by." Innovative television might increase the time people spent with TV by offering programs at hours the set normally went unused. Such initiatives would produce "more talk after the shows to keep television the dominating influence of our times." Like such critics of the mass media as Gilbert Seldes, Weaver assumed that radio and the movies had lost audiences in part because their products had become too predictable, too "safe." New types of shows, rather than more of whatever had worked on another medium, might even expand the total audience. More than half of all women at home during the day, Weaver noted in 1953, did not watch TV soap operas. A different kind of fare, he argued, might reach that nonviewer. With that unused TV set in mind, Weaver oversaw the creation of 90- and 120-minute daily information programs, "The Today Show" and "Home," which defined news broadly.

Weaver's innovations and CBS's more traditional and star-studded programming strategy assured the dominance of the home screen. Although some did cut their viewing time, people did not stop using their sets. In mid-1950s surveys in New York City and Charlotte, North Carolina, most respondents indicated that they preferred television to radio, film, or newspapers. "Television had established its place," Leo Bogart wrote in *The Age of Television*, "as the most important single form of entertainment and of passing the time."

Television's sudden and overwhelming popularity encouraged intellectuals who were decrying the evolution of a "mass society" to overestimate the newest medium's hold on viewers. What Gilbert Seldes liked to call "the great audience" was in reality made up of distinct viewing groups, connected by race, class, or ethnic tie. While each might watch a particular network program every week, they responded to it with different degrees of enthusiasm. Jackie Gleason, for example, enjoyed popularity among black Americans. Working-class Italian-Americans in Boston's West End whom the sociologist Herbert Gans interviewed preferred some programs over others. Most disliked the easily manipulated father in many situation comedies; traditional fathers had more will. "When the mass media depict family relationships," Gans wrote, "West Enders approve those which support their values and reject those which do not." Viewers ignored or even yelled at their sets. "We heckle TV," one told Gans, "just like we used to heckle the freaks at the circus when we were kids."

Television hardly worried those in power. TV might have the largest house, but its managers self-consciously respected authority. Advertisers made sure that the programs they sponsored honored conventional morality. TV shows, overall, were even more circumspect than the movies had been. According to John Crosby, "About the most pointed joke you could make then was how hard it was to get a taxi in the rain, because the rain didn't advertise, had no political affiliations, and fell on black and white impartially." Groucho Marx noted, "You crack a joke about a lawyer for example, you get a letter from the legal office of a legal office in some city. You can't kid anything anymore." Not all groups had such clout. Middle-class blacks' protest of the racial stereotyping on "Amos 'n' Andy" had the unintended effect of discouraging the networks from offering any programming with black actors, even in supporting roles, until the mid 1960s. The script to the TV drama *Thunder on Sycamore Street* was revised so that a parable about racial bigotry became one about prejudice against a white ex-convict. Africans on a Jack Benny program in 1954 were cast as cannibals, absurdly costumed and singing the Campbell's Soup song as they prepared to dine on Benny and guest Bob Hope. Only after the most protracted negotiations would CBS allow Lucille Ball in 1951 to play opposite her real husband, Desi Arnaz; the network did not want a Cuban husband in an American situation comedy. "I Love Lucy" did carry one larger message: every time Lucy left the home for a job, disaster befell her and her faithful companion, Ethel. The reporter of public disasters, Edward R. Murrow, may have made television news respectable, but those seeking penetrating insights into American politics in the 1950s had to rely on the printed page. "Politically Murrow was always on the safe ground of the ruling orthodoxy," British journalist Henry Fairlie observed. Most of the live dramas, for all their realism, had happy endings. Marty got a girl. Crises were personal, not societal. "Only in a very marginal and oblique way," wrote one student of the TV plays, do the anthology authors "challenge the values we are told to live by."

The New Forum

The introduction of television caused one more trepidation: the possibility that TV might reshape American politics. In 1950 some candidates for statewide offices hosted TV programs, a few held telethons modeled after ones Berle hosted on NBC. Two years later, Dwight Eisenhower appeared in a series of twenty-second "spots," carefully crafted by an advertising agent. To the horror of many sophisticated viewers, the general responded in the simplest fashion to a voter's question ("My Mamie gets after me about the high cost of living. It's another reason why I say, 'It's time for a change.'"). When Eisenhower subsequently won in a landslide, some bitter Democrats, out of power for the first time since 1932, blamed television.

As would be the case in subsequent campaigns, such criticisms were overstated. Democrats who assumed that TV commercials had so much authority in 1952 underestimated Eisenhower's appeal as a wartime hero and the relative obscurity of his Democratic opponent. Then, too, television set ownership probably had a slight Republican bias. That is, a TV set owner was more likely to be from the middle or upper class and already inclined to vote for the GOP. This built-in audience factor may have partly accounted for the favorable reaction to Senator Richard M. Nixon's televised appeal to the nation on September 23, 1952. Eisenhower's running mate, Nixon had been urged to quit the ticket after the *New York Post* reported that wealthy contributors had given him monies for a special, discretionary fund. The donations suggested a serious conflict of interest for the California Republican at a time when corruption had been a Republican issue. Although Nixon's thirty-minute talk possessed elements of a bad 1930s radio serial (he referred to his daughters' dog, Checkers, and wife's plain cloth coat), he probably had a disproportionately Republican audience predisposed to consider his corny pitch sincere. He remained on the ticket.

Nor did TV initially alter traditional voting patterns. Two political scientists, Herbert A. Simon and Frederick Stern, compared the 1952 returns in Iowa counties with "high television densities" (HTD) to those in counties with relatively few receivers (LTD), as well as with pluralities in earlier presidential contests. Simon and Stern argued that Republican margins in HTD counties were no greater and were consistent with earlier results. Eisenhower's advertising agents were not brainwashing those hapless Iowa residents who owned television sets. Indeed, some thought TV would change nothing. "Television, radio, etc.," a St. Louis Republican official wrote two years later, "will never replace the precinct captain and his workers."

There was, however, one disturbing indication of the distorting and powerful lens that TV might become. In 1951 the sociologists Gladys and Kurt Lang surveyed people who had viewed a Chicago parade in honor of General Douglas MacArthur, recently removed from command of U.N. forces in Korea. Those lining the streets, Lang and Lang found, divided over the controversial general. Many were mere spectators, simply watching the motorcade, but television's careful framing of the parade—its camera placement and omniscient commentary—suggested mass enthusiasm for a returning hero. "It has been claimed for television that it brings the truth directly into the home," the Langs wrote. "This assumed reportorial accuracy is far from automatic. Every camera selects, and thereby leaves the unseen part of the subject open to suggestion and influence. The gaps are usually filled in by a commentator."

Whatever TV's social effects, television had in less than a decade upset the republic of mass leisure. Many of those who had gone to the neighborhood movie house now stayed home. Families that in the evening had clustered around the radio now congregated before the home screen. Magazines and newspapers no longer drew the eyes of so many readers. TV was no fad. The light from the sets kept burning as competitors plotted ways to douse it.

THE WAR FOR ATTENTION   4
Responding to Television,
1947–1958

TELEVISION'S RIVALS had been warned: "Make no mistake about it— television is here and here to stay," the chairman of the Federal Communications Commission told a group of radio broadcasters in April 1949. "If there be those in this audience today who think they can lick it, who think they can stall the development of television in this country or in their community, I urge them to give heed because they know not what they see before them."

By the mid 1950s most of the older mass media accepted the obvious: TV had won the war for the largest share of time Americans spent consuming the mass media. Americans kept buying TV sets; a few, with more discretionary income, purchased second receivers for late evening, bedroom viewing or as a means of resolving intrafamily squabbles over what to watch. Viewing TV had become, in the words of one observer, "a routine activity." "Why go to the movies," remarked film executive Samuel Goldwyn late in 1955, "when you can stay home and see nothing worse?"

Printed Complacency

Television was also having its effects on the newspaper industry. Surveys in the late 1940s and early 1950s indicated that consumers continued their habit of taking one or more newspapers, though nearly all studies suggested that TV viewing caused Americans to spend less time reading them. Total newspaper circulation rose in the fifties but failed to keep pace with the sharply expanding number of individual households. The circulation per household, according to economist Bruce M.

Owen, fell 11 percent. Between 1948 and 1958 the number of cities with two or more papers fell from 109 to 70. On the other hand, the growth of suburbs encouraged establishing new dailies as the number of cities with daily papers rose from 1,392 in 1948 to 1,447 in 1958. Although newspapers' share of all advertising expenditures fell, from 35.8 percent in 1948 to 30.8 percent in 1958, gross revenues rose.

Rather than decry television, however, publishers complained most often about the costs of putting out a paper. Higher newsprint and labor expenses, they insisted, compelled newspapers to reduce the amount of news they carried. The shift was not abrupt, and most readers failed to notice. 'Papers did not become thin; most dailies actually grew in size, but advertising, not news, filled more of the additional pages. Publishers cut costs further by reducing the amount of news carried in favor of more photographs, larger print, and more white space.

Many newspaper owners regarded television as an investment opportunity. In small and large cities, daily newspapers sought a TV franchise. They liked being on the cutting edge of the latest communication technology. Starting a station, particularly in TV's earliest years, was considered a marvelous form of self-promotion and civic boosterism in cities like Milwaukee and Atlanta. Newspapers there and elsewhere, having owned radio stations, possessed the experience that was thought to be transferable to television. Harvey J. Levin estimated that by 1958, newspapers or newspaper chains owned one-third of all TV stations. Most found a TV outlet embarrassingly more profitable than a newspaper.

In the 1950s, few editors seriously considered television a competitor at news-gathering. A breaking big story, notably President Eisenhower's heart attack in 1955, might draw people to their television sets. Most of the time, however, neither the networks nor local stations took their informational function very seriously. "Television is going the way of radio as fast as it can: that is, toward entertainment," the editor of the *Louisville Courier-Journal* remarked in February 1956. News programs commanded relatively few viewers and virtually no advertisers. To limit their losses, networks and local stations ran fifteen-minute evening newscasts consisting of headline readings, stock film footage, and crude visual displays. A toy house might be set ablaze on camera to accompany an item on a house fire; model trains collided for a story on a train collision. "The best that TV can do," Jack Gould of the *New York Times* observed in 1956, "is a quick newsreel once-over of the day's events. There is no sustained coverage in depth, little helpful evaluation of the significance of the headline, and virtually no interpretive commentary to stimulate the viewer to do some thinking for himself."

Although several networks telecast portions of the Kefauver and Army-McCarthy hearings, relatively few Americans could take in these daytime congressional inquisitions, and most required a newspaper's mediation of the proceedings. "The Today Show" and "See It Now" notwithstanding, most network and station hours, especially during evening "prime time," were aimed at diverting rather than informing audiences. "In the new media of mass communication," newspaper columnist Marquis Childs complained in 1956 of both radio and television, "the effort at meaningful and vital communication simply has not been made."

Survey after survey indicated that the majority of TV users considered television a diversion. A poll of Atlanta set owners in 1952 found that the typical family "purchased television to be entertained. And, when asked what television had done for them and their families, the great majority answered it had entertained them." Viewers, sociologist Rolf Meyersohn observed, "seem to be entertained by the glow and the flow, regardless of whether [TV] presents a commercial, a second rate comic or an ancient Western."

Suburbanization posed a more immediate challenge to newspaper publishers. The new postwar family was quitting the densely populated city, where for three generations a daily newspaper had served as a bond for many of those crowded into a single great metropolitan area. In the 1950s, Jon Teaford notes, the population of the twenty largest cities increased by 0.1 percent; the number living in communities surrounding these core areas rose by 45 percent. Between 1940 and 1960 the proportion of Greater Los Angeles's population residing in Los Angeles County fell from 54 percent to 38 percent. The extension of freeways in Santa Monica, San Pedro, Pasadena, and the San Fernando Valley made living outside the city proper irresistible for many. Over the long run, the trend was even more pronounced for almost every metropolitan area. In 1930, 78.3 percent of Greater Washington's population resided in the District of Columbia; in 1980, 78.5 percent lived outside the district.

Many central-city publishers failed to understand this changing market. The Hearst chain continued to practice a hysterical journalism that appealed almost exclusively to the grim fantasies and prejudices of its publishers and some older urban dwellers. Newspapers owned by John S. Knight, in contrast, deliberately went after the younger, suburban audience by downplaying sensational crimes and such Hearstian causes as anti-vivisection in favor of stories designed for the new families, who were more concerned with children's cereals than with serial murders. Knight's foresight might have saved a struggling *New York*

Herald Tribune, whose editors in the 1950s ignored recommendations that the *Tribune* outflank its archrival, the *Times*, by putting out special sections for suburbanites. East of Manhattan, *Newsday* proved to be one of the great and largely unknown success stories of postwar journalism. Under publisher Alicia Patterson, the Long Island daily consciously played to the new geographical identifications of readers by publishing four separate "zoned" editions daily. Circulation rose from 32,000 in 1940 to 370,000 in 1960.

Suburbanization in the long run most affected the big-city evening daily. At least part of the big-city papers' earlier circulation growth had been due to consumers' need for diversion while taking a trolley or elevated train to and from work. In the 1950s, however, the percentage of families owning a car rose from 59 percent in 1950 to 77 percent in 1960, while passenger traffic on common carriers—buses, subways, intracity rail systems—fell by 34.7 percent. The new, individual commuter could not, except in the worst of traffic jams, read a newspaper; eyes had to monitor traffic, not wire service stories or a comic strip. In the Los Angeles area in 1960, workers spent as much as an hour returning from work. As traffic clotted freeways from midafternoon until six, delivering evening papers to surrounding communities proved more and more onerous. Morning dailies, in contrast, could be delivered to carriers in the early morning, when virtually no one used the highways. Yet in the fifties, publishers failed to anticipate the impact of individual commuting on evening papers. Most looked backwards, to the interwar years of laborers living closer to employers and using public transportation. Although *Los Angeles Times* publisher Norman Chandler correctly foresaw the vast migration to southern California after the war, he expected most of the area's population expansion to occur within the city itself, with the expanded work force relying largely on the city's red trolleys. This new resident, Chandler assumed, would need an evening tabloid modeled after those begun in New York a quarter-century earlier. Founded in 1948, Chandler's *Los Angeles Mirror* proved to be a $25 million forecasting error. Still, Chandler was only slightly more inept a soothsayer than the *Fortune* writer who in 1950 recommended that potential investors buy an evening paper to avoid a morning edition's higher overnight labor costs. Four years later, the owner of the *Washington Evening Star*, then the capital's leader in circulation and advertising, stood by aloofly as the *Post* bought the morning *Times-Herald*. The *Post* immediately assumed a circulation leadership which it never relinquished. With the *Times-Herald*'s morning run, the *Star* might have survived a losing battle with the *Post* for readers and advertisers. Not even Time Inc., which purchased the paper in 1978, could, after spending

$85 million and halfheartedly publishing five zoned editions, save the *Star*, which A. J. Liebling had described in 1959 as "a disgustingly rich newspaper with an unassailable position."

More successful editors in the fifties fought the complacency that eventually destroyed dailies like the *Star*. At *Newsday*, Alicia Patterson introduced a more readable, three-column layout. Knight's *Detroit Free Press* began experimenting with color photos in 1953. Drawing on surveys of readers, his chain championed a more accessible style, free of the multiple modifiers that denoted the wire service prose so many journalists utilized. Managing editor Turner Catledge sought to rid the good, gray *New York Times* of what he called "an unnecessary stodginess in the way the news was reported," notwithstanding the "general rule" at the *Times* "to do things today the way we had done them yesterday and not to worry about tomorrow."

Television and the suburban migration had more baneful effects on magazines. Compared with newspapers, periodicals had always been a luxury for most Americans. And having a television caused many families to take fewer magazines and spend less time reading those that still graced their coffee tables. The reduction in time allotted to magazine reading, surveys suggested, was far sharper than that for newspapers. The provincialism of newspapers served them well. The typical daily likely stressed local happenings—a state sales tax hike or county health board scandal—that all but commanded the reader's interest; thus the consumer did not feel the same imperative to scan a short story or profile of a Democratic presidential candidate in *Collier's*.

As a national medium, a magazine could not compete with television for the mass audience. As TV reached more households, the number of homes with television sets dwarfed the circulation of any single periodical. Television advertising became more efficient by reaching more consumers than did magazine ads. TV also offered would-be sponsors the visual display impossible with radio. According to Leo Bogart, between 1946 and 1954 the percentage of national advertising going to periodicals fell from 22 percent to 14 percent.

Nonetheless, some publishers found reasons for calm. Mass circulation periodicals like *Life*, *Look*, the *Saturday Evening Post*, and *Collier's* saw their circulation rise despite TV's advent. Between 1946 and 1954, Bogart reported, the circulation of the "Big Four" rose by 33 percent. The death of *Collier's* and *Women's Home Companion* in 1956 unnerved some monitors of the trade, yet in that same year, *Life* boasted a $16 million gain in advertising and circulation record of 5.7 million. The predominance of black and white television in the 1950s caused the advertisers who preferred color display to continue to buy space in magazines. All in all, the demise of certain periodicals appeared to be the result of bad management rather than the diffusion of television.

Like their counterparts at newspapers, magazine editors tended to dismiss the potential rivalry of TV news. There had been storm signals. For example, at the 1956 national party conventions, the networks received the best locations for their cameras, whereas four years earlier those locations had gone to *Life* photographers. Nevertheless, in Washington and New York, opinion leaders assumed that the newsmagazines, and not TV news, mattered. Former Time Inc. and *Collier's* writer Theodore H. White rejected an offer to work for CBS News in 1957; broadcast news, he had concluded, lacked the prestige of the printed page.

Finally, magazines that played to more specialized tastes prospered in the fifties. Perhaps the most spectacular success in periodical publishing in the decade, *Playboy*, ran nude foldouts between short stories and grooming tips, all meant for the young and self-conscious male. More established and prosperous, and rarely hidden, as were *Playboy*s, under mattresses, was the *New Yorker*, which actually rejected advertising for reasons of taste and spatial limitation.

In other ways, most magazines responded quickly to the twin challenges of TV and suburbanization. The exodus from the central cities caused a drop in newsstand sales and encouraged publishers to boost their subscription lists. Television and its new stars were opportunistically considered less as rivals than as sources of copy. Acknowledging TV's escapist preoccupations, mass circulation periodicals sharply reduced their run of fiction in favor of stories intended to help the "New Family" "cope" with such "problems" as juvenile delinquency, national highway policy, and the threat of rock 'n' roll.

In their coverage of national affairs, both periodicals and newspapers continued to respect the logic of the cold war. There were exceptions, including the *Progressive* magazine and I. F. Stone's weekly newsletter; more often, however, the press behaved, James Boylan observed, as a "yea-sayer to power," uniformly accepting most, if not all, confrontations with Communists abroad and largely imagined ones at home. In 1957 the press allowed disaffected scientists and Democratic legislative critics of the Eisenhower administration to frame the Soviet Union's launch of the Sputnik space satellite as a grievous blow to American prestige. "Let us not pretend," *Life* warned complacent readers, "that Sputnik is anything but a defeat for the United States."

The press normally treated inquiries into domestic subversion without any sympathy for the accused. One study of hearings into Communist influence at the University of Washington in the late 1940s found newspapers, in their construction of stories and their placement and use of sources, to be plainly biased against the targeted professors. Several years later, an obscure senator from Wisconsin, Joseph R. McCarthy, Jr., drew upon his familiarity with reporting practices, notably the deadline, to gain national notoriety. Like a few other masters of opinion management, including Franklin Roosevelt, McCarthy tried to time his news conferences so that there was no time for correspondents to contact a critical source. The practice often gave stories about him the look of a press release. And his most effective agents were the wire services, whose reporters were the least likely—as the most "objective" journalists—to doubt, let alone not file a story based on, a senator's allegation. They were captives of what Russell Baker called "the American faith in 'objective journalism,' which forbade a reporter to go beyond what the great man said. No matter how dull, stupid, unfair, vicious, or mendacious they might be, the utterances of the great were to be reported deadpan, with nary a hint that the speaker might be a bore, a dunce, a brute, or a habitual liar." Yet more than a manipulation of professional routine accounted for McCarthy's ample coverage; most reporters, including many who strongly disapproved of McCarthy's tactics, nevertheless agreed with his basic premise, that there were or had been Communist spies in the federal government. "McCarthy was a news diet of choice," Boylan wrote. "Almost to the end the press remained more accomplice than adversary."

Out of the Parlor

If television worried publishers, their product at least remained in the living room; radios by the late 1950s had been relegated to other parts of the house. Visitors to the family den rarely spotted the once large radio receiver, encased in wood and surrounded by the more comfortable chairs and davenport. Families had hauled their old sets to the attic, basement, or dump. Some more elaborate models with doors were preserved, after the radio apparatus itself was removed, for use as liquor cabinets.

Between 1948 and 1958, Americans who traditionally had listened to network radio shows in the evening by the mid fifties watched network television programs. According to the A. C. Nielsen Company, the average American family's radio listening per day dropped by 50 percent, from 4.4 hours in 1948 to 2.2 hours in 1956. "The Big Show," NBC Radio's costly attempt in 1949–51 to retain evening listeners, lasted only two seasons and cost the network millions. "Your radio show," Fred Allen told Groucho Marx in 1950, "is the only one that is mentioned by critics and listeners who, because they have dirty windows and cannot see the aerials of their neighbors' roofs, do not know about television and still listen to radio."

Advertisers followed the great migration. Although local sponsors remained loyal, especially in smaller markets without a TV station or in larger ones where TV spots were too expensive, radio's share of all advertising expenditures fell from 12 percent in 1948 to 6 percent in 1960.

The loss of advertisers and listeners most affected the radio networks, CBS, NBC, ABC, and Mutual. Three of the four radio chains, by entering TV programming, were, in effect, committing slow suicide. "Where outside of Alice in Wonderland could one expect to find an industry that would spend millions of dollars to ease itself out of business?" asked *Saturday Evening Post* contributor Milton Mackaye in 1952. The networks worsened matters by adopting what economists termed a "risk aversion" strategy, except in the case of NBC's "The Big Show." They stuck to old formulas and personalities who had worn out their welcome. Certain stars did make the transition to TV but simultaneously saw their radio audiences all but vanish. Jack Benny and Bob Hope did both TV and radio programs until their radio audience ratings became embarrassing. Hope, the medium's biggest draw in 1949, saw his Hooper rating fall from 23.9 in 1949 to 5.4 in 1954. He quit radio a year later. Although most stations continued to prefer having a network contract, affiliates rejected more and more network programming. Indeed, by the late 1950s, stations ordinarily accepted only brief network newscasts. By then, many individual operators, like many newspaper owners, had prepared for the worst by securing TV licenses.

For most Americans, radio became a supplemental medium, something consumed while they worked or played. If no longer in the living room, radio sets could be found in bedrooms and kitchens for use while people dressed for work or ate breakfast. Morning listening hours remained stable through the 1950s; before noon more people listened to radio than viewed television. New types of radios helped the industry. Manufacturers successfully introduced clock radios for bed tables; teenagers prized new "transistor" radios powered by batteries. More Americans who drove to work regarded a car radio as a necessary companion; between 1948 and 1958 the percentage of automobiles with radios doubled, and by 1963, 75.9 percent of all cars had radios. This new pattern of radio consumption benefited the individual station. With the vast evening audience all but lost, the radio networks reduced their costly entertainment programming. No longer did single stations operate at a comparative disadvantage; they could, indeed, easily offer what had always been popular fare, music.

Changes in radio broadcasting itself further strengthened the position of local stations. Until the late 1940s, broadcasters had assumed that listeners preferred live originations of music and other programming. Indeed, federal regulations had long required licensees to announce "transcriptions." Then, too, recording technology had been cumbersome for producers and dissatisfying for listeners. During the war, however, the Armed Forces Radio had developed a magnetic tape system that offered high-quality recording and quick and smooth editing. Performers like Bing Crosby and young news producers like Fred Friendly were impressed. In the late forties they began using tape in their productions. To the surprise of more tradition-bound radio executives, listeners had no objection. Radio analyst Judith Waller concluded in 1950, "The public is no longer disturbed by the announcement that 'this is a transcription.'" No longer did individual stations feel obligated to air a live performance of a "big band"; a tape or new, "high-fidelity" long-playing record would suffice.

Another innovation in radio programming accompanied improved transmission of recorded sound. Until the late 1940s, most musical programs were hosted by a popular singer or bandleader. One band or orchestra performed the music. But in Chicago and New York, listeners began to tune in to musical programs anchored by "disc jockeys," younger male hosts who selected different recorded tunes to air and offered commentaries between "plays." "DJs" like Dave Garroway in Chicago and Jack Eigen in New York appealed to a younger audience and soon had imitators around the country. On TV, Ernie Kovacs created sketches involving Wolfgang Sauerbraten, the all-night German disc jockey, dressed in lederhosen. "Dise nacht we blay zom heis moosiks let ein spreighen de newest b-bopper."

The disc jockey had ample opportunity for employment. Despite the advent of television, the number of radio stations increased fourfold in the fifteen years after World War II, from 973 in 1945 to 2,867 in 1950 and 4,306 in 1960. The FCC had encouraged the radio boom by awarding more frequencies; most were low-power stations that served smaller communities or were permitted to operate only in the daytime. The commission also began to issue licenses in the Frequency Modulation (FM) portion of the radio band (previous assignments had been in the Amplitude Modulation [AM] band). FM's superior transmission quality made it especially appropriate for classical and "easy listening" music. Doctors and dentists believed FM programs helped to relax their more nervous patients who were trying to thumb through *Life* in the waiting room.

The new stations struggled to win shares of a smaller total audience. They were, in effect, coming to dinner after the main course had been served. FM station owners had the worst of it: consumers were slow to buy radios able to receive the new frequency; the first generation of transistors were AM only.

The radio station expansion of the postwar decade encouraged some operators to develop more specialized "formats." And at a time when intellectuals bemoaned the centralization of America's culture, regionalism enjoyed a revival in many radio markets. In rural areas, newly formed, low-power stations offered the "country-and-western" (C&W) sound, recorded in Nashville and other southern cities. In northern cities, new outlets, owned by whites, played music that appealed to black audiences. Usually one or more offered rhythm and blues (R&B), which combined jazz and gospel melodies with racy lyrics.

R&B constituted music's urban underground, a musical genre that violated all the norms of the dominant culture and "pop" sound. Blacks performed R&B at a time when relatively few were allowed into the mainstream. In the 1930s black singers like Billie Holiday had interracial appeal, and in the fifties Nat King Cole ranked with the nation's most popular musical stars. Some in the upper middle class and on campuses prided themselves on their appreciation for black jazz. Even more enjoyed bandleaders Louis Armstrong and Duke Ellington. Yet except for some avant-garde jazz musicians, such as Charlie Parker, these performers had to varying degrees adapted their presentations to white norms. When formally attired, Ellington's band bespoke an elegance few whites could rival. In contrast, rythm-and-blues artists, like avant-garde musicians, favored by many upper-middle-class whites, conceded little to appearances. And their songs, full of sexual energy if not bravado, gave new life to the word *explicit*. In a decade when American couples in movies or on TV slept in separate twin beds, the Dominoes hailed "Sixty Minute Man" (1951), fifteen minutes of which went to "blowing my top." In "The Laundromat Blues" (1953), the Five Royales paid tribute to a girl who had "the best machine in town. . . . She can do it over and over."

To share their style with a larger audience, R&B artists found a publicist. At a record store in downtown Cleveland in 1951 a DJ named Alan Freed noticed white teenagers requesting rhythm-and-blues albums as they danced to the R&B tunes being showcased. Freed decided to produce an R&B musical program on WJW, heretofore another white music outlet. True to the R&B sensibility, Freed reputedly renamed the music after an R&B euphemism for sexual intercourse, "rock and roll." On his program, "Moon Dog's Rock and Roll Party," Freed broke with the cool or all-American DJ image; he shouted in rhythm with the music, "Go, man, go," and cried, "Yeah, yeah, yeah," while pounding his fist. To black and white adolescents in northern Ohio, Freed became a guru. A series of rock 'n' roll "parties" at the Cleveland Arena broke all records for indoor concerts. At one, twenty thousand reportedly had to be turned away; the facility could only seat ten thousand. In 1954, Freed took his act to New York and WINS, where he shook parents and music critics in the nation's largest city and cultural capital. A *New York Times* reporter listening to WINS wrote, "Alan Freed jumped into radio like a stripper into Swan Lake."

The supply side of the new sound began to change the year Freed hosted his first rock 'n' roll show on WJW. At first, Freed had played music by black artists. Then in 1951, a country-and-western bandleader in Philadelphia, Bill Haley, wrote the first rock 'n' roll song, that is, one that borrowed heavily but not exclusively from the rhythm-and-blues tradition. Haley mixed R&B with country elements, excising some, though not all, of R&B's ribaldry. "Rock a Beaten Boogie" began with the line, "Rock, rock, rock, everybody, roll, roll, roll, everybody." To teenagers having to endure Eileen Barton's "If I Knew You Were Coming I'd've Baked a Cake," Jeffrey Hart wrote, "Rock a Beaten Boogie" "was *The Kinsey Report* set to music." Bill Haley and the Comets possessed many of the characteristics that came to be associated with rock 'n' roll, what Hart called "an insistent, heavy beat with guitars and drums dominating the melody, the shouted rather than sung lyrics, the repetitive phrasing, the ear-splitting electronic amplification." Better yet, at least in the eyes of nervous radio station and record store managers, Haley's group was white; there was even less resistance to its sound. Anglophiles could take no comfort in learning that Queen Elizabeth requested a special screening of Haley's movie, *Rock around the Clock*, and Haley himself performed at the Duke of Kent's twenty-first birthday party.

The House of Windsor's preferences notwithstanding, many parents and public authorities in America worried. "Rock around the Clock" (1955) was Bill Haley's first big hit after his appearance in *Blackboard Jungle* (1955). The film's hoods listened to Bill Haley and, in one scene, destroyed the jazz and swing records their teacher had brought to play to his class. That year, the New Haven chief of police banned rock 'n' roll parties; other guardians followed. *Variety* spoke of rock 'n' roll "leerics."

Record companies tried to forestall censorship based on race. Although black groups had large followings, a white band had far greater market potential. Assuming that many white teenagers shared the bigotry of their parents, especially in the South, the larger record companies took up a longstanding industry practice: they produced new cuts of R&B songs with some or all of the more provocative lines bleached out. Joe Turner had sung, "You wear low dresses / The sun comes shinin' through"; Bill Haley offered, "You wear those dresses / Your hair done up so nice." The new recordings had white "covers" performing the tunes. As Jeremy Larner observed, in Los Angeles in 1954 an obscure black band, the Chords, cut "Sh-Boom," which quickly became the number one "gut song," or request, on local rock 'n' roll programs. Mercury Records then reproduced "Sh-Boom" with an unknown white group, the Crewcuts, and it became a nationwide smash. In the next two years, "covered" R&B songs outsold the originals. And mainstream singers like Eddie Fisher and Perry Como tried their hand at R&B.

"The King" of rock 'n' roll was no cover. Born to rural poverty in Mississippi, where his father was a white sharecropper, Elvis Presley masterfully combined the sounds of Pentecostal revival tunes, country, and rhythm and blues to become the dominant singer of the decade. Even black audiences initially cheered him. Like most rhythm-and-blues artists, in his appearance and presentation Presley flouted convention. He spurned middle-class or formal attire, let his hair grow long (one of the fifties male conventions was the crewcut), and worse, sported sideburns. More distinctive and, at the time, bizarre to those unfamiliar with the emotional singing style of southern revival sects was Presley's performing demeanor. Unlike the radio crooners and band singers of the forties, Presley gyrated around the stage. To the shock of one generation and the delight of another, he also shifted his hips back and forth with the rhythm. Police forbade "Elvis the Pelvis" from moving his body when he performed in Florida in 1955. Presley's singing style, together with his dress and "ducktail" coiffure, made him appear disrespectful toward authority. "Presley created a definitely 'antiparent' outlook," sociologist David Riesman noted later. "His music— and he, himself—appeared somewhat insolent, slightly hoodlum." Yet Presley was only so threatening to authorities. As a white boy, he could popularize R&B. An African-American singer, Otis Blackwell, wrote Elvis's 1956 hit, "Don't Be Cruel." Presley "had the hips and the hair and the skin," Blackwell recalled. "I had the music." RCA Victor bought Elvis's contract in 1955 and within six months had sold an unprecedented eight million Presley records. He earned a million dollars in 1956.

The triumphs of Elvis and others initially came at the expense of the dominant recording and music publishing firms. In the 1940s the record industry had become highly concentrated; *Fortune* estimated in 1948 that four companies controlled 75 percent of the total record market. This oligopolistic structure, sociologists Richard A. Peterson and David G. Berger argue, caused recording company executives to take up a risk-aversion strategy of their own. Companies signed bland, almost always white, singers to contracts. They performed tunes in a similar "sing-along" manner. The music and not, in most instances, the performer took precedence. A new song might be recorded by four different singers, each under contract with one of the four major companies, and released simultaneously. The Big Four in turn favored an older generation of white songwriters based in New York. In the 1930s Cole Porter, Jerome Kern, and Lorenz Hart had written tunes with sexual innuendoes at times almost as explicit as R&B yet packaged cleverly for the better-educated patron of Broadway and record stores. By the 1950s the total market for music had increased, and the percentage that could catch the meaning of Porter's metaphors was shrinking. Porter himself was weary, Hart and Kern dead. Survivors Irving Berlin and Oscar Hammerstein II had forgotten their youth; they and others continued to eye an older, adult, middle-class audience. The music industry as a whole disdained younger or black performers unless, like Nat King Cole and Frank Sinatra, they sang the old men's tunes and wore formal attire in concert. (Sinatra was allowed, on his album covers, to loosen his tie.) No one outside of the South and with indoor plumbing, the music moguls assumed, patronized country music. Black demand for R&B was similarly considered to be too small for concern. Until 1949, industry executives had called R&B "race music." The publisher of the mainstream music, the American Society of Composers, Authors, and Publishers (ASCAP), which had long enjoyed a virtual monopoly, had a similar fixation on the adult audience. Songs and singing styles must not offend this large market; they could only be so suggestive. A woman baked her lover a cake; she was not to be likened to a heavy-duty washing machine. All but neutered, the songs recorded by the big record companies, Douglas Miller and Marion Nowak wrote in *The Fifties*, "had the passionate impact of marshmallow whip."

The popular music industry's calculated moral innocence in the late forties and early fifties was not rewarded by the adult consumer. The middle-class families that music publishers had long coveted no longer had so many evening sing-alongs at the upright. They could watch Perry Como on TV. Television denied adults time for listening to music on the radio or record player. Despite the introduction of the LP in 1948, individual album sales per capita fell between 1948 and 1954.

One age group, however, was prepared to listen to more music. Teenagers, for various reasons, sought escape from parents and the tyranny of family togetherness in the room with the TV set. Adolescence was a time of being with friends who were the same age, of going with peers to "Coke" parties and sock hops to dance to Little Richard. Several factors made this new sense of teenage association more pronounced. Those entering their teens in the fifties had more time and more disposable income than any previous generation in the nation's history. The average weekly allowance had risen from $2.50 in 1944 to $10 in 1958. Fewer had to work to help support their families. Many of those who did take part-time jobs had more discretionary income than some older brothers and sisters with children and mortgages. Advertisers inspired by market researcher Eugene Gilbert began to play to this new market of youth. "The special charm that teenage income holds for Gilbert and his clients," social critic Dwight Macdonald wrote in the *New Yorker* in 1958, "is that it is, as they call it, free money—free from all claims except the possessor's whim." They could buy albums and radios and in the privacy of their bedrooms listen to Bill Haley while parents uneasily watched Eddie Fisher on TV trying to imitate him.

The disc jockey became all the more important. "This presiding angel (or devil) of adolescence underwrote the sense of generational difference," Todd Gitlin recalled. "He invaded the home, flattered the kids' taste (while helping mold it), lured them into an imaginary world in which they were free to take their pleasures." The DJ "played an important part in extending the peer group, certifying rock lovers as members of a huge subsociety of the knowing. Even as I sat home doing my homework, I felt plugged in."

Rock 'n' roll almost by definition appealed to adolescents. Songs made virtually no demands on the listener, especially after R&B originals had been sanitized. Lyrics never affected to the clever standards of the best 1930s tunes, which had alluded to current events, art history, or Helen of Troy. The double meanings were obvious (to New Haven's chief of police and others, too obvious). The very physicality of Presley's style drew younger audiences to him, while it appalled older performers like Frank Sinatra, who played by the old men's rules. Sinatra called rock 'n' roll "phony and false, and sung, written and played for the most part by cretinous goons."

Although not new to American culture, racy lyrics could not be aired until the 1950s. For two decades, the national networks, ever mindful of federal regulation and the sensitivities of various pressure groups, had blacklisted songs thought to be in poor taste. NBC had forbidden the broadcast of the lyrics to some 290 songs. Radio was considered a family medium, something everyone patronized. But by the mid 1950s fewer stations carried network programming, and more non-network outlets commenced operations. The black stations were among the first to ignore the old standard, and the FCC made little effort to "clean up" the airwaves. Then, too, older listeners who detested rock 'n' roll had choices: many stations that resisted the move to rock stuck with the older pop sound.

Simultaneously, smaller recording companies began to sign groups like Bill Haley and the Comets, Presley, and others. Based in Philadelphia, Los Angeles, Detroit, and Memphis, these firms suddenly increased their share of the album market. According to Peterson and Berger, total album sales rose 261 percent between 1955 and 1959; the number of firms producing Top 10 hits tripled. "A new company can be founded on one best-selling record by some hitherto unknown teenage 'composer,' who generally sings his own opus, with suitable guitar plonkings," Dwight Macdonald observed sourly. To the dismay of ASCAP, the rival Broadcast Music Inc. (BMI) shamelessly signed up the rock 'n' roll artist. ASCAP's Billy Rose screamed, "Not only are most of the BMI songs junk, but in many cases they are obscene junk, pretty much on the level with dirty comic magazines."

Still, all of the mass media came to terms with rock 'n' roll. Freed and Haley starred in their own movies. Presley made a series of films in which he was occasionally allowed to act and always expected to sing. Newspapers and magazines found that the most popular performers made almost as good copy as film stars; "teen" periodicals were much more generous. Even TV gave rock 'n' roll stars airtime. When Elvis first appeared on TV in 1956, his hosts were the Dorsey Brothers, popular forties bandleaders. Not even the ever-conventional Ed Sullivan, who had called Presley's act "unfit for a family audience," could resist the King. Sullivan paid Presley $500,000 to appear three times in 1956; and only on the third telecast, Todd Gitlin notes, were camera operators instructed not to shoot Presley from the waist down, gyrating.

Record companies persuaded more performers to try their hand at rock 'n' roll and, in the process, expanded the demand for the new sound. Although he would not gyrate, country ballad singer Pat Boone became a teen idol for many after doing covers, including one of Little Richard's "Tutti Frutti." Boone momentarily challenged the King's reign. When sociologist James Coleman asked some eight thousand teenagers in 1957 and 1958 to list their favorite singer, Boone ranked first among both males (43.5 percent) and females (45.2); Presley was a distant second. To subgroups of teenagers, perhaps sharing in their parents' distaste for Presley and black performers, Boone offered a wholesome alternative, and one that fit far more easily into the social conformism of the decade. College-educated (he had a B.A. from Columbia University) and habitually clean-cut, Boone reminded no one of a hoodlum or an extra on a motorcycle film. He could have attended a steak fry hosted by President and Mrs. Eisenhower without raising the eyebrow of a single Secret Service agent. Although most rock 'n' roll purists considered him an interloper, Boone helped to popularize the genre by bringing, Charlie Gillett wrote, "a little conservative respectability to the music's image."

The Lost Colony

Perhaps the least attractive aspect to being president, Eisenhower found soon after taking office in 1953, was the special pleading of different interest groups. Early in his presidency, Eisenhower was overwhelmed with requests for the removal of the federal excise tax on different goods and services. Among those approaching the president was the motion picture industry, whose representatives sought the lifting of the tax on theater tickets. Eisenhower ignored their entreaties. He had never been taken by the glitz of the movie colony; most "stars" bored him, he wrote in his diary. Yet he did admit that "the motion picture industry has gone through a very hard time because of the competition of television, as well as other influences."

Americans were not going to the movies as they had earlier. Average weekly motion picture attendance fell from 90 million in 1948 to 47 million in 1956. The number of theaters, which had peaked at 20,000 in 1945 with the wartime boom in moviegoing, fell to 17,575 in 1948 and more severely to 14,509 in 1956. Two studios, one of them RKO, part of the "Big Five," ceased operations in the late fifties.

Film producers and distributors tried unavailingly to reverse the trend. More theater operators installed and promoted air-conditioning. Huge "IT'S COOL INSIDE" signs under their marquees did bring in some suffering the summer heat. There were gimmicks, such as giving away a set of dishes once a week and bank nights. The studios pitched in with a national campaign declaring "Movies are better than ever!" and "Don't be a Living Room Captive—Step out and see a great movie." But nothing brought certain customers back, at least not with the frequency of the early forties. A romance had been reduced to a friendship. The marginal or neighborhood theaters that had shown second runs or B-movies closed. Medium-sized cities that had had five theaters in 1945 had two in 1960. In very small towns, operators gave up altogether; residents had to drive fifteen miles or more to see a picture. Abandoned theaters became laundromats or furniture and appliance stores.

The migration of millions of Americans to the suburbs did foster a new type of theater. With land plentiful in outlying communities, drive-in theaters became commonplace. Fences enclosed a large screen before a parking lot for two hundred to two thousand cars. Each space had a receiver for sound reception; in colder climates, operators provided portable heaters in the winter. The drive-in appeared to be ideally suited to the younger family all but lost to television. Parents did not have to find a sitter; the whole family could pile into the car and see a film. A 1950 survey of Minneapolis–St. Paul drive-ins found that 54 percent of the cars had parents with children. Outdoor theaters quickly proved to be a wise investment. They had better profit margins than indoor theaters; and, most agreed, because of more elaborate choices in food and drink, they earned more money on concessions. Such news encouraged more to enter the field; the number of drive-ins increased fivefold, from 820 in 1948 to 4,494 in 1956.

Whether they viewed a movie indoors or outside, many customers simply became more selective. The patron who attended a movie weekly in the 1940s went every other week or once a month in the 1950s. "Before the war movie-going was a habit," a Richmond theater operator told the *New York Times* in 1951. "Now people come when they really want to see a picture." "If a citizen has to be bored to death," President Eisenhower wrote in his diary in July 1953, "it is cheaper and more comfortable to sit at home and look at television than it is to go outside and pay a dollar for a ticket."

Some insiders and critics argued that the types of films produced after the war explained the empty seats. In a 1949 *Fortune* poll more of those surveyed were unhappy rather than pleased with recent releases. Veteran producer Sam Goldwyn admitted in late 1954 that "it was the continuous flow of pictures that didn't measure up to what the public expected that turned them to other forms of entertainment." To Gilbert Seldes, an almost juvenile sensibility denoted the late 1940s film: the tastes of the moviegoer had matured but those of the moviemaker had not. Another critic observed in 1953, "It's about time the movies—like the stage, grew up. The public did years ago."

The opposite assessment, that an excess of realism in many of the postwar films shocked and depressed audiences, was more frequent. During the Great Depression, Hollywood had given people hope and had reinforced traditional religious and family values. After the war, complained Frank Capra, one of the 1930s' most successful directors, came the "anything goes" period, "immortalized forever on film when Richard Widmark (in *Kiss of Death* [1947]) pushed a wheelchair with an invalid old woman in it down a flight of stairs—and laughed!" Three years later MGM's Louis Mayer remained outraged by Widmark's deed, likening it to throwing "mother's good, homemade chicken soup in the mother's face!" John Huston wanted to direct *Quo Vadis*, Mayer shouted in 1950, so he could "throw the Christians to the lions." Films that on the surface championed all the right causes nevertheless bespoke an unsettling exhaustion, or what Siegfried Kracauer called "the retreat into apathy" and "ideological fatigue." The banker played by Frederic March in *The Best Years of Our Lives* (1946) has to get drunk before he will defend loaning money to struggling war veterans. In *Crossfire* (1946), the district attorney in search of an anti-Semitic murderer appeared, Kracauer wrote, "overwhelmed by a mood of resignation, as though he had discovered that the struggle for enlightenment is a Sisyphean task." In *Knock on Any Door* (1949), a defense attorney (Humphrey Bogart) argues that poverty transformed the accused into a young killer; through its neglect of the underclass, society, not the defendant, was responsible for his actions. But Bogie cannot save the kid from the chair. To historian Warren Susman, such films reflected a darker side to postwar American culture. The nation's "moment of triumph" following victory in World War II and economic expansion "was accompanied by something disturbing: a new self-consciousness of tragedy and a sense of disappointment."

Blaming depressing movies for Hollywood's woes fails for two reasons. First, most films, as Seldes noted, eschewed the themes of realism and moral fatigue that Kracauer analyzed. Although Mayer correctly saw a heartlessness in directors like Huston, he had few imitators. The majority of movies were simply less sentimental in their support for the conventional values that Mayer's MGM movies had celebrated. Although dripping with cynicism about the theater, *All About Eve* (1950) concludes with the female lead (Bette Davis) describing marriage as a woman's true fulfillment. In Kazan's *On the Waterfront* (1954), a righteous priest persuades the film's protagonist to testify against corrupt union leaders. The leads in one of the most popular films of the 1950s, *White Christmas* (1954), played by Bing Crosby and Danny Kaye, were, if anything, the kind of men who lifted someone in a wheelchair up a stairway.

Then, too, surveys repeatedly showed that dissatisfaction with the content of movies did not in and of itself explain the half-filled picture house. According to a 1956 New York area poll, though 16 percent of those questioned believed that the quality of films had declined, 61 percent reported that they attended theaters less often. Hollywood had to look elsewhere, at the new and expensive piece of electronic furniture in the living room or den. Television had torn the entertainment pattern of a generation. But for the diffusion of TV, Frederic Stuart estimates, film receipts might have increased significantly between 1948 and 1954.

Did the studios anticipate what TV meant for moviegoing? In the late 1940s, TV had been one of many challenges besetting the industry. Film executives faced rising labor costs and union unrest, difficulties reentering certain foreign markets, the loosening of the studios' once chainlike hold on stars and directors, the forced spin-off of profitable theater chains, and allegations of Communist influence within the colony itself. With so many other problems besetting the industry, it became tempting to underestimate the effects of the newest medium. Many regarded as corporate propaganda RCA's David Sarnoff's predictions that the future lay in television. They could cite a Twentieth Century Fund study in early 1948 that assured Hollywood that "movie-going has become a fixed habit with the American people and is unlikely to be shaken by the advent of television."

Even as TV receiver sales rose sharply beginning in 1949, some in the movie industry simply refused to recognize the magnitude of this communication revolution. It did not, after all, occur overnight. Different people in different sections of the country bought their first receivers; that most homes would have one by the late 1950s was not assumed. Moreover, many if not most film executives momentarily convinced themselves that consumers would tire of the home screen. Their own show-business sense, developed, in many instances, after two generations in mass entertainment, largely accounted for this attitude. Few in Hollywood could regard TV as a true rival. Television seemed to rely on boorish New York comedians and very poor 1930s B-pictures. Not contemplated was the possibility that consumers for various reasons had lower expectations for TV programming. It was free, after all, and did not have to be compared with a feature film. Still, if nothing else, the studio heads could, like their counterparts in various newsrooms, remind themselves that Hollywood had survived radio.

In a far less passive response to the TV challenge, major moviemakers invested in rival telecasting processes. By creating their own distribution system, companies like Paramount intended to avoid having to deal with broadcasters at all. Hollywood would thus rid itself of the network or station middleman. All of the studios and theater chains experimented with "theater television," converting movie houses into giant TV rooms to screen important sports and other lavish live events. Theater television, however, quickly proved too costly. Some looked to pay- or subscription-television systems, whereby customers were charged to see films and other fare on a per-view basis. Yet this alternative to "free" TV took too long to perfect. With television sets in most households by the late 1950s, the great majority of viewers regarded pay-TV as a threat. The networks and individual stations had little difficulty orchestrating mass opposition to continued subscription-TV tests. Ever appreciative of free airtime, members of Congress forced the FCC, which had to approve the experiments, to delay further pay-TV tests in 1958.

In the late 1940s, several studios considered entering television directly by securing TV licenses and a struggling network. Immediately after the war, the FCC had begun to accept applications for TV station licenses. Some, even in the largest cities, were available for the asking, despite demands from radio networks and stations, newspapers, and TV set manufacturer Allen Du Mont. Paramount had invested in Du Mont's company and had the resources to aid the New Jersey inventor, but none of the major companies would take the plunge. Paramount, if anything, by refusing to lend Du Mont more money, frustrated his intentions to maintain a national network. Too late, Twentieth Century Fox tried to buy ABC in 1948. That year, the Warner brothers could not agree on purchasing stations in major markets and a year later withdrew from the competition for a Chicago frequency. Fox subsequently abandoned attempts to acquire TV licenses in five major markets. Within a few years, Hollywood's opportunity to challenge the networks on their own field disappeared. Big-city stations that served as the nucleus of a new network could no longer be acquired quickly. TV allocations in the potentially most profitable viewing regions went to others or were delayed by extended FCC hearings. An excess of caution had cost the film companies dearly. Studies repeatedly demonstrated that in the 1950s advertisers would only buy large amounts of time on two, perhaps three, TV networks. Had Fox been able to secure ABC or had Paramount helped Du Mont, one of the Big Five studios might have been able to compete against CBS and NBC.

Hollywood had been well-positioned to enter television. Although none of the studios could claim an extensive background in broadcasting, no radio chain had ever produced the visual entertainment that the studios had been assembling for decades. In the late 1940s the TV networks had to start literally from scratch, building sound stages in and around their headquarters in New York.

Nevertheless, it is by no means clear that the studios would have been allowed to enter television at this critical early stage. The FCC preferred to award TV licenses to those with a background in radio and a record of adhering to the commission's regulations. Moreover, the Big Five studios had just been found guilty of gross antitrust violations;

thus they hardly appeared capable of being trusted with another, possibly more important mass medium. FCC staff attorneys and the Department of Justice looked warily at any effort by the film industry to enter television. The FCC did allow United Paramount Theatres (UPT), the distribution chain created from Paramount Pictures as a result of the theater divestiture order of 1948, to purchase ABC in early 1953. ABC was then at such a severe competitive disadvantage that few protested the move. Yet the FCC simultaneously rejected Du Mont's application for several lucrative TV licenses because of Paramount Pictures' large, if passive, investment in his company. Denying Du Mont the revenue the large TV stations would have generated, the FCC in effect killed the network.

Having failed to enter free TV and still awaiting the development of pay-TV systems, the major studios determined to do battle with their new rival. Until the mid 1950s, most refused to sell their films to stations eager to run them on weekend afternoons and in the late evenings. Nor would most studios produce programming for the networks. The Warner brothers banned TV sets from the lot. After an initial involvement with live productions of television plays in the late 1940s, film actors rarely appeared on TV programs. Producers did encourage stars to appear on Ed Sullivan's popular show, but only to promote their latest release.

Smaller studios and United Artists ignored the Hollywood boycott. In 1948 United Artists began distributing half-hour series produced by small independent companies; nine years later, UA bought Warner Brothers's stock of pre-1950 films for release to TV. (UA had earlier sold its own film library.) Hal Roach sold copies of his 1930s serials, among them, "The Little Rascals," and produced several series for the networks, including a video version of "Amos 'n' Andy." Monogram and Republic Pictures made available old "B" Westerns and action dramas. Columbia formed Screen Gems in 1951 to produce programs and distribute old features and shorts starring the Three Stooges and others. MCA, one of the largest talent agencies, began producing series in 1949 and selling the rights to rerun programs to stations four years later.

In the midst of the tempest over television, the governors of the movie colony enjoyed a rare but important legal victory. Since 1915 the courts had refused to apply freedom of speech to films. Movie companies and theater owners had been subject to any and all pressures from state and local authorities that a feature deemed disrespectful toward prevailing political, sexual, or cultural mores be reedited or withdrawn from circulation. In 1951, however, a foreign-film distributor, Joseph Burstyn, challenged city and state officials who had ordered him not to show the Italian film *The Miracle*, directed by Roberto Rossellini. The feature's mockful treatment of rural Catholicism had enraged the city's church hierarchy. Unable to have the New York State Board of Regents' ban rescinded by the state's highest court, Burstyn appealed to the Supreme Court. In a unanimous decision, the court held for the distributor. *Burstyn v. Murphy* (1952) circumscribed (but did not eliminate) the power of state officials to censor movies. The Court had begun the process, with subsequent decisions based on *Burstyn*, of extending to films First Amendment guarantees provided newspapers and magazines.

Hollywood did not advantage itself of its new freedoms. The film industry, Garth Jowett notes, initially considered *Burstyn* a victory for the exhibitors of foreign "art" films in a few of the largest cities; the major studios did not make films like *The Miracle* or *Ways of Love* and had no plans to do so. That is not to say that the governors did not think about the potential of sex. "You want to make a million dollars in the movies?" Louis Mayer had asked a *Reader's Digest* correspondent in 1947. "Figure out a way to put fucking on the screen." Mayer and others had been pressing the industry's Production Code Administration since World War II to ease controls over projects and scripts. A few prominent directors, influenced by Italian realists like Rossellini, were even more demanding and, after many compromises with the PCA, won some victories. References to homosexuality were excised from the adaptation of Tennessee Williams's play *A Streetcar Named Desire* (1951), but not the rape of the female lead. PCA officials reluctantly waived another rule when they allowed a police officer to be killed at the conclusion of *Detective Story* (1951). The great majority of films, however, continued to respect social convention, if only somewhat less ritualistically. Movies by and large celebrated the decade's political and social conformity.

Films instructed no group to conform more than women. "From fifties movies," Benita Eisler wrote in *Private Lives*, "we learned that girls turned into wives. They traded in the ingenue's crinolined skirt, the smart hat of the career woman, the sex kitten's off-the-shoulder blouse for the homemaker's Peter Pan collar. No matter the convolutions of the plot, the outcome was never in doubt. We would become what we beheld." The exceptions, Marilyn Monroe or Jayne Mansfield, only made many women nervous or resentful. More acceptable, and generously portrayed, was Audrey Hepburn, "the patron saint of nice girls who waited." A more approachable role model (Hepburn was English) was Debbie Reynolds. In *The Tender Trap* (1955), Reynolds plays an aspiring actress who, despite a successful audition, confesses that marriage is "the most important thing in the world. A woman isn't really a woman until she's been married and had children." Reynolds in real life wed Eddie Fisher, one of the young white crooners that the big record companies had considered a safe bet for the nation's youth market.

In other ways, Hollywood struggled to conform in the fifties. Anxious about outward appearances, the major filmmakers continued to fret about the private lives and politics of their stars. The blacklist remained in effect. Studio employers regulated personal preferences. To squelch rumors of a promising male actor's homosexuality, a heterosexual marriage was arranged. Press agents carefully covered up the chronic drinking of a box-office champion. Stars had to wed rather than live with someone—and then endure frequent appearances in divorce court and being the butt of comedians' monologues.

Yet the movie colony was changing. In 1951, Louis Mayer was removed as head of MGM, the first of several longtime governors to be deposed in the fifties. Successors far less autocratically presided over a new, more modest and less centralized system of manufacturing illusions. This new Hollywood came to terms with independent production companies. Begun after the war, "independents" were centered around a prominent actor, director, or producer, who, rather than studio executives, commissioned and produced films. The studios provided some working capital and facilities and arranged for the distribution and promotion of the finished product. The talent involved in the independent company received less compensation in return for a split (usually 50 percent) of the film's profits. Huston and Bogart formed one independent company; actor Burt Lancaster led another. Although Mayer and others resented the independents' threat to their authority, other studios, led by United Artists, saw financial advantages to the new arrangement. Film executives continued to be unable to restrain bloated production costs; independents, in contrast, developed a reputation for efficiency. Independents were protecting their own investment, *Fortune*'s Freeman Lincoln wrote in 1955: "Everybody tries to save a dollar because it is his own dollar." According to Michael Conant, the percentage of films produced by independents rose from 20 percent in 1949 to 58 percent in 1957.

While they often took more artistic risks than the studios, the independents, film historian Tino Balio has noted, were no less interested in making money. Some independents made films with seemingly limited box-office potential, such as *On the Waterfront* (1954) and *Marty* (1955), which, because of low production costs, actually earned handsome profits. Other independents ignored the industry's longstanding philosophy that messages should be sent by Western Union. Stanley Kramer made movies about race relations (*Home of the Brave* [1949], *The*

Defiant Ones [1958], *Guess Who's Coming to Dinner* [1967]), as well as celluloid sermons against nuclear war (*On the Beach* [1959]) and creation-
ism (*Inherit the Wind* [1960]). Even the purposeful Kramer, however,
compromised by casting stars and, whenever possible, forcing romantic
interludes in his films, all in the hope of making his morality plays
more appealing.

Another independent producer of the fifties sought to prosper by
confronting those groups that had long restricted filmmakers' artistic
freedoms. Working for Darryl Zanuck of Twentieth Century Fox in the
1940s, Otto Preminger had been a dutiful employee. "I was turning out
a string of films," he wrote, "following rules and obeying orders, not
unlike a foreman at a sausage factory." He had accepted PCA admoni-
tions to make his features conform to the association's guidelines. But
as an independent director-producer in the 1950s, Preminger ignored
the PCA's objections to *The Moon Is Blue* (1953). PCA officials disapproved of the film's comical references to seduction and premarital sex;
when Preminger refused to edit the film, the PCA denied *Moon* its seal
of approval. A decade earlier, *Moon* would have been kept in a studio's
storage vault; and although Preminger claimed that he controlled the
final cut, his partner, United Artists, in fact retained the right to edit the
film to satisfy the PCA. It was a right that UA, under a new management that had little use for the old Hollywood, chose not to exercise.
UA anticipated making money on the feature and elected to stand by its
director. UA promoted the picture carefully. Although UA could not
stop Catholic church leaders and the Legion of Decency from organizing boycotts and protests at theaters screening the film, the company
did receive a boost from the direct targets of any pickets, the theater
operators. Angry over a shortage of films for exhibition, three of the five
largest theater chains agreed to book *The Moon Is Blue* without the PCA's
seal. Meanwhile, UA took to court local governments and state film
boards that sought to ban the movie. Relying on the *Burstyn* decision,
the courts held for UA. *Moon*'s box-office success—it placed fifteenth on
the list of fifty top grossing films released in 1953—made all the legal
and public-relations work worthwhile. And in the wake of the battle
over *Moon*'s distribution, and a more modest controversies over Preminger's *Man with the Golden Arm* (1955) and Elia Kazan's *Baby Doll* (1956),
the PCA's list of taboos was shortened. There were only raised eyebrows over the sexual images in Preminger's *Anatomy of a Murder* (1959),
in which a critical piece of evidence, alluded to in the film by a character
played by Jimmy Stewart, of all people, was a pair of women's panties.

Television indirectly figured in the controversy over *The Moon Is Blue*.
None of the big studios had challenged the PCA. The insurgent had

been United Artists, an upstart that since 1948 had been trading with the enemy, television. Most of UA's established competitors subscribed to the notion that films reached the same mass audience that they had entertained in the thirties and forties and that no segment of that audience should be offended. Inane comments in *The Moon Is Blue* about a character's virginity should have been sacrificed. Yet UA, if with less enthusiasm than Preminger, challenged the assumption that films still had to please every potential theatergoer. Like radio station operators who played racy rhythm-and-blues records, UA understood that television had changed the rules. Because they did not have the massive audience that TV had, movies no longer had to suffer exacting self-regulation; TV did. Preminger's films and ones like *Baby Doll* earned money despite the presence of pickets near some ticket windows. "No longer," Thomas Doherty wrote, "could the Legion of Decency spell box office curtains for a morally objectionable movie."

Moviemakers also discovered the new teenager of the 1950s. Like radio listening in the bedroom or dancing at a sock hop, moviegoing offered adolescents an escape from parents and younger siblings watching television. The box-office success of *Blackboard Jungle* encouraged a new genre: films about teenagers. Ones about rock 'n' roll and beach life were prominent examples. Horror films that cast adolescents as vampires or Martians followed. Cheaply produced—B-films for be-boppers—they proved highly profitable as drive-in movie fare. Teenagers, too, patronized the drive-ins, and if they were on a date, the quality of the feature often scarcely mattered.

The adult ticket-buyer, film executives reluctantly acknowledged by the early fifties, had become more selective. Many Americans continued to go to the movies, just less frequently. The challenge was to produce films that possessed qualities absent on television. "We're competing with TV," Dore Schary of MGM said in 1952, "and when the picture is good enough and big enough we know we can fill the theaters with the more discriminating people." Except for teen films and Westerns, sought by drive-in and small-town theater operators, the cheap B-pictures all but disappeared. Filmmakers, director King Vidor explained in 1959, "have to go scenic or go spectacular. I look for stories that can't be done on television." The moviegoer of the fifties was treated to lavish religious epics like *Quo Vadis* (1951), *The Robe* (1953), *The Ten Commandments* (1956), and *Ben Hur* (1959), filmed in color; and the studios experimented with wider and multiple screens. TV remained mostly black and white and twenty-one inches.

The strategy appeared to work to the studios' advantage in two ways. Although fewer Americans regularly went to the movies, those who did patronize theaters were willing to pay more for the lavishly mounted productions. Admission prices rose by 36 percent between 1947 and 1957. Between 1953 and 1956, thirty of Twentieth Century Fox's Cinemascope features each made more than $5 million; only one hundred films had earned that much before 1953. By the mid fifties, some spoke of a Hollywood "comeback." The new emphasis on the "blockbuster" also created a sellers' market for the filmmaker. Theater operators had to fight among themselves for the most promising release, which had the effect of upsetting the intent of the 1948 *Paramount* ruling separating exhibition from production. Between 1948 and 1963, Tino Balio noted, the largest studios' share of the total box office rose from 30 percent to just over 45 percent.

With fewer films being produced, and more production shifted abroad to save on labor costs, the old studio system underwent a dramatic contraction. Even before they realized the full effects of television, film companies had begun, in the late forties, to lay off longtime studio employees. Between 1940 and 1956 the number of full-time staff fell from 24,000 to 13,000. Women and men who had worked on sets and handled costumes lost their jobs. Skilled character actors and stars struggled as the studios ceased signing players to exclusive contracts. Many, like Ronald Reagan, ended up working in television. Such better box-office draws as Jimmy Stewart and William Holden remained in demand but found it more profitable to take a small salary in return for a percentage of the film's profits. To frustrate the Internal Revenue Service, payments were deferred. For appearing in *The Bridge on the River Kwai* (1957), Holden received $50,000 annually until his death in 1981.

The West Coast Plant

At the very moment when the movie colony appeared to have contained overruns in operating expenses and to be recovering from the worst effects of television, the major studios began to produce TV shows. Indeed, R. Christopher Anderson has argued that most large film companies deliberately waited until cost-cutting and the blockbuster strategy had stabilized operations and made feature films profitable again. Only then, when it was clear that the theatrical release could in fact survive television, did most of the movie colony seriously entertain offers to enter TV program production. Moreover, Hollywood had all but abandoned hopes that Americans would sharply reduce their television viewing and return to the movie house or subscribe to pay-TV processes. By the late 1950s virtually all of the studios made programs for television and were selling feature films for network telecast. *Printer's Ink* reported in August 1957 that "TV is becoming an industry with New York showrooms and a West Coast plant."

Network executives had not been uniformly willing to turn over program production to the studios. Although anxious to increase their sources for programming, the leading networks, NBC and Columbia, believed that the public preferred live telecasts. Moreover, NBC's chief programmer until 1956, Pat Weaver, held Hollywood in contempt; TV could be far more creative, Weaver averred, than the operators of the studios' assembly lines.

As Weaver and others scorned Hollywood, however, Lucille Ball and Desi Arnaz were demonstrating the possibilities of filmed series for NBC's archrival. The most successful situation comedy of television's first decade, "I Love Lucy" from the beginning in 1951 had been filmed in California. The series' married stars, Ball and Arnaz, did not wish to leave their small California ranch to do the program from New York; a live origination from California made little sense because of the difference in time zones; and a crude precursor of videotape, kinescope, was considered fit only for distribution to small, isolated stations and not network telecast. Filming the series appeared to be the only solution. Reluctantly, CBS and the show's sponsor agreed to pay the extra cost of filming the series. Insisting on live television's spontaneity, Columbia demanded that an audience be present during each production. Arnaz persuaded a former MGM cinematographer to devise a complex way of lighting and shooting each episode before a studio audience—heretofore not present during a filmed series' production—and with a "multicam" system of three or four cameras running at the same time. The best footage was then edited into an episode that was twenty-six and one-half minutes long. (Twenty-five years later, many situation comedies utilized Arnaz's technique.) Quickly drawing larger audiences than any live variety or dramatic program from New York, "I Love Lucy" severely undermined the argument that viewers wanted live originations. And Ball and Arnaz, having taken salary cuts in exchange for the rights to programs after their network run, made millions selling copies of the series as reruns to CBS and then stations beginning in the late 1950s. By then, Arnaz oversaw their production company, Desilu, in creating more programs, including "The Untouchables" (1959–63). Meanwhile his marriage to Ball deteriorated. "'America's favorite couple,'" a wag observed, "barely communicated with each other except as Lucy and Ricky Ricardo on 'I Love Lucy.'" Absorbing more of the shrinking movie colony, Desilu bought the RKO lot for full-time TV production in 1958.

ABC was too anxious to gamble on an independent producer like Arnaz. Almost immediately after acquiring ABC in early 1953, UPT President Leonard Goldenson drew on his many connections as a theater chain executive to approach various film executives. He was aided by ABC's blunt president, Robert Kintner. Their network, lacking the in-house production facilities of Columbia and NBC, was desperate to make a deal. Filmed programming had another advantage for the third network. ABC had far more trouble clearing programs for simultaneous transmission, making live telecasts problematical. In many smaller TV markets with two stations, channels "shared" their ABC association with Columbia or NBC and normally accepted only the most popular ABC programs and carried others at off-hours or days later. "We couldn't do the Ed Sullivan type of show if we wanted to," recalled one ABC executive. "There are too many places where we'd be saying 'Merry Christmas' in the middle of January."

Just over a year after the UPT-ABC merger, Goldenson and Kintner found a West Coast supplier. Although not the head of a major studio, Walt Disney had for more than twenty years produced America's most popular animated cartoons. He was willing to enter TV program production, but only in exchange for help in financing a vast amusement park he wished to construct in an Anaheim orange grove. Sharing the skepticism of most potential investors, NBC and Columbia demurred. ABC, however, agreed to become a partner after the cartoonist consented to produce a weekly series for the network. He named the program for his park, "Disneyland."

The Disney-ABC association succeeded beyond anyone's expectations. Disney's producers alternated animated and filmed fare, with generous plugs of the park and forthcoming Disney films. The program's success was all but assured after the airing in 1954–55 of three episodes based on the life of frontiersman Davy Crockett. More impressively mounted than the cheaper Western serials then available on the home screen and starring the likable Fess Parker as Crockett, the Disney version appealed to a nation that since the publication of dime novels a century earlier had admired the simple and heroic image of the frontier. In a short-lived but widespread "Crockett craze," the program's theme song, "The Ballad of Davy Crockett," made the top charts; its competition included "The Davy Crockett Mambo." Children cried for Davy Crockett shirts and hats. In April 1955 *Life* reported the manufacture of some two hundred different Crockett items, among them baby shoes and wallets, and projected midyear sales of $100 million. Disney spawned yet another preadolescent craze with the daytime "Mickey Mouse Club" on ABC. The cartoonist had kept the network afloat. Walking into ABC headquarters in May 1956, a *New York Herald Tribune* reporter spotted a secretary sporting Mickey Mouse ears. "Disney got the place off the ground," John Crosby wrote, "and nobody is going to laugh at Mickey Mouse ears on that network."

A year after the Disney deal, Warner Brothers agreed to begin producing a weekly program for ABC. Debuting in September 1955, "Warner Brothers Presents" comprised three alternating series, aired on Tuesday evenings, based on the successful Warner Brothers films *Casablanca, Cheyenne,* and *Kings Row.* Originally Warners used the final fifteen minutes of each hour to plug its newest theatrical releases; however, this promotional quarter-hour as well as the TV versions of *Kings Row* and *Casablanca* were dropped in the first year. Standing alone, the Western "Cheyenne," with its 6'7" star, Clint Walker, became another ratings victory for ABC. The movie-exhibitor philosophy of theater chain executive Goldenson had worked. "TV apparently can't help coming to the same observations that theater men formed years ago," *Sponsor* reported in November 1956. "For steady pulling power, nothing matches westerns."

"Cheyenne"'s success spurred all three networks West. Unlike early TV horse plays, Westerns like "Cheyenne" appealed to adults as well as children and enjoyed excellent ratings in the evening. In the 1958-59 season, seven of the ten most popular programs, according to the Nielsen Company, had a frontier setting. Compared with "The Lone Ranger," the new Westerns dealt with more mature themes. NBC's "Wagon Train" (1957–65) seemed like a Conestoga soap opera; *Variety* dubbed it a "horse oater." CBS's "Have Gun Will Travel" (1957–63) and ABC's "Maverick" (1957–62) contained elements of humor rarely seen in the best Westerns released to theaters. Their success bred imitation such that by the fall 1959 season twenty-nine Westerns graced the three networks' schedules. TV critic Terrence O'Flaherty, of the *San Francisco Chronicle*, decried the wave of "new hoof-and-mouth offerings."

By the end of the decade, the studios, led by Warner Brothers, were turning out another movie-house staple, the detective story, as weekly series. The ABC-Warners programs eschewed the stark realism of Dashiell Hammett and Raymond Chandler for a slick glamour thought to be palatable to the typical TV family. Private eyes in series like "77 Sunset Strip" (1958–64), "Bourbon Street Beat" (1959–60), "Surfside 6" (1960–62), and "Hawaiian Eye" (1953–63) were young and healthy and, though flip, lacked the cynical patina of Sam Spade or Phillip Marlow. Their assignments invariably involved the rich and famous. They were also all deliberately cut from the same cloth. The success of "77 Sunset

Strip," set in Los Angeles, had encouraged Warner Brothers producer William T. Orr to reproduce the series' format in other relatively pleasant or exciting cities, like New Orleans, Honolulu, and Miami. Two or three young private eyes formed a firm, with a slightly younger assistant, modeled after "Kookie" (Edd Byrnes), forever combing his hair on "77 Sunset Strip," to appeal to younger viewers. Byrnes and Connie Stevens, who played "Cricket" on "Hawaiian Eye," recorded a hit, "Kookie, Kookie, Lend Me Your Comb," in a cashing in of momentary celebrity. Critics like O'Flaherty, who several years earlier had been reviewing live teleplays, were appalled. Wise to the self-mimicry, O'Flaherty dismissed "Hawaiian Eye" as "77 Waikiki Beach" and complained that "The Warner brothers are turning out so many private eyes this season they ought to be forced to take out an optometrist's license."

By the late 1950s, Hollywood-based concerns produced the majority of the three networks' evening schedules. On one summer day in 1959, twenty-three TV programs were in production on the Warners lot, most of them for ABC. Although NBC denied it, it was widely thought that the network turned over to MCA chunks of airtime to fill with whatever its production wing, Revue, could produce. Revue purchased Universal Studios early in 1959. The movie colony, *Fortune* reported in 1958, produced three out of every five CBS programs. For its own creations, CBS needed more space, and a year later it bought the Republic lot.

The Hollywoodization of television horrified critics and those associated with other forms of programming. In November 1957 Rod Serling, who had written many early TV dramas, wrote a sharp rebuke of the networks' western migration. More than half of TV's live dramatic anthologies had been canceled since October 1956, Serling charged, despite the high quality of many of the teleplays. "The live hour or ninety minute dramatic show," Serling wrote, "has a feeling of theatre, a spontaneity and an immediacy that a filmed show can never hope to duplicate." Television, remarked another TV anthology writer, Robert Alan Aurthur, was "satisfied to become mainly a purveyor of the worst kind of Hollywood C-picture junk."

The movie colony was not, in truth, giving TV its best. Jack Warner agreed to work for ABC only after Goldenson assured him that he only expected a video version of the B-movie. ABC executives made no effort to disguise their model. "ABC believes that the B-Picture is the correct television show as it was the correct show in the neighborhood movie house," Martin Mayer noted in a profile of the company. "77 Sunset Strip," wrote another industry analyst, proved "principally that Warner Brothers could still make a B movie." Such series were being

run off the film company assembly lines, with individual episodes produced in two or three days. A CBS executive who uneasily observed the
trend in 1958 warned, "The trouble with buying too much from Hollywood is that you get belt-line, machine-made junk."

Hardly all Hollywood series deserved such scorn. One of the first, "I
Love Lucy," had drawn nothing but praise from critics. "'I Love Lucy'
is probably the most misleading title imaginable," *New York Times* critic
Jack Gould wrote early in 1953. "For once, all available statistics are in
agreement: Millions love Lucy." The birth of Lucy's child on the episode aired January 20, 1953, had disrupted celebrations of President
Eisenhower's inauguration. Westerns like "Have Gun Will Travel" and
"Maverick" had their admirers; their plots possessed more turns, and
their scripts more wit, than those of ABC's "Wyatt Earp" (1955–61) or
"The Rifleman" (1958–63). Weaver, the apostle of live and special telecasting, helped with the original "Maverick" episodes. Such series,
along with detective dramas such as "Peter Gunn," were every bit as
"good" as the more dreary teleplays on "Producer's Showcase" and
certainly more entertaining. Even a busy Senate majority leader in
the late 1950s, Lyndon B. Johnson, occasionally found time for "Gunsmoke."

Such programs, however, remained the exception rather than the
rule. The movie colony's embrace of television had been at best halfhearted. In the late 1950s, Hollywood regarded the production of TV
programs as a flotation device. Jack Warner thought so little of television that he placed in charge of his TV production a public-relations
specialist, not an experienced film producer. He and others lacked any
aspirations for the newest medium. "Most Hollywood video producers
still think in terms of pat formulas and fear experimentation," wrote
New York Daily News critic Ben Gross in 1954. "The worst catastrophe
that could befall TV would be for it to be dominated by the films."

Although the film industry and other manufacturers of mass diversions had conceded television's permanence, they did not give up the
mass audience altogether. Both the movie industry and radio stations
cultivated the smaller but important teenage market. Most film producers also eyed a larger and older audience. The lifting of old controls on
the content of movies did not, on the whole, bring about a new realism
about sex in particular or society at large. Filmgoers in 1960 could attend features almost as pure as those a decade or two earlier. Many if
not most radio stations contained their enthusiasm for rock 'n' roll. If
market forces compelled them to air the new sound, there was always
the palatable alternative of Pat Boone. Adults could find a place on their

radio dial that played to their musical sensibilities. Newspapers and magazines behaved much as they had before families bought their first televisions, if not their first radios, and in time would suffer the most for their obdurateness.

EVENINGS OF 5
AVOIDANCE
Television in the 1960s

When riots erupted every spring and summer in different American cities between 1964 and 1968, participants did not march on city hall or other citadels of political or economic power. If there were attacks on property, the targets were invariably neighborhood supermarkets and appliance stores, with the most coveted objects, TV sets. The new "Bastilles," Archibald MacLeish observed, were outlets of the consumer culture. "Mobs strike for the Bastille in any rising," he wrote, "and the Bastille in the United States today is whatever stands for the American Way of Life: the goods and services, the material wealth, which the majority claim as the mark of their Americanism and which the minority are denied."

In their fashion, the looters were demonstrating something more specific: the significance of television to American society in the 1960s. By 1965, 92.6 percent of all households had at least one TV set; 22 percent had more than one. And according to Robert T. Bower, television viewing hours in most households increased just under 20 percent during the decade. Daily set use per home, the A. C. Nielsen Company estimated, rose from 5.85 hours in 1963 to 6.50 hours in 1970.

Nielsen's data, it should be noted, were for total set use, not individual consumption. Not everyone sat in rapt attention. As earlier, many preadolescents attended the Saturday movie matinee downtown, while their older sisters and brothers avidly listened to a DJ playing rock 'n' roll. Still, virtually everyone born during the postwar baby boom regarded television much as their parents had looked upon network radio and the picture house in the 1930s: it was *their* medium. Glib commentators would later dub them the TV generation. Yet it was actually their grandparents, those over fifty years of age, who viewed the most television. They had the fewest distractions or, as age caught up with them, were too tired or infirm to do more than watch television.

Quieting the Guardians

Having come to dominate the republic of mass culture, television nevertheless remained uneasy about its standing in American society. Its leaders avoided offending any significant segment of the public. In terms of programming, that meant offering evenings of avoidance. At a time of racial turmoil, political murders, and a massive military intervention in southeast Asia, Americans viewed relentlessly escapist entertainment and rigorously "neutral" news programming.

Like the governors of the movie colony in the thirties and forties, television's operators in the late fifties and early sixties worried about the guardians, especially the Federal Communications Commission. Although the FCC limited the number of stations a network could own, the overwhelming majority of TV outlets—95 percent in 1959—were affiliated with one of the networks and normally carried their programming in the evenings, when most Americans watched TV. And the commission had the power to revoke individual TV licenses, including the profitable ones owned by the networks. The FCC might have become the biggest regulatory joke of the Eisenhower administration, yet older broadcasters such as Frank Stanton, president of CBS, could remember when the commission had taken its oversight duties very seriously. That spirit might be revived, if only halfheartedly, by congressional overseers of the FCC. Indeed, through the 1950s, congressional committees had met to study such topics as mass culture and juvenile delinquency, television station allocation and economics.

The House Commerce Committee late in 1959 uncovered the newest medium's worst scandal. Between 1955 and 1958, quiz programs that offered winners large cash prizes had been among the most popular on the schedules of two of the networks, CBS and NBC. Most critics had regretted the rise of shows like CBS's "The $64,000 Question," whose popularity had come at the expense of much praised but less popular programs like "See It Now." Unlike "game shows" aired in the sixties and later, the quiz programs appeared in evening prime time; their producers sought participants who displayed something other than a mastery of trivia. Expertise often ran against expectation: producers located a jockey who had studied fine art, a police officer who knew about Shakespeare. Spoiling the fun, however, were reports that the producers had coached their players and provided some with answers. One of the most popular, a young English instructor at Columbia University, Charles Van Doren, had taken a fall by forgetting the name of the King of the Belgians. Revealed in a series of confessionals conducted by the House committee, the quiz show "fix" greatly embarrassed NBC and CBS. The scandal seemed to confirm charges that TV had become excessively commercialized.

A guardian fury followed. Ministers had fodder for sermons. The press sharply condemned television. Politicians conveyed their shock and dismay. At a press conference, President Eisenhower, no proponent of cultural oversight, likened the scandal to the rigged 1919 World Series. And prominent members of Congress spoke of increased television regulation, including the licensing of the networks.

Network executives need not have panicked. The FCC had no taste for discipline; FCC Chairman John C. Doerfer stubbornly took issue with those members of Congress who demanded action. Doerfer cited the First Amendment, while his detractors pointed to his frequent social hours with broadcasters. Yet Doerfer had the public, if not their clergy and lay leadership, on his side. Although Americans followed the quiz show hearings closely, relatively few expressed the outrage heard from their elected representatives, ministers, or rabbis. The quiz programs had already lost much of their appeal, and virtually all had been removed from the evening prime time schedule by the fall 1959 season. Congressmen had received far more mail decrying the possibility of pay-TV in 1958—many elderly viewers had feared that fee-based programming proposed that year would in time have become the industry norm—than they received condemning the transgressions of free TV a year later.

If the networks could take comfort in the public's indifference, they could not ignore the opinion leadership. The quiz shows' very place on the evening schedule had upset those who wrote about television. Since 1957, TV critics for the nation's leading newspapers and magazines had been denouncing television's abandonment of the live anthology dramas in favor of quiz shows and filmed weekly series. As advertiser demand for television rose in the mid and late fifties, network executives felt more and more obligated to schedule nothing but popular programming, even at the expense of Edward R. Murrow. "See It Now" had been knocked off from the regular schedule in 1955 and was dropped altogether three years later. His many admirers were furious. Since his coverage of the Battle of Britain, Murrow had been a hero to the nation's liberal elite as well as among many others who admired the broadcaster's mix of irony and alarm. His widely covered public denunciation of television in October 1958 caused many to add TV to a larger concern that Americans had become materialistic and devoid of national purpose. As the country's major cultural machinery, TV had failed. "Why is television so bad, so monotonous?" the *New Republic* asked as the quiz fix story broke a year later. "In reaching for the largest possible audience at all times, television has betrayed its legal obligation to serve the public interest, convenience and necessity." Screenwriter Dalton Trumbo wrote of "the crime we have committed, not against ourselves alone, but against our children, our country, and even the broken victims of prostituted television."

The networks felt bound to act. Unable to plot a joint strategy with ABC, the two networks that had aired the fixed programs, CBS and NBC, moved to still their critics. Each network promised to regulate its own programs more closely. "Specials" with self-consciously high cultural aspirations were thrown together. To quiet those irate over the cancelation of "See It Now," CBS and NBC stepped up their telecasting of news programs. Even before the quiz scandals had been uncovered, Frank Stanton of CBS had announced that his network would produce an hour-long documentary program, "CBS Reports," to be aired in the evening and produced by Murrow's partner, Fred Friendly.

Stanton and his brethren were making a sacrifice, for news programs had never been popular. Murrow's only widely viewed effort in the 1950s had been "Person to Person," a celebrity interview program. The CBS and NBC evening newscasts had to be rescheduled to an earlier, less popular time period after ABC deliberately "counter-programmed" by airing entertainment programming that drew far better ratings. Most advertisers displayed no interest in news shows; for thirteen weeks in 1957, NBC's early evening news program, "The Huntley-Brinkley Report," had no sponsors. Most if not all news programs lost money. In April 1961, Richard Salant of CBS News contended that CBS's pretax profits in 1960 would have been 65 percent higher had the network not produced public-affairs programming.

In the heated atmosphere of October and November 1959, however, the networks had to offer more news programming. As a consequence of the scandals, the 1960 presidential election probably received more televised coverage than would have been the case had Van Doren uttered King Baudouin's name. All three networks donated time for TV "debates" between the major party candidates. And an average audience of 71 million Americans viewed Vice President Richard Nixon and Senator John F. Kennedy stiffly answer a panel of reporters' questions. The unprecedented forums caused most of the medium's detractors to forget the quiz show revelations of the previous fall. Walter Lippmann, who had earlier recommended the creation of a federal network, called the TV debates "a bold innovation." Other evening concessions came, most commonly hour-long "documentaries" modeled after "CBS Reports." NBC produced "Project XX" and ABC, "Close-Up!"

Through the decade documentaries tended to be dull, "objective" forays into public issues. When CBS aired an interview with former President Eisenhower in 1962, cartoonist Al Capp found the experience so numbing that he dubbed the program "Yawn Along with Ike." Most documentaries lacked the discernible point of view of "See It Now." "They don't jar convictions," Jack Gould of the *New York Times* wrote in December 1964. Reviewing a three-and-a-half-hour NBC special on U.S. foreign policy nine months later, Gould found the effort admirable yet lacking "some knowing editorial hand." The "total effect was strangely monotonous and enervating." Television, a *National Review* critic observed in May 1967, "becomes stuffy and self-conscious as soon as it puts on its Public Service toga." Then, too, the networks avoided certain topics or tones that might offend those in or merely possessed of power. "Too many men," Fred Friendly complained in 1963, "are trying to do 'safe' stories."

Documentaries normally finished last in the ratings. Despite heavy promotion, the CBS Eisenhower interview drew a dreadful 11 percent share of the TV audience. The networks all but guaranteed their news specials' last-place ranking by scheduling them against popular entertainment shows. In the 1961–62 season, "CBS Reports" faced ABC's popular series about prohibition agents, "The Untouchables," and NBC's sentimental music program, "Sing Along with Mitch." Yet neither program was impregnable: both "The Untouchables" and "Mitch" left the air once CBS challenged them with entertainment programming.

Telecasting news shows in prime time did placate TV's critics and, beginning in 1961, the Kennedy administration. Newspaper and magazine critics had regarded *any* informational programming to be superior television. They were forcefully seconded by one of their more avid readers, Kennedy's FCC chairman, Newton N. Minow. In a stunning attack Minow in May 1961 declared television a "vast wasteland" and insisted that the networks continue and increase their news coverage. *Variety* later compared Minow's address to William Jennings Bryan's famous "Cross of Gold" speech before the 1896 Democratic National Convention. "Like Bryan," *Variety* argued, Minow "electrified an army of supporters, angered his adversaries and jolted the nation."

Self-interest caused the new president to support television's newest guardian. In the late 1950s Kennedy had been among those displeased by reductions in news programming at CBS. He regarded television as *his* medium. Like Roosevelt and Truman, Kennedy assumed that the Republican leanings of most newspaper and magazine publishers affected their properties' treatment of Democrats. Broadcasters, in contrast, he considered to be virtual publicists. Network newscasts usually reported uncritically any administration announcement; documentaries, made with the full cooperation of the president's staff, tended to share their point of view on such issues as the cold war and civil rights. "Television news has become almost an agency of government," Ray Scherer of NBC wrote of TV's civil rights coverage. Kennedy put his own good looks and telegenic manner to good use in televised presidential addresses and press conferences. Watching a film of one session with reporters, he told an aide, "We couldn't survive without TV."

Independent of any governmental pressure, Robert Kintner, president of NBC from 1958 to 1966, had been increasing the budget and airtime of NBC News. A former journalist, Kintner took pride in television's informational potential; as president of ABC in the early 1950s, he had been responsible for his network's telecasting of the Kefauver and McCarthy hearings. The Kennedy administration's active promotion of TV news strengthened his position, as did the attitude of RCA, NBC's parent corporation. RCA, in effect, conceded the overall ratings leadership to CBS; Kintner was under little pressure to finish first as long as second place was respectable and profitable. News programming on NBC gave RCA goodwill. Kintner thought nothing, for example, of granting NBC News three hours in evening prime time in September 1963 to examine the civil rights movement.

Kintner also poured resources into the nightly newscasts. It was a perfect concession: as continuous efforts, the fifteen-minute programs were cheaper to produce and easier to promote than documentaries; they also enjoyed an increasing respectability. Until the late fifties, critics had singled out Murrow and the news documentary for praise. But more opinion leaders began to be impressed by the NBC newscasts, especially the coanchors, Chet Huntley and David Brinkley. Without resorting to the empty banter that came to afflict local news programs, both Huntley and Brinkley distanced themselves from the doomsday tone of Murrow and many of the old World War II correspondents. They displayed, a *Newark Evening News* critic wrote in 1960, a "relaxed, detached, low-keyed approach which was different and refreshing."

The significance that critics and opinion leaders attached to the nightly news increased enormously in September 1963, when CBS and NBC lengthened their newscasts from fifteen to thirty minutes. (ABC, still the laggard in public-service programming, waited until 1967.)

Many affiliates, resenting the loss of another fifteen minutes to the networks, had resisted the move, but most relented to placate Minow and others who raised their voices and eyebrows in Washington. And monitors of the medium were deeply impressed, believing that the longer format had finally made television a serious medium of information, comparable to daily newspapers. Theodore H. White compared the shift to the completion of the first transcontinental rail link in 1869. For the first time, network correspondents at the White House enjoyed greater access to the president than their colleagues working for newspapers, including the nation's most prestigious dailies. Kennedy personally agreed to be interviewed for the first thirty-minute editions of the "The CBS Evening News" and "The Huntley-Brinkley Report." The president had concluded, three scholars of his relations with the fourth estate observed, that the evening news programs "were more important in reaching the public than any newspaper or magazine."

The numbers of Americans who regularly and closely viewed the evening newscasts in the 1960s were actually far smaller than Kennedy and others realized. Although those viewers who were polled by the Roper organization beginning in 1963 listed TV as their primary news source, more systematic studies indicated that relatively few watched a network newscast four or more times a week. A survey by John P. Robinson suggested that more than half of the adult population had viewed no national news program during a two-week period in October 1969. Moreover, most preferred local to national newscasts. By comparison, most households still took one or more daily newspapers. Finally, those who did watch TV news programs were less attentive than when they sampled entertainment programming, perhaps because the early evening time slot clashed with the demands of preparing dinner or reviewing a child's day at school.

Why, then, did some assume that Huntley and Brinkley or their CBS rival daily visited the American living room? One explanation is that an element of the elite who started to watch TV news assumed that its own addiction was part of a much larger trend. Then, too, in times of crisis, most painfully during the four days following President Kennedy's death, millions of Americans did sit before their TV sets listening to Huntley and others as they tried to becalm themselves and their viewers.

CBS and NBC and, in time, many local stations did find evening newscasts to be profitable. "The Huntley-Brinkley Report," *Fortune* observed in May 1969, earned more money for NBC than any other network program. Although network news executives claimed that they spared no expense in bringing the world to viewers, they actually relied, Robert

MacNeil of NBC admitted, mostly on the wire services. (No network had a third as many overseas correspondents as did the *New York Times*.) Drawing on other news organizations helped to make the evening news programs cost-effective. NBC News spent about $28,000 per "Huntley-Brinkley" newscast in 1968, considerably less than the price of a prime-time entertainment program. The improved earnings from newscasts in turn reflected an overall demand for TV time from advertisers beginning in the 1960s, usually manufacturers of over-the-counter drugs who were interested in advertising to the network newscasts' disproportionately elderly audiences.

Nor did the longer evening newscasts overcome the essential superficiality of TV news. Producers normally used the additional fifteen minutes, Edward Jay Epstein noted in a study of the newscasts aired between 1962 and 1968, on light and inexpensive "features" (revealingly, NBC News forbade the use of the term). Anchors continued to be little more than uncritical readers of wire service leads. "The chief change for the moment," Gould wrote in 1963, "seemed to be only more headline bulletins, not any appreciable increase in true depth or diversity of coverage." Upset over such criticisms later in the decade, Richard Salant had a "CBS Evening News" broadcast set to type. To his horror, he discovered that it filled less than three-fourths of one page of the *New York Times*. "What the television viewer is getting essentially is a headline service," MacNeil wrote in 1968. "The effect was like that of a quick ruffle through a magazine."

The Other Television

The networks practiced a dualistic programming philosophy in the early 1960s. All three boosted news programming; none, however, slowed the trend toward filmed series. Indeed, Kintner and his rivals, while rededicating their companies to informational programming for an hour a week, encouraged producers to infuse more violence and sex into action dramas. The remaining dramatic anthologies left the air. News programming alone would have to provide each network with prestige. James T. Aubrey, president of the CBS Television Network in 1960, told Fred Friendly, "They say to me, 'Take your soiled little hands, get the ratings, and make as much money as you can'; they say to you, 'Take your lily-white hands, do your best, go the high road and bring us prestige.' "

Those who had artistic aspirations or pretensions and veterans of the old dramatic anthologies had to work within the confines of the weekly filmed series. Rod Serling produced and wrote many of the individual episodes of CBS's "The Twilight Zone" (1959–65). Compared with most series, "The Twilight Zone" was a hybrid of the old anthology and dramatic programs. Serling's series had no regular cast, only Serling himself, who was on camera at the outset to explain that a character or characters were about to enter a bizarre "fifth dimension." More conventional in their reliance on a regular cast were "The Defenders" (1961–65) and "Route 66" (1960–64), both on CBS. Veteran anthology writers participated in both series. "Route 66" concerned the odyssey of two young men traveling in a Corvette; above-average scripts and guest performers usually kept them off the road to melodrama. "The Defenders" marched for various causes, and in contrast to CBS's more popular defense attorney series, "Perry Mason" (1957–66). Created by pulp fiction writer Erle Stanley Gardner, Perry Mason only once lost a case. Nor did he handle any of social consequence: he always defended innocents accused of murder. The Prestons, the father-son team in "The Defenders," fought for those charged with violating selective-service laws, selling obscene literature, and distributing birth control information, an offense in most states in the early sixties. They helped the blacklisted and the atheistic. Their causes were always correct, liberal ones, fought calmly.

Series like "The Defenders" affected to a standard of realism not seen since the departure of the 1950s anthology dramas. Not surprisingly, the person most responsible for ending the golden age at CBS, James Aubrey, had opposed scheduling "The Defenders." The program was not enough like "Perry Mason," Aubrey argued. "The Defenders" rarely utilized the easy melodramatic trick, ritualistically employed on "Perry Mason," of having a climactic confession from the real killer, normally someone on the stand or in the courtroom audience. An episode of "The Defenders" might end with the Prestons losing a case or the verdict still pending. *Variety* in April 1962 called the program "a unique effort to combine the dramatic repertory program of the 'Golden Age' with the best qualities of the serials dominant these days."

Other adult dramas in the early sixties usually involved professionals. Most, modeled after old B-pictures and radio dramas, concerned the health professions: "Ben Casey" (ABC, 1961–66), "Dr. Kildare" (NBC, 1961–66), "The Nurses" (CBS, 1962–65), "Breaking Point" (ABC, 1963–64), "The Eleventh Hour" (NBC, 1962–64). Of these, "Dr. Kildare" and "Ben Casey" enjoyed the best ratings. And their success owed something to an old Hollywood casting formula: a handsome young male plays the lead, supported by an older, wiser superior; MGM had produced a series of "Kildare" films in the 1930s. It was a pattern reproduced in such 1970s series as "Marcus Welby, M.D." and many medical and private-eye programs in the eighties. Other adult dramas, laden with the liberal sympathies so pronounced on "The Defenders," featured social workers ("East Side / West Side" [CBS, 1963–64]) and a state legislator ("Slattery's People" [CBS, 1964–65]). Although ostensibly "action-adventure" programs, police dramas like "The Naked City" (ABC, 1958–59, 1960–63) and "The 87th Precinct" (NBC, 1961–62) possessed a maturity unseen in the typical cops-and-robbers series. Yet their realism never approached despair. The leads in the professional dramas wholly dedicated themselves to their jobs and their communities. Not coincidentally, Joseph Turow found, the American Medical Association cooperated with the producers of "Kildare" and "Casey"; the AMA seal appeared at the end of each episode. The AMA insisted that each physician appear to be hardworking and of modest means. Frantically fighting the enactment of a "socialized medicine" proposal, or Medicare, the physicians' association wanted the medical profession to be portrayed in the noblest light. The world of the professional dramas, Harris Dienstfrey wrote in 1963, "is a place that offers meaningful work, a public devotion to the common good, and secure, vital values."

The Network Oligopoly and the Creative Crisis in Programming

Until the quiz show scandals, the battle over programming had been waged privately between network executives and advertisers. The networks had each long plotted to break the power of advertisers, who as buyers of time could produce and all but force a program on the schedule. If, for example, CBS rejected a Procter & Gamble proposal or refused to air it at the time sought, P&G could go to NBC or ABC. This relationship persisted in the late fifties; by then, however, the issue of program control did not involve the advertiser so much as the independent producer. From the beginning, the cost and technical demands of TV production had caused most advertisers to have programs they sponsored produced by independent companies. They, and not the advertisers, had been responsible for most of the quiz show deceits.

To break the power of advertisers and independent producers, the networks were aided by the growth in demand for television time. Network billings to advertisers increased from $776 million in 1959 to $1,025 million in 1963 and $1,455 million in 1967. The networks maximized their sales potential by practicing what Raymond Williams has called "majority television." Although each network scheduled an hour a week of informational programming in prime time, each otherwise displayed a new ruthlessness about acquiring and holding large audiences. No longer could the single sponsors of the less popular "The Voice of Firestone" and "Armstrong Circle Theater" find a network willing to carry their shows. Their comparatively small followings created a poor "audience flow" to the next program and lowered potential network earnings. At the same time, the higher demand for airtime permitted the networks to boost their charges to advertisers. As network time became more expensive, advertisers gradually gave up exclusive sponsorship, that is, underwriting a single program. They instead "participated" with others, with the time costs pegged to the ratings.

By the mid 1960s, independent producers no longer worked for advertisers. Independents instead either approached the networks with proposals for series or pursued an idea for a show from network executives. If pleased with a "pilot" episode, the network accepted the program. Network executives, taking on the role once played by the advertiser or its agency, then oversaw the production of the series itself. And, in a classic example of achieving vertical control over an industry, the network, in exchange for investment in the costs of the production of a program, received a share of the profitable syndication or rerun rights for both domestic and overseas markets. As "packagers," independents working under this arrangement by the mid 1960s became the dominant source of network programming. According to the FCC's Office of Network Study, in 1957 packagers produced 38 percent of all network programming, compared with 33 percent provided by advertisers and 29 percent produced by the networks directly. By 1964 the packagers' share of all network fare had increased to 71 percent compared with the networks' 20 percent and advertisers' 9 percent.

This trend, by creating a structural conflict of interest for network programmers, raised a host of questions. An executive at ABC, CBS, or NBC had to choose between a program in which his network had an interest and one in which his employer held no financial stake. Often there was no choice, such as when the network originated the concept for a series and then funded a pilot episode created by the packager. The producer's effort might not be as creative as one offered by an advertiser, but the network stood to gain much more from the syndication of a packager's series.

With the network sharing more of the risks in programming costs and benefits, network programmers adhered to a risk-aversion strategy. New series tended to resemble old ones or "hot" trends in the industry. Compared with the late fifties, when the networks took up quiz shows, Westerns, and detective series to excess, the sixties saw a succession of minibooms. There were dramas about teachers and doctors, comedies and action shows set in World War II, action-adventure series about spies. One of the last type, "Mission: Impossible" (CBS, 1966–73), involved a special spy force that overcame extraordinary odds on behalf of the U.S. government; the series' wide distribution abroad left many in the Third World with a wildly exaggerated impression of the Central Intelligence Agency's capacities. ABC violated convention with only occasional success, as when it placed a soap opera, "Peyton Place" (1964–69), and a series about a comic book hero, "Batman" (1966–68), in evening prime time.

A staple of radio and early television, the situation comedy, flourished in the 1960s. Two-thirds of the programs that premiered in September 1964 were sitcoms; sixteen old sitcoms returned to the 1964–65 schedule. Most had a middle-class setting. With few exceptions, notably "The Dick Van Dyke Show" (CBS, 1961–66), the writing was uninspired. Some situation comedies possessed one incredible "schtick" or gimmick, such as a car or horse (Mr. Ed) that talked, a wife who was a witch, or a Martian roommate.

The blandness of most sixties sitcom scripts had several causes. Various taboos on discussions of sex or politics, enforced by the networks, inhibited writers. Then, too, there was the passing of most of the medium's great comedy variety programs, hosted by Berle, Sid Caesar, and others. They had insisted on having a talented team of gag writers, many of whom then went to work on the thirty-minute series. By the mid sixties, however, virtually all of these fifties-trained writers had left TV to labor in film or on Broadway. Sitcom producers discouraged potentially skilled replacements; to contain costs, they hired fewer writers per series and limited their salaries. Such practices dissuaded all but the mediocre or financially desperate to compose sitcom scripts.

Another illustration of TV's creative caution was the coming of the feature film to evening prime time. Although the studios had begun making their post-1948 features available in the mid fifties, stations and not the networks had scheduled films to fill their late-afternoon and late-evening non-network time slots. Network executives doubted that movies, especially ones that had fared less well at the box office, could compete with more popular series or variety hours; ABC's telecasting of British films in 1955 had been a costly failure. In the fall of 1961, however, NBC enjoyed unexpected rating success with recent Twentieth Century Fox releases aired on Saturday evenings. Viewers could see actors like Clark Gable, Susan Hayward, and William Holden, who either had never appeared on TV programs or had limited their appearances to one episode of "I Love Lucy," a segment on Ed Sullivan's program, or an interview on one of the new late-night "talk shows." ABC soon followed with Sunday telecasts of United Artists films. More "movie nights" came as the price of TV series rose. Network accountants discovered that the rights to air feature films cost less per hour than most entertainment programming, and they drew comparable or better ratings. CBS, with the largest number of popular series and the ratings leadership, waited until the mid sixties to air films. And by the fall of 1966, motion pictures absorbed just over 10 percent of evening prime time for all three chains. The number of TV series, in turn, fell from seventy-six in 1960 to fifty-seven in the 1967–68 season and forty-five in the fall of 1970.

By the late sixties Hollywood was producing "made for TV" movies for the networks. The practice began in 1964 when NBC commissioned Universal Studios to make three two-hour telefilms. The network's cost-consciousness, its wish to pay less than for theatrical features, made most early TV movies empty exercises. Ironically, NBC censors rejected the first Universal picture, *The Killers*, as too violent. Subsequently released in theaters, *The Killers* was skillfully directed by Donald Siegel and featured Ronald Reagan, cast against his type, as the villain. (In one scene, often screened later, Reagan slaps Angie Dickinson to the floor. Until wealthy friends persuaded him to run for governor of California two years later, Reagan had planned to finish his film career playing heavys.) Unlike *The Killers*, two other Universal movies, *See How They Run* and *The Hanged Man*, won network approval and in October and November 1964 earned, considering the amount of talent invested in each, respectable ratings. In the next few years, TV movies often served as cost-effective pilots for series like "Ironside" and "The Iron Horse." Normally, only a few network executives saw a thirty- or sixty-minute pilot. As a TV movie, however, such pilots could be sampled by millions of viewers. Critics were unimpressed, charging Universal and other studios with producing second-rate B-movies for the home screen. Charles Champlin of the *Los Angeles Times* called one NBC TV movie "long neither on imagination, nor cash."

By the mid sixties, those who wrote about television had concluded that the networks had abandoned any lingering creative tendencies. Series about police officers and spies, which relied heavily on violent confrontations, displaced other types of dramatic programs. Situation comedies were blandly imitative. Paul Jones of the *Atlanta Constitution* declared every new season the worst or, as he wrote in October 1964, "the most disappointing in years." A year later, Jack Gould called the fall 1965 season "the biggest yawn in the modern annals of broadcasting."

Although TV columnists rarely affected the popularity of programs, the more liberal members of the FCC read their commentaries and shared their low opinion of the home screen. Convinced that an oligopolistic control over the production of programming largely explained the medium's lack of creativity, the FCC attempted beginning in 1965 to curb the networks' role in creating series. Many regulators had long championed diversity, an article of faith that had inspired the breakup of NBC in 1943 and the rescue merger of ABC and UPT in 1953. In that spirit, the commission hoped that by decentralizing the program procurement process, it could make it possible for more types of programming, some of it more creative and more like that seen in the golden age, to appear on the home screen. Early in 1965 the FCC proposed to limit any network interest in programming to 50 percent of the schedule and end any network rights to syndication.

The "50/50" rule was placed on hold. Its proponents were all but undone by the cumbersome administrative process imposed on the FCC in the late 1940s. Those affected by a potential rule advantaged themselves of every right to slow things to a halt. Network lawyers won delays as they prepared long petitions forecasting the worst.

It was a deeply frustrating time for the more aggressive regulators. Briefly in 1961, Chairman Newton Minow had given the FCC a new visibility. Critics of television had hoped that Minow and his colleagues would somehow irrigate the "wasteland." But Minow had found the going rough: few of his fellow commissioners, named to the agency in the forties and fifties, shared his ambitious agenda for television "reform"; and Minow himself, stung by charges that he sought to censor programs, lowered his own voice. Change became incremental. Minow personally secured a powerful New York City TV station for the fledgling educational television system (ETV). With the support of most of his colleagues, he fashioned a long-term solution to the problem besetting UHF TV station operators. With most consumers still refusing to pay an extra thirty-five dollars to receive UHF signals on their TV sets, the chairman persuaded Congress to pass a law that required television sets manufactured after March 1964 to be able to receive channels 14–83. Such actions, however, had little immediate impact, and Minow himself quit Washington in mid 1963.

Minow's like-minded successor, E. William Henry, tried just about everything to keep his agency in the spotlight, including dressing up as Batman at a Washington party, to no avail. The concern among elements of the opinion elite that television had declined—and that the government had to reverse that trend—no longer existed. Many rightly turned their attention to the more immediate needs of the civil rights movement and the antipoverty war. No one turned more heads than Lyndon Johnson, who became president in November 1963. Johnson's wife Lady Bird had owned a CBS-affiliated radio station in Austin since 1942, and the new president had not numbered among Minow's fans. Although both Johnson and his wife sought to increase federal support of the arts, the president shared Kintner's view that television could fulfill its "mission" largely through news programming; entertainment programming need not aspire to much more than good ratings. Referring to the main character on "Gunsmoke," one of Johnson's favorite programs, *Variety* spoke in December 1964 of the new line in Washington: "Matt Dillon is in, Pablo Casals is out." Also "in" were two close friends of the new First Family: Kintner of NBC and Stanton of CBS, the targets of the 50/50 rule and other potential punishments. Kintner eventually went to work for Johnson as secretary of the Cabinet. Stanton personally repaired the president's Oval Office desk and installed the television sets. And the industry took Henry less and less seriously. Station managers who still worried about the FCC, one observer remarked in the late sixties, had "too few tasks to occupy their minds."

"There is no way to improve it"

With the FCC reverting to its customary irrelevance, the networks made even fewer concessions to television's guardians. The heirs to the anthology tradition, the professional dramas, left the air by the mid sixties. Not long after Kennedy's death, one network scrapped plans for a new series about the Department of Health, Education and Welfare. All of the networks reduced their prime-time news programming in favor of the more profitable, early evening newscasts. "Like live video drama and the bison," *Variety* observed in October 1965, "the hardhitting TV documentary is nearly extinct."

The Sunday afternoon "ghetto," one of the other, lost legacies of the golden age, fell to the larger audiences for sports programming. The number of professional football telecasts expanded with the creation of the American Football League (AFL) in 1960. ABC carried AFL games until 1964, when NBC won the rights. The league used some of the monies from the NBC deal to sign talented players like Joe Namath, of the University of Alabama, and in 1966 forced a marriage with the older National Football League. By then, watching a football game had become more exciting, for the technology of broadcasting the contests had improved. The networks utilized new and smaller cameras to pick up more of the action and, after 1963, videotape to provide instant replays.

For many American men, a TV game became excellent cause to escape Sunday afternoon chores. "People will arrange their day to watch an NFL game," one industry veteran observed. Premiering in 1960, "The Wide World of Sports" filled off-season hours and made ABC the leader in innovative sports telecasting. Only on "Wide World" could viewers see a rattlesnake hunt. The more genteel and such opinion leaders as John Kennedy could watch golf. Matches filled Sunday slots less because of the size of their audiences—the top-rated tournament in 1966 drew about half the audience of an NFL playoff game—than because of their composition. Advertisers then and later preferred the well-to-do fans of golf to the more pluralist followers of basketball. Although they and hockey addicts remain unsatisfied, the loudest cries came from TV critics and news-division personnel. By the late 1960s, sports had taken over Sunday afternoons, often at the expense of news and cultural programming. Whereas Murrow and others had once complained about being relegated to Sunday afternoons, the expansion of sports programming all but wiped out even that enclave. "Remember the old days when we used to talk about the Sunday ghetto?" recalled Salant of CBS News. "I'd like to have it back!"

The diffusion of color television marked another significant change for TV in the sixties. RCA and NBC had been promoting color TV since the mid fifties, but not for a decade did some more well-to-do consumers begin to purchase color sets. Of those homes with television sets, the number with color receivers increased from 1.2 percent in 1961 to 39.2 percent in 1970. In the midst of the color TV boom, NBC went to an "all-color" evening prime-time schedule in the fall of 1965. CBS and ABC soon followed.

In subtle ways, the colorization of prime time distorted the world that television presented viewers. Because color film picked up far more detail than black and white, most TV production designers cluttered sets with commodities—plants, flowers, paintings. These had the effect of making characters, even ones supposed to be of modest means, look affluent. On a TV show, a young adult's New York apartment was filled with fine furniture and wall-papered or painted blue or another lush color; in reality, most young Gotham renters furnished their places haphazardly, and landlords usually painted the walls white. The apartment of the middle-class nurse who starred on "Julia" could easily be mistaken for that of the chief of surgery. "The picture you get of American life on television," broadcast historian Erik Barnouw observed in 1972, "is one of extraordinary luxury."

Programming itself, as well as the most common program type, the situation comedy, did not change from the 1950s, though many individual stars could not match their earlier successes. Series starring Jack Benny and Ozzie and Harriet Nelson finally wore out their welcome. Other established performers like Phil Silvers and Lucille Ball never dominated the medium as they had earlier, though Ball's twice-revamped program, sans Desi, enjoyed an even longer run than had "I Love Lucy." Jackie Gleason had to revive "The Honeymooners" as a regular feature when his variety program's ratings began to slump.

CBS's comic schtick had a country flavor. In the mid 1960s, five of Columbia's fourteen sitcoms had a rural setting or rural-bred protagonists: "Andy Griffith" (1960–68), "Petticoat Junction" (1963–70), "The Beverly Hillbillies" (1962–71), "Green Acres" (1965–71), and "Gomer Pyle, USMC" (1964–70). The unusually broad humor of most of these shows appealed to largely white audiences in the countryside or to those who were unreconciled to the urbanization of America.

None found more success than "The Beverly Hillbillies." The series involved a poor family from the Ozarks, the Clampetts, who, enriched by oil discovered on their property, move to an exclusive Los Angeles suburb. The typical episode consisted of obvious confrontations between the newly moneyed but still pure Clampetts and various snobs. The series made few demands on its audience. "At no time," a *Variety* reviewer complained in October 1962, "does it give the viewer credit for even a smattering of intelligence. The lines were as cliché-ridden as the situations were obvious." And the program proved to be the most popular situation comedy of the decade; 44 percent of all sets were tuned in to the most-watched episode, aired January 8, 1964. The timing of the series held its ironies. The rural population was shrinking; and the real sufferings of some like the Clampetts, but not so lucky, had inspired the federal government, during the program's second season, quite unrelatedly to launch a war on poverty in the countryside.

The Alternatives

For those who were unsettled by the wasteland's expansion in the mid and late 1960s, there were few options. More UHF stations began operations as the percentage of homes with sets able to receive UHF signals increased from 7.1 percent in 1961 to 73.0 percent in 1970. But the frequency remained inferior to VHF; for many viewers, watching a UHF station meant moving the receiver or antenna and hoping for clear weather. The programming on UHF outlets made the struggle questionable. Although most new upper-frequency stations were unaffiliated with networks, they relied heavily on reruns of network programs

("The old film shows never die," *Variety* observed in February 1963, "they don't even fade away") as well as telecasts of sporting events.

By 1967 those who had hoped Minow would "better" TV had concluded that only a public network would serve their tastes. "Nothing can be done about commercial television," Gore Vidal wrote. "There is no way to improve it." President Johnson persuaded an indifferent Congress to pass the Public Broadcasting Act of 1967, which loosely joined the country's various ETV outlets into a Public Broadcasting System (PBS). An enthusiastic presidential speechwriter compared the creation of PBS to the Morrill Federal Land Grant Act of 1862. However, the inability of the president and Congress to agree on a permanent funding mechanism akin to that for the British Broadcasting Corporation and the federal network's heavy reliance on UHF channels severely hampered PBS.

Perhaps the most effective deliverer of diversity was community antenna or cable systems (CATV). First developed in the 1950s for consumers living in mountainous areas where terrain hampered reception, CATV had begun to be regarded as an alternative for those who sought more choices than local outlets presented. A cable subscriber might have twelve or more stations from which to chose, instead of the usual three or four. Yet cable operators found their opportunities limited by the FCC, which worried that CATV's continued diffusion would discourage UHF television. At a time when many if not most UHF operations barely broke even, CATV might reduce a UHF station's audience and the amount its operators could charge advertisers. Beginning in 1965, the FCC through a series of rules and regulations slowed cable's spread and all but banned CATV systems in the larger and most profitable TV viewing areas.

In the late 1960s, broadcast regulation of cable and the federal government's halfhearted support for noncommercial TV had the effect of reinforcing the three networks' dominance. They had little real competition: on a given evening more than 90 percent of all sets were tuned to a network program.

Self-Censorship

The networks did not take their hold for granted. Self-censorship of programming, once the preoccupation of advertisers who packaged radio and early TV programs, had become the responsibility of the networks. Like advertisers, they deferred to certain powerful critics. A 1961–62 Senate inquiry found that CBS and NBC had been all but compelling producers to infuse their programs with more sex and violence.

The networks swiftly responded by reducing the mayhem on their action dramas while introducing more situation comedies. Brute force on a sitcom was restricted to slapstick.

Respectful if not fearful of the repressed attitudes toward sex that were still common to many Americans who belonged to more conservative Protestant churches and those who resided in small towns, network programming avoided anything remotely explicit about sexual relations. Characters on afternoon soap operas kissed and hugged only so passionately. On evening programs, husbands and wives slept in twin beds. Single parents like Lucy Carmichael on "The Lucy Show" and Steve Douglas on "My Three Sons" were widowed, never divorced.

As in the 1950s, this preoccupation with audience "subgroups" had a racial dimension. The networks had been reluctant to cast blacks, even in supporting roles, in regular series. Southern station managers often protested giving blacks such prominence. Middle-class civil rights groups resented African Americans' being awarded supporting roles that might evoke memories of the fool servant perpetuated by Hollywood and network radio for two generations. Avoidance proved to be the best strategy: blacks were rarely seen on network programming until the mid 1960s, when NBC began scheduling programs in which blacks starred or costarred. Bill Cosby played an American secret agent on "I Spy" (1965–68); Sammy Davis, Jr., briefly hosted a variety show in 1966; and Diahann Carroll played a widowed nurse in the situation comedy "Julia" (1968–71). By the late 1960s blacks frequently had supporting roles as well. Yet not all programs were integrated: only one episode of "The FBI" in the program's nine-year run concerned a civil rights violation, despite the Bureau's heavy involvement in such cases.

All three networks devoted much of their news budget to covering protests of white segregation in the South. In the late 1950s and early 1960s each news division, under pressure from affiliates in southern states, had struggled to be "balanced" in its coverage. For a 1961 "CBS Reports" feature on racial turmoil in Birmingham, Alabama, Howard K. Smith sought to add a commentary assailing the city's police for standing by while white supremacists beat up civil rights demonstrators. The network accused him of excessive editorializing and forced his ouster. Within a few years, such controls ceased, and correspondents stopped cloaking their sympathies. "The tone of network programming has been emphatically liberal," wrote Robert MacNeil, then at NBC News, "identifying the advancement of the American Negro —toward equality as unquestionably linked to the health of this nation." As TV journalists shed their modesty, many began to assume credit for the wave of civil rights legislation passed in the 1960s. "There may have been no civil rights bill last year," Ray Scherer wrote in 1966, "if the country had not seen Bull Connor's police dogs in Birmingham on television."

Such comments tended to miscast television reporters and camera operators. Although subject themselves to verbal and physical attacks, they normally were witnesses to, not participants in, the racial protests. It was the civil rights leadership itself, and countless African Americans who enlisted in its campaigns, who daily risked imprisonment and injury. If TV news helped to advance the cause of the civil rights movement, it was on the initiative of the movement itself. As William B. Monroe, a New Orleans station manager, observed, "Negroes are the architects, bricklayers, carpenters, and welders of this revolution. Television is their chosen instrument."

Nonetheless, TV news did provide civil rights leaders a two-pronged weapon in their war against segregation in the South. As Monroe noted, network TV news allowed advocates of racial equality to overcome the indifferent or hostile coverage in local newspapers or on area television stations, most of which either opposed desegregation themselves or feared their communities' segregationists. Then, too, TV's record of the savage treatment of demonstrators by southern police had far greater impact, everyone agreed, than written accounts. "The difference between barbarity now and in other times," Russell Baker wrote, "is that now everybody sees it on television."

Yet elements of the news media other than TV must also be credited with presenting the civil rights protests of the 1960s to the nation. In his careful analysis of congressional reactions to the violence inflicted upon voting rights activists in Alabama in 1965, David J. Garrow stressed the importance of newspaper coverage, especially stories in the *New York Times* and the *Washington Post*. Constituents often mentioned a TV account; members of Congress, however, were likely to cite a newspaper story. Photographs in newspapers and magazines, especially *Life*, of attacks on marchers left deep impressions. Indeed, Garrow believes that one photograph of police dogs attacking a demonstrator, which ran in many dailies May 4, 1963, had the greatest single influence on behalf of the movement. "Now I've seen everything," a Maryland woman wrote the *Washington Post*. A twelve-year-old girl said, "It is a disgrace that here in the United States where we speak of liberty and justice for all that human beings should be attacked by dogs without committing a crime."

Militant black leaders later in the decade tried to use the networks as pulpits. Despite the news divisions' preference for the moderate leadership of Dr. Martin Luther King, Jr., few TV reporters could resist

King's flamboyant younger challengers, Stokely Carmichael and H. Rap Brown. In Cambridge, Maryland, in the hot summer of 1967, Brown declared, "If America don't come around, we going to burn it down, brother." And the networks did cut away from their evenings of avoidance to show northern cities set afire by angry ghetto dwellers.

Television entertainment programs actively avoided the other divisive issue of the late sixties, the Vietnam War. As America stationed some five hundred thousand troops in Vietnam by 1968, TV series eschewed any reference to the conflict. Espionage programs like "Mission: Impossible" almost never dealt with the war; one episode of the futuristic science fiction series "Star Trek" (NBC, 1966–69) allegorically justified U.S. intervention. But such efforts proved unusual. "In television drama in the 1960s," Geoffrey Cowan wrote, "the war in Vietnam didn't exist. It was too controversial for entertainment television." Controversy carried too high a price tag for the networks. Fred Friendly resigned as president of CBS News in February 1966 after his network refused to continue airing Senate hearings on Vietnam because too much money was being lost by preempting "I Love Lucy" reruns and soap operas. Senator Albert Gore denounced "the whole idea of a vast television network using the wave lengths that belong to the whole people to advertise soap, when we should be having critical examinations of the issue of war and peace."

Entertainment programming not only ignored America's intervention but lampooned its critics. Situation comedies and police shows like "Dragnet" ridiculed the counterculture's "hippie," and such stereotyping served to trivialize the antiwar movement. It became possible for much of "middle America" to dismiss war protest as the consequence of recreational drugs and long hair. No one more regularly mocked this type of war critic than Bob Hope. Every January, NBC aired a special based on the comedian's Christmas tours of American bases in Southeast Asia. His monologues included jokes at the expense of the war's more unusually attired critics. And he used his Vietnam specials to defend the war itself. His 1970 program ended with a plea for the government's policies. The Department of Defense, J. Anthony Lukas observed, having transported Hope and his entourage at great expense, "got its money's worth."

Two comedians a generation removed from Hope, Tom and Dick Smothers, tried to break ranks. On their popular variety program on CBS between 1967 and 1969, the Smothers brothers dared to include political satire, heretofore absent from the home screen. Doing so, however, rattled the habitually nervous CBS. Network executives forbade folksinger Joan Baez from dedicating to her husband, jailed for draft resistance, a song she performed on the program. Columbia tried to prevent Pete Seeger from singing an antiwar ballad. As fights between the brothers and network censors became more frequent and the show's ratings declined, CBS canceled the program. The network, *Newsweek* observed, "may have concluded that life with the Smothers brothers just wasn't worth the static."

Audiences for entertainment programming followed the flag or, more accurately, the flag-waver. Even as doubts over the war grew in 1967 and 1968, more than half the population, surveys suggested, either still supported America's involvement in Vietnam or deemed any criticism of it unpatriotic. Bob Hope's Vietnam specials did, after all, accrue far higher ratings than any Smothers brothers show. Hope's 1970 telecast commanded an extremely high, 46.6 percent share of the national audience. Mindful of such numbers, the networks regarded the war protest, like the civil rights movement, as a matter for their news divisions.

Covering the war itself proved an immensely complicated assignment. There were no easily tracked "fronts" as during World War II or Korea but seemingly endless American "search and destroy" missions against the Viet Cong and the North Vietnamese army. The VC and the North Vietnamese, in turn, did their handiwork at night, by which time American TV crews had returned to Saigon. Moreover, in the late 1960s the real "battle" involved the loyalties of the Vietnamese peasantry. "The challenge to American reporters is that of getting down to the villages where the war is going on," a TV correspondent wrote in the *Yale Alumni Magazine* in 1967. Yet network crews, lugging twenty-seven-pound Auricon cameras, were almost as immobile as an army division. In February 1966 an ABC News executive on the scene likened covering the conflict to "trying to cover our South in revolt, on a bicycle with one correspondent; it's like trying to keep on top if each of our states were producing what could be the top news story of the day."

With the fighting so complex, American correspondents depended heavily on Army information officers, who, at five-o'clock briefing sessions, tended to put the best face on the day's developments. TV reporters, like their counterparts for the wire services and newspapers, had little choice but to attend to the military spokesmen. Most had short tours of duty, no more than a year, which was not long enough to master military tactics and weaponry or learn the language or culture and nurture local contacts. Longer stays brought no career rewards. One CBS reporter confessed, "There was no premium on experience or expertise in our business."

Although the networks poured far more resources into war reportage than many big-city dailies like the *Chicago Tribune* or newspaper groups like Knight-Ridder, there were limits to their largesse. They refused to pay high satellite transmission fees and had their footage transported by air. As a result, most film from the war was forty-eight hours late. Nightly news reports on breaking stories most often consisted of an anchor reading wire service copy. Each network did offer special telecasts on the conflict; these programs rarely displaced popular entertainment series, however, but appeared, as did NBC's "Vietnam Weekly Review," on Sunday afternoons or during prime-time slots that a network had been unable to fill successfully. Even then, stations might rebel against a network's taking the war seriously. When ABC's documentary series, "Scope," began to focus on Vietnam in 1966, many affiliates refused to clear the program.

Some station managers' objections to programs on Vietnam had little to do with their tone. Rarely did viewers of "the living-room war" see blood: the TV audience, news producers reckoned, might be eating or about to dine when Chet Huntley or Walter Cronkite introduced a feature from Saigon. Most of the network footage surveyed did not show fighting. Of the 167 reports aired between 1965 and early 1968 and reviewed by political scientist Daniel C. Hallin, 22 percent included combat scenes; 24 percent had shots of the dead or wounded. More amazing was Lawrence W. Lichty's study of 2,300 network stories telecast between August 1965 and August 1970; Lichty found that 76 features, or 3 percent of those aired, actually involved "heavy fighting" with images of the dead or wounded. "It may be," Robert MacNeil wrote, "that television has built up a tolerance for the frightful, a feeling that war really is bearable."

Although network newspeople later claimed otherwise, television reportage of the war between 1965 and 1968 was anything but critical. Morley Safer's 1965 story on CBS showing American Marines using their Zippo lighters to burn a Vietnamese village proved to be one of the few segments that did not cast American intervention in the best light. The vast majority of Vietnam features took the opposite point of view. Anchors read neutral wire service bulletins on the war, George Bailey concluded after reviewing the evening newscasts. Observing a positive analysis of President Johnson's Manila conference on the war in 1966, *New Yorker* TV critic Michael Arlen wondered "if NBC's television news people really understand the degree of complicity with official government policy that they achieve by presenting government statements at face value and then simply not asking the questions that intelligent men are bound to be concerned about." An hour-long CBS News documentary on the U.S. air war in North Vietnam, Arlen complained, consisted of "58 minutes of propaganda" followed by brief interviews with critics of the bombing. The networks initially treated the budding antiwar movement with contempt, becoming only somewhat more respectful when a few congressional leaders began to attack American policies. But the networks took care to "balance" their stories with prowar voices in Congress and the administration.

The Tet offensive, a massive series of attacks in the cities and countryside of South Vietnam launched early in 1968 by the Viet Cong and the North Vietnamese, caused a transformation in the networks' handling of the war. Having been assured by military authorities that the search-and-destroy missions had made such a large-scale uprising impossible, correspondents in Saigon and producers in New York felt betrayed. Most, including CBS anchor Walter Cronkite, accepted the U.S. military command's assertion that Tet constituted a defeat for the Viet Cong; yet many TV reports began to express pessimism about the capacity of the United States to win in Southeast Asia. Army information officers had lost credibility. Fighting in Saigon itself, where the network crews lived, especially unsettled correspondents, as did the high number of civilian casualties. The percentage of footage showing combat increased dramatically. All in all, Daniel Hallin wrote, "Tet was the first sustained period during which it could be said that the war appeared on television as a really brutal affair." In time, TV newspeople would take credit for Johnson's March 1968 decision not to send still more troops but to reduce U.S. bombing of the north and begin negotiations. Forgotten was their earlier acceptance of the troop buildup, their tasteful sanitizing of the fighting itself, their shameless mockery of the few on the fringes who dared to challenge the cold war consensus. After three years, Lady Macbeth had indeed been able to wash the blood off her hands.

Most champions and critics of TV news subsequently overstated television's role in the direction of the Vietnam War. In fact, Americans had never embraced the cause of South Vietnam as they had Cuba in 1898 or Britain in 1941. Moreover, surveys indicated that support for the administration's conduct of the conflict had been falling prior to the Tet offensive. Johnson's rejection of another increase in American troop strength appears to have been shaped by the counsel of those immediately around him, and not by those appearing on his three television sets. These advisers, Melvin Small has argued, may have been affected by suddenly gloomy TV reports; more often, they shared the pessimism of friends and neighbors who had become disenchanted with the war before the TV news crews. Johnson himself, too tired to launch a public-relations counteroffensive, in effect handed the opinion leadership over to his detractors.

The Guardians Return

A more troubling assertion of television's power followed the murders of Martin Luther King, Jr., and Robert F. Kennedy and the wave of race riots in the spring of 1968. Some contended that television bore a responsibility for the senseless destruction of lives and property. Critics specifically cited the revival in the late 1960s of action-adventure programs that relied heavily on gunplay. Watching the president's three televisions shortly after Robert F. Kennedy was shot, Johnson aide Harry McPherson saw "a symbol of the problem we face. On the middle set, a reporter was talking from Good Samaritan Hospital about the dying Senator. On the left set, cowboys were shooting away at each other and dropping like flies. On the right set, a man was trying to kill a lady espionage agent." Violence on TV, McPherson complained, "was being treated as casually as my son Peter treats it when he squashes a bug. On the set in the middle, there was the real thing. Who knows to what degree it is the product of the universal presence of casual violence on television and in the movies?" A presidential commission subsequently investigated the relationship of violence to antisocial behavior, as did a Senate committee and the Surgeon General. Academics recruited to study the question struggled to confirm the lay critics' commonsense correlation, that fisticuffs on a program like "The Wild, Wild West" (CBS, 1965–70) somehow accounted for the burning of Newark or the death of a Kennedy. Such endeavors did remind the networks, however, that even the programming of escapism carried its risks.

So did news programming. Administration supporters resented the networks' Vietnam conversion experience and the prominence given antiwar protesters at the 1968 Democratic National Convention in Chicago. The airing of a violent police-protester melee during the time set aside for the nomination of candidates especially rankled convention managers. The "police riot" had actually occurred several hours earlier; the networks were running tape. Yet pro-administration Democrats regarded the screening of the footage as partial to the antiwar forces being clubbed so forcefully by Chicago's finest. And the networks could take no comfort in a Sindlinger survey showing that 56.8 percent of those polled approved the police's actions, while 21.3 percent regarded them as excessive.

From many more Republican homes came the cry that the network news divisions had become a virtual arm of the Democratic National Committee. In *The Newstwisters* (1971), Edith Efron tried to give such assertions a statistical basis, arguing that the TV networks had favored Democratic presidential nominee Hubert Humphrey over Republican candidate Nixon. Soon after Nixon's election, when the networks sought to balance coverage of his Vietnam policy addresses by interviewing prominent antiwar Democrats, Vice President Spiro T. Agnew accused the three broadcast chains of deliberately seeking to undermine the president.

The vice president struck a chord. Fifty-one percent of those polled in an ABC survey agreed with Agnew, while 33 percent sided with the networks. The overwhelming majority of calls and letters to affiliates supported Agnew as well. An Oklahoma City TV station reported 350 favorable calls, only 2 of them critical. Trying to put matters in perspective, NBC noted that it had received more mail opposing the cancellation of "Star Trek."

Even in the realm of entertainment, TV's main domain, there were signs of dissatisfaction. Although set use had remained steady through the 1960s, in his survey of viewers Robert T. Bower found a restlessness in the family room. Compared with respondents in a 1960 study, Bower's subjects showed a diminished enthusiasm for the home screen. Perhaps the popular passion for technological novelty had finally worn off, Bower speculated. There were other possibilities. One was that television entertainment had avoided reality too faithfully. Too many situation comedies, especially on CBS, had a small-town setting. Most TV program producers interviewed by sociologist Muriel Cantor late in the decade "thought their audiences lived in the smaller towns and the country." But this white-picket-fence America, once the fixation of MGM's Louis B. Mayer, was shrinking. More viewers were ready for humor more shocking, more like that of NBC's comedy revue "Laugh-in" (1968–73), though without the didacticism of the Smothers brothers. The success of several violent feature films suggested that action-adventure series, once people began to forget the horrors of 1968, might contain even more mayhem. TV news, able to forget Agnew's diatribe, might even become more adversarial.

COMPETING FOR 6
THE MARGINAL
Television's Rivals,
1958–1970

By THE EARLY 1960s all but one of television's major rivals had reconciled themselves to being secondary services. In strategies first formulated in the previous decade, magazine publishers, filmmakers, radio station operators, and popular musicians fought over that part of the consumer's time *not* devoted to television. Although most of TV's competitors prospered in the sixties, the decade ended with the future uncertain for most—and perilous for one.

Daily Struggles

Newspaper owners argued in the late 1950s that television was primarily an entertainment medium and no more a threat to them than movies had been a generation earlier. Networks and many stations aired fifteen-minute news summaries in the early evening; local outlets telecast fifteen-minute newscasts later in the night. But these programs were no more comprehensive than radio newscasts in the 1940s had been. Certain local happenings were missing. All in all, publishers expressed optimism about the newest competition. "The next twenty-five years," the editor of the *Philadelphia Bulletin* remarked in February 1959, "will see people returning to—or growing up to—the newspapers in droves. TV clearly is losing its mesmeric hold." Sharing in this consensus, the Hearst chain in 1962 combined its morning and evening Los Angeles dailies into an afternoon-only *Herald-Examiner*. The move spared the Hearst Corporation of having to contend directly with the *Los Angeles Times*. What had not been considered was the potential rivalry of TV news, which in time would cost the corporation dearly.

Newspaper reporters in the early 1960s treated TV news with contempt. Broadcast news smacked of show business; what self-respecting male reporter would, after all, wear makeup on the job? Still in its childhood or adolescence, depending on how one counted duty in World War II, broadcast news lacked newspapers' traditions. The majority of the most prominent TV newsmen, in fact, had originally worked for dailies or, like Walter Cronkite and Howard K. Smith, a wire service. Although newspaper reporters admired David Brinkley of NBC and a few others, most who worked in television drove their "print" colleagues to near madness. At the 1964 Republican National Convention, angry newspaper correspondents, tired of being jostled by the cumbersome equipment of network competitors, slashed the cables that provided their audio transmission.

Few reporters and editors could justify such behavior. Most American dailies in the 1960s failed to report the news with the completeness that they were more than capable of. And newspapers' inadequacies were never more evident than in their handling of the Vietnam War.

Without the limitation of time and the imperative for the visual that so handicapped television, newspapers should have better served Americans in covering the Vietnam War. With the exception of the *New York Times*, the nation's dailies did not. Relatively few had a Saigon bureau. The larger, more profitable papers contented themselves with sending a reporter briefly to Vietnam. Most relied on the major wire services, the Associated Press (AP) and United Press International (UPI). In a survey of eighteen hundred Vietnam stories in six dailies, Clarence R. Wyatt found that papers varied in the amount of wire service copy they ran. In one sense, quantity hardly mattered. AP and UPI dispatches, Wyatt concluded, often lacked coherence or context. Like the TV networks, the wire services merely described individual encounters and posted body counts of the enemy. Relatively few dailies, of course, had ever invested heavily in overseas reportage, and Vietnam was, after all, a "conflict" and not a "war" in the sense of World War I or II. Taking cues from their readers, most newspapers emphasized local occurrences.

Granting its essential provincialism, the typical American daily nevertheless left much to be desired. Few papers reported the poverty of the inner cities, with the result that most readers were unaware that the economic boom of the fifties and sixties had not touched all Americans. Not until President Johnson declared his War on Poverty in 1964 did most papers begin to consider the problem. While many northern big-city dailies covered with distinction the civil rights movement in the South, they remained largely ignorant of the growing black resentment in their own communities that would inspire a wave of urban rioting between 1964 and 1968. Worse, few had any black reporters to help in or coordinate the coverage. The *Los Angeles Times,* which was becoming one of the nation's best dailies in the early sixties, paid very little attention to Los Angeles's largest black neighborhood, Watts. The *Times'*s policy toward Watts "starkly illustrated the neglect so often characteristic of inner-city reporting," Jack Hart wrote. Before Watts erupted in 1965, "every *Times* reporter was white. Total *Times* preriot coverage of the black community came to 120 inches dating back to 1943. All but two of those stories ran less than eight inches and the majority were city hall handouts on Watts municipal projects."

Newspapers by and large defined local news as official pronouncement or unexpected transgression. Like many dailies, Jack Hart observed, the *Los Angeles Times* played up police reports early in the decade. The April 12, 1960, edition included twelve local crime stories in the first section. Reporters on the police or local government beats rarely applied a critical perspective; doing so might end a productive relationship with their sources. As a result, Hart wrote, "a smug feeling of shared authority with government" pervaded the newsroom of the *Times* and, in truth, the vast majority of America's dailies. Most newspapers "still cover their local governments wretchedly," wrote Ben Bagdikian in 1972. The wire service temptation proved too great even for many dailies in news centers. "Over half the papers in state capitals get most of their coverage from sources outside their staff, like wire services, outside papers or press releases," Bagdikian found. "Some quality coverage has been outstanding, but a mass of indifferent local papers remain."

Such indifference in reporting came despite a landmark libel case that seemingly unleashed the watchdog. In *New York Times v. Sullivan* (1964), the Supreme Court greatly restricted the right to bring libel action against newspapers and other news organizations. An aggrieved party had to prove "malicious intent" on the part of the journalist. That is, attorneys had to demonstrate conclusively that a reporter knowingly included false and negative information in a story. Initially at least, the *Sullivan* doctrine did not encourage a more contentious attitude on the part of reporters. They by and large remained tradition-bound, respectful of those in power, and repelled by the sensational practices of some British tabloids that, by giving personal character more play, might invite libel cases. Those periodicals that carried critical investigative pieces, notably the *Saturday Evening Post* and *Life,* found themselves subject to libel suits. Indeed, *Sullivan* notwithstanding, the number of libel actions actually increased after 1964, despite the tendency of reporters on a regular assignment or beat to treat officials and their aides with a certain deference. Behaving otherwise jeopardized their access to newsmakers and to their calculated leaks. (Not surprisingly, the few journalists to challenge those in power, notably I. F. Stone, avoided official contacts and relied instead on reviewing often obscure public documents.) The overwhelming majority of those reporters surveyed in the late sixties and seventies failed to list *Sullivan* and subsequent libel precedents, not all of them supportive of the fourth estate, as a factor in their story selection and tone.

Economic circumstances did not explain this cautious reportage. Most newspapers, especially in medium-sized towns, continued to make handsome profits in the sixties. And fewer had competitors for advertisers and readers. An analysis by James N. Rosse found that the number of cities served by more than one newspaper fell from seventy in 1958 to thirty-seven in 1973, and the percentage of papers sold by firms in multipaper cities dropped from 51.7 percent to 32.2 percent.

Editorial sloth was, in fact, one consequence of more "one-newspaper towns." The loss of rivals caused most dailies to invest less in investigative stories, which occasionally had been critical of officials. With a competitor in the same community, such pieces might be the basis for winning or retaining reader loyalty. Lacking a rival, newspapers saved money by running wire service copy or simply more advertising. On the other hand, most publishers, realizing their readers no longer had a choice in local reportage, did try to eliminate bias in their news accounts and make their editorial page less opinionated. "When one speaks or thinks of 'the power of the press' in the United States," Robert J. Manning wrote in 1964, "he is almost certainly not referring to a power, or even a consistently demonstrated desire, of its editorial writers to inflame the gizzards or tousle the minds of their readers."

A newspaper's prejudices could still be located on the opinion page. Syndicated political cartoonists like Herblock, Manning noted, pulled no punches. A Republican publisher loath to antagonize his many working-class readers might order his editorial writer to speak of nothing more controversial than the advent of spring and the need for mime garbage collectors, while to the right of such blather his daily regularly ran only conservative nationally syndicated analysts such as William F. Buckley, Jr., and James J. Kilpatrick. In a study of columnists carried in American dailies in 1959, Bagdikian concluded that just over 20 percent of 599 papers sought to balance liberal and conservative columnists; more than half gave most or exclusive space to conservative commentators.

The monopoly newspapers' editorial sleight of hand worked, making them profitable and desirable commodities. Studying changes in newspaper ownership, Gerald L. Grotta concluded that those dailies that had gained a monopoly in their communities between 1950 and 1968 were likely to charge more to subscribers and advertisers without significantly increasing their staffs and editorial content. "No economist will be surprised," Bruce M. Owen observed, "to find that monopolists charge monopoly prices."

Newspapers without competitors became coveted properties, and at a time when, the French publisher Jean-Louis Servan-Schreiber noted, social theorist Marshall McLuhan was predicting the end of the printed word. In perhaps the single most stunning refutation of McLuhan's thesis, fellow Canadian Roy Thomson purchased twelve American dailies on August 25, 1967. According to Christopher H. Sterling and Timothy Haight, the percentage of dailies owned by newspaper groups rose from 31.8 percent in 1960 to 50.3 percent ten years later. The chains' length increased even more in terms of circulation, with their share of the total daily circulation increasing from 46.1 percent in 1960 to 63.0 percent in 1970.

Despite the nostalgia of many newspaper critics for hometown ownership, the growth of chains in the 1960s was not in and of itself detrimental to American journalism. Some papers improved after being purchased by out-of-town owners, notably John S. Knight and the New York Times Company, which were not only committed to enhancing their purchases but, as well-heeled outsiders, more than willing to see their papers challenge the excesses of local elites with which a hometown owner might have identified. Other chain dailies, however, suffered from inattention. S. I. Newhouse had garnered much praise for promising sellers local autonomy. Unlike earlier newspaper tycoons, Newhouse would not dictate opinions; yet he carried this pledge to extremes. He refused to check the segregationist stance of his *Birmingham* (Ala.) *News*. Nor did he care, especially after the mid 1950s, about the quality of his properties. Having begun to borrow heavily to purchase more papers, he was determined to get his money back. As his biographer Richard H. Meeker notes, Newhouse himself only read the *New York Times*.

Nor did all chains prosper in the 1960s. The best performers, groups like Gannett and Ridder, quietly emphasized the purchase of dailies in smaller towns without competition. The more visible chains, like Scripps-Howard and the Hearst Corporation, which earlier in the century had founded or acquired dailies in the largest, most competitive markets, had become the captives of an outdated corporate strategy. Publishing in America's great cities for most newspaper owners had become a losing proposition, Russian roulette with five bullets in the chamber.

Between 1958 and 1965 the number of dailies in Detroit, Houston, Pittsburgh, and Indianapolis decreased from three to two and in Los Angeles and San Francisco, from four to two. New Yorkers, as was their custom, suffered most; they had seven dailies in 1960 and three seven years later. Among the casualties was one of the nation's most admired newspapers, the *Herald Tribune*. The most notorious victim was the Hearst chain, which between 1956 and 1967 sold or closed outlets in Chicago, Pittsburgh, Detroit, Milwaukee, and New York. Hearst's "empire" had become a principality.

There was more bad news: According to Bruce Owen, while total circulation of all newspapers rose in the decade, circulation per household, as in the fifties, dropped 11 percent. The expansion of early-evening local TV newcasts from fifteen to thirty minutes or more in most markets partly explained the relative decline in demand, especially for evening papers. Yet as late as 1967 academic monitors of the fourth estate such as William Rivers of Stanford University insisted that longer newscasts notwithstanding, a new evening newspaper could prosper in New York City. In an article reviewing all of the factors explaining the May 1967 death of the *New York World Journal Tribune*, George Merlis did not mention competition from television news.

Merlis and others instead lamented the rising cost of doing business. Higher operating expenses—labor, paper, delivery—placed publishers in a dilemma. Most owners dreaded raising the price of the paper for fear of losing even more readers. A Tulsa, Oklahoma, publisher claimed in 1967 that the expenditures for news-gathering and wire services, as well as the wages of craft union employees, had increased fourfold since 1942. Newsprint, ink, and delivery costs had trebled. Subscription prices, however, "are not even twice what they were twenty-six years ago."

Publishers looked to advertisers to pick up more of the tab. Advertising charges rose such that ads constituted 75 percent of the typical daily's revenues. Papers became bigger, though Bagdikian concluded that most of the new pages went to advertisements, not news. For their part, advertisers went along with the new approach. Local retailers had little recourse. Although some advertisers did shift parts of their budgets to individual TV and radio stations, time- and price-specific information, indicating bargains on ground chuck and Washington State apples, for example, could not be adequately conveyed in a sixty-second broadcast commercial but required a full-page news-paper ad. By 1970, observed Servan-Schreiber, such local advertising, along with classified notices, constituted 82 percent of all newspaper advertising revenues compared with 18 percent from national adver-tisers.

Advertisers were unsentimental in their selection of newspaper space. In two- or three-newspaper towns, advertisers usually went with the circulation winner. Thus a daily with a 60–40 percent circulation ad-vantage might accrue 75–80 percent of all advertising. The second- or third-place newspaper had no choice, given its new reliance on adver-tising revenues, but to consider closing down. Most failing papers sold to competitors, as in Houston or Pittsburgh, ended operations. And the predictions of some newspaper critics to the contrary, no new dailies came in their wake. New newspapers came to the suburbs, not the city. No new *Herald Tribune* arose from the ashes of the old one. Scripps-Howard could not locate a purchaser for its moribund *Indianapolis Times*. "We beat the bushes literally trying to find somebody who would buy the paper," complained a Scripps-Howard executive in 1967. As to the *New York World Journal Tribune*, the result of a merger of the New York operations of Scripps, Hearst, and the *Herald Tribune*'s owner, "nobody would take it as a gift."

One solution in competitive newspaper markets was the Joint Op-erating Agreement (JOA). First developed in the late 1940s, JOAs al-lowed rival papers to consolidate their printing and business operations while maintaining separate news staffs. One JOA daily published a morning edition, the other an afternoon edition. Diversity of opinion would be welcome. One might endorse Johnson for reelection in 1964, the other his Republican opponent, Barry M. Goldwater. In theory, only advertisers suffered. The consolidation of business operations meant that advertisers had no choice but to buy space in both papers. Nor did consumers benefit from the end of competition for newsstand and subscription sales that came with operating agreements: in JOA communities, publishers, bereft of rivals, increased their papers' price.

Many publishers, faced with rising operating expenses, declared war on their unionized employees. For years, newspapers had abhorred work stoppages. A walkout by those who set the type in the composing room or drove the trucks to carriers was, to publishers, akin to a power outage at a hospital operating room, something to be avoided at any price. Publishers, the *Detroit News* commented in 1962, had "accepted any alternative as better than an interruption of regular publication." As a result, newspaper owners had routinely accepted demands for wage hikes and job guarantees that, with the introduction of new machinery, caused excess or rigid staffing, or "feather-bedding." Such arrangements had bought labor peace. Until 1962 the New York local of the International Typographical Union (ITU) had only struck twice, in 1883 and 1919. But cost-cutting pressures filtered down to the press shop and truck bays. Papers with unionized employees, which sought to increase their profit margin, no longer regarded a strike as the worst-case scenario. Dailies like the *Herald Tribune* considered new automated typesetting equipment to be the only hope for continued operation. In New York and many other cities, newspapers had been slow to take up new printing processes. "The composing rooms, where the printers did their work, had remained fundamentally unchanged since the invention of the Linotype nearly a century ago," labor reporter A. H. Raskin wrote in 1979. Yet the inflexibility of the ITU in New York toward automation all but assured the failure of that city's struggling dailies. The *Herald Tribune*, the *Journal-American*, and the *World, Telegram and Sun* had deferred investing in new equipment and then expected the ITU and other unionized employees to make sacrifices that they themselves had shirked earlier. Moreover, unions correctly regarded such new technologies as automated typesetting equipment as threats to their jobs. They were also in no mood to be reasonable about wage demands that, in New York at least, merely reflected gains by white-collar newspaper employees in the 1950s. There were strikes that lasted months in New York, Detroit, and Cleveland. Between 1956 and 1968, work stoppages cost Motor City readers the equivalent of two years of a daily paper's run, and many Detroiters, in need of a newspaper, became accustomed to a suburban paper or the *Toledo Blade*, published sixty miles away.

Changes in newspaper publishing in the 1960s involved more than confrontational labor relations and the introduction of new technologies. A few industry leaders had been urging their colleagues to alter newspapers' layout and prose; otherwise, younger readers could not be expected to continue their parents' habit, Barry Bingham of the *Louisville Courier-Journal* had warned in 1959. "Journalists [must] make their product more appealing, more magnetic, more enjoyable to younger readers. If we fail, we in America at least will be confronted in a few years by a generation that absorbs all its information through sounds and pictures." The American newspaper, a *Portland Oregonian* editor observed a year later, "continued to cover the city hall, the police station and the baseball park as though its audience were the same, with the same needs and the same tastes, as its audience in the days when William McKinley used to saunter into the press room and exchange a few harmless jokes with his personal friends among the first members of the White House press corps."

Aware of such criticisms, several editors, in what constituted perhaps the greatest innovation in the presentation of news in the 1960s, began to give new emphasis to synthesizing information for readers. The *New York Herald Tribune* and the *Los Angeles Times* led in digesting more news. In their greater mediation of information, they resembled the *Wall Street Journal* and the newsmagazines; for a brief time in the early sixties, former newsmagazine editors ran both the *Trib* and the *Times*. Under their direction, more of the news came in summary form, often, as in the *Journal*, on page 1, with digests of the biggest stories atop one another in one long column. Formats like the *Trib*'s "In the news this morning" gave readers the sensation of knowing what they *had* to know. They also allowed dailies to invest more heavily in investigative stories generated by the newspaper's own staff and not a public-information officer or public-relations agent. Papers could escape the tyranny of news as nothing more than a string of events and analyze information in a more sustained fashion than any TV newscaster could achieve. Yet this new formula, widely and sometimes badly imitated in the 1970s, had unintended effects: by rejecting comprehensiveness, the digested format allowed the editors and writers more power to decide what to summarize and what to investigate. As the *Los Angeles Times* discovered with the Watts riot, ignoring certain stories carried risks.

The *Trib*, anxious to distinguish itself from the *New York Times*, encouraged a novel form of reporting borrowed from *Esquire* magazine. In the early sixties, the *Trib*'s Sunday magazine began to carry a colorfully written and irreverent "new journalism." Giving lip service to canons of objectivity, reporters often allowed their own presence at an event or attitude toward an issue to intrude upon a story. They could be cruel toward subjects and careless about the facts. More tradition-bound journalists expressed outrage. They were, Tom Wolfe wrote, "better than railroad men at resisting anything labeled new." But the new journalism impressed many younger reporters, and its practitioners continued to find outlets long after the *Trib*'s death. New journalists such as Wolfe, Joan Didion, and Hunter Thompson wrote for *New York Magazine*, the spin-off of the old *Herald Tribune* Sunday supplement, as well as *Esquire* and *Rolling Stone*.

There were other new conventions. Some dailies followed *Newsday* in breaking with the pattern of placing virtually every story and headline in eight columns. Many papers self-consciously became consumer-oriented in ways not seen since the crusading "new journalism" of the turn of the century. Readers who dialed special telephone numbers, listed on page one, could ask "action line" reporters for help with a defective product or delivery of governmental service. Immensely popular, action lines accompanied the consumer revolt of Ralph Nader, all the while self-servingly building circulations. In a heretofore large and impersonal institution like the *Detroit Free Press*, readers could find a "friend" and advocate. Telephone crews at first felt otherwise: demand for the *Free Press's* action line proved so enormous in January 1966 that Michigan Bell briefly had to shut down the line.

A few newspapers actually improved or maintained a high standard of news reportage. While long-respected dailies like the *Atlanta Constitution* and the *Portland Oregonian* waned, others, led by the *Los Angeles Times* and the *Washington Post*, greatly upgraded their news-gathering operations. The death of the *Herald Tribune* did not, as A. J. Liebling had cynically forecast, cause the *Times* to abandon its long-held commitment to being the newspaper of record. No other American daily or television network had so many overseas correspondents. No other paper dared challenge the nightly consensus on the war by sending a reporter to North Vietnam, as the *Times* did late in 1966.

Yet in the late 1960s it was by no means certain that even the *Times* could forever remain so exceptional in its devotion to news. The *Times* and other papers had to continue to modernize their make-up and printing facilities and, in the process, to win the cooperation of intransigent unions. At the same time, advertisers and readers had to remain faithful. For seductively in the background rested one or more television sets in virtually every home and apartment. The expansion of early- and late-evening newscasts on most TV stations in the sixties, as well as the networks' news programs, could not be ignored forever. TV might after all be a competitor for the consumer's loyalty, or more of one than radio news had been in the thirties and forties. The publisher of a daily in a one-newspaper town might be in battle with three local TV news shows aired in the early evening, a time that residents had devoted all but exclusively to the reading of the paper.

Periodical Problems

As TV competed successfully for some advertisers and readers in the late 1950s, several magazine publishers launched a short-lived campaign against watching television. In March 1959 popular periodicals ran two-page notices admonishing Americans to "trade a few hours of viewing for *extra* hours of reading." The effort failed: forced to chose between watching TV or reading a periodical, the typical American selected the home screen. Not surprisingly, *TV Guide*, a weekly schedule of television programs, was the most popular magazine of the sixties. Those who subscribed to periodicals did not cancel their subscriptions so much as they spent less time with them or began to read those that appealed to the smaller, specialized audiences that TV ignored. According to former *Life* editor Chris Welles, 160 magazines failed between 1962 and 1972, while 753 others started, "nearly all with a sharp focus."

Although many magazines prospered in the sixties, those that provided general-interest entertainment—*Look, Life,* and the *Saturday Evening Post*--struggled to survive. Many consumers who before the advent of TV had loyally subscribed to one or more of the Big Three had continued to do so out of habit in the 1950s. By the sixties, however, such readers were having second thoughts; TV had marginalized many publications, and once-loyal readers began to let their subscriptions lapse. This forced publishers to fight for new readers, many of whom would only take *Look, Life,* or the *Post* at bargain discounts, which proved increasingly burdensome to publishers. According to Welles, by 1971 a *Life* subscriber paid twelve cents for an issue that cost forty-one cents to publish. The Post Office Department added to the expense of subscriptions by boosting the second-class delivery rate beginning in 1962. As before, the Big Three executives looked to Madison Avenue for relief, but advertisers had grown skeptical. The expense for them of reaching a thousand magazine subscribers, *Business Week* reported in March 1962, was two to three times greater than the cost of reaching a thousand TV viewers. Circulation gains resulting from subscription deals did not impress all space buyers, who looked warily on new readers who had been virtually given their subscriptions. Indeed, the strategy may have been counterproductive. Advertisers preferred magazines whose readers, by paying more for their subscriptions, conveyed a greater probability of actually reading each issue—and its ads—more closely. By the late sixties the circulation war had all but ended. "The numbers game is over," *Look* publisher Gardner Cowles admitted in April 1970. "The multi-million circulation magazine just didn't have the strong appeal for advertisers it used to."

The general-interest magazines tried to make their content more appealing in the age of television. The *Post* abandoned its former stodgy look, which for so long had appealed to small-town America. In 1960 a nostalgic Dwight Eisenhower had sold the rights to his forthcoming memoirs to the *Post,* upsetting his old political booster, *Life* founder Henry Luce. The new *Post* all but wrote off not only the aged president's boyhood friends in Abilene, Kansas, but also its readership in favor of the younger, more well-to-do suburbanites living around

Kansas City and other major metropolitan areas. The *Post* ceased carrying middle-brow short stories. In their place came new and intense investigative pieces that brought costly lawsuits on the *Post*'s owners, Curtis Publishing. In other ways the strategy backfired. By altering its format so quickly, the new *Post* dismayed many long-loyal subscribers, thus losing, Stephen Holder observed in 1969, "its value as a ritual experience" for such readers. (A rival for the "family readership" market, *Reader's Digest*, remained unchanged in the sixties, Holder added, and saw its relative position improve.) The potential new subscriber that the *Post* coveted proved unable to disassociate the magazine from its provincial past and refused to take the periodical. And the *Post*'s thoughtful editorial page, more skeptical than most in the mid 1960s of America's intervention in Vietnam, reached fewer and fewer readers every year.

Life remained seemingly unassailable through most of the decade. The claims of TV news notwithstanding, *Life* gave the greater visual record of the world. While most Americans' TV sets were capable of receiving signals only in black and white (not until 1972 did most homes have color), *Life* provided color representations of culture and news. The magazine paid $150,000 for the rights to the color footage filmed by a bystander to the assassination of John Kennedy. (Their pretensions to realism notwithstanding, *Life*'s editors could not bring themselves to reproduce the frame that showed the president's head explode. The end product had to be reasonably tasteful.) Hugely popular, the special number drove some to thievery as many subscribers reported that they never received their issue. Thousands with better neighbors saved their *Life* account of Kennedy's death. Television viewers could not preserve the initially clumsy coverage of the networks. *Life* similarly made the horrors of Vietnam more plain than did any TV newscast or special report. As in World War II, *Life* showed blood and pain, not a correspondent in fresh khakis usually saluting the courage of men under fire. Finally, the networks, unwilling to pay the high cost of live satellite transmission in the 1960s (a miserliness they later denied), lost their potential advantage in delivering a big overseas story like Churchill's 1965 funeral, most of which was shown on tape and not live. By contrast, *Life*, which spared no expense to secure photos of the Churchill services, presented the permanent record, in color. Such initiative appeared to make *Life* a necessity for millions. In the musical *Company* (1970), a jaded female observer of upper-middle-class housewives sings of "the girls who play wife, keeping house but clutching a copy of *Life* just to keep in touch." Reporting *Life*'s record advertising and circulation figures in 1967, British journalist Magnus Linklater described "an orgy of self-congratulation" at the magazine's headquarters.

But *Life* too was in trouble. Advertisers who preferred color display slowly began to shift more of their accounts to television. Although most homes in the late sixties had black and white sets, well-to-do consumers, coveted by the promoters of certain goods, were likely to have color receivers. And TV's evening audiences continued to be larger than *Life*'s or any other magazine's readership. In 1968 one sales representative for a group of TV stations offered audiences "bigger than *Life*." At the same time, according to Linklater, postal rates climbed 170 percent, a burden for *Life* in that subscriptions constituted 90 percent of its total circulation. A drastic redesign of the magazine, intended to cut operating costs and appeal to a younger, more intelligent yet more television-dependent reader, only made *Life* less lively. It had become thinner; there were fewer pictures, more commentary. Like the *Post*, the periodical began to lose its identity to subscribers and its appeal to advertisers. In their worst moments, *Life* editors imagined the only copy of their weekly in the American home being one with a martyred president on the cover.

In contrast to the general-interest periodicals, the newsmagazines flourished in the sixties. TV, if anything, made a weekly synthesis of the news—and there was so much information to absorb in the decade—all the more vital to the cosmopolitan consumer of information. The total circulation of the three newsweeklies—*Time, Newsweek,* and *U.S. News & World Report*—rose from 5.38 million in 1961 to 8.74 million in 1970. Although *Time* continued to lead in circulation (4.26 million in 1970) and in circulation growth (62.0 percent between 1961 and 1970), *Newsweek* not only prospered but adopted a new editorial tone in the decade. Acquired by the *Washington Post* in 1961, *Newsweek* ceased to be a pale imitation of Luce's *Time*. It also gained from the widespread perception that Luce's periodical had become too prejudiced in its treatment of Democratic leaders, including President Kennedy. "We realized that *Time* was very frozen in its ways and was a sitting duck," *Newsweek* editor Osborn Elliott recalled. "*Time* didn't have our access [to] and empathy with the Kennedy administration." And compared with *Time, Newsweek* questioned America's Vietnam adventure. "Did the U.S. really belong in Vietnam in the first place?" *Newsweek* asked in April 1966. "Could the war still be salvaged? Or had the moment arrived to begin thinking seriously of withdrawal?" By the late sixties, with the war a regret, Luce dead, and *Newsweek*'s successes unnerving his successors, *Time* moved back toward the national center.

The Crowded Dial

Although entrepreneurship in radio, as in magazine publishing, carried risks in the 1960s, they were not as great as in the previous decade. Television's growth no longer inhibited sales of radio spots to advertisers; if anything, the increased cost of TV time caused some companies with more modest advertising budgets to shift more of their promotional expenditures to radio. According to *Broadcasting* magazine, except for 1967, radio times sales annually increased 7.0–13.7 percent between 1962 and 1969.

Like television, radio in the late fifties suffered momentarily from scandal. In 1959 and 1960, congressional investigators revealed that various record companies had been paying station managers and some 335 disc jockeys to play songs on their labels. On ABC-TV's "American Bandstand," Dick Clark had been giving special consideration to records in which his company held an interest. Incredibly, Clark himself survived and the industry pledged no more "payola."

Although radio remained a secondary mass cultural activity for most, the opportunities for listening increased over the decade. The transistor revolution continued unabated. The tiny receivers even inspired a hit 1961 single, "Transistor." By the late sixties, every member of a family of fairly modest means could have a personal radio. Then, too, the larger numbers of Americans who commuted to work by automobile were more likely to have car radios; indeed, for most a radio had come to be regarded as "standard" rather than optional equipment. The percentage of cars with a radio increased sharply from 68.1 percent in 1960 to 92.5 percent in 1970. Advertisers had a captive market. In *Broadcasting* magazine one cartoon character told another, "Don't ever forget our thousands of car radio listeners who never leave the room when the commercial comes on!"

Radio tempted many an entrepreneur. With most VHF licenses awarded by the early sixties, many would-be broadcasters, especially in communities too small to support a television outlet, settled for a radio station. The FCC encouraged such local expression, especially on the FM band. Between 1960 and 1970 the number of commercial AM outlets increased from 3,456 to 4,292, while the number of commercial FM stations rose from 688 to 2,184.

The FCC promoted FM both directly and indirectly. Government regulations made new AM allocations less desirable. While increasing

the number of AM outlets, the commission restricted the power or operating hours of many of the new frequencies allocated to smaller communities. These stations thus lacked the larger potential listening area
that had made AM more attractive to potential radio investors. Further-
more, after 1962, more exacting technical standards for AM assignments
made an FM license easier to obtain. Other FCC rules in the 1960s discouraged FM "repeater" stations, that is, stations that carried AM
broadcasts simultaneously in the same community. The commission
also promoted FM stereo, which in time had a special appeal to fans of
rock music.

More consumers began to listen to FM stations in the 1960s. According to Christopher H. Sterling, by 1969 about half of all radios purchased could receive FM stations, though relatively few car radios were
AM-FM. By then, about half of all households had AM-FM or FM-only
radios, compared with only 10 percent in 1960. The larger cities were
the most hospitable to FM. Between 1960 and 1969 the percentage of
homes with radios able to receive FM stations in Milwaukee increased
from 30 percent to 78 percent; in Philadelphia, FM's penetration rose
from 38 percent to 84 percent; and in Miami, from 32 percent to 65
percent.

As in the fifties, the augmented number of stations encouraged more
operators in all but the smallest markets to appeal to specialized tastes.
Stations adopted a "format" in which the stations played only one type
of music. In New York City, WINS dropped rock 'n' roll, the sound of
too many rivals, in favor of "pretty music," older hits and vocalists, and
celebrated the shift by playing sixty-six hours of Sinatra. The station
then returned to rock, only to switch again early in 1965 to an all-news
format, the nation's first. "The replacement of disk jockeys by editorial
writers," a hopeful Jack Gould wrote in June, "could be the sociological
surprise of 1965."

Country-and-western music stations prospered in cities as well as
small towns. Many assumed that the migration of white southerners accounted for the popularity of such outlets. But the size of the audiences
for C&W stations and country-music concerts, Richard Peterson and
Paul DiMaggio argued in 1975, was far greater than the number of
southern émigrés in cities like Philadelphia. Nor, they added, would it
explain such overseas C&W phenomena as the Tokyo Grand Ole
Opry: few southern whites lived in Japan's greatest city. Rather, white
working-class and lower-middle-class Americans, many more than a
generation removed from the farm, took up southern artists, almost all
of whom, James T. Carey contended in 1969, upheld older attitudes toward love and honor.

The Fab Four

No audience subgroup held more potential for the radio station operator than the teenagers of the 1960s. The percentage of Americans in their adolescence had increased since the mid fifties, when many DJs and music companies had begun to attend to their preferences for rock 'n' roll. The sixties saw "baby-boomers," those Americans who were born in the decade after V-J Day, reach adolescence. They constituted a lucrative, specialized market. It was a market Pepsi-Cola sought when, in the early sixties, the beverage maker radically redesigned its advertising to appeal to the youthful ("Now it's Pepsi, for those who think young"). Ford Motor Company prospered with the sporty Mustang, the perfect first automobile for the adolescent children of the well-to-do. Although the typical teenager in the sixties did not have the money for a new car, most adolescents did have the cash for transistors and albums. The young consumers also had the time for radio listening. Like those who went to drive-ins to see *Rebel Without a Cause* in 1955, the typical teenager of the sixties preferred the company of peers and listening to a rock DJ on a local station to sitting with parents and younger siblings before the TV set.

Those in radio who coveted the teenage rock 'n' roll fan tried to limit their risks. In the mid fifties, Robert "Todd" Storz had developed a "Top 40" format for his chain of rock 'n' roll stations. Adopting the practice of jukebox operators, Storz ordered his DJs only to play the forty best-selling songs, with the Top 40 list based on the weekly sales of 45-rpm records. (Most jukeboxes at the time only carried forty tunes.) Other broadcasters soon followed Storz, turning their DJs into marionettes. "The era of free-willed deejays was rapidly drawing to a close," R. Serge Denisoff wrote. Although the Top 40 format minimized the possibility of payola, it also denied airtime to new or experimental groups, as well as black rhythm-and-blues artists. In markets served by two or more stations competing for the teenage audience, it was thought, playing such performers caused listeners to switch stations. Adults, depending on such factors as race and class, preferred different sounds. Many liked older, "mainstream" vocalists like Sinatra, Tony Bennett, Patti Page, and Nat King Cole, who sang material from movies and Broadway musicals. Most rural and many working-class and lower-middle-class whites listened to country music, though virtually no African Americans took up C&W, which seemed to be the sound of southern white sheriffs and vigilantes. The young in larger cities tended to disdain country music. Charlie Gillett blamed the producers of C&W albums, who had deliberately written off teenage listeners by all but forsaking the "rockabilly" rock 'n' roll sound of the fifties.

American teenagers in the early sixties were left with a potpourri of musical performers and performing styles. Some better-educated teens and young adults, while spurning C&W, began to enjoy Peter, Paul, and Mary and Bob Dylan, who gently fused country ballads with the protest sound of Pete Seeger and Arlo Guthrie. Many more young consumers remained loyal to Elvis Presley. At the King's Memphis palace, sycophants, mediocre songwriters, and a child bride kept Presley happy. After 1962, however, Presley had to compete with groups like the Beach Boys, who offered a southern California sound perfect for a decade of surf movies and far less threatening to parents than the early Elvis or Little Richard.

While white groups as before "covered" black songs, African-American performers had a larger, multiracial following in the new decade. No one initially had more crossover appeal than Chubby Checker. His single "The Twist" topped the charts in 1960 and brought the inevitable invitation from Ed Sullivan's TV producers a year later. Doing the twist while he sang, Checker caused millions of white adolescents and young adults to mimic a black rock 'n' roll dance style. At the Kennedy White House, men who waged cold war during the day danced the twist at night.

More than Checker's momentary success broadened the demand for African-American performers. Critics attributed the larger white audience partly to the "Motown" sound of Detroit album producer Berry Gordy. Forming Motown Records in 1960, Gordy, unlike earlier producers, invested the same care in preparing albums for such African-American groups as the Temptations that white performers enjoyed. "The Motown policy," Charlie Gillett writes, "always depended on fierce 'quality control.' "

Motown's emergence and Checker's celebrity notwithstanding, rock 'n' roll fans had their frustrations in the early sixties. Some radio outlets tried to placate parents and their older children by giving both rock and the older sound equal play. They satisfied aficionados of neither. Worse, the major album producers failed to realize the intensity of the teenage demand for rock—adolescents would be willing to purchase far more records than their parents—and mistakenly limited their production and promotion of rock 'n' roll. The biggest recording companies, their executives well past adolescence and based in New York, had never reconciled themselves to rock music. Its origins were too southern and too oriented toward teenagers, Gillett found, "part of a culture that was generally patronized and even despised." Such condescension took its toll. Total record industry sales, as measured by Richard A. Peterson and David G. Berger, were sluggish in the early sixties. In 1963, Ed Ward wrote, "it looked as if there would never again be a time when the land was rocking in harmony, when teenagers communicated in a secret language and adults shook their heads in bewilderment."

Rock 'n' roll was reborn with the arrival of the Beatles early in 1964. The English foursome's swift and overwhelming popularity made it the dominant force in American popular music for the next six years. As teenagers, John Lennon, Paul McCartney, George Harrison, and Ringo Starr had, like most British teens, listened to American rhythm and blues and rock 'n' roll. Presley's "Heartbreak Hotel," Lennon's Aunt Mimi recalled, transfixed her nephew. "From then on, I never got a minute's peace. It was Elvis Presley, Elvis Presley, Elvis Presley." "I'd sit in Liverpool and dream of America," Lennon remembered. "Who wouldn't? America was Chuck Berry, the Leonardo of rock 'n' roll. America was Little Richard." When Lennon met McCartney, he was playing Little Richard's "Tutti Frutti." After the four played in obscure Hamburg clubs and decided on a name, their agent secured them a record contract. Press manipulation, good timing, and the group's own charm with the press and audiences created a "Beatlemania" in Britain in 1963. In America early the following year, the top five pop hits were Beatles tunes. Publicists carefully orchestrated their arrival at New York's Kennedy airport in February 1964. (The story persists that one agent paid a group of Catholic high-school girls to be on hand and scream as the boys deplaned.) When TV host Ed Sullivan announced that he would anoint them, more applied for tickets to see the program than had sought entry to Elvis's first appearance in 1956. Mothers who had once become hysterical over Sinatra watched in amazement as their daughters treated the "Fab Four" as so many deities.

The Beatles were a record producer's dream. Having played in the worst holes imaginable in England and Germany, they had suffered enough. Coffeehouses held no lure. They wanted to perform in packed stadiums and amphitheaters. They professed no interest in the less popular, if critically more acceptable, rock of Dylan and others. After being urged in 1963 to consider Dylan a model, Lennon replied, "Dylan. Dylan. Give me Chuck Berry. Give me Little Richard. Don't give me fancy crap." The Beatles' nationality also worked to their advantage. An English group was a novelty in 1964. The year before, only one of the ten top-selling albums in America had been British-produced. The Four also possessed a unique look: cereal bowl haircuts and jackets without lapels, similar to those worn by some black groups. Without donning the khaki pants and prep school blazers of many white performers, they avoided the unkempt and disconcerting, to adults, appearance of beatniks. The compromise gave them a modish respectability. David Riesman told *U.S. News & World Report* in February 1964 that the Beatles lacked Presley's once "sinister quality" and " 'antiparent' outlook." A few parents actually shared in their children's enthusiasm. "They were marvelous," the wife of New York's governor told the *Herald Tribune* after seeing the Beatles perform in February 1964. "They have a lot of talent."

The success of the Beatles' first U.S. tour related in part to their spontaneity as performers, something Charlie Gillett, for one, found absent among most white singers. By the mid 1960s, Gillett writes, album producers had again seized artistic control. At white and black recording companies, the performer had become less important than the song, individual instruments less important than the total effect of a rendition. The Beatles' casual, often self-mocking wit and charm made them, and not elaborate production values, all-important. They also restored, albeit briefly, the guitar orientation of early rock. "They were doing things nobody else was doing. Their chords were outrageous, just outrageous, and their harmonies made it all valid," Bob Dylan thought as he listened to their songs on the radio while on a cross-country drive in 1964. "Everybody else thought they were just for the teenyboppers, that they were gonna pass right away. But it was obvious to me that they had staying power. I knew they were pointing the direction where music had to go."

The Beatles' staying power also related to their conscious rejection of adult values. Previous white teen idols like Pat Boone, Ricky Nelson, and Frankie Avalon had been presented, Carl Belz writes, "as young adults rather than teenagers." They did not all dress in tuxedos like Frank Sinatra, Jr., or Johnny Mathis, but they were intended to be "symbols for teenagers to emulate, since they were supposedly more mature than the young members of their fan clubs." The Beatles, in contrast, made no effort to seem grown-up. The Fab Four, Belz observed, "had conquered the adult world without submitting to it." And the notion that a popular musician could avoid maturity, if only in public, stuck. Male rock 'n' roll performers came to embody the Peter Pan syndrome.

Other English groups and a new version of American R&B followed. In 1964, thirty-two British-produced albums ranked in the American weekly Top 10. The Beatles quickly had to compete with fellow Britons. Their greatest rivals, the Rolling Stones, made fewer compromises in their appearance or manner. Their songs, more deeply affected by rhythm and blues, and performance style moved all of rock toward a more explicit sexuality, though Sullivan forced one hit, "Let's Spend the Night Together," to be performed on his program as "Let's Spend Some Time Together." At about the same time, a new black sound emerged. "Soul" performers like James Brown and Wilson Pickett borrowed heavily from R&B while encouraging the improvisation that was missing from Gordy's Motown productions.

The popular music industry and many radio stations had once again been converted to the gospel of youth. Presley's successes in the mid fifties should have been enough warning. Yet what Gillett called "the imported reverence" that record company executives had for the British groups, the tendency to be more impressed by white British performers, made producers take rock 'n' roll seriously. Although some album makers failed to seize full advantage of the demand for rock, never again would the popular music industry as a whole or radio stations discount the power of rock 'n' roll. By 1966 some opportunists tried to manufacture the look and charm of the Fab Four by casting four unknowns as the Monkees, a domestic imitation that enjoyed momentary popularity starring in a TV series. Rock purists were disgusted. The Monkees were a "totally synthetic success," Geoffrey Stokes wrote. "Serious rock fans hated them."

The Beatles' dominance continued unabated through the decade, even as they began to challenge political and cultural conventions. After several years, the Beatles, led by Lennon, started to resemble the Stones and some American folk singers. Several Beatles became social critics. Their changing coiffure and dress both led and reflected a teen rebellion against conformity. By then they could claim larger congregations than Jesus Christ and suffer little for such blasphemy. Such behavior would have been unforgivable in the late fifties. A decade later, the Beatles and the rock sound they had brought with them from England had become too powerful for all but the most religious record producer and station manager to fight.

Like the Beatles, much of rock began to embrace the counterculture of the late sixties. Sexuality became more obvious as rock lyricists rejected the romantic passivity that had been common in the fifties and was still a constant in most C&W tunes in favor of a new aggressiveness. "The affair is actively sought by lovers rather than passively longed for," James T. Carey wrote. In many songs, "love seems to be reduced simply to physical desire." Just under a third, according to Carey, dealt with political or social themes or even subtly advocated recreational drug use. As in the fifties, some older adults objected to the new sound. When his daughter died from an overdose in 1969, Art

Linkletter, a radio and TV talk show host, complained, "Almost every time a top-40 record is played on the radio, it is an ad for acid, marijuana, and trips."

Linkletter and other angry parents were, in fact, giving both the songwriter and the audience too much credit. A 1967–68 survey of Michigan high-school students by John P. Robinson and Paul Hirsch found the great majority of those polled unable to remember or comprehend rock lyrics. Moreover, adolescents, like their parents, did not share one taste. Large numbers of white teenagers disliked racy R&B songs; comfortable middle-class students, not ones from Detroit's working-class and poor neighborhoods, favored protest tunes.

Some station owners seized upon this fragmentation of the rock market in the late sixties. Market surveys suggested that Top 40 radio appealed too exclusively to adolescents. Young adults, much more likely than their teenage siblings to purchase cars, stereos, and other expensive consumer items, had tired of the format. Yet they would hardly abandon rock altogether and join in their parents' preference for older vocalists or, worse for status-conscious urban dwellers, take up country music. Relief came in several cities where FM station owners, frantic to boost their share of the audience, gave new freedoms to their DJs. Led by Murray "the K" Kaufman of WOR-FM in New York and Tom "Big Daddy" Donahue of KMPX-FM in San Francisco, FM DJs deliberately ignored the Top 40 compilations and played a more sophisticated, more demanding sound rich in allusions to weeds and war. Many of these songs and performers came to be associated with the "progressive rock" movement. Such stations aired Dylan, who with "Lay Lady Lay" in 1969 finally made the charts. They also played some of the more challenging cuts from the Beatles' experimental "white album," which included a spoof of Dylan.

Crises in the Colony

Hollywood, too, sought the attention of teenagers and young adults. As in the fifties, the movie colony, or more precisely, smaller and less prestigious companies such as American-International, produced films intended for adolescents. These were almost always B-films. Young actors, sometimes obscure or better known for their singing, played the leads; Chubby Checker appeared in *Don't Knock the Twist* (1962); the Beatles starred in several successful films, such as *A Hard Day's Night* (1964) and *Help!* (1965). Settings for teen pictures varied. A common type in the early sixties was the beach movie, including *Where the Boys Are* (1960) and a series of releases starring crooner Frankie Avalon and

Annette Funicello, who had earlier been on TV's "The Mickey Mouse Club." Smaller studios specialized in the manufacture of the "teen horror" film. Some, directed by Roger Corman, had their critical admirers. Others, like *Teenage Psycho Meets Bloody Mary* (1964) and *Monster a Go-Go* (1965), were intended to be the second bill at the drive-in.

For the larger studios, the home screen continued to be a substantial source of revenue. By the early sixties, every film company produced TV series. With the success of NBC's "Saturday Night at the Movies" in 1961–62, selling the rights to telecast recent feature films became far more profitable. Fees rose steadily. When in 1966 ABC paid the then record $2 million for the rights to air *The Bridge on the River Kwai*, Hollywood regarded the transaction, Charles Champlin wrote, "as only slightly less epochal than the premiere of *The Jazz Singer*," the first sound picture. The average charge for two network telecasts of a film rose from $150,000 in 1961 to $800,000 in 1968. Such fees allowed movies that had enjoyed mixed or poor success at the box office—*Fortune* estimated in November 1966 that half of all feature films lost money during their theatrical release—to break even. In the late sixties, the film colony's bonds to the networks tightened as some studios began producing made-for-TV movies.

While allied to television, filmmakers adhered to the "two-screen" strategy they had developed in the mid fifties. For the networks, the studios offered their recent releases and produced series. But the theatrical film continued to be their major concern—and great passion. Television was a financially rewarding association, but one usually handled by vice presidents. The top executives devoted their hours to moviemaking.

The experience of one major studio, Twentieth Century Fox, fostered a new emphasis on the "blockbuster." Early in the decade, Fox was in serious financial trouble. Cost overruns on *Cleopatra* and bad luck with recent releases produced an after-tax loss of $39.8 million in 1962. Darryl Zanuck, who had left Fox in 1956, returned and together with his son Richard cut costs drastically. The studio sold its back lot to an aluminum company and closed its commissary. These steps, together with the success of *The Longest Day* (1963), a drama about the D-Day landings of 1944, helped to save the company from receivership. And the phenomenal popularity of the film version of the syrupy Rodgers and Hammerstein musical *The Sound of Music* (1965) turned Fox completely around; the company earned $12.5 million after taxes in 1966.

Like most great success stories in show business, the boffo box office of *The Sound of Music* had been unanticipated. Set in Austria in the late 1930s, *The Sound of Music* tells the story of a governess who befriends the Von Trapp children and eventually wins the heart of their widowed father. Although the Broadway version had enjoyed a healthy run, theater people had not considered *The Sound of Music* to be Rodgers and Hammerstein's best work. Nor had the studio plotted a hit. Zanuck had expected *The Bible* (1965) to be the bigger grosser. When *The Sound of Music* opened, the most prominent New York–based critics were unenthusiastic. Pauline Kael's review in *McCall's* was so harsh (she called the film "a sugar-coated lie") that the magazine fired her. Then, to the surprise of Fox executives, people poured into theaters. Whole families— children and grandparents—went to see the movie. Some older patrons had not been to a film in years. Many screened it repeatedly—one Los Angeles woman watched it a hundred times; and an Oregon man sent Fox a transcript of the script he had composed from memory. *The Sound of Music* played for a year in some towns, to the dismay of some with more bittersweet tastes. "49 Weeks of Schmaltz is Enough," a Moorhead, Minnesota, group protested. The film earned over $100 million at home and abroad, and its first run surpassed the total box office for the previous all-time leader, *Gone With the Wind* (1939).

The "Sound of Money"—as *Mad Magazine* dubbed the movie—as well as two 1964 releases, *Mary Poppins* and *My Fair Lady*, caused a rush to film expensive musicals. The Zanucks quickly committed Fox to three musicals—*Dr. Doolittle*, *Star!*, and *Hello, Dolly!*—tying up more than $50 million in the process. The elder Zanuck's premise was simple: one hit would keep the entire operation in the black. Yet he had his uneasy moments. "If we hadn't made such an enormous success with *The Sound of Music*," he admitted, "I'd be petrified. You can never be sure of a hit in that category. You're never sure of a hit any goddamn time, but when you're talking $20 million, it's a bigger gamble."

While millions patiently stood in lines to see *The Sound of Music*, some filmmakers were winning the right to produce very different types of features, ones not designed to appeal to the grandparents or children enchanted by the Von Trapp saga. For more than a decade, a coalition of directors and writers had been demanding the relaxation of production codes. By forbidding the use of "dirty" words and nudity, the codes had inhibited the portrayal of sexual activity; the success of some foreign releases, which were far more explicit in matters of the heart, suggested that American films should be allowed to mature. In 1965 the Production Code Authority awarded its seal of approval to (and, in effect, permitted the distribution of) *The Pawnbroker*, despite two scenes of nudity. The PCA subsequently allowed the release of *Who's Afraid of Virginia Woolf?* (1966), despite obscene language. Both actions were conditional: exhibitors were expected to bar those under eighteen from attending either feature. Two years later, the Motion Picture Producers Association of America (MPAA), under Jack Valenti, who had become president two years earlier, created a ratings system from "G" (all ages admitted) through "X" (no one under sixteen years admitted) for films according to their language, treatment of sexual matters, and, less often, violence. In effect, the MPAA placed the burdens on parents and theater owners. The studios moved cautiously, fighting the MPAA ratings board and sometimes their own directors over a possible X rating. According to Leo Bogart, 32 percent of the films reviewed by the MPAA in 1968–69 had a G rating. But many producers and directors did take risks, to the delight of critics like Pauline Kael. More daring and usually younger moviegoers could watch simulated murders in *Bonnie and Clyde* (1967) and *The Wild Bunch* (1969). After *The Graduate* (1967), *Goodbye, Columbus* (1969), and other sex comedies of the late sixties, the Doris Day-Rock Hudson romances filmed only a few years earlier seemed quaint. One of the few X-rated films by a major studio, *Midnight Cowboy* (1969), won the Academy Award for best picture. The MPAA overcame its historic prudishness in part because of the changing audience for films. Notwithstanding the draw of *The Sound of Music*, fewer Americans actually went to the movies. According to Garth Jowett, weekly moviegoing per household had fallen from 2.22 in 1948 to .96 in 1956 to .77 in 1965. Many of those who did regularly patronize theaters had a different set of expectations than the larger television audience. Younger or better-educated moviegoers wanted a realism about sex and violence absent on TV or in *The Sound of Music*. Relatedly, religious and state officials had been encountering more and more resistance to bans or organized boycotts of films that violated their standards. Those likely to obey a church condemnation of a film rarely went to the movies anymore, except to see the Von Trapps' life story. The final blow to the guardians came in 1968 when the Supreme Court, in *Ginsberg v. New York*, ruled that state boards could not ban a film. The burden fell to exhibitors, who were expected to honor the spirit of the new ratings system and prevent minors from seeing a feature considered to contain material inappropriate for children.

Just as filmmakers began to savor their new freedom, many suddenly found themselves dealing with owners with little or no background in motion pictures—and no memories of Hollywood's decades-long struggles with its own or state and religious censors. An outside takeover trend began with Jack Warner's sale of his studio to a Canadian film exhibition chain, Seven Artists, in 1966. A year later, Gulf & Western, a conglomerate, secured Paramount. TransAmerica, a banking and insurance holding company, took over United Artists in 1968. In 1969,

Kinney National Services, which operated funeral homes and parking lots, purchased Warners–Seven Artists, and a hotel magnate, Kirk Kerkorian, bought MGM.

Why had Hollywood attracted such interest from investors? Until the late 1960s, companies not directly involved in entertainment had scorned the movie colony. To someone without a background in show business, successful filmmaking seemed to be a sort of modern alchemy; it was far easier to forecast demand for washing machines or snow tires than for *The Sound of Music*.

Several factors explained the movie colony's appeal. The transformation of some businesses in the 1960s into conglomerates, that is, corporations that owned companies providing a variety of unrelated goods and services, made acquiring a film company less frivolous. Ego, the *Economist* suggested mischievously, drove some executives, excited at the prospect of accompanying a glamorous actress to a premiere. More important, studio stocks in the mid sixties, like others in the entertainment business, were undervalued; and a sustained boom on Wall Street made most stocks dear. Then, too, as Tino Balio has written, most film companies owned valuable property and recording units. And no matter how uncertain the prospects of a studio's theatrical releases or the value of its physical plant, each company's stock of features made it a bargain at a time when the networks outbid one another for the rights to air features. Indeed, the value of the telecasting rights alone was greater than the price of their common stock. "If Paramount's new management can't make the production end of the business pay," a Wall Street analyst told *Fortune*, Gulf & Western's president "can still come out well via the real estate and the film library."

However, the movie colony's new rulers had seized power too soon. The industry's overall good health in the mid sixties had encouraged the start of new film companies, which, by trying to lure away talent from the older studios, caused production costs to increase sharply. While confronting escalating operating expenses, filmmakers received bad news at the box office. The wave of movie musicals released after *The Sound of Music* fared poorly. Children who had loved the Von Trapp story had entered adolescence by the time many of the subsequent musicals were released; their tastes had matured. Then, too, few of the late-sixties musicals had all of the elements—the book, score, and skillful or lucky casting—that had made *The Sound of Music* a triumph. Most adults would only go to a movie if the word of mouth was good. And few were talking up *Paint Your Wagon* or the musical version of *Good-Bye, Mr. Chips* (both 1969). The studios that had banked on them faced extinction. In 1969 most of the major film companies lost money: MGM reported pretax losses of $72 million, Fox of $65 million, and Warners of $52 million. Observers blamed the blockbuster musical strategy. The studios had put too many of their chips on one number. According to Arthur Krim of United Artists, "Instead of playing red or black on the roulette table," they played one "number in the hopes of hitting the jackpot."

From the East Coast came another blow. Late in 1968 the networks began to curtail their expenditures for TV film rights. Instead, orders for the less expensive (and for the studios, less financially rewarding) made-for-TV films rose. The new realism of some filmmakers had created another dilemma: certain movies, in their language and relatively explicit treatment of sexuality, simply could not be shown on TV without editing. Although bared breasts and four-letter words had become permissible on the big screen, they remained taboo on television. The new realism appealed to a subgroup that regularly attended movie theaters; it offended the larger audience that, after all, had been able before TV to impose a church school morality on the film industry. All too aware of such sensitivities, Michael Dann of CBS stunned movie executives in January 1970 by attacking many recent releases' easier morals. "People do things in these pictures—boys and girls, boys and boys, and girls and girls—that are naughty," Dann said. "The film companies are going to be in for a surprise when they come to the networks with them."

Business reporters traveled to Hollywood in 1969 and 1970 wondering whether what was left of the American film industry would survive the new decade. The costly musicals had flopped, leaving their producers and studio partners awash in red ink and angry creditors banging on the door. With the networks complaining about the relaxed standards of other new movies, the studio vaults full of recent releases no longer brought smiles to the outsiders who had bought the film companies expecting to sell TV rights at ever higher rates. Not since the spread of television itself and sharply declining ticket sales of the early fifties, a Bank of America analyst reported in 1969, had Hollywood faced such a crisis.

The film industry's crises of the late sixties served as a warning to all of television's competitors. Battling for the marginal leisure time of Americans left the rival mass media with the smallest room for error. The profitability or even the survival of most individual movie companies, newspapers, or radio stations could not be taken for granted. Strategies that had worked in the fifties might not stave off the Fates two decades later. The film companies and other mass media could only sustain themselves by accepting their marginality. And some egos would not allow it.

NETWORK TELEVISION   7
TRIUMPHANT, 1970–1981

In the 1970s, network television's hegemony seemed complete. At no time in the history of American TV had the three giant chains so dominated the nation's culture and politics. The networks' paramountcy came despite new competition from individual stations, public broadcasting, and cable systems. On a typical evening in the late seventies some 90 percent of those homes watching television viewed a network program. In 1977, David G. Grote noted, more people watched one episode of the TV situation comedy "Laverne and Shirley" than had seen the year's most popular theatrical film, *Star Wars*. Seeking a new host for its annual awards program, the Academy of Motion Picture Arts and Sciences selected Johnny Carson, the popular host of a network late-night talk show. "He fits the small screen," Vincent Canby of the *New York Times* remarked in April 1979. TV news people hectored public officials; many appeared to have eclipsed them. In 1980 CBS news anchor Walter Cronkite, about to retire, spoke of "inaugurating" his last chief executive; few found his conceit excessive.

The decade began with good tidings from Madison Avenue. For the first time in the medium's history an economic downturn that cut into advertiser patronage of the older mass media failed to reduce TV time sales. Television appeared to be recession-proof. As Martin Mayer observed, more pleasant surprises for network executives followed. Congress had imposed a ban to take effect in January 1971 on all TV cigarette advertising; television had accrued some $150 million in revenues from tobacco companies in 1970. But after three months in "cold turkey," television time sales rose again. First CBS, then NBC and ABC, recovered some losses by offering thirty-second spots at more than half the cost of a sixty-second segment. Then, too, governmental intervention unintentionally strengthened the networks' position. The Federal Communications Commission, ever anxious to increase individual "local expression," had promulgated the Prime Time Access Rule, which limited network programming to three hours nightly beginning in October 1971. In a classic illustration of the law of supply and demand, the access rule made network spots all the more precious. National advertisers, anticipating shortages of airtime, rushed to the networks well before the restriction took effect. At the same time, companies that had not advertised on the home screen, notably the McDonald's fast-food restaurant chain, as well as ones like Coca-Cola and Avon Products, which had heretofore dealt exclusively with individual stations, began to purchase network television time.

With TV a seller's market all through the decade, an advertiser could no longer exercise any significant control over a program. Virtually all shared the sponsorship of each series. "No advertiser today is really in the program business," an agency executive told Mayer in 1970. None intent on hawking wares to the great television audience had any option but to accept network programming.

For their part, the networks kept their customers happy. A strategy of majority television, of seeking to schedule popular programs for virtually every evening hour, continued through the seventies. Occasionally a network threw in the towel and, against an especially popular program, aired a news documentary. Such "public service" at least placated critics and regulators.

Majority television enriched all three networks. According to Sally Bedell, the total revenues of ABC, CBS, and NBC increased in the 1970s from $1 billion to $3 billion. In 1970 the cost of a sixty-second spot on a hit program on the most popular network was $60,000; by the decade's end it had risen to $200,000. In August 1979, former CBS executive Michael Dann calculated, every new ratings point for a network brought an additional $75 million in pretax profits.

Entertaining the Millions

The leading network in the first half of the seventies was CBS. The popular favorite since the early 1950s, Columbia had relied heavily on well-crafted situation comedies. After the extraordinary success of "The Beverly Hillbillies" in 1962–63, CBS began to carry sitcoms with a decidedly rural orientation. Such series, along with several variety programs ("The Glen Campbell Goodtime Hour," "The Jim Nabors Show," and "Hee Haw"), added to the network's country flavor. CBS, Les

Brown observed, "had an excess of corn." Long-established CBS variety shows hosted by Jackie Gleason and Red Skelton had large followings, but among older, less well-to-do viewers. And they were proving harder and harder to sell to Madison Avenue. Simply put, the wrong consumers—the very young and very old, often in small towns—preferred such programs. Although behind CBS in the overall ratings, NBC had an easier time offering "Laugh-In" and other programs that appealed to audiences having superior "demographics," those who lived in larger suburban and urban markets and were more likely, as younger adults, to spend money on the goods and services sponsors hawked. In contrast, CBS's canceled programs, Bedell wrote, were "all proven successes that happened to appeal to the viewers with the least amount of money in their pockets."

Early in 1970, CBS TV President Robert D. Wood announced a drastic revamping of his network's evening programming. Despite strong or respectable ratings, the Gleason and Skelton shows, as well as "Petticoat Junction," would not be renewed. CBS axed other straw-strewn sitcoms, including "The Beverly Hillbillies" and the country-music variety hour "Hee Haw," in the next year.

In their place came more situation comedies, some of which broke new ground while intentionally appealing to the sorts of viewers NBC had captured in the late 1960s. In most instances, CBS's comedies shared two related characteristics. First, they sought to be, in the jargon of the times, "relevant," more oriented to urban or suburban consumers and to the social and political transformations of the era. "What we need to begin the rebuilding," Wood said, "are programs that are relevant to what is happening today, instead of the make-believe. That's what will get us looking young again." Second, the new sitcoms marked a restoration of the TV scriptwriter's status. In the sixties, sitcom producers had tended to downgrade the writer's role, and not surprisingly, the scripts had suffered. In addition, the networks relaxed once rigid guidelines that had made slapstick the only possible schtick.

"All in the Family" was one of two CBS programs to set the pace for the 1970s sitcoms. The series began its run as a mid-season replacement in January 1971. Columbia had scheduled the program, which had been rejected by ABC, with mixed feelings. CBS's research indicated that "All in the Family" had little prospect of capturing a significant share of the audience. Gradually, however, viewers turned to the series; and for five years beginning with the 1971–72 season "All in the Family" ranked first in the Nielsen ratings. And its success encouraged a new type of sitcom that constantly dwelt on political and cultural controversies.

Modeled after the British series "Till Death Do Us Part," "All in the Family" involved the everyday lives of the Bunkers: husband Archie, his wife Edith, daughter Gloria, and her husband Michael. "All in the Family," like past successful sitcoms, was well-cast. Carroll O'Connor played Archie, and Jean Stapleton, Edith, with an authenticity few TV performers could have achieved. In contrast to most previous sitcoms, "All in the Family" concerned a blue-collar family. No one would confuse Archie with the soft-spoken, college-educated father on the vast majority of family comedies. Like Ralph Kramden on "The Honeymooners," Archie frequently lost his temper and engaged in various forms of verbal violence. But there was a far rougher edge to Archie's language. Even Edith, normally pliant, broke a TV convention by calling Archie an "S.O.B." (to which Archie would reply, "Stifle yourself"). With similar frankness, "All in the Family" conveyed Archie's politics (liberal Michael was always "Meathead") and his racist attitudes. Never before had such blatant bigotry been displayed by a TV series character. One had never known Ralph Kramden's ideology or position on minority rights. The political duels between Archie and Michael were both new to television and well-timed. They reflected the deeply ideological aftertaste to the sixties and the political frustration of the white working-class male. "All in the Family," Don Freeman wrote in the *San Diego Union,* "is outrageous, shocking, probably offensive, undoubtedly insulting and it is also extremely funny. Certainly it stands alone in American television, an adult social satire reflected in farce comedy with a bite that cuts nearly, with surgical precision, to the bone."

Series producer Norman Lear, a liberal Democrat, and his scriptwriters took pains not to celebrate Archie. If anything, the white upper-middle-class professionals who worked for Lear or hailed his program dismissed Archie's attitudes as irrational. "Mike is always the one who is making sense," Lear wrote in October 1971. Absent was the possibility, later observed by Christopher H. Lasch, no champion of political reaction, that Archie's real-life counterparts had legitimate grievances. Instead, Lasch argued, the series posited a patronizing "New Class" stereotype of blue-collar males as mindless blowhards incapable of accepting the new political and cultural order. "It's about time," civil rights leader Whitney M. Young, Jr., wrote in February 1971, "that clever liberal writers started easing up on their portrayal of working-class whites as bigots. Some are; some aren't." Other commentators worried that many viewers not from the New Class sided with Archie. "By making the expression of hostility more commonplace, do we really exorcise it?" a *New York Times* guest columnist asked. "Or do we, in fact, make it more acceptable?" Lear and CBS assured doubters that the program struck a blow for tolerance. But like most of those who worked in or wrote about the mass media, they failed to consider the hypothesis of selective perception; it had not occurred to them that others might respond differently to Archie's commentaries. From their 1974 survey of "All in the Family" viewers, Neil Vidmar and Milton Rokeach contended that those who watched the program often brought fixed attitudes with them. Whatever the overriding "message" of an "All in the Family" episode, Archie's xenophobic tirades often reinforced a bigot's own values. "Too many viewers," Vidmar and Rokeach wrote, "did not see the program as a satire on bigotry, had identified with Archie rather than Mike, saw Archie as winning, did not perceive Archie as a character who was the most ridiculed, and perhaps most disturbing, saw nothing wrong with Archie's use of racial and ethnic slurs."

"All in the Family"'s robust ratings, and not the different ways viewers interpreted its characters' values, made Lear a "hot" producer, precious in an era when two out of every three new series failed. He produced more sitcoms, some with black leads; almost all regularly dealt with ideological and racial conflict. The lead on "Maude" (CBS, 1972–78) had an abortion. "Mary Hartman, Mary Hartman," "Forever Fernwood," and "America 2Night," all non-network originations, ridiculed an old Hollywood ideal type, small-town America.

"The Mary Tyler Moore Show" (CBS, 1970–77) also helped to transform the American sitcom. The program involved a single woman working in the news department of WJM in Minneapolis. The star's own company, MTM, produced the show. Like Lear's group, MTM elevated the role of its writers. "MTM was founded on writers," MTM president Grant Tinker told Horace Newcomb and Robert Alley. Freed of the constraints that had inhibited many of their colleagues elsewhere in Hollywood, MTM writers created a cast of true characters, less stereotypical and more complex than ones before. They collectively played a large role in each episode. (Jane Feuer, who studied the MTM productions, dubbed "The Mary Tyler Moore Show" a "character comedy.") Most activity occurred in the WJM newsroom or involved its personnel. As Ella Taylor notes, Mary's apartment, which would have been the primary set in most earlier TV comedies, became an annex.

Together, Newcomb wrote, Mary's coworkers at WJM—and not the lead's own children and spouse—constituted "the family" of the new, work-based sitcom. The gruff boss, Lou Grant, was capable, if the crisis was of sufficient magnitude, of showing the consideration an ideal father or brother displayed toward his wife or sister. At the same time, Ella Taylor argues, Lou Grant and other characters, in their occasional displays of temper, conveyed the tensions common to most families. "If

WJM provides a primary haven of love and shelter," Taylor writes, "it also crackles with the hostility and ambivalence that form the other side of the coin of family intimacy."

Despite their setting in a newsroom, characters on "The Mary Tyler Moore Show," David Grote observed, never discussed contemporary stories like Watergate; instead, the politics of MTM concerned the life style of the new woman of the seventies. Single, Mary Richards (Moore) came to Minneapolis at the end of an unhappy romance; in one episode, she and a boyfriend spend the night together. Ten years earlier, as the married Petries in "The Dick Van Dyke Show," Moore and her husband had slept in separate twin beds. Female leads in other sixties comedies had been married or widowed. A few had been single and worked, but they were younger than Mary Richards and only marking time until the right man came along to propose marriage. Mary was different: she had a career. "When our show went on," Moore recalled in 1977, "we were considered very radical—so radical that there were prophecies of instant disaster. Mary Richards was not a widow. She'd never been married. She even hinted at having an affair! She was a mature woman in her thirties, not a young girl having a fling before marriage. She wasn't even hunting for a husband! She was an ambitious career woman interested in her work and making it on her own." "In terms of human relationships and changing social mores, from Women's Liberation to sexual freedom," Geoffrey Cowan wrote, "Mary Tyler Moore" and "Rhoda" (CBS, 1974–78), a subsequent MTM production, "were as real, innovative, and poignant as anything on television."

MTM, like Lear's company, became a sought-after manufacturer of series. Many were spin-offs of the original series. One, "Rhoda," briefly enjoyed better ratings than "The Mary Tyler Moore Show." In the late seventies and early eighties, MTM made dramatic programs as well, including "Lou Grant" (CBS, 1977–82), "Hill Street Blues" (NBC, 1980–87), and "Remington Steele" (NBC, 1982–87). As in "The Mary Tyler Moore Show," the best MTM series had their characters change and not, as in the worst sitcoms or action dramas, remain cutouts from the series pilot who, through the miracle of make-up, even failed to age.

If only in the presentation of situation comedies, TV in the early seventies was enjoying a second golden age. Other well-written, work-based character comedies included "M*A*S*H" (CBS, 1972–83), "Barney Miller" (ABC, 1975–82), and "Taxi" (ABC, 1978–82; NBC, 1982–83). MTM and Lear had fathered a competition that had not been seen in television since the mid fifties. "From 1971 to 1976 was a tremendously exciting time in television comedy," James L. Brooks, a writer and producer for MTM, told Newcomb and Alley. "We felt a need to be better than Norman and his shows and we respected them and watched them and we watched 'M*A*S*H' and we watched 'Maude' and 'All in the Family.' There was an enormous amount of respect that I think was mutual amongst the shows then."

Nevertheless, TV writers and producers like Brooks did not draw their inspiration just from each other. Based in southern California, television's creative talent closely followed the film industry, and much of the decade's relative realism in TV programming reflected changes on the big screen. In the late sixties, motion picture makers had acquired new freedoms in portraying human relations and sexuality. Scripts included obscenities and had lovers in bed and in various states of undress. Those in TV production wanted to enjoy some of the same liberties. Indeed, an artistic envy permeated TV production companies. They, too, sought to break ground and enjoy, at weekend parties, the praise of colleagues and company executives who worked in the older medium.

Such aspirations took on new importance because of a shift in economic relations between Hollywood and New York in the 1970s. Since 1965 the FCC had been attempting to check the networks' growing financial interest in programming. The commission contended that the networks' co-investing in series only added to their power over producers, all in all lessening the diversity of the medium. Network attorneys successfully delayed any action for five years. Then in 1970, as part of its Prime Time Access Rule, the commission forbade the networks to participate financially in any evening entertainment programming. The program participation rule forced the networks to be less dictatorial in their dealings with producers, though they still retained the power of the schedule.

If no longer the program producers' loan officers, the networks would not, and could not, grant them the same discretion that motion picture companies had awarded their creative talent. Although they were willing to relax many rules, some four-decades old, the networks insisted on maintaining certain standards. Challenging too many social conventions, network executives worried, might anger viewers, especially in the South and Midwest. Anticipating such concerns, each network insisted on changes in individual episodes or characters. No chain was more uneasy than CBS, which had the largest number of affiliates in smaller communities, thought to be the most conservative culturally. CBS had always been the most preoccupied with its public image, and Lear constantly fought the network over story ideas and scripts for his programs. Although he usually resisted their demands, others had to relent. MTM had originally planned to present Mary Richards as a divorcee. "M*A*S*H" excised the adultery rampant in the original film version and pilot episode. A script for "Rhoda" during the 1977–78 season had to be rewritten so that the heroine's decision to bed her lover came after three weeks, rather than one evening, of courtship. ABC delayed introducing a comedy about two women and a man living together, "Three's Company," until audience research indicated an acceptance of such coed living arrangements. Such new "sexcoms," Sally Bedell wrote, only teased the viewer. "Today's videosex remains almost exclusively verbal rather than visual," Newsweek commented in February 1978. "Nudity and explicit portrayals of sexual acts are still taboo." Viewers saw just so much of Chrissy on "Three's Company." For a February 1978 cover, Newsweek had Suzanne Somers pose revealingly in sexy nightwear. Yet, Geoffrey Cowan wrote, "nothing sufficiently risque had appeared on the air."

Such restraint was logical. Americans with more traditional values did not welcome the new type of sitcoms. Many, led by the Southern Baptist Convention, actively protested their advent. CBS received some twenty-four thousand letters objecting to the abortion episodes on "Maude"; thirty-nine CBS affiliates refused to carry the programs. "While Norman Lear was winning awards from groups concerned with civil rights and civil liberties," Cowan wrote, the head of CBS TV "was getting nasty telephone calls and letters from irate citizens and government officials. Even some of his own affiliates had become his most severe critics." His counterparts at ABC received even more critical abuse for "Soap" (1977–80), a sitcom that relied heavily on sexual situations for humor. As a result, ABC, normally the most feckless of the three chains, forced "Soap"'s scriptwriters to alter certain scripts. In perhaps the most egregious example, a Jesuit priest would not, as originally planned in one episode, be seduced by the daughter of one of the leads.

CBS and the FCC had tried to placate the traditionalists. As in the sixties, some members of Congress and lay critics of the medium continued to worry about the effects of television, especially of violent programming, on children. Under pressure, the FCC and Arthur Taylor, who had succeeded Frank Stanton as president of CBS, fashioned a voluntary, three-network agreement that in the fall of 1975 created a "Family Viewing Hour," the first sixty minutes of network evening prime time. The planners assumed that younger children went to bed by nine (and by eight in the Midwest); programs telecast before they donned their pajamas were to be free of violence or sexual innuendo. All of the networks juggled their schedules. "All in the Family" was moved from eight o'clock on Saturdays to nine on Mondays. For programs to be aired before nine, producers struggled to meet the expectations of Taylor and FCC chairman Richard Wiley. "Is it too late for Rhoda to become a virgin?" wondered one CBS underling. A superior vetoed one "M*A*S*H" script concerning venereal disease. NBC's fidelity to the new order gutted a promising sitcom, "Fay," starring Lee Grant as a divorced older woman, which had been slated for the early evening. The program's hilarious but adult humor panicked network officials. When NBC canceled "Fay" after three weeks, Grant bitterly remarked, "That's life and death on television in the Family Hour, folks."

Soon after "Fay" left the air, the family hour died, and with it, the last vestiges of the FCC's oversight of programming. Lear and other writers had challenged the FCC and the networks in court, and in November 1976, Federal District Judge Warren Ferguson ruled the plan unconstitutional. The FCC, Ferguson maintained, had forced the idea on the networks and thus violated their First Amendment rights, though Taylor of CBS deserved half the credit or blame for initiating the proposal. Ferguson's ruling, by expanding the First Amendment's protection to TV entertainment, effectively denied the FCC even an indirect role in shaping the content of American television. The industry's new freedom was not unrestricted: TV performers might not use certain words considered "dirty" by the commission; but otherwise, it allowed all of those in television to be even more dismissive of the FCC than they had been since the mid sixties.

The networks were free, in so many words, to be greedy. For his attempted "statesmanship," Taylor was fired as CBS president. In an earlier decade he might have survived, might even have been the subject of a flattering *New Yorker* profile or *Time* cover story. But not in the 1970s: with so much money to be made, altruism had become irrelevant.

At NBC, frantic activity related closely to the condition of its parent, RCA. Traditionally, NBC executives had been under less pressure to finish first than their counterparts at CBS and ABC. NBC could be a respectable second. But RCA's attempt to transform itself into a conglomerate had been poorly managed, leaving the corporation saddled with debt. In the late seventies, RCA under chairman Edgar H. Griffiths began to sell off assets to pay for new ones and maintain earnings. RCA had a liquidity problem, and Griffiths insisted that his broadcast operations earn more.

At all three networks, new programs had to demonstrate audience appeal quickly. Formerly, a network had given a series at least thirteen, usually twenty-six, weeks to nurture a following. By the mid seventies, programs were being canceled after four weeks. CBS dropped "Khan," a private detective show set in San Francisco, after four telecasts. Two years later, Columbia shelved "Young Daniel Boone" after a month on the schedule; the network never aired several episodes already filmed. NBC, in one of its many moments of high anxiety, canceled one series without ever telecasting any episodes. One producer complained, "Television has changed from a program business to a ratings business."

No one TV executive typified the new mentality of networking more than Fred Silverman. The son of a television repairman, Silverman had been fascinated by the home screen since his father bought the family's first receiver in 1949. He majored in radio and television at Syracuse University; earning his M.A. at Ohio State University, Silverman wrote a long and admiring thesis on ABC's rise to competitive status in the 1950s. A technician's celebration of skillful scheduling rather than a considered analysis of what was being scheduled, Silverman's essay ignored the charge that ABC's programming strategy had helped to destroy the golden age. But then Silverman rarely weighed the views of TV critics. He gave every appearance of being unburdened by a great familiarity with high- or even middle-brow culture. Many other programmers, with more refined tastes and self-consciously seeking the approval of outsiders in New York who derided the medium, regarded their task with a certain distaste. Not Silverman. He did not privately scorn television or the TV audience; he *was* the TV audience. And he had a showman's eye for detail, such as whether a joke in a script worked or a set possessed a flaw, and what was far more important, an extraordinary knack for placing programs in the right time slot. Kept too far down the ladder at CBS, Silverman went to ABC in 1975 and became the network's chief programmer. Under Silverman, ABC set the tone for television for the balance of the seventies.

A combination of factors made Silverman and ABC winners. Several potential hit series and miniseries, the success for which Silverman would wrongly be credited, were in production when he moved to ABC. He and his new employer also benefited from broadcast regulations. The FCC's Prime Time Access Rule had spared ABC having to offer three and one-half hours of programming. Traditionally, ABC had had the most difficulty filling out a schedule; the least popular series were usually ABC shows. The rule thus eased ABC's programming needs. Then, too, the steady diffusion of UHF television into more homes helped ABC, which had been forced to rely disproportionately on stations in the upper band for affiliates.

With ABC an option for viewers, Silverman settled on a mix of situation comedies and action dramas, some already being telecast or, like the eight-part "miniseries" "Roots," about to be aired when he joined the network. Targeting younger viewers, Silverman had little use for the more subtle humor crafted by MTM. Nor did he seek Norman Lear. Indeed, Silverman believed that viewers had lost much of their enthusiasm for CBS's "quality" comedies. Other insiders concurred. The audience, *Broadcasting* suggested, might be tiring of what it called the Norman Lear "comedy with a message." Silverman thus committed ABC to programs that virtually no critic likened to the best CBS efforts of the early seventies. He worked tirelessly on the details of each show and character. As part of his overall plan, he at first concentrated on promising new entries on the schedule, including two sitcoms, "Happy Days" and "Welcome Back, Kotter." He insisted that the brittle side to seemingly antisocial characters like Fonzie on "Happy Days" be softened. Sex was given prominence in ABC's TV movies, with sexual assaults deliberately incorporated into each episode of "Roots."

Sex figured prominently in a program about three female private investigators, "Charlie's Angels." The series premiered in September 1976, with two models and one actress in the leads. Initially, Aaron Spelling's scriptwriters hoped to make the heroines illustrate the women's movement by providing examples of women succeeding at a male's occupation. By the time "Charlie's Angels" went on the air, however, the series favored action and displays of female fashion over intelligent sleuthing. The series' writers, *Newsweek* complained, "use any pretext to get the buxom trio into an equatorial clime, then into wet T-shirts and finally into whatever run-and-jump situation that best displays their unfettered charms."

Silverman's video voyeurism paid off. In 1976, his first full year at the network, ABC's earnings rose 186 percent. "Charlie's Angels" and "Roots" (some 130 million Americans, or 85 percent of all TV homes, watched all or parts of the miniseries) had allowed ABC to overcome CBS for the overall ratings leadership for the 1976–77 season.

The following season, sexual innuendoes formed the basis of two more hit ABC comedies, "Soap" and "Three's Company." Silverman had told the producers of "Three's Company" to make it "the same kind of breakthrough in sexiness that 'All in the Family' was in bigotry." "Breakthrough" for Silverman meant what Bedell and others considered broad, fraternity-style jokes about sex. "Three's Company" "epitomized the leering voyeurism that passed for sex on television in the late seventies," Bedell wrote. "Television characters seemed content instead to chatter about sex in a strikingly immature manner as they leered at the possibilities undulating around them." Yet Silverman knew what worked. The program quickly rose to the top five in the

Nielsens. The more endowed of the two female roommates, Suzanne Somers, enjoyed her moment of celebrity. "If you've got it," she remarked, "bump it with a trumpet."

Somers's character represented the other side of TV's portrayal of women in the 1970s. Mary Richards had quietly reflected the gains of the women's liberation movement. She was a single, working woman who liked men but had not organized her life or career around one. Chrissy suggested the era's more sporting and, in many instances, exploitative sexuality.

In other ways, the ABC comedies little resembled the best CBS sitcoms of the early seventies. They were designed to attract younger, teenage viewers. Research subsequently confirmed Silverman's own hunch that in family viewing situations, children most often determined what was watched. The Silverman sitcoms made few demands; indeed, the ABC shows were relentlessly cheery. "Stress the positive, not the negative," was a Silverman maxim. "Happy Days" and "Laverne and Shirley" also sought to cash in on the decade's nostalgia for the fifties. "Parents can relax when we show Richie and Potsy running around," the producer of "Happy Days" said of his program's main characters. "They know that Richie's not going to pull out a needle any minute." Such an approach to comedy, however, exasperated critics, most of whom, it appeared, had fallen in love with Mary Richards. "The current lineup at ABC," John J. O'Connor of the *New York Times* complained, "is totally devoid of the class production once represented by 'The Mary Tyler Moore Show.' It doesn't take a disgruntled critic to realize that the level of television entertainment in recent years has been dropping rapidly to kiddie levels, and that ABC has been mindlessly leading the way."

Silverman's rivals at first dismissed his approach to programming. Paul Klein, chief programmer at NBC, had concluded that the TV series was passé and that his network could succeed by stressing special events that would appeal to the well-to-do viewer (Klein was, in effect, reviving Pat Weaver's approach to scheduling). Silverman's success, Klein remarked, could be attributed to such schticks as the jiggle, that is, having "a young female television personality running at top speed with [sic] a limited amount of underwear." A more righteous Robert J. Wussler, Wood's successor as CBS TV president, compared ABC's programs in September 1977 to "junk food." "Maybe we've been stupid or naive this year, but we've tried to do programs that are more adult."

That emphasis appeared less justifiable as ABC held its lead in the 1977–78 season and began to lure away CBS and NBC affiliates. Between 1976 and 1979, ABC signed contracts with seventeen stations that had been associated with CBS and nine that had been with NBC; most had been tied to one of the older networks for more than a generation. Although the typical switch occurred in smaller markets, NBC found itself dropped by outlets in Minneapolis–St. Paul and Indianapolis. Silverman's successes were overcoming his network's two-decade-long disadvantage in the quality of affiliates.

CBS and NBC felt compelled to take up his strategy. Paley fired Wussler; his successor, Robert A. Daly, not only praised ABC's hit shows but tried to imitate them. In the fall of 1978, CBS offered two series modeled after "Charlie's Angels." Klein oversaw the production of TV movies for NBC that promised to go beyond anything ABC offered in their emphasis on sex. "If ABC is doing kiddie porn," an NBC executive remarked, "NBC will give the audience adult porn." Lesley Ann Warren, who had once played Cinderella in a CBS musical, portrayed a high-class madame in NBC's 1977 miniseries "79 Park Avenue."

At NBC nothing worked. For the remainder of the decade, CBS remained second, NBC a distant third. And not even television's Svengali could save NBC. Silverman went to NBC in mid-1978 but was unable, after three frantic years, to improve the network's woeful position. Awarded more authority than he had ever enjoyed at ABC or CBS, Silverman proved unequal to the challenge. His reckless spending on talent and programs actually added to NBC's woes; the network's earnings fell from $152.6 million in 1977 to $75.3 million in 1980. Silverman promised to put NBC ahead in the ratings by Christmas 1980. But the network continued to finish third, and the corpulent Silverman's image as "the man with the golden gut" was shattered. "Many ballyhoos were ballyhooed when he arrived as president and chief executive officer in June 1978 to resuscitate the seriously ill network," N. R. Kleinfield wrote in the *New York Times* in July 1980. "But, if anything, NBC is aching worse than before."

As in the late fifties, ABC had won largely at the expense of more creative forces or impulses at the other networks. ABC had shamelessly played to the broadest taste and, by winning the ratings wars so conclusively, set the terms of battle for its rivals. Successfully cultivating the twelve-year-old viewer, or the viewer with a twelve-year-old's cultural preferences, ABC made life much more difficult for those producers who proposed series that would appeal to an older, more mature sensibility. What was indefensible, then, about TV in the late seventies was not, as the medium's most priggish critics moaned, that "Happy Days" and "Charlie's Angels" found places on the airwaves but that they had become the ideal types of all three networks, too often all that they aspired for. Tinker of MTM spoke gloomily in 1980 of what the new network rivalry had done to television. "The excitement of the mid-seventies and its shows, the work that excited the creative people, are casualties of a fierce high-decibel competition," Tinker remarked. "It means networks reaching for the lowest common denominator programming. Shows of the quality of ['The Mary Tyler Moore Show'] no longer get started, and to the extent that they don't, the kinds of people who do that kind of work have perhaps been lost to television."

Tinker's company and others still fashioned some programs that critics admired. Work-based situation comedies like "Barney Miller" and "WKRP in Cincinnati" (CBS, 1978–82), comparable to "M*A*S*H" or "The Mary Tyler Moore Show" in their attention to character and avoidance of slapstick, remained on the air. MTM's "Lou Grant" could be likened to the best of the liberal professional dramas of the sixties. Although most made-for-TV movies resembled the forgettable B-films of the 1940s or seemed to be merely sexed-up successors to that cultural form, a few, beginning with "Brian's Song" (1971), won praise from many of the home screen's monitors. Veteran film stars who had never before thought themselves suited to the smaller screen began to appear in TV films. "Roots" deeply affected both white and black Americans. "The American people saw what television entertainment had shown rarely, if ever, before," Robert Sklar wrote, "admirable, heroic black people struggling to survive the degradations of slavery; black men and women raising families, loving and grieving, and living the human story from generation to generation."

Nevertheless, as Sklar and others observed, aside from "Roots," African-American performers and viewers had few victories on television in the 1970s. The disappointing ratings for a 1977 NBC TV movie about Martin Luther King, Jr., discouraged the networks from scheduling dramatic series with black casts. White viewers, network executives concluded, preferred TV dramas with all or mostly white leads. "It's a white country," an ABC programmer told Todd Gitlin, "and [TV] a commercial business." None of the decade's promising dramatic series about African Americans, Rick Du Brow of the Los Angeles Times noted, was given sufficient time to nurture a following. The black actors and actresses who starred in "Roots" found subsequent television work hard to find. "If you had been a white actor, and you were in the most popular show in television history," Lynne Moody recalled in 1986, "you would have had—at the very least—a job." One Hollywood agent told another "Roots" star, "I love your work, but I just don't want to handle any black actresses. They're too hard to get work for."

The networks instead promoted black situation comedies that evoked new or old stereotypes. George Jefferson on "The Jeffersons" (CBS, 1975–85), though a financial success, was a buffoon. To Henry Louis Gates, Jr., George Jefferson was one of many TV characterizations of male blacks that suggested "their domestication, in direct reaction to the questing, macho images of black males in the '60s news clips of the civil rights movement, the Black Panthers, and the black power movement." More often, black sitcoms reinforced the image of the fatherless African-American family. Writers eliminated the strong father character on "Good Times" (CBS, 1974–79), a Norman Lear production, while giving more attention to the shiftless "J.J." figure. The series lead, Esther Rolle, quit in protest for a year. "I just had to be relieved of any sense of responsibility for the kind of idiocy that program was perpetuating," she told an interviewer in 1977. White audiences, however, rewarded the predominately white producers and writers of such programs, which remained popular into the eighties. "Blacks," Gitlin wrote, "are still entertaining as comic relief."

More representative of television in the seventies was the police drama. Technical innovations added to their appeal. Mobile cameras eased filming car chases, popularized in the motion pictures *Bullitt* (1968) and *The French Connection* (1971). Like *The French Connection*'s Popeye Doyle, the leads of the 1970s crime series reflected the conservative preoccupation with law and order. In the fifties the crime-show heroes had often been private investigators or defense attorneys; in the seventies they were usually police officers. And they did not, in instances recorded by Stephen Arons and Ethan Katsh in 1977, much respect suspects' civil liberties. "The overall image the shows project," they wrote, "is clearly one that is alien to the Constitution."

More commonly, critics complained about the brutality of the 1970s police dramas. For one week in 1974 the *New Yorker*'s Michael Arlen recorded violent episodes on network programs. On "Kojak" (CBS, 1973–78), Arlen wrote, "an old man was shot to death by gangsters, and two men were killed in a gunfight. On 'Columbo' [NBC, 1971–77], a woman was strangled to death, and another was drowned in her bathtub." Two nights later "a man was murdered with a harakiri knife" on "Hawaii Five-O" (CBS, 1968–80), and "one man was killed in an overturned car, and another man was shot to death by a rifle" on "Cannon" (CBS, 1971–76). Arlen had located a common structure. "In most detective programs," he concluded, "there is usually a key murder of an unknown but significant figure within the first five minutes; there is sometimes a throwaway murder of a secondary character in the middle; and there is invariably a gunfight which kills off one or two secondary or unknown characters, within the last five minutes."

"No more controversial issue bedevils American television," Robert Sklar wrote of TV violence. As earlier, parent groups and members of Congress protested the brutality on television crime dramas in the 1970s. But even larger numbers weekly tuned to programs like "Columbo" and "Kojak." In the 1973–74 season, "Hawaii Five-O" finished fifth in the Nielsens, "Kojak" seventh, and "Columbo" tenth. Their appeal undoubtedly had far more to do with strongly written and acted leading roles than the explicitness of the mayhem that accompanied each episode. Still, the guardians fretted. They pointed to individual incidents of children imitating antisocial behavior shown on a TV program (hardly surprising with tens of millions watching). Far more systematic inquiries in the seventies collectively indicated a causal relationship between TV violence and antisocial behavior among the younger viewers, especially those who watched great amounts of television. At the same time, however, most analyses stressed the child's predisposition, suggesting that what he or she brought to the experience of TV-watching was far more important than the programming itself. To confuse matters further, the networks periodically released their own research denying a link. They probably could have spared themselves the expense. By the mid seventies, voluntary efforts by the networks to protect the child viewer by creating a family viewing hour had been ruled unconstitutional. The courts were enfeebling the FCC's programming authority, thus permitting the networks to give the guardians little notice.

Informing the Millions

Few scholars studying the American mass media dismissed the rise of TV news in the 1970s. With the publication of *The People's Choice* (1944), which had suggested that radio and newspapers had limited effects on voters, most scholars had regarded the mass media as merely one of many influences on individuals. But slowly in the seventies, various academic callings, notably political science, began to come to terms with television. Many, discarding the "limited effects" model, asserted that TV was tremendously powerful.

In the seventies, television news did appear to assume a new importance in America. Local and national TV anchors became celebrities, none more than Walter Cronkite, the anchor of "The CBS Evening News." In the late 1960s, Cronkite's newscast had overtaken NBC's "Huntley-Brinkley Report" in the ratings. Cronkite's success was one of the ironies of the new decade's journalism of personalities. In a profession that increasingly prized youth and appearances, Cronkite was older and relatively untouched by fashion. His mustache, pipe, and hairstyle (he refused to disguise his receding hairline but combed his hair straight back) had not been in vogue since the late forties, if then. Unlike his rivals at NBC, he found joke-telling a struggle—he was a newsman, not an entertainer. A former wire service reporter, he honored journalistic tradition by broadcasting from a set that resembled a newspaper newsroom and having himself billed as "chief editor." Yet it was precisely the old-fashioned stolidness of Cronkite and his newscast that made them appealing—and feared. When a Republican senator accused the CBS anchor in 1971 of favoring the Democrats, an aide to President Nixon wrote, "Taking on Walter Cronkite cannot do us any good whatsoever. It is like attacking the Lord himself." Three years later, Cronkite headed the list of the most "trusted Americans" and was subsequently considered for the vice-presidential nomination of a major third-party candidate. His interviews with Egypt's President Anwar Sadat and Israeli Prime Minister Menachem Begin in 1977 were thought to have brought two longtime adversaries to the bargaining table in 1977 and led to a historic peace treaty two years later. Although virtually all scholarly accounts of the negotiations dismiss the claim (as usual, newspeople denied the possibility that newsmakers were simply using them), the impression of influence proved more important than the reality. Cronkite's retirement in 1981 received enormous coverage, unimaginable to those broadcasters "reading the news" a generation earlier.

In fact, the numbers who watched the early-evening network newscasts in the seventies increased slightly, though mainly because more ABC affiliates started to run their network's news program. In the late sixties, about one-third of ABC's stations, including those in Boston, Houston, and Miami, had refused to air "The ABC Evening News." More ABC affiliates began to carry the program in the early seventies. And many station managers then adopted a "roadblocking" strategy; that is, in areas served by only three outlets, all telecast the network news programs simultaneously, leaving viewers no choice but to take in a network newscast. The networks' excessive coverage of the crisis surrounding the hostage-taking of American embassy personnel in Iran encouraged more news-watching in 1979–81.

Despite roadblocking, the total audience for network news programs remained lower than for entertainment shows. Only one news program, "60 Minutes," beginning in 1976 could compete in evening prime time. Cronkite, in reality, only occasionally entered some American living rooms; a poorly worded survey question partly accounted for the confusion. Since 1963 the Roper Organization had been reporting that most Americans—64 percent in 1976—relied on television for news. More systematic measures, however, that attempted to calculate individual use, as opposed to *claims* of individual use, indicated that Americans examined a newspaper more frequently than they viewed a network newscast. The greatest fallacy was the tendency of social observers, then and later, to regard TV and newspaper consumption as dichotomous variables and to assert that citizens obtained all their information from television. A survey of Alabama voters in 1982, for example, suggested that voters who changed their minds about a candidate did so on the basis of multiple sources. Overall, viewers were more likely to watch the local newscast, with many skipping the network newscasts altogether. In their study of surveys of some fifty-six hundred adults in November 1974, Robert L. Stevenson and Kathryn P. White found that just under half of those sampled viewed no network nightly news program during a two-week period. "On any single, average day, the television news audience includes only about half of the adult population while only one adult in five sees the showcase of the medium, the evening network news." CBS itself admitted in 1982 that just 4.2 percent of all homes viewed "The CBS Evening News" four or more times a week. Moreover, analyses by Stevenson and White and others showed viewers to be relatively inattentive during a newscast (they were more disrespectful only toward commercials). Subsequent studies by John P. Robinson and others indicated that most TV viewers retained little information presented on the newscasts.

Viewers' indifference toward newscasts may be explained by the TV news's true function for many. Some scholars suggested that most who watched a newscast mainly sought reassurance. That is, they turned on the programs after a day at work to be sure that they had not missed a story of enormous significance—and that all was right with the world. The producers of the two most popular network newscasts in the 1970s apparently sensed this need for consolation. Critics dubbed the older, mustachioed Cronkite, with his avuncular delivery, "Uncle Walter." Todd Gitlin called Cronkite "the sturdy meta-father." Family metaphors could be extended to his rivals at NBC. If smug by comparison, David Brinkley and John Chancellor could still be regarded as favored uncles with an excess of cynicism.

Television's personalization of news delivery strengthened the mass perception of TV as the nation's information machine. Even those Americans who still relied on newspapers could not see or hear their dailies' reporters and columnists in their living rooms. A newspaper or newsmagazine was a group enterprise, with hundreds shaping its contents; there was no individual with whom to identify. Although dozens likewise fashioned a network news program, its presentation by a few on-camera performers implied otherwise. "To some degree the public's expression of reliance on 'television news,' " George Comstock wrote in 1978, "represents a response to the medium as symbol or eternal presence at the hearth rather than a measure of its actual importance as a regular news source."

The networks and stations privately had few illusions about the mass appeal of TV news. During evening prime time, news programs usually appeared against an unbeatable combination. On the night in 1977 that NBC broadcast the NCAA basketball finals and ABC the Motion Picture Academy awards, CBS aired an hour-long documentary on Africa. Despite a writers' strike that forced the rerunning of programs in the fall of 1980, no network aired a special on that year's presidential campaign. Each limited its election coverage to TV debates and late-night thirty-minute wrap-ups. Individual stations were reluctant to preempt a network entertainment program in favor of a locally produced examination of a campaign or public issue.

Broadcasters, however, made money on the early-evening news programs. *TV Guide* reported that the three network newscasts earned $760 million in 1979. Although their audiences were smaller than those for entertainment programs, their viewers were older, which appealed to the makers of laxatives and arthritis remedies. ABC, which had long neglected its news division, realized that it was missing an important source of revenue and began to pour resources into its news programming.

ABC sparked an intense rivalry with NBC for the early-morning news viewership in the 1970s. NBC's "The Today Show," like its nightly newscast, had long made money for the network; "Today" was relatively inexpensive to produce and, despite its small audiences, attracted many advertisers. ABC's "Good Morning, America," however, by de-emphasizing public affairs and politics, began to appeal to viewers who had heretofore ignored "Today"'s more traditional agenda. Predictably, NBC responded by slashing its coverage of national affairs. At "Today," producer Steve Friedman in 1976 sharply cut the time given to newsmaker interviews. William F. Buckley, Jr., recalled that "Today" gave him and John Kenneth Galbraith fifteen to twenty minutes to debate the 1972 presidential election; four years later, they had six minutes. "Anything that requires us merely to exchange wisecracks doesn't work," Galbraith complained. The time allotted such encounters was sacrificed in favor of more "features" on "coping" with modern life and interviews with (and free publicity for) the stars of forthcoming network programs and motion pictures. On ABC's "Good Morning, America," *Time* observed in 1980, "bad news is provided almost apologetically." A year later, ABC fired "Good, Morning, America"'s producer when he forgot the new order and extended the program one hour to cover the murder of Egyptian President Sadat.

Although the nightly network newscasts by and large avoided the new, softer agenda of the early-morning programs, they remained marginal instruments when compared with the nation's best dailies. The producers of the NBC and CBS newscasts, Herbert Gans observed, based their selection of stories on those emphasized by the *New York Times*. "The broadcast media are in the rear guard of the informational process in this society," remarked one critic in *Performance* in 1972. "Television gets all its news from the newspapers. The newspapers still define what is news."

The *Washington Post*, and not one of the networks, broke and then pursued most heartily the biggest story of the decade, the Nixon administration's attempt to cover up its involvement in political espionage at the Watergate complex. Although of the three networks, CBS covered the affair early, its reports were usually summaries of accusations and refutations. "Each charge about Watergate," Lawrence W. Lichty wrote in his analysis of network coverage, "was almost always neatly balanced with a statement of denial." The networks left to the *Post*'s Bob Woodward and Carl Bernstein the initial task of uncloaking the conspiracy, CBS White House correspondent Dan Rather admitted. "In the important early going," Rather wrote in 1977, "our coverage was less than outstanding."

In overseas coverage, no network matched the *New York Times*. According to Michael Arlen, NBC in 1975 had twenty foreign correspondents, and CBS fourteen, compared with forty at the *Times*. Six years later, Lichty listed twenty-three full-time overseas correspondents at CBS, compared with thirty-two for the *Times*, thirty-six for *Time*, nineteen for the Knight-Ridder newspaper chain, and about three hundred for AP. Such staffing priorities conveyed the networks' bias toward domestic news. International stories normally involved a presidential trip abroad or a plane crash only if Americans were on board the ill-fated craft. "Organic, ongoing, interpretive coverage of the world as a whole by United States broadcast journalism seems right now to be at a minimum," Arlen wrote, "and—despite the profitability of the three networks—shows no signs of becoming more ambitious."

Nonetheless, the network news programs' overall standards surpassed those of local newscasts. Profiting all the more from the demand for TV time that enriched the networks in the 1970s, stations came to consider producing newscasts as the most efficient and profitable way to satisfy local advertisers. Although they were not cheap, producing early- and late-evening newscasts cost less than the rights to telecast old network entertainment programs, and the station did not have to share the profits with a 1950s TV star like Lucille Ball. And production expenses fell as stations began to use videotape, which could be processed immediately and later reused, instead of film for stories. Portable cameras also made news-gathering easier and less expensive. By the late seventies, the *Wall Street Journal* reported, TV news programs could generate as much as 60 percent of a station's revenues. Newscasts accounted for 15 percent of all expenses for Milwaukee's three network-affiliated stations in 1981 yet produced one-third of all revenues. Ratings thus proved all-important. Stations shamelessly hired news "doctors," outside consultants who studied the set's design and the appeal of various anchors and offered ideas for feature stories. Money was poured into constructing a new set or purchasing an expensive piece of hardware, not for hiring additional correspondents. In 1977, Leo Bogart reported, the typical TV station, which usually reached several daily newspaper "markets," had a news staff of eleven. A single daily with a circulation of about twelve thousand had a staff of nineteen.

News doctors and their patients emphasized the news "team" reading headlines. To make newscasts more relaxing and pleasant for viewers, producers directed on-camera personnel to convey an affected warmth and engage each other in "happy talk," the empty banter first tried at two of the stations ABC owned. Looks were paramount. In the 1960s, stations often had an older male hosting the newscast; in the 1970s, most had been replaced by the young and the handsome, some of whom had little or no reporting experience. Although women had more opportunities to read or report on air, stations tended to select them on the basis of their appearance. One indication that a show-business mentality had overtaken TV news came in the spring of 1980 when a Chicago talent agent tried to persuade Linda Yu, the weekend news anchor on WMAQ, to audition for the vacancy left by the departure of one of "Charlie's Angels." For women especially, being an on-air reporter or anchor could be as precarious as fashion modeling. Station executives had no qualms about dismissing a female employee for not aging gracefully. "The faces of television newswomen are never wrinkled," Russell Baker wrote in March 1981. On-camera looks almost as often determined a male newscaster's career. At a Chicago locker room in 1978 newspaper columnist Mike Royko watched a local TV newsman take thirteen minutes to blow-dry and then comb his hair.

"His hair doesn't look like it is starting to fall out," Royko wrote, "so he'll probably last in television for another 20 years or so."

A similar attitude affected the pacing of reports and "story selection." To secure maximum ratings, a newscast should be "lively," consultants maintained, and emphasize the visual. The coverage of "hard" news, notably government and politics, was even more superficial than that offered by the networks. Although state governments were expanding faster than the federal machine in the sixties and seventies, they received relatively little airtime on local newscasts, William T. Gormley, Jr., pointed out in 1978. News directors preferred stories with good pictures. Many local TV news executives had begun to disdain political reporting altogether. At California TV stations, Mary Ellen Leary wrote in the *Columbia Journalism Review*, reporters since the early seventies "had been actively discouraged from specializing in political coverage." In her analysis of TV's handling of the 1974 California gubernatorial race, Leary concluded that stations largely avoided the campaign. Producers regarded the contest as "a bore" and a hazard to ratings. In the place of such reportage, local stations ran soft features that would not wear out the attractive anchors' welcome. Cleveland's outlets always found time for a story on the annual return of the buzzards to Hinkley, Ohio.

Stations increasingly tried to help viewers deal with a variety of everyday experiences. Producers frequently hired a local doctor to dispense free advice. Sometimes it came from on-air personnel. In May 1979, New York's WABC aired multipart stories on infertility and childrearing. On one level, such story selection appeared innocent, even "responsible." But stations promoted these items heavily, with a conceit that implied that the reporter would somehow "solve," in a few minutes, a potentially complicated problem for the viewer. Under a picture of a newborn, an ad for WABC had the headline, "Unfortunately, it doesn't arrive with a set of instructions." The promotion then promised those instructions, with WABC's Rose Ann Scamardella casting herself in the role that heretofore had been the preserve of relatives and family physicians.

Network news did share some of the local TV news's weaknesses. Dan Rather and others granted that they had to stress stories with "visuals." That is, a serious report on inflation had to be diluted by interviews with unhappy and not necessarily representative patrons of a Washington-area supermarket that did nothing to explain the phenomenon. Complex developments or trends were either oversimplified or, more likely, skipped altogether. Linda Ellerbee, who had worked for NBC News in the seventies, wrote, "Television news producers often

turn down certain stories because, they say, the stories are too complicated or too dull to mean anything to the plumber in Albuquerque." But
the network newscasts avoided happy talk and until the 1980s refused
to make their agenda fit the needs of a market researcher. Veteran anchors could not be handled as easily as a younger station news host.
Cronkite himself called news consultants "idiots." Then, too, network
news executives, unlike their local counterparts, paid close heed to TV
critics. The network producers knew that any serious attempt to model
national newscasts after local efforts would be damned by the *New York
Times* and *Washington Post.*

Most TV columnists at first celebrated the incredible ratings victory
of CBS News's "60 Minutes." Beginning in 1968, Columbia experimented with a new "magazine" program. Unlike the documentary,
which devoted an hour or more to one great or light topic, "60 Minutes"
consisted of three or four different stories, some features, an interview,
and an investigative piece. This mix in time proved far more palatable
to audiences than the old documentary. Finally granted a permanent
weekly slot on the schedule in the late seventies, "60 Minutes"
achieved the impossible: it competed successfully with entertainment
shows to be among the most popular programs on television. In the
1981–82 season it ranked number one. No other news program had ever
commanded so many followers in evening prime time. "60 Minutes"
"has been the only non-entertainment series consistently to attract a
vast and seemingly unflagging following," E. J. Kahn, Jr., wrote.
"While the show is under way, restaurant employees who might at that
hour normally expect to be staggering under trays can minister to their
arches."

The triumph of "60 Minutes" could be attributed in part to its place
on the schedule. The program did not reach the Nielsen top twenty until 1976, when CBS elected to carry the program immediately following
its West Coast National Football League game. "60 Minutes" thereafter
enjoyed a spectacular "lead-in" audience, with sets already tuned to
their CBS affiliates. That season "60 Minutes" rose to eighteenth place
in the ratings of all network programs. A year later the program finished fourth.

CBS News only owed so much to the NFL. Other programs had enjoyed good lead-ins yet failed. "60 Minutes," however, was as calculat-
ingly paced as any good entertainment drama. Like innumerable local
TV station managers, "60 Minutes" producer Don Hewitt dreaded boring viewers. He preferred "what's got good pictures, what's got sex appeal," he told *TV Guide* in 1973. Personality was paramount. "I hate
issues per se," Hewitt told Kahn. "I'm not interested in the issue of the

environment but I'm interested in somebody who's dealing with the environment." Hewitt carefully edited investigative pieces to have the dramatic, storybook structure of a beginning, middle, and end. Closely choreographed, correspondents became in effect performers delivering lines. Mike Wallace, Harry Reasoner, Dan Rather, and Morley Safer narrated the weekly exposé (insiders called it "the scam of the week"), intended to leave viewers with little doubt as to the evil or wrongdoing reported. Producers routinely oversimplified the complicated and in some instances painted black and white what had been only gray. "I want to package reality as attractively as Hollywood producers package fiction," Hewitt told *TV Guide*. "The Lone Ranger" was one model to Hewitt. Arlen likened "60 Minutes" to "Perry Mason" and other old courtroom melodramas. Not surprisingly, "60 Minutes" faced numerous lawsuits for maligning the "villains" of various segments. "Too often," one admirer wrote in *Channels of Communication* in 1981, "the show has impaired its own effectiveness with theatricality or slanted editing."

The hostile approach "60 Minutes" assumed toward some subjects denoted a larger trend in network news. TV news in the fifties and sixties had tended to treat government policies and mainstream politicians uncritically. A wish to appear "professional," that is, as objective as any reporter on a good daily, and the reality of regulation—and possible governmental revenge for excessive criticism—had kept the news divisions in line. In the late sixties, however, younger network producers and correspondents had begun to assume a more searching attitude toward elected officials. This new pose, however, came only after the collapse of the broad cold war consensus among those in power whom TV newspeople covered. Prominent members of Congress critical of foreign-policy pronouncements by Presidents Johnson and Nixon became increasingly easy to track down, if not unavoidable. The deceit and incompetence that many in and out of the industry associated with America's Vietnam effort further discredited those in the executive branch.

A 1971 CBS documentary signaled the new relationship between the networks and the federal government. Ten years earlier, Cronkite had been narrating films for the U.S. Air Force. In "The Selling of the Pentagon," his employer attacked the Defense Department's publicity machine. Producers edited creatively for effect. To carry the thesis, several interviews and speeches were placed out of order of the question, or out of context. The network withstood a firestorm of criticism centered in the House of Representatives, and CBS President Stanton survived an attempt to cite him for contempt after he refused to supply a House committee with the material edited out of the program.

The forcefully adversarial tone of "The Selling of the Pentagon" appeared to suggest that TV news might finally be emerging as a serious, independent force in American policymaking. In fact, the network was probably being used, or allowing itself to be used, by a prominent Senate critic of the administration. As in the reporting of the Vietnam War in the late 1960s, CBS News had not become a "fourth" branch of government. It was instead conveying congressional dissatisfaction with high defense spending. In their analysis of "The Selling of the Pentagon," Jimmie N. Rogers and Theodore Clevenger, Jr., found repeated similarities between the documentary's indictment and one prepared earlier by Senator J. William Fulbright. Although the program's narrator had assured viewers that "no politicians pleading special causes" had been sought, CBS had apparently fobbed off a congressional opinion as its own, and very effectively. Refusing to challenge CBS News's claims of disinterestedness, the vast majority of newspaper and magazine TV columnists hailed the network. Subsequent ham-handed attempts by the Nixon administration to force favorable coverage ("objective reporting," its operatives insisted) only made CBS and White House correspondent Rather appear more heroic.

After Nixon resigned in disgrace in 1974, there was seemingly no turning back for the networks. The office of the presidency, once commonly revered, and used by different chief executives to enhance their power, had become open game. With network correspondents modeling their questioning after Rather's tough handling of Nixon, press conferences became duels. Immediately after presidential addresses to the nation, a panel of newspeople and politicians participated in what Vice President Spiro Agnew called "instant analyses," which invariably included several contrarian deflators. Reports of administration actions normally ended with a skeptical "last word," a smirk and raised eyebrows from a trench-coated correspondent.

The new tone was less ideologically driven than some assumed. Although conservatives then and later saw the networks as liberal instruments, such an assertion was hardly borne out by the networks' rough treatment of President Jimmy Carter and his liberal challenger for the 1980 Democratic presidential nomination, Edward M. Kennedy. The networks, like all mainstream mass media, coveted the center. Newspeople Herbert Gans observed at NBC and CBS appeared only slightly left of center. To Gans, they had more in common with the middle-class progressives of the early 1900s than the liberal activists of the sixties and seventies. They promoted "responsible" capitalism and abhorred bureaucratic waste. Then, too, though more liberal than many of their viewers, network newspeople normally strove to be objective. According to Michael J. Robinson and Margaret A. Sheehan, though CBS was more critical of the 1980 candidates than were writers for UPI, three-fourths of that network's election reporting could be considered neutral. "The campaign reporting we watched and read," Robinson and Sheehan wrote, "stayed inside the laws and truth and fairly well inside the rules of responsible reporting."

In earlier work, Robinson had worried that the relatively more critical stance of TV newspeople had antidemocratic consequences. To Robinson and others, TV's occasionally adversarial or sneering tone toward elected officials discredited the political process for many viewers. Writing on the network anchors and commentators during the 1976 campaign, British journalist Henry Fairlie concluded, "Everything about an election is reduced by them to so miserly an estimate of human motives that there can be no sense of the sheer hopefulness of a free people when they vote." For many TV-dependent viewers, that is, those who relied only on television for information, Robinson argued in 1977, TV caused a "videomalaise." "The television news system helped to foster and to amplify the changes in our political culture—changes such as the increasing levels of cynicism, pessimism, alienation, and estrangement."

Proof of the videomalaise thesis was elusive. The strongest support came from controlled experiments in which subjects sat together in a room, monitored by a professor or research assistant, and watched an instant analysis, critical documentary, or portion of the Watergate hearings. Many of those participating in such studies then reported having less trust in government. Yet relatively few Americans consumed television news under such laboratory conditions. Many shunned informational programming altogether or gave it only partial attention. Other research, relying on surveys, undercut the videomalaise thesis. In interviews of Dane County, Wisconsin, residents, Jack M. McLeod and others found that the networks' coverage of Watergate failed to have a significant impact on voters' involvement in politics generally or on the 1974 elections. Moreover, the Wisconsin project suggested that any mass dissatisfaction with America's leadership had begun well *before* the Nixon scandals, when TV news had behaved more respectfully toward those with authority. Then, too, television's impact may have been more ephemeral than its detractors realized. In a review of studies of the 1976 televised presidential debates, David O. Sears and Steven H. Chaffee determined that TV news analysts, though anxious to announce a "winner" or to declare one of the candidates, Ford, a bumbler, only momentarily affected the decisionmaking of most voters. "The impact of the press analyses," Sears and Chaffee wrote, "appears to have been short-lived and did not make an appreciable difference in the final electoral result."

TV alone could not be blamed for the decline in participatory democracy. Political parties, which had actively promoted voting, had been declining since the early 1900s. In the nineteenth century many Americans had voted out of self-interest. Party affiliation might mean a job or canal contract; in the cities, party machines helped many struggling newcomers. However, as Michael McGerr and others have written, the growth of a nonpartisan civil service and state-run welfare agencies marginalized elections. By definition, the permanence of the modern administrative state caused some Americans to doubt that their vote really could change matters. "The increasing complexity of society," Gans observed, "encourages a centralization of functions and power that reduces the ability of individuals to affect the society through their participation." Moreover, as British political scientist Alan Ware argues in his study of the Democratic party between 1940 and 1980, suburbanization, the decline of labor unions, and growing involvement of middle-class professionals all combined to make political activism—and voting itself—less compelling for many working-class Democrats.

Lay political observers, however, increasingly assumed otherwise. Television, they had concluded, had become the main factor—for some, the only one—in deciding elections and the success of a president. Joining President Carter's staff in 1980, Lloyd Cutler was astonished at "how much television news had intruded into both the timing and substance of the policy decisions that an American president is required to make."

In many ways, such perceptions overtook reality. A November 1979 CBS special on Carter's rival, Edward M. Kennedy, received abysmal ratings. With rival networks airing the feature films *Jaws* and *MacArthur*, "Teddy" drew only 15 percent of the TV audience. Nevertheless, it was not how many as much as *who* watched the documentary that mattered. Advance word on the program had encouraged many influential journalists to view the documentary, and they were stunned by Kennedy's poor handling of an interview with Roger Mudd. These political analysts then began, in commentaries carried in newspapers and magazines across the country, to describe Kennedy in far more hostile terms. His candidacy never fully recovered, and Carter won renomination. Still, Carter could take little pleasure in besting his intraparty foe. In November the president faced the former governor of California and host of "G.E. Theater" and "Death Valley Days," Ronald Reagan. And the latter's unexpectedly lopsided victory (he carried forty-one states) seemed to be another confirmation of television's ascendancy over politics.

Alternatives to Networking

On the evening of October 28, 1980, 71 percent of those watching television viewed the only debate between the two major-party presidential candidates. Those avoiding the Carter-Reagan match switched their dials to a non-network station, usually on the UHF portion of the spectrum. The number of UHF outlets had increased in the decade. With few, if any, stations available on VHF (channels 2–13), those who sought a TV license had to obtain an assignment on UHF (channels 14–81). Although UHF remained inferior, most TV sets—92 percent in 1977—could obtain both UHF and VHF signals. With this greater potential audience, UHF stations in larger markets had become profitable enterprises by the late seventies. Advertisers contributed to UHF's success. The demand for TV time outpaced supply, forcing some would-be sponsors to turn to UHF outlets. Earnings for all UHF stations doubled between 1974 and 1978. For the first time parties competed for a UHF station allocation, and buyers began to pay large sums for upper-band licenses in the bigger cities. Nevertheless, unless the UHF station affiliated with one of the three networks, and only 36 percent had a network association in 1981, it normally ranked fourth in the ratings and showed reruns of network programs or old movies.

Some distance behind independent outlets in popularity were public broadcasting stations. Most PBS stations had been established in the sixties, and in 1979 two-thirds of them were stuck on UHF. They did not enjoy the success of their commercial UHF competitors; the most popular PBS programs might secure a 5 percent rating, or less than half of that for the least popular network show. PBS did have some programming successes. On Sunday nights, "Masterpiece Theatre" carried British-produced anthology dramas, usually costume pieces, that appealed to some of the upper middle class that in the 1950s had watched the networks' anthology dramas. They also savored "The French Chef," a cooking program hosted by Julia Child. Far more successful were the daytime children's programs, "Mr. Rogers' Neighborhood" and "Sesame Street." Both sought to rescue youngsters from the cartoon programs aired by the commercial stations. Each garnered impressive ratings and, for PBS programming, unusual familiarity. Mr. Rogers's opening song served several TV comic sketchwriters; and the peculiar appearance of rookie Detroit Tigers pitcher Mark Fidrych in 1976 caused him to be nicknamed for the "Big Bird" on "Sesame Street."

Taken as a whole, however, PBS ranked as one of the great disappointments in American television in the 1970s. Inadequate funding hampered the system severely. On a per capita basis, America spent far less on its federal network than any other developed nation; Japan, *TV Guide* reported in August 1977, spent four times as much. Lacking broad viewer support, PBS could not prod Congress into providing more funding. Congress rejected a "spectrum use" fee on TV license holders, which had been proposed in 1979 by the Carnegie Commission on Public Broadcasting. Still, the system had not been neglected: federal appropriations had increased from $10 million in 1969 to $118 million ten years later. The fault, several commentators suggested, rested largely with PBS itself. Authors of the Public Broadcasting Act of 1967, who wished to avoid the network model, namely, of a few New York–based executives determining all programming, had deliberately invested power in individual PBS stations. In yet another illustration of the law of unintended effects, different PBS outlets in larger cities vied for programming money from corporate and federal sponsors. Instead of one strong, centralized bureaucracy, PBS spawned dozens of them, preoccupied with fundraising and, as Benjamin DeMott argued, the purchase of expensive transmission equipment and office furniture, as opposed to creating programs. Of $103 million in federal funds appropriated for PBS in 1976, $13.3 million went to programming. Rather than produce shows, stations often merely imported British series. "At its most sublime moments," Carnegie Commission Chairman William J. McGill remarked in 1979, public television "is a national treasure; the problem is that the sublime moments do not come sufficiently often [and] many of them have British accents." PBS's wish not to offend potential viewers, DeMott contended in 1979, fostered an artistic timidity. "On occasion, public TV leaves an impression of energy, excitement or daring," DeMott wrote, "but it's far more often predictable and mild, even downright prim."

Then, too, by the late seventies PBS had become the virtual captive of those who put money in the hat. Potential contributors, usually upper-middle-class, would only pledge money if stations offered programs like "Masterpiece Theatre" and old films, not all of them acknowledged to be classics. WNET's telecasting of *Mother Wore Tights* enraged John J. O'Connor of the *New York Times*. "Even when first released in 1947, this Betty Grable and Dan Dailey musical was several cuts below top-quality levels," O'Connor wrote. "However *Mother Wore Tights* is now being elevated by WNET/13 to the kind of attraction that it is hoped will induce viewers to contribute $25 or more yearly to the station." Indeed, most PBS viewers, however snobbish about mainstream television, shared a middle-brow sensibility. They did not patronize avante-garde plays or films; rather, they preferred conventional dramatic forms, like the soap opera, in the British upper-class trappings of "Upstairs, Downstairs." (The vast majority of critics in the 1970s, enamored of PBS, failed to note the similarity of some BBC series to soap operas or MGM costume dramas a generation earlier.) And those who contributed money to PBS stations controlled a disproportionate part of the schedule. Although individual donations constituted 10–25 percent of a station's revenues in 1977, PBS executives regarded them as having the best growth potential, especially after a longtime patron, the Ford Foundation, withdrew support for programming. As a result, though public stations spared viewers commercials, they did have to suffer frequent one- or two-week-long fundraising events that nightly consumed all or part of the schedule. "This constant panhandling drives everyone crazy," the president of New York's WNET admitted in June 1977, "but what we raise from the public represents 25 percent of our operating funds." "Public television stations," Stephen Chapman wrote in 1979, "have replaced Alka-Seltzer and Pepsi ads with their own whiny solicitations and telethons, which are at least as obnoxious as anything on commercial television and longer-winded to boot."

In the many discussions of PBS's woes in the late seventies, Chapman was among the few to suggest that public broadcasting's original mission of providing more diversity might be better achieved through community antenna (CATV) or cable systems. The expansion of commercial television services, Chapman argued, and not governmental ones, could solve the "TV problem."

Cable television's spread had been slow and unimpressive. Broadcasters until the mid sixties considered CATV systems, common in some less populous areas whose terrain complicated TV reception, to be nothing more than an expensive means of enhancing reception. In 1965 only 2.4 percent of all TV homes had been wired to a cable system. At about the same time, however, interest in CATV among color TV set owners, a growing constituency, grew because cable improved their set's picture. Major corporations like Warner Communications and Time Inc. began to buy or start CATV systems. Yet, they soon faced unexpected local obstacles. Because special cables had to be laid for a CATV system and because of the expenses such work involved, only one firm would normally seek to serve a given community. That company needed the cooperation of local authorities. More time was then lost as individual city councils decided, with less efficiency than the FCC, which petitioner would "wire" their towns and how much of the

CATV firm's take the cities would receive. These municipal "shake-downs" continued in some larger cities, such as Milwaukee and Chicago, into the 1980s.

The FCC itself had greatly hindered CATV's growth. The commission's own research in the sixties tended to reinforce the position of commercial broadcasters that CATV, by providing three or four times as many stations from which to chose, would siphon off audiences for local outlets, especially struggling UHF operations. Mandated to protect "local expression," the FCC, beginning in 1965, promulgated cable regulations that slowed cable's diffusion in the larger markets and discouraged many early CATV investors. Time Inc. began to sell off its cable systems. To a close student of federal cable policy, Don Le Duc, the commission's concern for small-town UHF operators contradicted its expressed wish to provide viewers with more choices. Only CATV could increase the number of stations significantly. "An agency charged with the responsibility of encouraging communications service," Le Duc wrote in 1973, "now seems a primary cause of its restriction."

Gradually, cable freed itself of the most inhibiting FCC regulations and entered more American living rooms. The commission voted in 1972 to permit the use of satellites to beam signals to cable operators across the country. Begun four years later, satellite transmission proved far more efficient than the alternative microwave process. Any system with a receiving "dish" could offer a far greater array of distant signals. The first satellite user, Home Box Office (HBO), a Time Inc. service that offered recent feature films, which CATV subscribers could obtain for an extra monthly fee, suddenly had access to cable operations across the country. So did another early satellite patron, Ted Turner; his Atlanta-based WTBS became the first of several "superstations." A year later, HBO successfully challenged in federal district court the FCC's restrictive cable rules. The commission had no option but to free CATV's hand. And by the late seventies the greater number of choices on cable systems made them a necessity for more and more Americans; the percentage of TV homes with cable increased from 14.3 percent in 1975 to 27.0 percent in 1981.

The networks watched cable's diffusion with mixed feelings. In 1975, Thomas Whiteside noted, the networks had urged Congress to contain cable's growth. Although Congress had traditionally deferred to the industry, by the mid seventies more liberal senators and representatives had become chairs of the committees overseeing the communication industries, and they paid broadcast lobbyists little mind. The networks could only hope for the best.

They did not, in fact, worry too much. If anything, network executives, having found the seventies so prosperous, behaved like the crowned heads of Europe in the summer of 1914. Few thought the old order might change and their empires be lost. Superstations like WTBS were not taken seriously. They relied on sporting contests, old network programs, and even older feature films. They were not affecting the networks' audience share, or at least not enough to cause panic. Few realized that the 1980s would see cable alter all of the mass media—and end the networks' hegemony. "We were enjoying the profits," a CBS executive recalled in 1989. "But the world changed around us and we failed to notice."

THE BABEL BUILDERS   8
Television's Rivals, 1970–1990

In the 1970s the baby boomers got their revenge. The first generation raised in front of television sets entered adulthood. And those rivals to TV who had best adjusted to being an alternative service, often for the younger adult audience, prospered. Those who failed to adapt to the new adult market suffered, none more than newspaper publishers.

The Ordeals of the American Newspaper

Until the mid 1970s, newspaper owners had concerned themselves more with internal organizational difficulties than with competition from television. Most of these were overcome in the seventies. Dailies across the country had become fully automated. Union locals either had accepted the consequences or, in the case of typesetters at the *Washington Post*, among others, had been ousted from the workplace altogether. When the energy crisis of 1973–74 caused sharp increases in the cost of paper, newspapers had to raise their subscription and newsstand prices.

Most publishers convinced themselves that their product was worth the extra charge. The nation's larger dailies had finally distanced themselves collectively from a presidential administration. Perhaps never before had American newspapers revealed more about their government and, in the process, been as directly involved in newsmaking as in the early 1970s. And the experience left journalists convinced that their profession had well served the republic.

The first sign of this detachment came in June 1971, when the *New York Times* began to print excerpts from a top-secret Defense Department history of the Vietnam War. The timing was a complication. On the one hand, though the history included documents that suggested the worst about policymakers (racism toward the North Vietnamese, duplicity toward the American people) in several administrations, support for the war had already been dropping. Yet the continued presence of American troops in Vietnam made publishing the "Pentagon Papers" appear unpatriotic to some, including printers in the *Times* composition room. In an extraordinary turn of events, the Nixon administration, arguing that printing the secret history compromised national security, won an order in U.S. district court blocking the continued publication of the papers. Never before had the federal government embraced such a priori censorship against a major newspaper. "The Nixon Administration is launching a frontal assault on the First Amendment," the *St. Louis Post-Dispatch* cried. Undaunted, the *Washington Post* then began to carry materials from volumes of the secret history that the *Times* had not obtained. The U.S. Court of Appeals in the District of Columbia, however, honored a Justice Department motion to stop the *Post*. The executive branch, Judge J. Skelly Wright wrote in dissent, "has enlisted the Judiciary in the suppression of our most precious freedom." The *Boston Globe* joined the newspaper tag team by starting to excerpt the papers and then confronting Justice Department officials in federal court. Other dailies, including the once ardently anti-Communist *Los Angeles Times*, ran stories that quoted generously from the secret history. In subsequent appeals, the administration could not demonstrate that the papers' release endangered the nation. If anything, the case had the opposite effect, indicating that the federal government excessively labeled materials "top secret." By a vote of 6 to 3 the Supreme Court upheld the newspapers' right of publication. And normally conservative dailies such as the *Arizona Republic* and the *Indianapolis Star*, while critical of the newspapers that printed the secret history, hailed the court's decision.

In publishing the Pentagon Papers, longtime *New York Times* correspondent Harrison Salisbury wrote, "*The Times* was taking a quantum leap toward a new role in history." The *Times* argued in its brief to the Supreme Court that the rise of an objective press in the twentieth century created a new relationship, sanctified by the Bill of Rights, between the federal government and the fourth estate. Modern newspapers, freed of party ties, served all citizens. Although the government had "the greater power," the *Times* maintained, "the press wields the countervailing power conferred upon it by the First Amendment."

This philosophy of "countervailing power" would in time be institutionalized and affect both Democratic and Republican presidents.

In the short run, however, readers had difficulty believing that any reinvention of the press's role had taken place. Indeed, press critic Ben Bagdikian, after surveying coverage of the president in 1972, found "a retrogression in printing newsworthy information that is critical of the Administration and a notable decline in investigation of apparent wrongdoing when it is likely to anger or embarrass the White House. This, coupled with the shrewd manipulation of the media by Nixon officials, has moved the American news system closer to becoming a propaganda arm of the administration in power." Although some journalists reported individual administration actions skeptically, most accounts strove to be neutral. Presidential aides worked constantly to assure favorable coverage and harassed those who criticized the president. A consistent abrasiveness cost a reporter what access he enjoyed to administration spokesman Ronald Ziegler, who by 1972, the *Columbia Journalism Review* reported, "had become a king." During Nixon's reelection campaign, Ziegler and other aides kept reporters from the president. "You can't cover this guy," a Philadelphia correspondent complained in 1972. "They won't let you." Nixon's strategy of being a "touring emperor," David Broder wrote, largely worked. White House and campaign correspondents had little to report, Tim Crouse wrote; even *The New York Times* would not normally allow correspondents to do much more than summarize what the president said. "The press," said Crouse, "needed some new form of journalism to deal with the obscurantism and dissimulation of the White House." Then, too, an aggressive correspondent risked upsetting editors, almost all of whom still expected objective accounts. Publishers, in turn, overwhelmingly favored Nixon over the Democratic nominee, Senator George McGovern. Of the 1,054 dailies surveyed by *Editor & Publisher*, 753, or 71.4 percent, endorsed Nixon; only 56 supported McGovern. Of the newspapers that recommended a candidate, 93 percent favored the president.

Most papers at first dismissed the June 1972 break-in at Democratic National Committee offices at the Watergate complex as a minor, partisan caper. In what Bagdikian called "twinning," the wire services and most dailies routinely gave equal space to both a Democratic charge that Nixon's managers had known of the misdeed and a denial from the accused party or, more likely, its "spokesman." Twinning thus lessened the impact of the allegation. Few papers pursued the story. According to Bagdikian, of 433 correspondents based in Washington, only 14 initially investigated the Watergate "cover-up."

From July through October 1972, two *Washington Post* reporters, Bob Woodward and Carl Bernstein, most actively pursued the Watergate story. Both had been assigned to the police beat and had experience at having critical information from law enforcement officials "leaked" to them. As Edward Jay Epstein noted, neither uncovered much that would not in time have been revealed in legal proceedings. "It was not the press which exposed Watergate," Epstein wrote, "it was agencies of government itself." Woodward and Bernstein did locate bureaucrats and Nixon appointees who, resentful of the administration's handling of the affair, offered more details. Angry supporters of the president then publicly attacked the paper, while administrative operatives privately placed severe pressures on the *Post* to drop the story. Although Woodward and Bernstein, by not being on the White House beat, did not have to worry about revenge at the hands of Ziegler and his superiors, some Nixon aides engineered challenges to the renewal of the licenses for several of the *Post*'s profitable television stations. But the *Post*'s editor and publisher stood by Woodward and Bernstein.

The *Post* displayed a nonconformity rarely seen in American journalism. "For months we were out there alone on this story," a *Post* editor recalled in 1973. "What scared me was that the normal herd instincts of Washington journalism didn't seem to be operating." In fact, the *Los Angeles Times* had carried some Watergate features in October and, unlike the *Post*, never had to retract any stories. Many smaller dailies that subscribed to the *Post*'s news service ran some of the Woodward and Bernstein items, but most editors appear to have downplayed their labors. Many other papers gave the story little space. The *Chicago Tribune*, which endorsed Nixon's reelection, did not place a Watergate story on page 1 until August 27. Republican leaders had deliberately and successfully made Watergate appear to be nothing more than a partisan issue. Nixon won reelection overwhelmingly, carrying forty-nine states.

Most voters, including many of those who subscribed to papers that carried the *Post* stories, ranked Watergate well below other issues in the 1972 campaign. Ample coverage of Watergate did not at first necessarily set the "agenda" for readers; that is, it did not tell them what to think about. Relatively few Americans tracked the story intensely. For most voters, Gladys and Kurt Lang have written, Watergate was a "high threshold" issue, easy to skip because it did not directly affect them as did such "low threshold" concerns as crime or inflation. As James A. Capo notes, though an April 1973 Gallup poll showed 83 percent of those surveyed to be familiar with the Watergate story, just 31 percent agreed that it revealed corruption in the Nixon administration.

The Watergate story suddenly appeared to be a more serious matter in April 1973. Although the men who had broken into the Democratic offices had initially refused to name their employers, Federal Judge John J. Sirica persuaded one of the accused, E. Howard Hunt, to talk. He in turn revealed that members of the Nixon campaign committee and White House staff either had known of the espionage or had tried to buy his silence. With details of Hunt's meeting with Sirica leaking and then pouring out, Nixon on April 30 announced the resignation of two of his top aides and the firing of his legal counsel, John Dean. *Post* editor Ben Bradlee told his staff, "The White Hats win."

After April 1973, others in and out of the fourth estate shared in the *Post*'s glory. All of the major news organizations assigned reporters to the story. This constant, extensive coverage, Lang and Lang write, transformed an issue that had engaged a cosmopolitan minority into a "politically relevant" one for a much larger audience. Surveys indicated that fewer dismissed the scandal as a partisan matter. Televised Senate hearings that spring and summer revealed more excesses, though anti-Nixon Democrats appear to have followed the congressional proceedings and the detail elsewhere most closely. FBI agents and a special prosecutor's office unraveled more of the conspiracy. By the spring of 1974, many conservative mainstream papers had taken Nixon to task. On May 8 the *Chicago Tribune,* a decade earlier conservatives' journalistic equivalent of Napoleon's Old Guard (it would never surrender), called for Nixon's resignation or impeachment. Soon after the president released tapes of conversations implicating himself and his aides, the House Judiciary Committee approved articles of impeachment. A man who, *Esquire* had observed, enjoyed referring to his administration's "firsts" had the ignominious distinction of being the first president to resign from office.

Nixon's destruction was a heady experience for Woodward and Bernstein and an inspiration to many newspapers. "One effect of Watergate has been to make investigative reporting more fashionable than ever," a *Time* editor wrote in 1974. Woodward and Bernstein's own book-length account of their exploits, *All the President's Men,* was a bestseller; a film based on their memoir cast them in the most heroic light. All in all, Watergate, the poet Robert Penn Warren observed, had given Americans a taste for melodrama that they might never outgrow. Even *Post* publisher Katharine Graham soon after Nixon's ouster remarked, "To see conspiracy and cover-up in everything is as myopic as to believe that no conspiracy and cover-ups exists." Yet at her paper and many other large news organizations, the constant search for and emphasis on "conspiracies" and "cover-ups," sometimes reported hurriedly and sloppily, became the norm. Columnists and headline writers gave every subsequent scandal a nickname ending with "-gate." "Of all the crimes committed by President Richard Nixon and his aides," Stephen Chapman wrote in 1986, "none compares to the damage they wrought on American journalism. It brought out the prosecutor latent—and in some cases not so latent—in many reporters. The search for scandal is now synonymous with the pursuit of news." Neglected, Chapman maintained, were other more complicated items, like the budget deficit or the Middle East, which did not offer the dramatic "closure" of a conspiracy's—and conspirator's—uncloaking.

According to political scientist Samuel Huntington, this approach to reportage created "a democratic distemper." Like critics of TV news in the 1970s, Huntington saw the press's search for conspiracies and cover-ups and what he regarded as its oppositional tone contributing to a destabilizing of constitutional government. The *Times* and the *Post* now rivaled the presidency itself in authority, Huntington argued. The press in effect removed from office "a President who had been elected less than two years before by an overwhelming popular majority. No future President can or will forget that fact." The fourth estate's relatively rough treatment of Presidents Ford and Carter, their failures at leadership, and their defeats for reelection appeared to confirm Huntington's thesis. "All reporters want to have impact," a *Washington Post* reporter told *Rolling Stone* magazine in May 1987. "And all reporters want to take down the government." Only the most sustained press management and orchestration of television news permitted Ronald Reagan to enjoy his first six years in office, then once again the press's pursuit of the Iran-Contra scandal temporarily weakened his command. The news media, historian Morton Keller wrote a year later, "have come to be seen as an independent political force operating outside of the constitutional order of checks and balances."

Nevertheless, two factors kept everyday stories from being as critical as some in power and observers such as Huntington assumed. Most dailies continued to rely heavily on neutral wire service copy for national and international news. Moreover, reporters on regular beats relied on sources, and a hostile story risked the loss of daily contacts. "The first fact of American journalism," newsman Walter Karp wrote in 1989, "is its overwhelming dependence on sources, mostly official, usually powerful." Indeed, Karp continued, "sources are nearly everything; journalists are nearly nothing." Correspondents, for example, depended heavily on aides to President Reagan for stories and quotes. Yet presidential assistants carefully provided only so much "news" to reporters. A Lebanese paper, and not one with a reporter on the White

House beat, broke the Iran-Contra story. The flood of stories that followed, Mark Hertsgaard contended in his history of Reagan's press relations, "was limited, and softened, by Washington journalists' dependence on official sources."

Then, too, if the presidency had in fact been weakened in the 1970s and 1980s, Huntington and others did not give Congress sufficient credit. Huntington regarded the press and Congress essentially as partners, when in fact Congress appears to have been the major player. By the mid seventies, conservative southerners, who had chaired most congressional committees, few of whom had aspirations to national leadership, had been replaced by more aggressive, liberal colleagues, who, in turn, had given more power to subcommittee chairs. New leaders on Capitol Hill also had a larger supporting cast: the number of congressional aides more than doubled between 1973 and 1985. The expanded congressional leadership and staff then used leaks or carefully crafted commentaries to attack presidential policy. "On matters of public consequence," Karp maintained, "it is not news editors but the powerful leaders of Congress who decide what is news and how it will be played."

The presidency had also been weakened by the legacies of the Vietnam War and Watergate, which combined to subject the nation's chief executive to greater scrutiny. The presidency had lost an impression of infallibility. Journalists who had covered presidential visits overseas said as much. In the sixties such summitry had been reported relatively uncritically; in the seventies correspondents watched for missteps (literally in the case of President Ford, who had a bad knee and sometimes had trouble deplaning). After Ford's successor visited Europe in 1977, Haynes Johnson of the *Washington Post* wrote, "The tone of criticism that dominated [coverage] of Carter's trip from beginning to end is another indication of how much harder it is to perform as President these days." Kennedy's press secretary confessed to Johnson, "If Kennedy had been in office today we'd have been thrown out after six months for some of the things we did."

The decline of deference toward the presidency also owed much to the changing status of reporters for the larger papers. The Washington correspondents Leo Rosten interviewed in the mid thirties tended to come from lower-middle-class families from the Midwest and to be the products of state universities. By the seventies and eighties, studies by Stephen Hess, David H. Weaver, and G. Cleveland Wilhoit indicated, more reporters were from more affluent backgrounds, northeasterners and graduates of prestigious private colleges. "Journalism has attracted some of the best brains in the country," political scientist James David

Barber wrote in 1980. "In the colleges, very bright students insist on struggling their way into that overcrowded line of work." Not coincidentally, they had far higher self-esteem than the self-deprecating crew who labored in the late 1940s. Reporters forty years later compared themselves favorably with many, if not most, of those public officials they covered. Contrasting the press corps over the forty years he had lived in Washington, David Brinkley observed in 1982, "In terms of educational background, experience and intellectual ability, [it is] generally superior to the people it covers." Five years later, a prominent Democratic campaign adviser remarked, "We have a generation of reporters less and less likely to be in awe of the people they write about."

More established reporters enjoyed a professional's autonomy, suffering an editor's scowl and blue pencil far less frequently than previous generations (in part because cost-conscious newspapers had fewer editors). Journalists increasingly drew from each other judgments about selecting stories and deciding which issues "mattered" or "should matter" to their readers. In November 1980 Haynes Johnson complained of his colleagues' isolation and the "astonishing, almost aggressive, assurance with which many [in the press] claim to know what's on people's minds."

Such claims to omniscience were unsettling considering that reporting and especially editing remained overwhelmingly the callings of white males. According to Weaver and Wilhoit, the percentage of women who worked for dailies increased from 22.4 percent in 1971 to 34.4 percent in 1982–83. Although more women became columnists and editors, few served as managing editors. When the *Los Angeles Times* complained in December 1988 that the incoming Bush administration was recycling Elizabeth Dole as its token female Cabinet officer, a few readers noticed only one woman on the *Times*'s list of fifteen company officers, publishers, and editors. Blacks were even harder to find at newspapers. Hopes in the late sixties that newspapers would hire more African Americans were unrealized. A 1984 survey by the American Society of Newspaper Editors (ASNE) indicated that blacks held 5.8 percent of the editorial staff jobs at the nation's newspapers.

Ideologically, too, correspondents with the most influential newspapers were unrepresentative and in ways that affected reporting. America's journalistic elite frequently was more liberal, and on such issues as abortion far more liberal, than most of their readers in the 1970s. That caused the national press, David Broder noted, to ignore the rise of the religious right in that decade. It "was outside my experience and that of most of the people I talked with on the political beat." Similarly, journalists at first downplayed the antiabortion movement and the resentment in the West toward the environmental regulations by the Interior Department. They and many of their readers were left largely unprepared for the Republicans' recapture of the White House and Senate in 1980.

Some of the liberalism common to journalists in the seventies faded in the eighties. Many reporters had grown disenchanted with liberalism and its certainties. Those who joined the profession in the late seventies and early eighties had been untouched by the leftist passions that rocked numerous campuses in the late sixties. Reporting for them was simply a job, not a chance to change the world. In a survey conducted by Weaver and Wilhoit, the percentage of journalists who described themselves as being even "a little to the left" fell from 30.5 percent in 1971 to 18.3 percent in 1982–83. As earlier, conservative columnists filled more dailies' editorial pages.

A few newspaper people who appeared on TV news programs became celebrities—greatly distanced from their readers' world. Newspaper columnist George Will earned a network contract and by the late 1980s made perhaps $1 million a year. Will was one of about two dozen who gained notoriety after appearing regularly on TV talk (or more accurately, talk-and-shout) shows like "The McLaughlin Group" and began to command impressive fees as public speakers. The gulf separating such correspondents from the mass audience widened. "The world of the have-nots," a veteran correspondent admitted in 1990, "is a world we no longer know." Another commented, "Reporters seem to have lost any grasp of the frustrations of blue collar workers and the lower middle-class."

Reporters at smaller dailies bore little resemblance to their big-city counterparts. They had no agents arranging large-fee speaking appearances. Their salaries and often their reporting instincts were painfully modest, their ideology more centrist. A 1983 Gallup poll indicated that journalists who worked for smaller-circulation dailies tended to share their readers' views. Moreover, in covering officials, such reporters were far gentler than colleagues in some of the largest cities. That a governor had a drinking problem, or a Senator, touted for national office, chronic superficiality, was not considered news. Compared with their counterparts at the largest dailies, few journalists at smaller dailies manifested a great interest in political reporting. Those reporters surveyed in 1978 by Peter Clarke and Susan H. Evans disliked having to cover elections, an assignment that enjoyed little prestige at their newsrooms. Editors, like local TV news producers, were no more enthusiastic. "Elections are planned for; they are coped with," Clarke and Evans wrote. "Electoral politics is the dog beat of newsrooms."

Newspaper editors in most small and medium-sized communities similarly resisted pouring resources into inquiries that might embarrass government leaders. Often part of a community's power structure, they did not—and could not—regard themselves as watchdogs. Instead, like many of their nineteenth-century counterparts, they sought largely to "boost" their communities and deny serious divisions within them. In their study of eighty-eight Minnesota papers in the mid 1960s, Clarice N. Olien, George A. Donohue, and Phillip J. Tichenor found that the smaller the community the more likely conflict went unreported in newspapers. Moreover, many readers, they concluded, preferred to have disagreements handled personally. The press should serve "as an instrument for tension management."

In small and large markets, there were economic disincentives to investigative journalism. Assigning one or more reporters to work for an extended period absorbed too many workhours. Sending a staffer to cover the mayor's speech to the Rotary Club was far cheaper than having that reporter spend days reading city records of sewer contracts improperly given to the mayor's best friend. By the 1980s some large-city dailies, having become as indifferent to investigative journalism, began to be scooped by local TV news programs. More and more viewers saw their TV news programs fulfilling a function once exclusively handled by their newspaper.

In larger cities, the newspapers' complacency related to competitive factors. Many dailies no longer had rivals trying to scoop them. The trend toward "one-newspaper towns" that had begun in the smaller markets early in the century finally arrived in many of the largest communities in the late seventies. Advertisers singled out the circulation leader for patronage; a daily that had a 60–40 percent edge in circulation often enjoyed a 70–30 percent advantage in advertising revenues. In Washington, D.C., in early 1981 the *Star* had 34 percent of the circulation, but the *Post* received 85 percent of the advertising revenues. Economic downturns proved especially burdensome for the second-place daily, as advertising demand for newspaper space was more elastic than that for TV time, and many of those families who took two papers dropped one during tough times. The 1981–82 recession hastened the end of several of the nation's big-city papers, as did the lower inflation rate. As inflation slowed in the early eighties, publishers had more difficulty passing along stiff increases to advertisers, who quite understandably complained that other costs were falling. Owners lost millions of dollars a year trying to keep their enterprises afloat, and most gave up the ship. Newspapers that ranked third in circulation in Chicago in 1978 and Philadelphia in 1982 ceased operations. Second-place dailies scrambled to stay alive. By the late 1980s Baltimore, Buffalo, Cleveland, Columbus, Ohio, Des Moines, Duluth, Fort Worth, Hartford, Los Angeles, Louisville, Memphis, Miami, Minneapolis, Newark, New Orleans, Portland, Rockford, St. Louis, and Tampa all joined the ranks of one-newspaper communities. Elsewhere, only dual ownership or a Joint Operating Agreement kept the second daily alive.

Several studies suggested that the decline of intracity rivalries caused citizens to be less informed. In a 1973 survey, Steven H. Chaffee and Donna G. Wilson asked a sample of Wisconsin residents to list the most important issues facing their state. Those residing in two-newspaper towns offered a greater variety of problems than did people in one-newspaper areas. Peter Clarke and Eric Fredin found parallel results in a study of voters' knowledge about U.S. Senate candidates in 1974. Those in two-newspaper communities had more reasons for liking or disliking candidates than those in communities served by one newspaper.

Local ownership of newspapers also waned in the seventies and eighties. Stiff federal inheritance taxes discouraged many publishers from passing ownership to their heirs. Some families, like the Grahams, owners of the *Washington Post*, "went public," that is, offered shares on the market while retaining effective control. Other owners sold out to newspaper groups. The Gannett Company and other chains in the mid 1980s paid record prices for dailies, many of which, like the Louisville papers, had been owned by imperious families for several generations. According to John C. Busterna, the percentage of independently owned daily newspapers had fallen from 68 percent in 1960 to 30 percent in 1986. Although no one chain dominated the American newspaper industry as in Canada and Australia, or as Hearst had threatened to eighty years earlier, the twelve largest U.S. newspaper chains accounted for 47.2 percent of the total daily circulation in 1986.

The advent of absentee ownership often had unpredictable consequences for newspapers. "Locally owned" dailies were not necessarily superior to those that belonged to chains such as Knight-Ridder. A nonresident editor in search of a story was less concerned than his home-grown predecessor with the feelings of the local elite, members of which might bear the paper's scrutiny. Regardless of an owner's residence, however, an editor had to be organizationally loyal. Although newspapers owned by Knight-Ridder had long been regarded as editorially independent, an analysis of their coverage of the Gary Hart scandal implied otherwise. When a Knight-Ridder paper broke the Hart story in 1987, other newspapers in that chain gave the affair significantly more display than did newspapers controlled by other groups.

There were no memos ordering an editor to place a certain item on page 1, only a powerful organizational understanding. Other owners did impose editorial styles, formulated in Los Angeles or Sydney, that were simply inappropriate for many American communities. Assuming that Hartford's citizenry shared Angelenos' indifference to democracy's details, the *Los Angeles Times* reduced the *Courant*'s coverage of local government in favor of stories on self-help and self-gratification. Town meetings mattered to Hartford area residents yet were alien rituals to editors imported from Los Angeles.

In other cases, the new bosses, some of whom had borrowed heavily to purchase the property or planned to buy still more, insisted on high profits. This cash-flow mentality often meant editorial neglect and firing or failing to replace experienced reporters. The Thomson chain was considered among the greatest offenders. After being taken over by Thomson, one rival publisher contended in 1987, a newspaper had "smaller news holes, fewer reporters, less locally produced news, more wire news, higher paid editors fired and replaced by less experienced people, lower editorial budgets, and lower quality." While newspaper critics bewailed the shortcomings of Gannett's national daily, *USA Today*, which began publication in 1982, few noticed the deterioration of the chain's other, far less visible properties. One study of Gannett's *Idaho Statesman* indicated that between 1975 and 1985 the number of columns devoted to local news fell 28 percent. "The amount invested in news at the *Idaho Statesman* today is pitiful," a *Lewiston* (Idaho) *Tribune* columnist wrote. "The local section is lucky to have two pages of news before the classifieds start." Such attacks had no effect on Gannett, a former *Statesman* editor observed. A good cash flow impressed Wall Street, and "it's the opinion of the Gannett management that the foremost thing is to keep its stock healthy."

Gannett and other groups understood that the most desirable newspaper properties were based in the suburbs. Most who mourned the death of big-city dailies failed to note the rise of new papers in the ring of communities surrounding the old metropolitan areas. Suburbs continued to grow in the seventies and contributed to massive highway tie-ups that greatly complicated the delivery of afternoon editions. While owners contemplated putting the *Washington Star* out of its misery, rivals publishing in the District of Columbia's surrounding counties tried to keep up with growing demand. New printing technologies lessened production expenses, while smaller circulation zones kept delivery costs in line. Between 1972 and 1981 one Washington suburban publisher increased circulation from 2,000 to 138,000. In the late 1980s,

Los Angeles's second most important paper was no longer the bare-bones *Herald Examiner*, which expired in 1989, but the suburban *Daily News*. The only new entrant to the New York City newspaper market in the eighties was *Newsday*, based on suburban Long Island. By 1986, 73 metropolitan areas had about 3,500 suburban weekly or daily papers.

A change in the suburban experience in the seventies and eighties challenged the very purpose of the metropolitan daily. Most big-city papers had thrived early in the century by presenting themselves as agencies of a new urban identity. A newspaper had inculcated a sense of the city as a community for residents in very distinct neighborhoods. Covering and boosting a city often self-servingly proved to be a metropolitan paper's single greatest role. Competition from rivals in the suburbs, however, signaled an end for many to this urban orientation. Suburbs had become increasingly self-sustaining places. Smaller numbers of workers commuted to the city to work. In 1977, Jon Teaford notes, about 60 percent of the work force in Philadelphia labored in the collar communities and not the city proper. Twelve years later, Sears prepared to move its corporate headquarters from downtown Chicago to a suburban site near O'Hare Airport. Fewer suburban dwellers in Chicago and other cities even visited the older urban areas' parks, museums, and stores. The era's new cathedrals of consumption, the elaborate indoor suburban shopping malls, and not the center city department stories and specialty shops, lured consumers and bored teenagers. Recognizing such preferences, the *Orange County Register* had a mall reporter.

Most metropolitan dailies finally awakened to the suburban challenge in the 1980s. Some dropped their city identification altogether. The *Minneapolis Star Tribune* became the *Star Tribune*, the *Cleveland Plain Dealer* became the *Plain Dealer*. Many followed the *Los Angeles Times* in putting out special zoned editions with news about a specific suburban area. And by directly competing with suburban dailies for news, the metropolitan papers, Stephen Lacy argued in 1987, increased the amount of local reporting available to readers, thus effectively substituting for the loss of a second daily in the core city. "Metropolitan papers," an industry analyst wrote in 1987, "are no longer inept, vulnerable competitors of the suburban press. Not long ago they were."

The reading habits of the baby boomers provided another reason for change. As the cohort born between 1945 and 1960 entered adulthood, newspaper circulations, contrary to industry expectations, began to drop. Between 1974 and 1977 circulations fell from 63.1 million to 60.7 million. Studies suggested that adults under thirty were the least likely to read a newspaper. According to John P. Robinson, 42 percent of adults in their twenties surveyed in 1977 estimated that they read a paper, compared with 64 percent in 1967 and 75 percent in 1957.

Why were baby boomers not reading papers? One obvious explanation was television. By the time most of the baby-boom generation entered adulthood, TV news, at least on the network level, carried an air of professionalism and authority ("That's the way it is," Cronkite of CBS nightly declared at the end of each "CBS Evening News" broadcast), suggesting that newscasts were, in effect, substitutes for newspapers. Then, too, compared with previous generations, a larger percentage of women born during the baby boom not only entered but stayed in the work force and had less time for newspaper reading. The full-time homemaker had been a heavy newspaper reader. A related factor, Leo Bogart of the Newspaper Advertising Bureau suggested, was a fall in the size of individual households. Between 1940 and 1989 the average household size declined from 3.67 to 2.62 persons. No longer did so many young adults continue to live with their parents or marry early, thereby making a newspaper, which could be shared with several members of the same household, a reasonable expenditure. More young people had their own apartment and almost always had a TV set. The percentage of Americans living alone grew at a rate of 5 percent annually in the 1970s.

Anxious to reverse the trend, publishers commissioned consultants, similar to those TV stations hired. And by the late seventies and early eighties, most newspapers had reinvented themselves. The news doctors had recommended that national and international news be deemphasized in favor of features and "life style" items. The substantial coverage so many dailies had given the Watergate scandal had left many readers tired of serious news. In response, dailies reduced their diet of "hard" news. Foreign news in the country's ten largest papers, H. Brandt Ayers reported, dropped from 10.2 percent of the news hole in 1971 to 2.6 percent in 1988. Even the *New York Times* under A. M. Rosenthal launched a "Living Section," to the horror of Harrison Salisbury and other old hands at the paper. Salisbury spoke bitterly of the good gray *Times* running long features on "tofu, aerobics, and anorexia." Still, Rosenthal's compromise allowed the paper to be profitable enough to continue, between features on gourmet pizza, to be America's newspaper of record.

The news doctors encouraged newspapers to recognize their secondary status. Television and a host of unrelated factors—longer driving time to work, a commitment to jogging or strutting about health clubs, the greater likelihood that middle-class women held full-time jobs—appeared to reduce the time that many Americans had to read newspapers. To win a larger share of this time-conscious, primarily young, adult market, the consultants urged that stories be shortened. A *Milwaukee Journal* editor in 1985 spoke of redirecting his struggling daily toward the younger readers, "the skimmers and scanners." The slick summaries and graphics in *USA Today* served as a model for many smaller dailies. The more prestigious papers increasingly practiced what two critics called "trust me" journalism; that is, news stories offered less information and more analysis. Instead of telling what the president said, the mediator commented on the address and why it was delivered.

None of the doctors' prescriptions—the more analytical or shorter stories, the colored weather maps—boosted circulation. As William B. Blankenburg noted, while the number of households increased just over 40 percent between 1970 and 1988, daily circulation rose only 1 percent. The ratio of newspapers per households, Leo Bogart observed, had fallen from 111:100 in 1960 to 71:100 in 1987. Part of the decline stemmed from a drop in the number of homes that took more than one daily. Yet an increasing number no longer read even one paper. When in 1990 a Times-Mirror Center survey asked a national sample if they had looked at a newspaper the previous day, 48 percent said yes, compared with 71 percent twenty-five years earlier. For younger consumers the trend was even more disheartening: of those under age 35, 24 percent said they had read a paper the day before, compared with 52 percent in 1965. Those who continued the newspaper habit appear to have spent no more time with their papers than before, even though increases in the number of advertising pages permitted many dailies to carry more material.

Notwithstanding their declining share of the national audience, the overwhelming majority of newspapers prospered in the late 1980s. Even in a downturn, Alex S. Jones reported in 1990, newspapers had profit margins "most businesses would envy in good times." Shrinking circulations were not, in and of themselves, bad for newspaper owners. Indeed, more and more publishers in effect unconditionally gave up the mass audience to television. They instead cultivated an upper-middle- and middle-class readership desirable to advertisers. One chain newspaper executive warned against worrying about the lost readers of the seventies and eighties. "They don't read, period, and don't buy."

Periodical Specialization

With three great exceptions, periodicals accepted the new order wrought by television. By December 1972 all but one *(Reader's Digest)* of the great mass-circulation, general-interest magazines had ceased production. The *Saturday Evening Post* expired in 1969, *Look* in 1971, and *Life* a year later. None could overcome rising operating and delivery costs and falling advertiser interest. Each was revived as a monthly later in the decade, though only *Life* persisted past its initial run.

Almost all surviving periodicals followed the new axiom of magazine publishing, namely, that a magazine should appeal to a clearly defined audience. Nothing better manifested television's effect on a rival mass medium. No more could periodicals compete directly with the TV audience. Some, *Reader's Digest* and *TV Guide*, came close in their popularity. Early in 1972, *Reader's Digest* had a circulation of 18 million and, with the pass-along factor, had an estimated total audience of 42 million. *TV Guide's* circulation was 17.6 million, and its total audience was 34 million. The vast majority of periodicals, however, settled for far smaller followings.

The specialty magazine had several advantages. Subscribers, precisely because of their intense interest in *Tennis, Antiques, Trailer Life* or *Model Railroading* or in riding a *Dirt Bike*, would pay more, sometimes all, of the cost of producing the periodical. Advertisers who did buy space in specialized publications had every reason to believe that subscribers actually read them. One of *Life's* great disadvantages in the late 1960s had been the uneasy feeling on Madison Avenue that cheap subscriptions—offered to boost circulation—had created a class of readers who only skimmed the weekly. The bargain rate had figured too much in their decision to take the magazine.

The specialization strategy appeared to work. At a time when newspaper reading declined, a comparison of studies asking those surveyed whether they had read a periodical the previous day suggested that slightly more Americans (28 percent) read magazines in 1976 than in 1965–66 (25 percent). Those polled, John P. Robinson found, read specialized publications far more frequently than they did such general-interest magazines as *Time* or *Ladies Home Journal*. Similarly, the sample reported spending more time with periodicals in 1976 than in the previous decade. Most impressively for the magazine industry, younger adults, many of whom were forsaking the newspaper, shared in the overall interest in periodical reading.

Nevertheless, the greatest success story in magazine publishing violated the new rule. Begun by Time Inc. in March 1974, *People* ran numerous pictures of "personalities" in politics and, more often, mass entertainment, especially popular music. There was little text. "*People* is essentially a magazine for people who don't like to read," Nora Ephron wrote in 1975. Editors, though careful to place people identified by most of the adult population on the covers, occasionally celebrated "unknowns" and obscure people who enjoyed brief notoriety. Momentary trends such as celebrity roller-skating filled pages of a week's issue. And to the surprise (and embarrassment) of some top executives at Time Inc., *People*'s circulation rose sharply. With a circulation of 2.6 million in its tenth year, *People* had the high pass-along rate of the old *Life* and the third-highest total readership, perhaps as many as 21 million a week, of any weekly in America. Like *Life* in the 1940s and 1950s, *People* was the sort of magazine almost always found—and read—in dentists' waiting rooms and beauty and barber shops.

In plotting the magazine, Time Inc. deliberately avoided some of the problems that had hurt *Life*. By comparison, *People* was cheaply produced; it was smaller, 8" × 11" to *Life*'s 10½" × 14". Publishers limited potential production problems by running only black and white pictures (color prints might smear). And the magazine did not depend on advertisers and subscriptions for revenues. Rather than place itself at the mercy of the Postal Service, *People* offered no discounts to subscribers but instead depended on newsstand sales. Having a popular celebrity on the cover therefore greatly affected sales.

The more cosmopolitan consumer of magazines took one of the three newsmagazines, *Time, Newsweek*, or *U.S. News & World Report*. *Time* led in circulation and advertising revenues, though *Newsweek* scored the greatest circulation gains, from 2.61 million in 1970 to 3.31 million in 1988. Under new ownership in the mid eighties, *U.S. News* saw its circulation rise from 1.9 million in 1970 to 2.4 million in 1988.

Once noticeable differences between the two leading newsmagazines in layout and ideology narrowed in the seventies and eighties. Both *Time* and *Newsweek* covered Watergate extensively, with the latter, owned by the *Washington Post*, the more enthusiastic. Between June 1972 and August 1974 *Newsweek* carried some thirty-six cover stories, or about one in three, on the scandal. *Time* in November 1973 rattled its many longtime Republican readers by urging, in its first editorial in fifty years of publication, that Nixon resign. In handling other stories, as well as declaring cultural trends or trendsetters, the two periodicals increasingly resembled one another, though *Time* remained the more conservative. Herbert J. Gans, in his study of the two magazines in the 1970s, underscored their shared ideological and cultural values. Even covers came to have a redundancy. Between 1979 and 1984, William Safire noted, the newsmagazines had the same cover subject eighty-two times, or 26.3 percent of the time. Everette M. Dennis of the Gannett Center for Media Studies in 1988 found "a dulling sameness to them."

Time and *Newsweek* "marketed" themselves to those who were reaching adulthood in the seventies. To appeal to the first television-bred generation, *Time* and *Newsweek* ran more photographs and less text. Sensing a growing indifference among the young to politics after Watergate, editors included more features on entertainment figures. *Newsweek*, Peter S. Greenberg observed in 1978, ran twice as many cover stories on show-business figures in 1977 as in 1976. These normally fawning assessments cheered innumerable press agents. By the late 1970s each tried to anticipate film "blockbusters" by doing cover stories on films about to be released, like *King Kong* (1976) and *The Empire Strikes Back* (1980). Both periodicals, in the process, fecklessly became publicity arms of the moviemakers. (One of Nora Ephron's six rules to writing a newsmagazine cover story was, "Try, insofar as possible, to imitate the style of press releases.") For a filmmaker, David Thomson wrote in 1985, a *Time* "cover is one of the sesames to the new heaven." Forty years earlier, a movie actor had to achieve stardom first and then wait ten or more years before adorning a newsweekly's front. No more. The newsmagazines were competing with other magazines, most of all *People*, devoted to celebrities and with those many TV talk shows that deemed them all-important.

In the 1980s the newsmagazines went in still other directions. Although none prized reporting so much as synthesis, both *Newsweek* and *Time* did more investigative journalism and interviews with prominent newsmakers. But serious news competed with more diversions. Hall's Editorial Reports, a company that measured the content of leading periodicals, indicated that between 1980 and 1987 the percentage of space given to national affairs fell in both *Time* and *Newsweek* from 30 percent to 25 percent. Cover stories, when not on national or international news, more often concerned matters thought to be of importance to the suddenly health-conscious middle class (headaches, back pain, the new sobriety, and the hazards of salt). There were covers on ice cream, consumer catalogues, and cats. All told, the "soft" sections not only had grown but had become for much of the middle-class readership, one observer told the *New York Times* in 1988, "the respectable way to get material that's gossipy and light." A less generous Everette Dennis sensed an editorial confusion, if not desperation. "They are still not sure what they should cover."

All three magazines gradually lost their importance to the cosmopolitan consumer of news. The better-produced network newscasts of the seventies and eighties offered the short and knowing summary that the cosmopolitan news consumer had long found only in *Time*. TV, a *Vanity Fair* contributor observed in 1985, "has pre-empted the art of news digestion." The spread of news programs on cable channels in the 1980s provided instant omniscience for information-hungry Americans who forty years earlier had eagerly awaited the latest issue of *Time*. Leaders abroad who in the early sixties had taken *Time* to gain some measure of American opinion relied thirty years later on the Cable News Network. CNN's regular viewers included Cuba's Fidel Castro and Iraq's Saddam Hussein, both of whom, like enterprising Americans who "pirated" the service, paid no fees to a local cable company.

Newsmagazines suffered too with the improvement of some dailies and the greater availability of the nation's best newspapers. Most dailies by the late sixties and seventies ran the news analyses, prepared by the *New York Times*, the *Washington Post*, or another large paper, that had been the newsmagazines' specialty. "Twenty years ago," Martin Mayer wrote in 1987, "anyone writing about news in America would have had to reserve considerable space for the newsmagazines, which were more serious and wider-ranging than any but a handful of the best American papers. Today, the papers present a higher horizon and a wider focus, while the newsmagazines are more mired in Washington and more dominated by the cult of celebrity." Then, too, cosmopolitan consumers of news had more access to the country's most prestigious newspapers. The *Washington Post* began a national weekly edition in 1983. The *Wall Street Journal*, then the *New York Times*, utilized new technologies to publish daily national editions. The *Journal*'s "What's news" front-page summaries promised to tell busy business leaders what they had to know. In its detail, the *Times* offered as much as anyone could possibly want to know. Americans with the time to read and the discretionary income to take either newspaper had no fear of being underinformed, and no need to subscribe to a newsweekly.

On the Radio

In October 1975, *Time* and *Newsweek* ran the same person on their covers the same week. Although public officials occasionally scored such a coup, the subject in this instance was not a newsmaker in the traditional sense. Singer Bruce Springsteen had begun to gain popularity by combining many rock 'n' roll traditions with an energetic but grim working-class perspective of central New Jersey. State legislators in 1980 briefly weighed making his "Born to Run" the "unofficial rock theme of the State's youth." And the simultaneous long profiles of "the Boss" in *Time* and *Newsweek* had been one of many cynical attempts to capture young middle-class adults.

As the newsmagazines paid more attention to rock stars, they took themselves more seriously. John Lennon and his wife had a bedside "love-in," open to reporters, for peace. In 1971 fellow Beatle George Harrison organized a concert, which was recorded and then produced as a three-record set, with the proceeds to go to civilians suffering from the war in Bangladesh. A nine-year Internal Revenue Service audit revealed that none of the money had actually gone to the affected. Although rock musicians, mindful of Harrison's fiasco and perhaps sharing in the self-centered mood of the decade, did fewer benefits in the late seventies, more came in the eighties. Singers performed on behalf of struggling family farmers and other causes. Fifty singers and musicians participated in a 1985 album for Ethiopian famine relief and, in what one rock critic called "nauseous self-gratification," exaggerated the time and labor they put into the effort. "Give us your tired, your poor, your huddled masses yearning to breathe free," Joel McNally of the *Milwaukee Journal* wrote in 1985. "We'll play rock 'n' roll for them all night long." McNally could recall "a time when young people aspired to become rock stars to pick up girls, ride around in limousines and consume mass quantities of pharmaceuticals. Today, it is for the public service." Sting, objecting to the deforestation of the Amazon, defended his involvement. "We have access to information," he told *Time* in 1989, "and can transmit it through the media."

The publicists of various causes rarely recruited the practitioners of an antisocial rock emerging in the late 1980s. "Bigot pop" was led by the heavy metal band Guns N' Roses, whose songs attacked Asian immigrants, blacks, and homosexuals. Some black "rap" groups similarly mocked "faggots." Women fared no better. 2 Live Crew, a *Boston Globe* columnist wrote in 1990, "use[s] every hideous adjective for women."

"A bunch of sexist louts," music critic Jon Pareles of the *New York Times* wrote mockingly, "had become a threat to public decency." Bigot pop's critics, usually unknowingly, did have more support in social science. Surveys in the 1960s had suggested that adolescents frequently did not comprehend most of rock songs' innuendoes; two decades later, John P. Robinson reported, teenagers had far less difficulty with their musicians' more explicit metaphors. Some parents starting in 1985 mobilized to force the labeling of some albums as unfit for children. In 1990 an aggressive Florida police official arrested a retailer selling a 2 Live Crew album.

Such crackdowns threatened to make the offenders martyrs. "Suppression confers importance on rock songs," Pareles argued, "putting them under the spotlight and wrapping them in outlaw romance." Angry pop music critics and performers championed the offenders' cause.

British vocalist David Bowie likened rock censors to those a generation earlier who had forced the removal of the novels of Hemingway and Ray Bradbury from public libraries. "What's happening," Bowie told a Philadelphia audience, "is the thin end of a very fat wedge." "The only thing worse than Guns N' Roses," the *Economist* maintained, "is censorship."

Record companies ostentatiously, and self-servingly, defended their clients. It was a courage that the music industry had lacked in the thirties and forties, when it had routinely self-censored lyrics and performers, especially African-American groups. Music publishers and album producers then had eyed an audience of easily offended adults as well as their offspring. By the late twentieth century, however, adolescents, many of whom relished having every social and cultural value assailed in their music, constituted the recording industry's primary market. Censorship of rock performers thus threatened profits as well as civil liberties.

Rock 'n' roll was, after all, in America to stay. As in the fifties and sixties, competition among radio stations, notably those on the FM band, encouraged the form. So did the greatest patrons of rock, the pre-adults. Radio continued to provide adolescents with an escape from the family and the family viewing of television. A 1985 Nielsen study estimated that teenagers spent 27 percent less time watching television than the average American. And TV could not begin to meet the adolescent demand for rock music. There were not enough teenagers to justify placing a program aimed at rock fans in evening prime time. Series in the sixties that had featured rock musicians—"Shindig!" (ABC, 1964–66), "Hullabaloo" (NBC, 1965–66), and "The Monkees" (NBC, 1966–68)—had been unable to compete with programs that appealed to more age groups. Successful shows featuring rock stars, like "Saturday Night Live" (NBC, 1975–), appeared late in the evening, when most adults had gone to bed or had yet to return from an evening out. Beginning in 1981, adolescents and their younger siblings could view the all-music cable channel, MTV, which aired "music videos" showing performers in concert or "lip-syncing" their way through an overproduced fantasy.

The culture of adolescence had been thoroughly commodified in the seventies and eighties. Teenagers proved almost as willing as ever to purchase rock albums and tapes and, beginning in the mid eighties, expensive compact disc recordings. Their bedrooms became little entertainment centers. They decorated them with posters of rock singers, and themselves with t-shirts announcing a group's tour. By 1990 the music merchandising industry—the makers of New Kids on the Block pillowcases and the like—had become a $500 million business. Most of these consumer goods did not come cheap. And the adolescent need for discretionary income—of 16,000 high-school students surveyed in 1987, 80 percent reported working for spending money—staffed thousands of mall stores and fast-food restaurants. A paycheck allowed the purchase of a CD player or a portable AM-FM tape deck, or "boombox." Less expensive "Walkmans," small earphones attached to portable tape decks and radios, permitted users to escape parents on a family trip or traffic noise on a bike ride or jog.

As earlier, however, not all popular music was rock. The jolting lyrics an adult might hear by mistake while trying to get another station in San Diego or St. Louis could, in fact, be avoided. The largest cities had all-news stations; most listeners had access to a public broadcasting outlet. Millions of older, white Americans patronized the country sound, and country music eventually had an all-music cable station. Several country singers, like Willie Nelson, had crossover appeal. Outlets serving black communities continued to play rhythm and blues, soul, and gospel music. Many stations had an "easy listening" or "beautiful listening" format of older popular music performed by an orchestra gently and often without inspiration. Of the 505 top ten stations in the fifty largest markets, *Broadcasting* reported in September 1979, 17.7 percent had an easy-listening format.

Perhaps cultural historians, betraying their age and prejudices, paid rock too much heed. Yet easy-listening and most other formats did not have rock's spillover effects. People did not purchase Mantovani posters or wear Johnny Mathis t-shirts, though some in the 1970s could buy ones sporting Beethoven's likeness. Rock fans decorated themselves and their world with their musical idols. Rockers bought albums and tapes; the other three-fourths of the population rarely if ever visited a music store. Rock was a cultural conglomerate, most other musical preferences a corner grocery store.

Rock itself split into several directions in the seventies. Although the Beatles broke up in 1970, the British invasion continued. British vocalists Elton John and David Bowie proved to be among the decade's most popular performers. A smaller share of the popular music audience patronized American vocalists like Joni Mitchell, who mixed folk and rock. On stage with a guitar and little else, Mitchell and other singer-songwriters, Ken Tucker writes, "took great care to maintain the illusion of intimacy with their audience." The Carpenters offered a sugary and immensely popular variation of this singing sensitivity. Very much in contrast was "hard" or "progressive" rock. Its elaborately orchestrated compositions, performed at full blast, encouraged, Simon Frith noted, the purchase of still more expensive record and tape players.

Hard rock lyrics, when not pretentious ripoffs of Bob Dylan, smacked of a banal nihilism. Pink Floyd's album *The Wall* (1979), Tucker writes, spoke of the "evils of education, the perils of rock stardom, and the inhumanities of all bureaucracies."

Rock's diversity was frustrated by "format radio." As Tucker notes, FM station owners in the early seventies had begun to take their properties more seriously. Most FM outlets, especially those that played rock music, had been money losers. Yet there were indications that FM stations might become profitable, or even substantial moneymakers, through a calculated marketing strategy that drew larger numbers of listeners to the frequency. "Radio doctors" recommended rock formats based on demographic profiles of listeners; the doctors counseled stations to follow a rigid formula developed by two Metromedia outlets, WNEW-FM in New York and KMET-FM in Los Angeles. To achieve the demographics most pleasing to potential advertisers, stations should air Album Oriented Rock (AOR), which appealed to white males between the ages of thirteen and twenty-five. Ordered to follow the AOR format, FM DJs, like their AM counterparts a decade before, lost the freedom they had enjoyed to grant different, sometimes innovative, but obscure groups airtime. An individual DJ could make no exceptions; the performers tended to be white and male.

One phenomenon briefly compelled integration. In the mid 1970s, dancing at clubs or "discotheques," a sixties fad, enjoyed a revival. In 1969 and 1970 at Woodstock and elsewhere, very casually attired rock patrons had largely listened and not danced to the music. At discos, women and men dressed up and danced elaborately to performers not in the AOR mold. Black and gay groups, excluded from the rock mainstream, performed an electronically rich "disco" sound with a repetitious beat. The lyrics were sexually obvious; one disco hit was "Push, Push in the Bush." Disco also enlisted female groups and soloists. Donna Summer simulated orgasms while singing "Love to Love You Baby." As before, white performers moved in, with an Australian group, the Bee Gees, the most popular. Bee Gees singles finished second and fourth in the *Billboard* charts in 1978 and first and fourth a year later. With their help, Paramount's *Saturday Night Fever* (1978), a film about an aspiring disco dancer, was one of the decade's top-grossing films. AOR-format station managers started to receive calls from listeners demanding disco. Some impatiently switched to "all-disco" outlets available in the largest cities. "Roll over rock," sociologist Richard A. Peterson wrote in 1978, "disco is here to stay."

Some rock enthusiasts would not roll over. Fans of folk rock could not stand the elaborate attire of disco patrons and the sound's simple beat. Others could not abide the gay, female, and black dominance of the form. Emotion spilled over when the Chicago White Sox hosted "Disco Demolition Night" between games of a doubleheader in 1979. The Sox had hired an AOR station DJ to oversee the burning of thousands of disco albums. A riot ensued, and the hapless Pale Hose had to forfeit the second game. Disco died soon thereafter.

Even before disco's wake came other types of rock and new rock stars. Punk rock, which had begun in Britain, managed to outshock hard-rock fans in the brutality of its lyrics. The Sex Pistols' Sid Vicious sang "I am the Antichrist." The Pistols, Sid Vicious declared, had "finished rock and roll." But a month after murdering his girlfriend, Vicious died, in February 1979, and Punk faded away. New Wave groups like the B-52's offered a tasteful alternative. Female singers, many affected by both Punk and New Wave, rose in the charts in the early 1980s. "Male-dominated rock has increasingly gone coed," the *Wall Street Journal* observed in May 1985. Being costumed provocatively on stage and in music videos briefly brought stardom for singers like Patty Smyth of Scandal, Apollonia, and Vanity. The *Journal* called them "negligee rockers." Another, Madonna, had greater talent and far better publicists. It was hard to find a magazine rack in the late 1980s that did not have one or more periodicals with her picture gracing the cover. The nation's most popular female singer, she reportedly earned $44 million in 1988. Even more successful was a male rival for pop dominance, Michael Jackson, whose confusing sexual identity did not prevent him from being rock music's top moneymaker.

Radio management and technology in the eighties strengthened popular music's star system while enforcing a racial quota system on rock listening. Competition among rock stations made owners even more unwilling to give airtime to new and experimental groups, as well as many African-American performers. White audiences, it was assumed in many markets outside the largest cities, preferred the known and the white. MTV's managers, preoccupied with capturing for advertisers the suburban children whose parents subscribed to cable, initially shared this view. "Of the over 750 videos shown on MTV during the channel's first eighteen months," *Rolling Stone* reported in December 1983, "fewer than two dozen featured black artists." MTV would not air Jackson's elaborately produced videos until civil rights groups and his record company complained. Many radio operators avoided decisionmaking altogether by carrying weekly Top 40 reviews from Hollywood and, beginning in the mid eighties, by subscribing to the Satellite Music Network, complete with DJs.

Still, the expansion and dominance of FM constituted the greatest technical change in radio in the seventies and eighties. The number of commercial FM stations rose from 2,184 in 1970 to 3,059 in 1979. The FM boom both anticipated and reflected a dramatic increase in the number of AM-FM radios in American homes, parks and streets. Auto dealers began offering AM-FM radios as a standard feature in the mid seventies. By 1979, three-fourths of all cars had AM-FM radios. Although outnumbered by AM outlets that year, FM stations had a slightly larger total audience. While it offered a variety of formats from classical to country to easy-listening, FM by the late seventies had become the preferred frequency of rock fans. Hard rockers in particular wanted the better-quality transmission of FM. A well-run rock FM frequently led both AM and FM outlets in the most competitive big-city markets. By 1987, industry surveys suggested that only three out of every ten listeners tuned in to AM stations. AM stations fell in sponsor interest and value. In 1987 FM stations claimed $4.9 billion in advertising sales, compared with about $2 billion for all AM outlets. A year later, NBC sold its owned-and-operated AM stations; they had once been the crown jewels of the nation's most popular radio network.

AM responded to FM's rise by abandoning rock and its youthful audience altogether. Rock had never been taken up by most AM outlets, especially those serving small towns. Some had halfheartedly given a few inoffensive rock hits playing time. Nonetheless, more and more AM stations moved to a mixed format of music, talk and news, intended to appeal to adults driving to and from work. "Drive time" ratings could make or break the careers of station managers. Those AM stations with the right "program mix" and on-air personalities frequently led in fierce fights for ratings and advertisers. "Call-in" programs promised an "electronic back fence"; in truth, they permitted the often marginal and resentful members of the audience to air their grievances. "Those poor phone-besotted howlers," Russell Baker complained in August 1989. "Their cries pierce the night, burden the afternoon, make somber the sweetest morning." One hundred years after Whitman heard America singing, Baker wrote, "We can only hear America snarling." In a variation of the call-in format, stations and national syndicators offered hosts posing as experts on personal relationships or finance. Others dabbled in politics and considered themselves vital opinion leaders. Early in 1989, some were credited with the outpouring of opposition that delayed awarding Congress a huge pay raise. Baker likened them to picadors, "their task to intensify the furious callers' rage."

Radio's changing competitive environment marked a triumph of sorts for the Federal Communications Commission. The scarcity of radio services in the 1920s had been a justification for broadcast oversight by the government. Because only a small number of AM stations could serve most communities, proponents of regulation had maintained that the government had to mandate that each license holder serve all citizens. The diffusion of FM, however, eliminated this regulatory rationale. The number of stations had grown from 6,237 in 1965, when the commission started to act on FM radio's behalf, to just over 9,000 in January 1981; new FM outlets accounted for most of the increase. By the late 1970s the FCC, led by chairman Charles Ferris, named by President Carter, began to "deregulate" radio. Gradually the FCC ended requirements, some from the 1920s, that stations air newscasts and public-affairs and religious programs. "When we create a more competitive environment," Ferris said in January 1981, "we are compelled to reconsider our earlier prescriptions." Carter's successor filled the FCC with even more enthusiastic champions of deregulation.

Deregulated, many stations ended or reduced their public-affairs programming. Some broadcasters did find frequent news and weather reports attractive to their share of the audience. Others, notably those specializing in rock, dropped their newscasts, thereby reinforcing the tendency of many popular music fans to avoid reality altogether. By 1984, an AP radio network official noted, "a station with a full-time news director and a full-time newsperson is fast becoming a rarity."

Porky's in Space

Television's marginalization of moviemaking, like that of radio, had its advantages. With most adults rarely going to the movies, filmmakers could be much more realistic or exploitative about sexuality than ever before. The guardians, who earlier would have tried to shut down the exhibitor of the offending feature, had either died or were at home watching television.

No longer did Hollywood rigidly respect social conventions. The collapse of the studio system freed stars from small-minded publicists. Actors and actresses no longer had to marry. They lived together, and *People* magazine celebrated their life style. So many actresses began to have children out of wedlock in the mid eighties that columnist Ellen Goodman, no moralist, decried "the celebrity of unwed motherhood, and the unwed mother as celebrity." Goodman called for "a moratorium on heartwarming stories about the rich, the famous, the unwed, and the pregnant." No one, however, suggested that they suffer the fate of Ingrid Bergman.

In politics, too, Hollywood rewrote its history. Earlier, the movie colony participated in an industrywide blacklist of Communists and fellow travelers. But by the late 1970s, with one of the Second Red Scare's most prominent anti-Communists, Richard Nixon, in disgrace, "anti-anti-Communism" became the fashion. Films beginning with *The Front* (1976) hailed the victims of the blacklist. "Anyone [in *The Front*] who was blacklisted," John Simon contended, "was ipso facto a hell of a nice guy, manifestly superior to anyone who did not make this honor roll." Those who had cooperated with the Red hunters fell into a revisionist abyss. In 1989 Lorimar, which had purchased the old MGM offices, honored the petitions of those who insisted that a building named for actor Robert Taylor be rechristened. Taylor had been a friendly witness before the House Un-American Activities Committee.

By the 1980s the Hollywood that had once uniformly treated government officials as honorable, vital members of society had turned against them. In a minor classic science fiction film released in 1958, the police and others had worked with the hero in seeking to overcome the evil Blob. In the remake of *The Blob* twenty-eight years later, Janet Maslin noted in 1988, law enforcement personnel are of no help. Indeed, government-sponsored research is responsible for the Blob itself. An outcast motorcyclist aids the protagonist in destroying the beast. Even the hugely popular, violent and ostensibly conservative *Rambo* films, critic Andrew Sarris contended, had antistatist overtones. Rambo is constantly at odds with government bureaucrats.

The new Hollywood tone often borrowed from journalistic exposés of institutional excesses. The TV sequel to a 1963 feature film about Allied prisoners of war during World War II, *The Great Escape*, deals critically with American forces' cooperation with Nazis after the war. In the 1988 TV film, some surviving POWs after the war track down Gestapo officers who had shot escaping Allied prisoners, only to be informed by an American intelligence officer, "Nobody cares about Nazis, except how they can be used against the Russians." Since the original motion picture, Americans had learned that some in the Army had, in fact, offered such lines. "In the first version of *The Great Escape*," John O'Connor of the *New York Times* observed, "this interpretation of the American role would have been unthinkable. Now, after years of headlines about questionable deals with Nazi criminals, it becomes a passing piece of information in a television movie."

The movie colony similarly turned on the once sacred Federal Bureau of Investigation. For nearly forty years beginning in the 1930s, FBI

Director J. Edgar Hoover had carefully courted the film executives, who returned the gesture with heroic treatments of the bureau. This myth-making culminated in *The F.B.I. Story* (1959). But after the 1960s, Hollywood stopped turning out FBI agitprop. The Bureau had been embarrassed by revelations in the 1970s of Hoover's excesses, and it became another institutional target. Scriptwriters, Barbara Isenberg of the *Los Angeles Times* wrote, recast the heroes as fools. While *Mississippi Burning* (1989) grossly exaggerated the Bureau's tenacity in tracking down the murderers of civil rights activists, FBI agents bumbled their way though such 1988 releases as *Feds*, *Midnight Run*, *Married to the Mob*, and *Die Hard*.

Filmmakers frequently exaggerated rather than mirrored national attitudes toward government in the seventies and eighties. Although surveys showed a declining respect for government, screenwriters and directors as a group were to the left of the American audience. One of the new Hollywood's most honored directors, Oliver Stone, denounced America's 1989 invasion of Panama and declared, "We have a fascist security state running the country." If with more care during interviews, actors took up various causes. Most had a liberal or progressive tilt.

Although Hollywood had long been involved in politics, its participation did take on more significance in the 1980s. As the cost of campaigns rose, politicians with national ambitions found industry executives, producers, directors, screenwriters, and actors cheerful givers. Then, too, many movie stars, like rock singers, began to use their celebrity to gain access to the forum. "If my privacy is going to be invaded and I'm going to be treated as a commodity," Susan Sarandon remarked, "I might as well take advantage of it." Such politically active actors believed that a society (or news media) that awarded celebrities so much more attention would undoubtedly take seriously their opinions on the environment, infant formula, or family farming. Actresses Jessica Lange, Sissy Spacek, and Jane Fonda, after appearing in films about rural life, testified in 1985 on behalf of the family farmer, and for subsidies opposed by the Reagan administration, before a House committee. A horrified Indiana minister wrote *Time*, "I know the U.S. is truly an entertainment-crazed society. Our conscience and attitudes are no longer molded by the logic and expertise of the speaker but simply by the magnitude of the celebrity."

Republicans could not object too much. A former film star, Ronald Reagan, had taken them to the promised land. Charlton Heston, who had played Moses, had marched on Washington with civil rights activists in 1963, only to turn sharply to the right. Heston appeared in TV spots for the National Rifle Association in 1990. Republican presidential candidates had no difficulty recruiting Heston and others to appear on their behalf. "I only played the terminator," actor Arnold Schwarzenegger declared in 1988, "George Bush is the real terminator."

Ironically, film stars' greater political visibility came at a time when they entertained a smaller and less representative portion of the national audience. As John Izod and others noted, individual ticket sales had not risen between the 1960s and 1980s. Regular moviegoers tended to be better educated and more often lived in the largest cities. Many were less sentimental about American institutions. The typical theater patron was also young. Just under three-fourths of moviegoers polled in a 1972 survey for the Motion Picture Association of America were twenty-nine or younger. According to a 1985 Newspaper Advertising Bureau survey of adult film patrons, 70 percent of those who reported attending a motion picture in the previous four weeks aged eighteen to thirty-four, compared with 8 percent aged 55 and over.

Older adults, who were most likely to take offense at the filmmakers' irreverence, rarely went to the moviehouse. "There is a lot of talk in Hollywood as to what happened to *The Sound of Music* audience. I mean adults over twenty-five and children under twelve," screenwriter William Goldman wrote in 1983. "It's gone, simple as that—lost and by the wind grieved, never to come back again, locked forever with their living-room tube." The distinct audiences for films and television could be seen in theatrical releases' ratings on TV. By the 1980s, made-for-TV movies normally drew more viewers than did telecasts of feature films. ABC's TV movie "Lace" (1984) obtained better ratings than the blockbuster *Star Wars.*

The demographics of the movie audience also partly explained Hollywood's new sexuality. The percentage of films rated "R" (usually denoting nudity) by the MPAA rose from 23 percent in 1968–69 to 56 percent in 1985. The percentage of films rated "G," or for "all audiences," fell from 32 percent to 4 percent in the same period. A 1981 Newspaper Advertising Bureau poll indicated that the young adult moviegoer, aged eighteen to thirty-four, was twice as likely to want "vivid sex scenes" as the older ticket purchaser. This audience expectation of sex or the sexy affected most moviemakers. Certainly some directors dismissed the opinions of an eighteen-year-old from Edina, Minnesota, responding to a movie poll. Envying the realism of the French cinema, many filmmakers shot torrid love scenes in the name of art. Others exploited the ratings system and the women, who normally bared more, with an eye to that large audience of adolescent moviegoers.

Remakes offered one sign of this new cinematic sexuality. In the 1960 beach movie *Where the Boys Are*, the female leads "came across as innocent and incurably good-natured," Harry and Michael Medved write. "The very worst anyone could say about them is that they were 'boy crazy.'" In *Where the Boys Are '84*, "the best anyone could say about the featured femmes is that they are sex crazy, and the worst is that they are sleazy, jaded, self-indulgent tramps." They come to Florida with diaphragms and "Dave," an inflatable "Party Doll."

To be sure, sexual behavior had changed between the release of the original *Where the Boys Are* and the 1984 remake. For producers to ignore that shift would have been culturally dishonest and commercially disastrous. Undergraduates in the mid eighties did not go to Florida over spring break to work on their term papers. But had screenwriters overstated the transformation of sexual mores? Some moviemakers, perhaps betraying their own casual morality, in effect tried to deny audiences any lingering innocence about sexual relations. Then, too, many American women were insulted by frequent cinematic characterizations of them as boy toys. Like many TV program producers, rock musicians, and advertising agents, however, filmmakers could not reconcile their need to exploit women for box-office purposes with their wish to appear politically correct.

High potential profit margins caused some film producers to offend feminists. Although many teen-sex pictures failed at the box office, their relative cheapness made them a good risk. Twentieth Century Fox spent about $5 million to produce *Porky's* (1982), a very broad, R-rated comedy about Florida teenagers in the 1950s. *Porky's* enjoyed a $100 million box office worldwide. In several sequels, cast members continued to play adolescents despite the fact that they had clearly passed into adulthood. Television partly justified such foolishness for filmmakers and their accountants. Although network programs became more explicit about sex in the 1970s, the older TV audience and federal overseers kept program producers in line. TV remained a tease. Those who wanted more had to see an R-rated film.

Television also reinforced an earlier movie colony predilection for blockbusters. Possessing production values far higher than anything seen on television in the fifties and sixties, they were shot on location with state-of-the-art technology. Filmed TV series were produced live on a New York stage or in an old sound stage in Hollywood. One or more successful blockbusters would cover the losses of other releases, as well as the studio's administrative costs.

Yet the blockbuster strategy had been perilous. Like all mass entertainment entrepreneurs, motion picture executives had trouble forecasting hits. An individual film's popularity almost invariably owed more to luck and chemistry than to elaborate market surveys. When *The Sound of Music* set box-office records in 1965, motion picture companies excitedly committed themselves to more musicals. The failure of these costly ventures to break even, let alone repeat the success of *The Sound of Music*, left the studios facing angry creditors, and several, the prospect of bankruptcy. Only severe cost-cutting and asset liquidation saved the most endangered film companies.

Beginning in the mid seventies, high interest rates forced a dramatic restructuring of the movie industry. To spread the higher interest expenses, most studios in effect gave up their remaining autonomy over production. Since the late 1940s the major filmmakers had frequently split production costs and profits with independent producers. By the late seventies the film companies had further diluted their role. "Deals" were struck with different sources of capital. Columbia Pictures, for example, put forward only 60 percent of the costs of *Annie* (1982). Individual studios increasingly served as brokers or distributors.

Despite the sharing of financial risks, filmmaking remained a gamble. Production costs continued to rise. To guarantee a feature's success, deal-makers sought stars, whose agents aggressively won higher fees for their clients. Robert Redford received $6 million for appearing in *Out of Africa* (1985); Tri-Star Pictures paid Arnold Schwarzenegger $10 million to star in *Total Recall* five years later. Nonetheless, no star or his agent could assure a hit. In the eighties, industry analyst Harold Vogel estimated, up to seven out of ten features lost money for every one that broke even. Not surprisingly, with so much more at stake, running a major film company, never the most tenured of positions, became a still more unstable calling. Between 1984 and 1985 all but one of the heads of the largest film companies either were fired or resigned. The *Chicago Tribune* observed, "Executives come and go like smog alerts."

Hollywood persisted, however, in banking heavily on the big grosser. On *Variety*'s January 1980 list of the ten box-office champions of all time, only two, *The Sound of Music* and *Gone With the Wind*, had not been released in the 1970s. Even a studio that downplayed the blockbuster strategy, Paramount, produced three of the seventies' top-ten grossers, *The Godfather* (1971), *Saturday Night Fever*, and *Grease* (1978). Nor did the emphasis on the megahit lessen in the eighties. Theater owners pressed moviemakers for a sure thing. Moreover, the blockbuster strategy, when effective, strengthened the industry's oligopolistic tendencies. The largest film companies collectively produced less than a third of the films released in 1988, the *Economist* noted. Yet their features accounted for 80 percent of box-office receipts. With the playing field so uneven, Sony Corporation paid $3.4 billion for one of the biggest studios, Columbia Pictures, and then, to protect its investment, spent $500 million to hire the two producers of 1989's top grosser, *Batman.*

A variation on the blockbuster mentality was an emphasis on sequels. As expenses continued to rise, movie interests tried to protect their return by making another film based on a hit. The average production cost for a studio film, the *New York Times* reported in 1990, increased from $2.3 million in 1975 to $23.5 million fourteen years later; this did not include an average promotional expense of $7.8 million. A sequel had more appeal for outside investors. This had not always been the conventional wisdom. Until the early eighties, analysts had assumed that sequels had a limited draw. But the strong box office for *Rocky III* (1982) caused the movie colony and its financial angels to embrace the sequel with new enthusiasm. *Rocky IV* (1985) subsequently outperformed its immediate predecessor. Perhaps, some thought, years of viewing TV series, with their established setting and regular cast of characters, had conditioned some moviegoers to accept sequels. Filmmakers, a *New York Times* correspondent wrote, "see sequels as a way to lure the public with bait it has swallowed before."

The decade's most popular films shared certain characteristics. Almost all appealed primarily to younger consumers or adults who shared their children's fascination with the comic strip characters *Superman* (1978), *Batman,* and *Dick Tracy* (1990). Although most did not carry an R rating, many contained violent scenes that would offend some older adults. A TV director could not show a horse's head in a character's bed as Francis Ford Coppola did in *The Godfather.* Nor could television easily ape films like *Star Wars* (1977), which, Harold Vogel noted, utilized new and often costly computer-aided design and electronic editing and composition devices. More than ever, filmmakers used technological innovation as an advantage over television. The large screen and special sound systems enhanced special effects that TV could not or could not afford to duplicate. An attempt to imitate *Star Wars,* "Battlestar Galactica" (ABC, 1978–79), flopped.

The two greatest beneficiaries of the blockbuster strategy were Steven Spielberg and George Lucas. After Spielberg directed *Jaws* and Lucas, *Star Wars,* each became bankable properties to would-be dealmakers. Indeed, the young duo had taken over the toy store. "The industry has to a degree abdicated to directors," the *Wall Street Journal* reported in 1980. Unlike other momentarily hot directors, Spielberg and Lucas did not lose their new-found wealth on subsequent, artistically ambitious projects. They made hits. As of 1990 the two had directed or produced eight of the ten all-time leaders in theater receipts in America and Canada. Most of their projects, fantasies based on science fiction, old movies, and TV shows, benefited from their mastery of special effects. These proved easy to promote, and in what became an industry practice, children could purchase toys modeled after characters in the *Star Wars* films. Lucas's Star Wars Corporation, selling film-related books and artifacts, earned some $200 million after the release of the first feature. Mel Brooks, in his parody of the genre, *Spaceballs* (1987), showed the evil leader's bathroom having "Space Balls—The Toilet Paper." Spielberg, the *Economist* reported, earned more in 1988—$105 million—than any popular culture figure except Michael Jackson.

With Lucas and Spielberg went most of the movie colony. *Star Wars*, Gene Siskel observed in 1985, had marked a turning point in American cinema. Hollywood moved "toward subject matter that is typically escapist and juvenile." The banner box office for Spielberg's *E.T.* (1982), about a boy's befriending an extraterrestrial, strengthened the trend. "The problem with the movie industry today," Siskel wrote, "is the overwhelming number of writers, producers, packagers and studio executives who cater only to a primarily youthful 'E.T.' audience that can make a popular movie a megahit and give a mediocre movie a better chance of breaking even."

Not all feature films in the seventies and eighties played to adolescent or childhood fantasy. Even Spielberg, to his credit, tried to make movies for adults. It simply proved harder to find the financing and talent to produce a feature lacking special effects or a teenage temperament. Director Peter Yates spent some six years trying to interest a studio in *Breaking Away* (1979), a film about coming of age in small-town Indiana that, once made, proved to be a minor critical and popular success. Richard Zanuck needed four years to raise the money and produce *Driving Miss Daisy* (1989), about a Southern matron and her African-American chauffeur. "The basic ingredients of movies are action, sex, violence and stars," Zanuck admitted. *Miss Daisy* had none of those attributes, though it won the Oscar for best picture and had a healthy box office.

The motion picture industry's preoccupation with blockbusters and adolescents gave TV movies a new respectability in the 1980s. Some made-for-TV films dealt with an individual's health crisis ("the disease of the week") or familial crises, such as incest or wife-beating, that filmmakers thought too sober to appeal to the younger moviegoing audience. "Television is far more likely than any current movie to grapple with pressing realities, from domestic abuse to the homeless to AIDS," John J. O'Connor wrote in 1990. "I don't think films today are better than what's on television," director William Friedkin remarked. "Films today are directed at 12-year-olds."

The relative maturity of some TV movies had an economic explanation. Many appealed to women, who, market research suggested, had far more control over the TV set than over the selection of a feature film to see on a date. Then, too, TV producers found it easier and less expensive to show a wife setting her sleeping husband's bed afire than to mimic George Lucas and blow up a planet. That said, some made-for-TV films aspired to be spectaculars. In 1989 NBC aired a TV remake of the extravagant 1956 feature *Around the World in Eighty Days*. The ABC miniseries "War and Remembrance" cost more than the 1963 theatrical feature on the invasion of Normandy, *The Longest Day*.

Finally reconciled to television, the movie industry came to terms with pay cable companies, led by HBO. The *New York Times* estimated in January 1983 that HBO, which needed about 150 motion pictures a year, spent about $600 million for the rights to broadcast movies. Although some in the movie colony had feared that pay cable would discourage subscribers from seeing films in theaters, a boom in box-office receipts beginning in 1987 becalmed Hollywood. Three years later, Harold Vogel estimated, pay cable accounted for 8.3 percent of the movie industry's revenues.

By the late eighties the film industry hailed the newest household technology, the videocassette recorder (VCR), which could record from and play on a television set. About 70 percent of all American homes had VCRs by 1990. Millions rented cassette tapes of feature films at least once a week. "VCRs enable viewers to do something not even cable allows," Tom Shales wrote, "to program their own personal television station in the home." Small towns whose one movie theater had closed a generation earlier had at least one outlet offering films for VCRs, often more than one. By 1986, Leo Bogart noted, there were more videocassette stores (about 24,000) in the United States than moviehouses (20,000). Receipts from tape rentals that year provided filmmakers with more revenues than did theaters. For Hollywood, VCRs appeared to have won back some of the Lost Audience. The monies of millions of Americans who would not leave their dens or family rooms to go a moviehouse had been captured after all.

Or had they? Perhaps the motion picture industry was experiencing another false spring. Beginning late in 1986, VCR owners began to cut back on the number of films they rented. "Six or seven years ago," a video store executive told the *New York Times* in 1990, "people would charge in and out with armloads of movies. Now they don't have that insatiable appetite." "The first few months were heaven," a Milwaukee journalist wrote of owning a VCR. "But that was just the first few months. I've had my VCR for a year now, and the honeymoon is over." There were also indications that some VCR users rented tapes instead of attending theaters. "What is gained in one market," Harold Vogel wrote in 1990, "may be at least partially lost in another."

Income from VCR tape sales and rentals, Vogel noted, masked two pressing problems for the larger companies. In the 1980s, individual theatrical ticket sales were flat; only hikes in ticket prices made the total demand for films appear to be unprecedented. Yet the higher admission charges did not keep pace with the greater production and promotion expenses. Revenues from home video and pay cable, then, allowed profit margins to be maintained rather than boosted. "New-media revenues," Vogel argued, have been "more important as a prop than as a source of improved aggregate industry profitability."

Some foreign investors ignored such assessments. Honoring the new economic mantra of a "global economy," they envisioned a world joining the cable and home video revolutions and in need of "software." That led them to Hollywood. For all the problems besetting American filmmaking, it remained far and away the world's leading producer of motion pictures. Few other domestic enterprises could make that claim. The American advantage in so many other industries had been squandered or given away in the previous half-century. Not moviemaking. "Hollywood, unlike Detroit, has found a product that the Japanese can't improve upon," said the Roberto Croizueta, the man who sold Columbia Pictures to Sony. Would-be rulers of the "communication age" such as Sony had no choice but to take over an American studio. And at the end of 1990, foreign interests had acquired four of the country's eight largest film companies. In addition to Sony's ownership of Columbia Pictures, an Italian concern held what was left after the merger of MGM and United Artists; Australian newspaper mogul Rupert Murdoch operated Twentieth Century Fox; and Matsushita, another Japanese electronics conglomerate, had secured MCA-Universal.

Would the new owners prove any more successful than previous outsiders? Hollywood had always been the "colony" of investors, conglomerates, and film exhibitors headquartered in New York, San Francisco, and elsewhere. That said, the entry of Sony and Matsushita was intriguing. To many Americans at the end of the twentieth century, the Japanese seemed infallible business managers. But had they finally taken on too much? Had their entry been predicated on estimates of ever-growing, worldwide video revenues, which would prove unrealistic if not so much globaloney? If so, the movie colony's new and old governors in time might join AM radio station owners, newspaper circulation managers, and newsmagazine editors in cursing themselves for having to live in an age of communication.

THE SHRINKING MASS 9
Television and Mass Culture
in the 1980s

AFTER ALMOST THREE DECADES of television, political scientist Richard Neustadt observed in 1976, America had yet to have "a presidential master of the medium." The nation "had a brief precursor under Kennedy, although political conditions were not then as ripe as they are now. The medium is even more pervasive now, and its technology still more advanced. We await the potential master."

The master came four years later. For the first time in American history, voters elected as their president someone with a background in show business, former film and television actor Ronald Reagan. Unlike the lawyers and generals and technocrats who had heretofore held the office, Reagan did not need to be instructed in the ways of the home screen. Having hosted two television programs, Reagan skillfully used the medium in campaigns for governor of California and for president.

Television, many of Reagan's critics maintained, largely accounted for his success as president. Old hands had expected the new president, on coming to Washington, either to abandon his conservative agenda or to find himself frustrated, as Nixon, Ford, and Carter had been, by an "iron triangle" of opposition from special-interest groups, Congress, and the bureaucracy. When Reagan unexpectedly won a major tax cut in 1981 and rewrote the national agenda, stunned observers groped for an explanation. Presidential appeals on television, members of Congress and the press corps agreed, had turned the tide. Moreover, Reagan's TV image, which political scientist Thomas Cronin later called a mix of Mr. Rogers and John Wayne, allowed him to maintain his popularity. He became the first president to win reelection since Richard Nixon in 1972. The day after the balloting, Reagan's opponent, Walter

Mondale, blamed his overwhelming defeat on his inability to relax on television. "Image," it seemed, had triumphed over substance. Mondale could not best "the Great Communicator." "Historians can decide if Ronald Reagan was a great president," Tom Shales of the *Washington Post* wrote in October 1988, "but any TV viewer can see he has been a great leading man." "There is little question that more than any other modern politician," the *Wall Street Journal* remarked, "Mr. Reagan understands the TV medium. At times this attribute has been accorded powers less appropriate to an American President than to Merlin the Magician."

Such tributes were, like most investments of power in television, remarkably free of statistical support. They revealed much more about the commentators, namely, their aversion to Reagan's ideological mission and their simpleminded notion of TV's effects on the audience. As Elliot King and Michael Schudson later showed, journalists frequently asserted that Reagan was personally popular or enjoyed far more favor than did his policies. They virtually never carefully read polls indicating that the fortieth president, his telegenic prowess notwithstanding, had comparable or lower approval ratings than most of his immediate predecessors. Nor did surveys suggest any greater enthusiasm for him as an individual than they had for most postwar chief executives. King and Schudson found that reporters simply ignored evidence contradicting their own conclusion. "The buzz of Washington about the skills of the Great Communicator," King and Schudson wrote in 1986, "powerfully amplified by the news media, helped to establish a myth as truth."

"No Longer the Single Courthouse Square"

Those decrying the "presidential television" of the 1980s similarly overlooked the impact of cable on the national forum. Presidential television addresses in the 1970s had commanded up to 80 percent of the audience. All three networks normally honored a White House request for airtime. And viewers, most of whom were served by stations with a network association, had to watch a presidential appearance or view nothing at all. As Joe S. Foote observed, however, the diffusion of cable allowed more Americans to avoid televised presentations by their chief executive. The share of the audience that viewed Reagan's State of the Union message fell from 81 percent in 1981 to 58 percent in 1987. And Reagan's TV ratings had been declining well before the Iran-Contra scandal caused a sharp fall in the percentage of Americans who approved of his labors. "More than 25 million persons had defected to other programming during Reagan's presidency," Foote wrote. President Bush's ratings shot up when he announced U.S. air attacks on Iraq in January 1991. Yet it seemed a ghastly commentary on the information age that an American president had to begin a war to raise his audience share.

All in all, cable's spread had not promoted self-government. Some champions of CATV had hoped that cable news services and live coverage of Congress on C-SPAN would stimulate democracy by offering every American with cable expanded forums for great debates on great issues. In fact, only a small percentage advantaged themselves of such fare. In the 1980s, the highest rating for the Cable News Network (CNN), 7.4 percent, for the coverage of the 1987 rescue of a little girl trapped in a Texas well, was still below those for each of the network newscasts. Subscribers normally found cable's other, noninformational programming far more tempting. The percentage of Americans who viewed presidential debates fell. In 1980, the Nielsen Company estimated that 71 percent of all TV households watched the Reagan-Carter confrontation. Eight years later, the first joint appearance between the major party candidates drew a 38 percent share. "It's apparent," the *Washington Post* observed, "that TV is no longer the single courthouse square of American politics."

By the late 1980s, new technologies were relaxing the once tight grip the networks had on the television viewer. A majority of Americans had non-network sources of home entertainment. As more communities were wired, cable became a common staple. According to the Nielsen Company, the percentage of homes with CATV rose to 55.6 percent in May 1989. More nettlesome for the networks and advertisers was the steady diffusion of remote-control devices, which allowed those who were momentarily bored by a program or advertisement to switch channels without leaving their seats. "The rapid rise of remote-control devices," Roger Simon wrote in the *Baltimore Sun* in July 1988, "has eliminated walking to the TV set to change channels as the major form of exercise for most Americans."

Although about 70 percent of all homes had a VCR in 1990, they did not prove to be a great threat to television. VCRs did cut into the total potential audience for network programming on Friday and Saturday nights, when films were rented to placate children or impress a date. Yet owners most often used their VCRs to engage in what jargonists of new communication technologies called "time-shifting," that is, recording a network program for viewing at another time. One could record an episode of "Dallas" (CBS, 1978–91) while attending a party Friday evening, or tape a weekday soap opera while sitting or dozing through a professor's lecture.

Cable, however, together with new independent TV stations, did greatly undermine the network hegemony. More than two hundred non-network stations commenced operations in the eighties. By the mid eighties there were more television stations than newspapers. Many independent outlets beginning in 1987 became affiliates of the new Fox Network. Although Fox did not offer a full schedule, and its programs with a few exceptions had modest ratings, it combined with more popular CATV outlets, such as ESPN, WTBS, and the USA Network, to tempt viewers away from the Big Three. In the late seventies about 90 percent of all television sets in use during evening prime time were tuned to programs on the three national chains. Ten years later the three networks' share had fallen to just under 70 percent. Cable channels' percentage of the TV audience had increased from 6 percent in January 1982 to 20 percent in January 1989; the independents' had risen from 12 percent to 18 percent. The networks' share continued to drop, to 61 percent late in 1990. Not surprisingly, perhaps, public television had failed to draw more converts; 4 percent viewed PBS programs in 1982 and seven years later, PBS had an average evening prime time audience of 2.7 million out of 92.1 million homes, or 2.9 percent of all households, in 1989.

All types of network programming suffered. In an "information age," the ratings of the nightly network newscasts fell steadily. Just under half of those who used their sets watched the networks' coverage of the 1988 national party conventions. Entertainment programming also lost viewers. According to Elizabeth Jensen of the *New York Daily News*, the average rating in 1981 for a prime time program on the third-place network, then NBC, was 17.4. Eight years later, NBC had become the first-place chain, with an average program rating of 16.0.

NBC was the first network to come to terms with cable. Grant Tinker, who had replaced Fred Silverman as network president in 1981, believed that prime time had to include series that appealed to the more well-to-do viewers with cable and VCRs. Three hours of variations on "Three's Company" would no longer work. Ironically, a police drama first conceived by Silverman, "Hill Street Blues," marked the new approach to scheduling. Despite initially weak ratings, "Hill Street Blues" enjoyed the favor of many in the upper middle class (Mercedes Benz was an early sponsor), who savored the series' realism and black humor. "Hill Street" gradually developed a larger following. Tinker and his chief programmer, Brandon Tartikoff, relying on MTM Productions and MTM veterans, placed more professional dramas on the schedule. While they resembled those aired twenty years earlier, series like "St. Elsewhere" and "LA Law" possessed comic elements and humorous supporting characters that were new to the genre. With superior scripts and acting, such series, together with the detective series "Remington Steele," cultivated the middle-class cable subscriber and VCR owner marginalized by Silverman and rivals at ABC and CBS. Tinker and Tartikoff, an industry analyst observed in April 1983, "are trying to bring back viewers who had left the medium because they felt it has become trite, mindless and banal."

Tinker also displayed a patience that had not been seen in a network programmer in more than a decade. In the 1970s a network usually had canceled a series that ranked near the bottom of the Nielsens, as "Hill Street" had, after a few weeks. But Tinker had refused to drop "Hill Street" and other programs. He correctly realized that with cable cutting away at a network's normal audience, a series required more time to nurture a following.

Still, Tinker did not run his network only for those who could correctly pronounce *croissant*. NBC's first big success during his presidency was "The A-Team" (1982–87), a tongue-in-cheek action drama about a group of vigilantes led by a cigar-chomping George Peppard and his bejeweled aide-de-camp, Mr. T. Without "The A-Team"'s humor, "Miami Vice" (1984–89), another NBC hit, gave a conventional police drama the look of a long music video, an approach that, among other things, disguised consistently weak performances by the leads. Three well-cast and often well-written situation comedies—"Family Ties" (1982–89), "Cheers" (1982–93), and "Night Court" (1983–92)—helped the network as well. Another, "The Cosby Show" (1984–92), was so popular that in the years when NBC carried the World Series, the network forced major league baseball to delay the start of Thursday night contests one-half hour. Bill Cosby came before the National Pastime. He had earned NBC some $400 million, the *Chicago Tribune* reported in July 1989. That month, Diane Haithman of the *Los Angeles Times* noted, NBC had finished first in the prime time ratings for fifty-five weeks in a row, breaking the old record set by CBS in 1962–63.

ABC and CBS dropped behind NBC in the ratings. ABC had stuck too long to its 1970s comedies and action programs to retain its leadership. CBS, despite the success of lavish prime time soap operas like "Dallas," fell to third place. To promote CBS's fall 1989 schedule, what critics had dubbed "the Tiffany of the networks" began a promotional tie-in with the K-Mart chain of discount retail stores. Outlets were decorated with posters of CBS stars. "We've got to grab people," a network executive admitted in July 1989. "Look what's happened in the last ten years: independent television, cable, VCR."

All three networks, competing with unedited films on pay movie cable channels and rented tapes on cassette recorders, relaxed standards on the treatment of sex and violence. Shootouts on "Hunter" (NBC, 1984–) and "Miami Vice" began to resemble those on feature films. On one sitcom, a teenage boy worried about not having lost his virginity; on another, a high school student had an abortion. The female lead on "Moonlighting" (ABC, 1985–89) was violently raped by her costar. Such explicitness would have been unthinkable in TV series twenty or thirty years earlier, when the networks only had to worry about small-town moralists.

Cable and VCRs also affected the TV movie. The tendency of Hollywood in the seventies and eighties to produce motion pictures that appealed to only a segment of the mass audience had caused feature films to have relatively weak ratings when they were aired on the networks. The ease with which VCR owners could rent recent films or see them on pay cable further diminished theatrical pictures' appeal to TV audiences. As a result, the made-for-TV movie, which had its "world premiere" on the home screen, continued to flourish. And as in the case of their entertainment programming, cable competition encouraged the networks, in many TV films, to ignore older moral conventions. "Kicks" (ABC, 1985) dealt with a couple's preference for sex in elevators and while skydiving. NBC's fall 1988 miniseries "Favorite Son" portrayed a U.S. senator's sadomasochistic relationship. The following spring, another NBC TV movie, "Full Exposure: The Sex Tapes Scandal," cast Lisa Hartman as a district attorney investigating the death of a call girl who had specialized in whipping her clients. Hartman goes undercover and dons a leather bra and miniskirt. Monica Collins of *USA Today* called "The Sex Tapes" "exploitative and degrading on many levels." NBC, Collins wrote, should be redubbed "S & M-BC."

The network newscasts also tried to adjust to the more competitive environment, but without success. To reverse falling ratings, producers carried fewer stories from overseas and from Washington in favor of features. Comparing two months of network newscasts in 1975 and 1986, Robert M. Entman calculated that the number of stories on domestic policy dropped by 37 percent, while human-interest features increased by 50 percent. Producers also gave their programs a faster pace. The length of "sound bites," the unmediated excerpts of newsmakers, dropped steadily. The average sound bite for a major presidential candidate in 1988 was 9.8 seconds long, Kiku Adatto reported, compared with 42.3 seconds in 1968. Yet the swifter choreography and softer agenda were not working. They had new rivals. A decade earlier in many markets, viewers who turned on their sets at 5:30 or 6:30 P.M. found all three of the stations that served their community, each affiliated with a network, carrying the national newscasts. The entry of new, non-network and cable outlets in the late seventies and eighties gave these consumers more choices. And they increasingly turned to syndicated quiz programs such as "Wheel of Fortune" and "Jeopardy," which were scheduled against the newscasts on independent channels, or a rerun of "The Andy Griffith Show" on one of Ted Turner's outlets.

Local news continued to outdraw the national broadcasts. Observing people watching the news while he traveled across the country in 1984, British journalist Henry Fairlie noticed that when the national news followed the local newscast, people kept their sets on but turned down the sound. Members of Congress, if not *USA Today* profilers of network anchors, understood such routines. Being on "The NBC Nightly News," a Kansas congressman remarked in the late 1980s, "is not nearly as important to my reelection as being on the NBC affiliate in Wichita."

Another network news program suggested that the demand for information television was overestimated. ABC's "Nightline," modeled after PBS's "The MacNeil-Lehrer Report," aired at 11:30 P.M. (ET) and hosted by Ted Koppel, had impressed opinion leaders since the program's premiere in 1980. But Koppel's ratings, too, fell steadily, from 8.0 (with a 25 percent share) in 1980 to 5.8 (and a 17 percent share) in 1987. Early in 1987, *Broadcasting* reported, 52 percent of ABC's affiliates in the seventy-five largest markets either refused to clear "Nightline" or carried it later in the evening. Four years later, the St. Louis ABC affiliate dropped "Nightline" in favor of the syndicated "Arsenio Hall Show" and "The Party Machine."

The networks usually scheduled informational programming in prime time for reasons other than audience demand. Only "60 Minutes" consistently enjoyed ratings success against prime time entertainment. Although NBC and ABC continued to offer similar programs, their relative cheapness—the *New York Times* estimated in 1989 that they cost 25–50 percent less to produce than entertainment series—partly explained their appearance on the schedule. So did FCC regulations intended to encourage the airing of news programs in prime time. The 1970 Prime Time Access Rule, while limiting the networks' financial stake in entertainment programming, had placed no restrictions on informational programming. The networks could own and produce a news show, and not share the profits with a Hollywood producer. Although CBS's "48 Hours" had lower ratings and thus earned less money than entertainment series, the network did not have to split the earnings with an independent filmmaker.

Accountants assumed even more importance as each network underwent a change of ownership in the mid eighties. Capital Cities, a station chain, purchased ABC in March 1985; General Electric bought RCA nine months later. Laurence Tisch became CBS's major stockholder the following year. The new owners insisted on economies. By April 1987 each chain had eliminated some twelve hundred jobs.

The conglomeration of network television has yet to have the consequences dreaded by some Jeremiahs. Although the mass dismissals of 1986–87 were painful exercises, movingly captured in the film *Broadcast News*, the network news divisions had in fact been overstaffed. Reductions in personnel, *Electronic Media* noted in March 1987, left CBS News with more employees than it had in 1978, "when Walter Cronkite was riding high." Budgets remained twice those of a decade earlier. All in all, TV news did not become any more superficial than before.

A more serious charge, raised by Ben Bagdikian, Edward Herman, and Noam Chomsky, among others, was that as the networks and other news organizations became parts of larger corporate institutions, newspeople would lose a measure of their independence; certain stories would go unreported, for example, ones critical of General Electric by NBC News. To date, the evidence suggests that ownership or "structure," with some exceptions, does not explain the selection of or play given individual news items. Journalists and editors take no cues from distant board chairmen. Efforts to control them would invite bad publicity from rival news organizations. Then, too, the vast majority of newspeople working for a mainstream news organization like NBC simply do not share the hostility to large-scale capitalism of their more liberal monitors (nor did they before the trend to conglomeration). Those who do tend to work for alternative publications such as the *Nation*.

The more immediate problem for commercial television—cable—remained. For perhaps the first time in TV history, the market value of stations affiliated with a network fell. "Overall," a broker in station sales remarked in November 1988, "the potential growth of cash flow is being questioned."

Subgroup Culture

Would cable displace network television altogether? Would NBC, CBS, and ABC go the way of the Big Five film studios and lose their leadership in the republic of mass culture? All three networks needed to sustain profits at a time when, as the film companies well knew, the costs of entertainment programming kept rising. One option was to carry more news programming or carry cheaper entertainment shows like "America's Funniest Home Videos" (ABC, 1989–). The weakest of the three networks might have to cut back on programming or even cease operations.

Nevertheless, network television, if no longer the nation's "courthouse square" and likely to endure further viewer defections, would probably remain the first medium. Despite smaller audiences, the networks reported $9.39 billion in advertising billings in 1987 compared with $910 million for all cable program services. No one cable channel in the foreseeable future would be able to claim the networks' viewership. In the third quarter of 1987 three wrestling programs placed in the top five most popular cable series; the other two were old movie programs on Turner's WTBS. None had a higher rating than 3.6. Although all cable outlets increased their share of TV time sales, to 21 percent in September 1990, national advertisers and major producers still approached the networks first. "When you chose to buy [time on] cable," an agent told the *Wall Street Journal* in 1990, "you have to put together so many little pieces to reach the audience size you're used to when buying a network show."

That said, cable has ended the networks' dominance of the home screen. Combined, cable channels have been the most successful practitioners of the anti-network TV strategy formulated by some radio station managers in the fifties. Cable programmers sought subgroups targeted by certain advertisers—the upper-middle-class cosmopolitans viewing CNN or their children temporarily transfixed by MTV—not the mass audience.

Although social and behavioral scientists will long argue over television's effects on Americans, TV's impact on the other mass media is beyond dispute. Television's enormous appeal forced rivals to attend to the tastes of subgroups that the older mass culture had slighted. Radio and popular music were the first to seek subgroups, often adolescent ones. The fancier of classical music usually had her station, and country fans, like George Bush, had at least one outlet. Beginning in the mid fifties, the motion picture industry emphasized blockbusters that in time appealed to a minority that constituted the regular moviegoing population. The slowest to adapt to the television challenge proved to be the publishers of newspapers and magazines. Some periodicals, to be sure, capitalized early on the potential of smaller audiences. Others in the 1950s and 1960s assumed that television was only slightly more of a competitor than radio had been. By the 1970s, however, the deaths of three mass circulation magazines—*Life, Look,* and the *Saturday Evening Post*—forced publishers to rethink their place in the republic of mass culture and to devote their energies to smaller clusters of readers.

TV's fostering of cultural choice had not been forecast by some social observers. In the 1950s many American intellectuals, condemning what they regarded as an emerging "mass society," insisted that individual or group taste and aesthetic aspiration were being smothered by mass-produced entertainment. They carried a picture in their heads of soul-less consumers, watching the same television programs, humming the same tunes, paging through the same newspapers and magazines. Yet television, the supposed primary instrument of this new cultural con-formity, had in fact encouraged a diversity in all of the popular arts, and in ways unimagined by mass culture's detractors.

If television forced the other mass media to provide more choices in culture, its consequences for information services were less posi-tive. Newsmagazines, which had never, in truth, lived up to their claims of completeness, began to imitate television. Taking national news and traditional culture less seriously, they diluted what had al-ready been a weak drink. Most newspapers, belatedly recognizing TV as a deadly foe, lengthened and often trivialized their definition of news while shortening the length of stories, sometimes regardless of their significance.

Television, by its very entry onto the battlefield for audiences and ad-vertisers, had created rivalries that eventually distorted news judg-ments. TV station managers and network news producers as well as their competitors in the older mass media worried more about which stories had appeal. Information's entertainment value assumed greater precedence. The older tradition, which had weighed more heavily the "importance" of an item, was hardly infallible and could at times smack of a professional smugness. Nor was this "socially responsible" atmo-sphere found in every newsroom. Many big-city newspapers, to in-crease or maintain circulations, had long defined news as diversion. All in all, the news media's behavior before television's diffusion should not be idealized. Still, there is some evidence that many in the older news media, when operating in a less competitive atmosphere, did try to balance concerns over profitability with public service. By the late twentieth century, market forces, or, more accurately, a perception of the market, more often drove the information media. Many editors and TV news producers began to share authority with consultants, who, poring over demographic tables, suggested magazine covers, "sexy" documentary topics, or local newscast features. They instructed editors, for example, not to allow a story to "jump," that is, run beyond one page, no matter how important.

Many of the changes in newspapers in the late seventies and eighties had been based on the assumption that readers had less time for the news or attentively watched a network newscast or cable news program. Although the audience for information on TV rose markedly with the Persian Gulf crisis in 1990 and 1991, the resolution of that conflict restored former patterns of viewing less television news. Nevertheless, newspaper editors continued to believe that consumers either already knew from TV the basic elements of a story or trend or preferred to have them summarized. Newspapers mediated more and more information for readers. More and more dailies behaved, as A. J. Liebling had once complained of *Time*, like the restaurant maitre d'hotel who not only seated the patrons but ordered their meals for them.

This greater synthesis of information was to a great extent unwarranted. That Americans no longer had the hours to consume a more detailed journalism and, indeed, faced a crisis over "time management" in the 1980s became a common complaint. However, because many baby boomers had fewer or no children, leisure time, whatever the common perception, had actually increased since the 1960s. What was new was the news media, taking up what had been a newsmagazine chant, repeatedly telling Americans how busy they were and how much they needed to have information synthesized for them. Nor was it clear that an "information overload" justified a journalism of summary. Few Americans viewed cable public-affairs channels or read the nation's small number of relatively comprehensive newspapers.

In the end, Americans lived in an essentially imaginary "information age." The excessive mediation and superficiality of most dailies and TV news programs left many with the barest sense of the world about them. Viewers typically finished watching a TV news program without remembering its major points. TV electoral reportage, political scientist Eric A. R. N. Smith concluded in 1989, "was entertaining but not very informative" and had contributed nothing to Americans' political knowledge since the 1960s. A more bitter Ben Stein observed, "It's the information age and no one knows anything."

NO COUNTERVAILING 10
MOTIVES, 1991–1996

IN THE 1990s, all of America's mass media had to reckon with new competitive realities, and competition played its own tricks on longtime advocates within the federal government and the academy. Upsetting the traditional expectation, more intense rivalries for consumers and advertisers did not always result in more choices. Diversity might, in fact, decline. Intermedia battles for consumer's attention in the 1990s undermined American journalism. In the field of entertainment, more and more of the mass media pampered certain demographic subgroups while neglecting others. Meanwhile, the largest media industries tried to lessen their ever-burgeoning risks through mergers with companies in other media.

"Dinosaurs Can Still Bite Your Head Off"

For much of the established mass media—network television, motion pictures, and newspapers—the 1990s started badly, and there were ample reasons for any industry executive who thought past the next quarterly earnings report to fear that the worst was yet to come. Motion picture box-office attendance was flat, while costs for production, talent, and promotion continued to soar. Newspaper publishers saw their once-healthy profit margins narrow. Network television executives scrambled to keep more viewers from defecting to cable channels.

The Persian Gulf War of 1991 appeared to portend a new information order for the republic of mass culture. Americans had followed World War II by listening to CBS and NBC radio and by reading local papers. Twenty-five years later, they and their children depended heavily on both newspapers and network television for coverage of the Vietnam War. But with the commencement of armed hostilities in the Persian Gulf early in 1991, many Americans turned to an upstart news service on cable—CNN, the only television news organization with correspondents and a direct satellite hook-up in Baghdad when the bombs and missiles began falling on Iraq's capital. Fifty years earlier, Americans had heard CBS's Edward R. Murrow calmly report the Battle of Britain, usually from atop BBC's Broadcast House. Many of their children and grandchildren listened to CNN's Peter Arnett, John Holliman, and Bernard Shaw describe the events as they huddled in their Baghdad hotel room.

The established networks had surrendered well before Iraq's forces. Planning their coverage late in 1990, NBC, CBS, and ABC tried to do it on the cheap. All three networks, having suffered sluggish advertising sales, had been engaged in serious cost-cutting since 1987. International reportage was sharply cut; overseas bureaus were closed. In the early 1990s, a *New York Times* editor complained, "the television networks in the United States have in effect given up trying to cover overseas news on a regular basis." This shift could be witnessed during the first days of the Gulf War. Most of the best-paid network anchors and correspondents remained in New York studios, impeccably dressed and made up, talking to "experts"—ex-generals and scholars whose qualifications had been established by being quoted in the *New York Times*, the *Washington Post* and the *Los Angeles Times*.

The experts, in turn, did little to explain a region about which most Americans knew next to nothing. Despite the casting of many academics, historian Janet Steele found that network hosts avoided discussion of context. Instead, they stressed the analytical angles that both defined and delimited mainstream American journalism. They gave greatest weight to tactics and predictions ("When will the ground war begin?"), with some pop demonology ("Is Saddam insane?") tossed in as a flag-waving effect. "With one or two exceptions," Steele concluded, "there were no stories that meaningfully presented the background of the crisis."

Soon after the war broke out, the networks abandoned their studio-centered strategy, however cost-efficient, and shifted more of their resources to the Gulf itself. Even many large-market TV stations sent crews to Allied headquarters. And CNN's audiences began to shrink; some 11 million CNN converts, Tom Rosenstiel reported, switched back to one of the big three networks. CNN's ratings "bump" had been only that, a temporary spurt; when the war ended, CNN's ratings were actually lower than they had been before the conflict began. "Like George Bush," Elizabeth Kolbert of the *New York Times* wrote, "CNN never really managed to build on its gulf war success, and its ratings still rise and fall precipitately with world events." Many Americans turned to CNN in a crisis, but only then. "When some emergency happens somewhere in the world," President Clinton admitted late in 1993, "there's a 50/50 chance I can look at it on CNN quicker than I can get a report from the State Department."

In 1992 CNN and other "new media" again upset the traditional three-network monopoly on national news. As in planning the Gulf War coverage, the networks had decided to cut back their presidential election coverage (they had expected President Bush to win reelection easily). More reportage was studio-centered, with correspondents sitting in Washington and New York analyzing polls and strategy and talking to Washington-based campaign consultants. During the primaries, fewer reporters followed the candidates. The mediation of political news only increased, reducing each candidate's sound bite to new lows. Finally, responding to the excesses of the 1988 campaign, the networks inaugurated critical assessments of each candidate's political advertising. (This last innovation was carried out with such tendentiousness that it may have had the unintended effect of discouraging some voters from supporting *anyone*.) All in all, information-hungry voters seeking details about individual candidates and their positions had to turn to CNN, CSPAN, and other cable outlets. "If they want more," CBS chairman Laurence Tisch remarked, "they can go to CNN." Four or eight years earlier, Tisch's dismissive approach might have worked. With the economy then strong, most voters had followed politics at a distance; campaigns had not mattered. But the recession of 1990–92 had a greater impact on the middle class than had previous postwar downturns, and the middle class was much more likely to vote than were the poor. Not surprisingly, then, the networks' reduction in campaign coverage drove many voters to switch to other sources.

Several candidates quickly recognized the appeal of non-network television. One, journalist Patrick J. Buchanan, had gained national prominence by cohosting a CNN talk-and-shout program, "Crossfire." He managed to embarrass President Bush in the early 1992 GOP primaries. More incredibly, Texas billionaire Ross Perot used CNN's "Larry King Live" as a springboard to his independent candidacy. When campaign managers showed Perot a pricey projected advertising budget, he replied, "Why do I want to pay for this, when I can go on Larry King?" Mindful of Perot's appeal, NBC's "Today" reversed a decades-long trend and expanded the length of his interviews; the ratings actually improved. In the fall, Perot spent millions of dollars on half-hour "infomercials." They were dull television, reminiscent of off-hours

1950s fillers. Perot was decidedly untelegenic. Michael Kelly later called him "a deeply unattractive campaigner. He talked funny, he was short and homely." When Perot spoke of his pet issue, the deficit, he sounded like "the crazy aunt in the basement." But Aunt Ross proved to be an effective television pitchman. An *Advertising Age* reviewer dubbed the programs "as primitive as can be. Also brilliant." Perot had something to say, and his infomercials garnered good ratings. On election day, his TV-dependent candidacy attracted just under 19 percent of the vote, the highest for a third-party candidate since 1912.

No one better understood the new or alternative media and their potential than did Governor Bill Clinton of Arkansas and his advisers. Early in 1992, the Clinton campaign had been hammered by accusations of the candidate's marital infidelity. The governor and his circle cleverly responded by contending that the issues, especially the sluggish economy, mattered more than tabloid-generated charges concerning the governor's character. Clinton's people noted that reporters probed him incessantly about his marriage, while the voters he encountered asked about him about the issues. "Demand for political information—especially a specific plan for the economy—was high," wrote campaign aides James Carville and Paul Begala. "When the traditional media were unable or unwilling to give Bill Clinton time to discuss these issues, we turned elsewhere." "Elsewhere" included local TV news and talk radio programs. As in the case of Perot, the networks played catch-up. Clinton appeared for two hours on CBS's "This Morning" and the program's ratings ran 10 percent above average. "Today" allotted him two hours and allowed twenty-seven call-in questions. On some occasions, Clinton sought merely to cast himself in a more favorable light, the policy wonk as good ol' boy. Running third in the polls in June, he appeared on the syndicated "Arsenio Hall Show" sporting sunglasses and playing the saxophone. To many observers, this appearance turned his campaign around. Clinton continued to use alternative media, notably MTV, to advance his candidacy. A befuddled George Bush eventually (and very reluctantly) appeared on MTV and twice on "Larry King." But it was too little, too obvious, and much too late.

The alternative media strategy had its advantages, both for Clinton and for many voters. Compared to their snarling counterparts at ABC, CBS, and NBC, cable newspeople like Larry King and MTV's Tabitha Soren, as well as local TV anchors and talk-show hosts, were uncritical if not supportive interrogators. Larry King, wrote Maureen Dowd, "is the resort area of American journalism, the media's Palm Springs, where politicians and other figures of controversy or celebrity can go to unwind, kick back and reflect on what a wacky and wonderful trip it has been." That said, the questions from audiences or callers, several media monitors noted, were more likely to concern issues than those posed by journalists who mocked King.

Clinton's victory appeared to suggest that in the 1990s, mastery of the alternative media could assure effective national leadership. At first, Clinton largely ignored the White House correspondents, cutting their access and hosting fewer news conferences, in favor of interviews with individual TV station anchors and televised town meetings, including several on MTV and Larry King. "You know why I can stiff you on the press conferences?" the president asked a group of Washington reporters. "Because Larry King liberated me by giving me to the American people directly." "'Larry King,'" Sidney Blumenthal wrote early in 1993, "has become Clinton's metaphor for the diminishing influence of the Big Media." Clinton's strategy, Blumenthal wrote admiringly, "was not really possible until the world of three-network media became anachronistic." They and the country's largest newspapers were mass media dinosaurs. The president's director of media affairs dreamed of creating a Clinton cable channel, "BC-TV."

Clinton and many others soon realized that the alternative media strategy would not work. The alternative remained just that; they could not substitute for the mainstream. Just under a third of all U.S. homes did not subscribe to cable. The ratings of the networks' nightly newscasts had fallen; according to a Times Mirror Center for the People and the Press survey, the percentage of Americans who said they regularly watched the network newscasts dropped from 71 percent in 1987 to 42 percent in 1996. Yet viewers for any one of the networks dwarfed the average audience for "Larry King" or any other CNN program. "On a good night," wrote one show business correspondent late in 1993, "King's audience [represented] about 1 percent of the nation's TV-viewing households." When King interviewed both the president and vice president in mid-1995, he secured a 1.6 rating—under a fifth of the rating that evening for ABC's "World News Tonight." In 1994, CNN ranked sixth in the cable ratings—behind, among others, the Cartoon Network.

Then, too, newspapers continued to have a disproportionate effect on other news organizations. Circulations may have been flat, but the nation's largest dailies still covered the federal government in greater detail than any broadcast service. In Washington, Stephen Hess wrote in 1994, "news is manufactured mainly by print journalists, who far outnumber those working for the electronic media." Broadcast news remained largely dependent on the *New York Times* and, to a lesser extent, the *Washington Post*, in selecting stories to include in their newscasts. "You can get elected from outside the media mainstream, and the 1992 election may even have set a permanent precedent," observed Frank Mankiewicz, a veteran campaign aide and journalist. "But it is just as difficult to govern without the Establishment Media as it has ever been." To Clinton's fury, the establishment media initially reported his presidency in a largely critical tone. As Jonathan Alter remarked, "Dinosaurs can still bite your head off." "However you feel about Bill Clinton," Adam Gopnik wrote, "no other American President since the eighteen-seventies has been hung up by his thumbs so soon, and left there to hang for so long." An annoyed president cried late in 1993, "I have fought more damn battles here for more things than any president has in twenty years, and [I] have not gotten one damn bit of credit from the knee-jerk liberal press, and I am sick and tired of it."

No mainstream news medium administered more pain than some elements of the alternative media. Nationally syndicated radio talk show hosts gave the president no honeymoon, only hell. "More and more of our citizens," the president complained in his 1995 State of the Union address, "now get most of their information in very negative and aggressive ways." Earlier, the first lady had blamed the "overly information-loaded society" for the defeat of her health care bill. In fact, the explosion of radio and cable talk shows, personal computer internet messages, fax machines, and the like was transforming Washington into a modern Babel. "This cacophony of voices is deafening," Debra Goldman of *AdWeek* wrote in August 1994. "The cumulative effect," observed the *New York Times*'s Michael Wines, "has been to turn a somewhat slow and contemplative system into something more like a 500-channel democracy, with the clicker grasped tightly in the hands of the electorate."

Some political scientists and journalists insisted on faulting the messengers for a new and destructive political culture. A new "attack journalism" had emerged in the 1970s and 1980s and was continuing to flourish in the 1990s. "While there is probably less genuine corruption in American politics than ever before," Jacob Weisberg of *New York* magazine wrote in April 1994, "more careers are destroyed by revelations of unseemly behavior. There's no more cash on the floor of Congress. But politicians can be stopped dead in their tracks by memberships in discriminatory clubs, nanny violations, rubber checks, boorish comments at work, boozing, adultery, you name it. Peccadilloes in the literal sense—tiny sins—have become intolerable lapses." "The reporter used to gain status by dining with his subjects," Gopnik observed. "Now he gains status by dining on them."

To a large extent, much of the problem with contemporary journalism related to an outwardly manifest adherence to objectivity. As Thomas E.

Patterson noted, to assess the merits of a federal health care proposal might force a reporter to reveal an ideological bias. So might a careful review of a candidate's position on balancing the budget. It was better to fall back on appearances and the tactical: complain about the enormous time a president took to name an attorney general or Supreme Court justice, or ask a candidate if he would win the next crucial primary. An early 1995 "CBS Evening News" assessment of the Clinton presidency eschewed mentioning "any substantive aspect of his proposals or plans in office," James Fallows wrote. "Its subject was exclusively Clinton's 'handling' of his office—his 'difficulty making decisions,' his 'waffling' at crucial moments." Later in the year Fallows watched CNN's Judy Woodruff interview New Jersey Senator Bill Bradley shortly after he had announced his retirement. "Every answer Bradley gave concerned the substance of national problems that concerned him. Every question she asked was about short-term political tactics." A study of the leading news media found that most accounts of the debate over Clinton's elaborate health care plan stressed which side was winning—and not the merits of the plan itself. John McLaughlin routinely ended his thirty-minute talk-and-shout program by questioning his panelists, "Who won the week?" There was no ideology in such a "horse race" concentration. It also betrayed a professional indifference toward complex public issues. "A lot of reporters dislike policy making, they dislike the process of it," observed Stephen Hess, "and so they like to do the sport of it."

Such "who's ahead" treatments were increasingly overladen with a cynicism that appeared born not of experience, but of immaturity. Indeed, television reporters especially cast themselves too often as the children in 1970s and 1980s sit-coms, knowingly smarting off to parental authority. "Much of journalism today is really a form of institutionalized early adolescence," Steven Stark wrote in 1994. Reporters took enormous pleasure in inflating politicians' inconsistencies, as if America's greatest leaders had never changed their minds on any matter of import in the past. For the press, Stark argued, "the cardinal sin in American politics today is not to run up a deficit or lose an important court case but to change one's mind: like a fourteen-year-old, the press always takes a switch as evidence of hypocrisy." Patterson decried reporting that "assumes that politicians are manipulators and liars."

Many, including some within the fourth estate itself, feared that cynicism was adversely affecting both the quality of information available to Americans and even their very belief in democratic institutions. Patterson and others noted that journalists' more hostile approach coincided with a nationwide loss of faith in politicians and government. "Critics are beginning to fear that cynical press coverage is helping to create a nation of cynics," journalist Paul Starobin contended. Cynicism certainly restricted the news agenda. Reporters, Starobin observed, largely dismissed the Republican "Contract with America" during the 1994 campaign as a public relations stunt. Voters were thus left largely unaware of the Republican blueprint once the GOP won control of Congress for the first time in forty years. Several months later, 60 percent of those surveyed by Times Mirror agreed that journalists focused too much "on the misdeeds and failings of public figures."

The flood of new news organizations and talk shows only worsened matters. Facing marginalization in a more crowded media environment, newsmagazines adopted a tone James Fallows likened to the most biting sports commentary. As one newsmagazine writer admitted, "Pieces that are harsh and snide and critical and quizzical always do better and get bigger play and attract more attention." The increased competition had other negative consequences. In the 1970s, many editors and producers had normally delayed or refused to report stories without reliable sources; in some cases, a personal scandal went unpublicized because an editor considered its release to be unrelated to the public—as opposed to prurient—interest. Such caution became markedly less common in the 1980s and 1990s. A charge, widely covered early in 1992, that Bill Clinton had indulged in extramarital affairs, originated with a supermarket tabloid. "Reporters dove for it like unreconstructed drunks diving for a jigger of whisky," wrote two of his aides. "Sober reporters who had once been content to record the candidate's views on budget-balancing," *Newsweek* admitted, "now wanted statements on his sex life." What had ended the traditional editorial discretion? One factor was the adolescent mentality of many reporters. "Political coverage tends to focus on gaffes, girlfriends, and youthful indiscretions while far more important, 'adult' issues go underreported," Steven Stark complained. Moreover, as Larry Sabato found, the new, more intense news-reporting environment of the 1990s all but forced the hands of editors and producers. The possibilities of being scooped were too many and too immediate, even if it meant "bottom-feeding," that is, reporting items from a scandal sheet. David Shaw, the media critic for the *Los Angeles Times*, admonished his peers not "to allow the men and women who publish supermarket tabloids and who broadcast tabloid television shows to distort our news judg-ment. And that's happening more and more with each passing day." Former *New York Times* editor A. M. Rosenthal later wrote of the "exploding movement in newspapers, magazines and TV toward the specialized form of garbage collection known as gossip. The 'Gee, Dad, they did it first' Syndrome—picking up damaging, unsubstantiated stories from [the] gutter press and TV."

Stressing scandal or tactics had another advantage. It was much less boring, especially on television, than a thoughtful review of public policy. And this dread of dullness was the bane of America's news cultures, with few exceptions, at the end of the twentieth century. In the age of the remote control, only a handful of news organizations found anything but the devil in the details. "We need to delve more deeply into issues," one TV station general manager admitted late in 1993. "When we do, nobody listens and nobody watches."

It became tempting as well for mainstream news media to attend excessively to stories which earlier would have been relatively under-covered. These were "sensational" items. In 1994 two stories stood out. First, Olympic skater Tonya Harding tried to take out one of her rivals, Nancy Kerrigan. Later in the year, former professional football player O. J. Simpson was arrested for two brutal slayings. The networks, especially the prime-time news magazines and interview programs, as well as many daily papers and newsmagazines, awarded enormous space to the Harding and Simpson stories.

None commanded more attention than Simpson's trial. In many ways Simpson was the product of the modern celebrity cultural machinery. After an outstanding football career, Simpson achieved even greater success in show business, not as a leading film or TV performer, but as a spokesperson for a rental car agency and an on-air personality on network football telecasts. An African American, Simpson appeared relaxed and likeable to whites. Two historians had referred to his "good-natured decency." That long-cultivated image made all the more grip-ping the charges that he had brutally murdered his ex-wife Nicole and another man, both white. Although the plots to countless TV crime dramas had often involved celebrity crimes, Hollywood personalities were in fact rarely accused of much more than drunk driving, speeding, or boorishness. It should not have been astonishing, then, that millions of Americans were drawn to the Simpson story. Reality mimicked prime time. When CNN covered Simpson's flight from the police, the network almost matched its Gulf War ratings. Between June 1994 and April 1995, CNN's audiences increased fivefold when airing Simpson-related pro-ceedings. (As before, CNN could not sustain its popularity once the trial ended.) With about a quarter of America's population regularly viewing the live coverage of the trial, the ratings for afternoon soap operas and the nightly network newscasts fell. More Americans could identify the judge in the trial than the new and controversial Speaker of the House. One law school dean called the American people "the thirteenth juror." Nevertheless, too much can be made of the Simpson coverage and its audience. The spectacle came to tire many, if not most, Americans.

Tellingly, jokes and sketches involving the case helped Jay Leno of NBC's "Tonight Show" seize first place in the late-night ratings for the first time since he became host in 1992. Still, the conclusion proved to be a national media experience; Americans rushed to TVs much as they had done to follow the first moon landing or the murder of John Kennedy. When the jury announced its verdict, 154 million Americans were watching—70.6 percent more than viewed the second-highest rated TV event of the year, Super Bowl XXIX.

The massive resources poured into the Simpson story infuriated professional evaluators of the press, who as usual overlooked the larger reasons behind the tabloidization of the news. One, already noted, was the greatly increased competition. A network that downplayed the Simpson proceedings risked losing viewers to CNN and other news organizations that heavily covered the trial. To a large measure, the established news media had lost their traditional gate-keeping role. Then, too, the end of the cold war opened up the news agenda. The great and dangerous rivalry with the Soviet Union had ended. Perhaps more than anything else, the cold war had ultimately accounted for the "responsible" behavior of the nation's larger newspapers and broadcast networks. With the threat of a third world war removed, what were the news media to cover? There were important international stories, to be sure, but none directly involved national security. A similar shift had occurred in the 1920s, when the United States ostensibly retreated into isolationism; then the nation's newspapers had channeled their energies into covering spectacular crimes and stunts like Charles A. Lindbergh's flight across the Atlantic.

As Americans again retreated inward during the 1990s, most mainstream news media sharply reduced their international news coverage. CBS, which at one time had maintained twenty overseas bureaus, had four in 1994. Between 1984 and 1994, Tom Rosenstiel reported, the number of stories and amount of time devoted to international news on the network evening newscasts fell by half. "'Foreign news' is considered an expletive best deleted in most local station newsrooms and has fallen from favor even among networks," Dan Rather remarked. To a certain extent, the networks and other news organizations were simply following (and, in the process, hardening) public opinion. "Speak of world affairs and most eyes glaze over," Max Frankel of the *New York Times* admitted in early 1995. "Americans are again withdrawing into their shell, trying to hide from the strange and the distant."

Despite occasional claims to the contrary, television had always been better at providing entertainment than information. The networks' great advantage in the 1990s continued to be in telecasting the most popular entertainment programs. And there were signs that the networks, together with Fox, had found a means of holding off cable. Between the 1976–77 and 1991–92 seasons, the combined network share of evening prime time had dropped from 93 percent to 63 percent. For the next two seasons, however, the networks' share remained relatively constant.

The turnabout had several explanations, beginning with the feminization of the network TV audience. Network schedulers had come to recognize that a majority of adult television viewers were women, about 6.5 million more per evening in 1995. The female plurality increased as cable sports channels (and, to a much smaller extent, internet use on personal computers) siphoned off some male viewers. The female majority encouraged networks to air more series such as "Sisters" (NBC, 1991–96), "Dr. Quinn" (CBS, 1993–), "Ellen" (ABC, 1994–) and made-for-TV movies appealing to women. The percentage of female major characters in prime-time series gradually rose. In 1994, CBS transformed the Winter Olympics into what the *Boston Globe*'s John Powers termed a "global soap opera." The network framed the competitions as so many human interest stories: the skater with a blind mother, another whose sister had been killed by leukemia, and "Little Orphan Oksana" of the Ukraine. Overproduced features about these and other Olympians dominated CBS's coverage, sometimes at the expense of the events themselves. Nevertheless, CBS earned the ratings gold.

The networks also self-consciously pursued audiences by race and age. A spate of hip 'n' single situation comedies crowded the schedule. The casts were increasingly segregated, with Fox carrying shows that featured all-black ensembles, and the other networks reverting to a sit-com apartheid. "It's a trend in television towards a sort of separatism," complained the creator of Fox's "Martin" (1992–). The enormous popularity of NBC's "Friends" (1994–), about a group of young white singles who sit around drinking flavored coffee all day, received much of the blame. The series "spark[ed] a white bread wave of sitcom clones about young Caucasian chuckleheads," wrote one TV industry reporter. "Any more 'Friends' on network TV," cracked another, "and you could organize a Quaker meeting group."

These and other shows ignored old taboos about discussions of sexuality. "N.Y.P.D. Blue" (1993–) led the way, using explicit language and nudity heretofore disallowed by network censors. Organized protests seemed prudish and proved ineffectual, until sit-coms airing earlier in the evening, when many more children watched TV, began to share the same creative freedom. Characters on "Mad About You" (NBC, 1992–) spoke of having sex on the kitchen table, or of simply having great sex. "Friends" characters referred to making love on a copying machine. And words such as "bitch" and "hooters" came into use, as well as references to foreplay and condoms. One study indicated that the use of profanity on network programs aired between 8 and 9 p.m. (EST) had doubled between 1990 and 1994. Rick Du Brow of the *Los Angeles Times* concluded in mid-1995 that "at the moment, sexy material—or at least what TV regards as sexy, although many would consider it juvenile—is clearly considered a priority at the networks, even in the early prime-time hours once reserved for more innocent family viewing." After twenty-five years of innocently teasing viewers about sex, wrote a Milwaukee TV critic in 1995, "the networks have discovered the sexual revolution."

Critics of the new explicitness frequently compared 1990s shows to ones aired ten years earlier or even to older chestnuts enjoying new life on cable's Nickelodeon channel. Yet the networks were not just competing with one another, as in the 1970s or 1950s, while trying to placate the Baptist preachers who occasionally sent them nasty postcards. CBS, NBC, ABC, and Fox had to abandon programming standards, some dating from TV's very start, out of fear of the remote control. Most viewers had choices that were not available to them or their parents a generation earlier. Network shows, their producers and schedulers averred, could succeed only if they seemed up-to-the-minute, smart, and sexy, not colorized versions of "The Donna Reed Show" (ABC, 1958–66).

Enhanced competition had other consequences that cheered many critics. The best 1990s sit-coms ranked with classics from earlier periods. Fox revived the science fiction series, which had long struggled to find prime-time permanence. And the decade's TV dramas underwent an extraordinary renaissance in the early 1990s—even greater than the MTM-led revival of the 1980s. In an extended tribute to TV dramas in 1995, Charles McGrath, the editor of the *New York Times Book Review*, spoke of "a sort of golden age." "The weekly network dramatic series," he argued, "are flourishing in a way that they haven't since the very early days of the medium." There was actually less financial pressure on the producers of prime-time dramas like "E.R." (NBC, 1994–) or "Law and Order" (NBC, 1990–), McGrath maintained, than on counterparts doing Broadway shows or movies. As a result, the TV drama could take more risks and better develop its characters. "TV drama is also one of the few remaining art forms to continue the tradition of classic American realism, the realism of Dreiser and Hopper: the painstaking, almost literal examination of middle- and working-class lives in the conviction that the truth resides less in ideas than in details closely observed. More than many novels, TV tells us how we live now."

Although the network business appeared to have righted itself—the audience-hemorrhaging had been stopped and advertising sales were strong—not all networks shared in the good times. CBS had seized the ratings leadership in the early 1990s only to be undone by a shift in programming strategies. In the fall 1992 season, ABC and NBC, partly inspired by Fox's "Beverly Hills, 90210" (Fox, 1990–), began scheduling more series appealing to younger adults. CBS deemed this emphasis heresy; a successful network should telecast shows attractive to all audience subgroups. CBS stuck with popular programs like "Murder, She Wrote" (CBS, 1984–96). To the network's horror, however, Madison Avenue began rewarding the heretics and punishing CBS.

Television advertising was undergoing a transformation. For nearly four decades, sponsors had sought bulk. Size had been network television's niche. It could deliver larger numbers than any other medium; a network could charge top dollar for advertising during a program in the Nielsen top ten. But in the late 1980s, several factors combined to upset network-advertiser relations. The first were improvements in audience measurements that gave sponsors a much better sense of the composition of those viewing a specific program. Clients, coveting greater cost efficiencies, welcomed these demographic breakdowns; they had been pressing agencies to deliver messages with more precision. Companies were no longer content to throw millions at large audiences; they sought to toss them at subgroups more likely to purchase their products.

A demographic bias began to seep into the network business. Fox had few hits, but they included programs especially appealing to younger adults and adolescents, who were generally less likely to watch television than other audience subgroups. During the 1991–92 season, NBC's "Matlock" (1986–95) and ABC's sit-com "Family Matters" (1989–) had similar ratings. "Matlock," however, had "older" demographics. And advertisers were prepared to pay 58 percent more for a thirty-second spot on "Family Matters." In the fall 1992 season, ABC and NBC elected to emphasize youth by ushering in shows with younger casts. "In the 1992–93 season," Bill Carter of the New York Times wrote, "network television will enter a new age. The age is about 22." ABC and NBC dropped series that, while still popular, had aging followings. Advertisers termed it "granny dumping."

Although canceling popular series because of their demographics was not new—CBS in the early 1970s had discarded long-successful programs that had older, small-town followings—the demographic emphasis of the 1990s was much more ruthless. In the new economics of network TV, a smaller body of viewers was more equal—or more coveted by advertisers—than others. None was more favored than young adults. Programs had to have a special appeal for them; though they were less likely to watch TV, they were more likely to consume. They had less of their income tied up in fixed assets (homes, mutual funds) and were less loyal to brand names. NBC and ABC thus sought series that young adults would want to watch every week; a network could then charge advertisers more than would be assessed for shows like "Matlock" or "Murder, She Wrote." In the fall of 1994, NBC was charging more to advertisers for "Seaquest, DSV" (1993–95), a futuristic adventure series, than CBS demanded for "Murder, She Wrote." "Seaquest" ranked sixtieth in the Nielsens, "Murder" seventh. The difference was the 18-to-49 demographic group. Nielsen estimated that per 100 households, 107 adults in the 18-to-49 year group viewed "Seaquest," compared to 42 per 100 for "Murder." "That demographic advantage," Bill Carter of the *New York Times* explained, "showed why NBC and CBS are going in opposite directions." CBS waited too late to take up the new approach. On Madison Avenue, remarked an industry executive in August 1994, "CBS is the Geritol network." The average age of a TV viewer in November 1994, a Fox executive observed, was 36 years old; the average age of a CBS viewer was 51.

This demographic bias upset one of the earliest conventions of network television. In the late 1940s, Frank Stanton of CBS had defended television as a true cultural democracy. He had likened broadcasting to a political ideal: the majority ruled. A half-century later, network television practiced a tyranny of the minority. In a way, the networks were mimicking many radio stations, which had found success in the late 1980s and early 1990s by offering music that appealed to one demographic subset and to no one else. Wrote a Knight-Ridder correspondent in mid-1995, "Television viewers over age 50 are slowly but surely being told to get lost by the big TV networks."

Television's demographic tyranny carried one great risk: if the networks played too exclusively to younger adults, other viewers would flee to cable. "This emphasis on younger demographics is especially risky," an industry analyst remarked in September 1995. "There are too many look-alike programs and everyone is targeting the same smart, young sophisticated urban viewer." CBS's trip to the Fountain of Youth that fall proved disastrous. All in all, there were some signs during the 1995–96 season that cable might be capturing viewers who did not let their friends watch "Friends." Cable's total rating increased. "Viewers in the younger and older ends of the spectrum in particular are turning more and more to cable," reported Lawrie Mifflin of the *New York Times*. One of cable's great success stories in 1995 was Nickelodeon, which relied on programs first aired in the 1960s and 1970s, when the networks practiced cultural democracy. By persuading their children to view "The

Dick Van Dyke Show," parents did not have to worry about Rob and Laura Petrie discussing the great sex they had had the night before, or Lucy on "The Lucy Show" (CBS, 1962–74) referring to her late (never divorced) husband as "Frosty, the Sperm Man," as on CBS's "Cybill" (CBS, 1995–).

Unfavorable demographics constituted only one of CBS's woes. Ownership proved the main one. CBS owner Laurence Tisch determined to run his company like the worst corporate takeover artists of the 1980s. He slashed costs—CBS's New York work force shrank from 9,900 in 1981 to 4,700 eleven years later—and greatly depressed morale internally and among CBS's affiliated stations. He sold so many subdivisions that by 1992 the CBS headquarters building in New York had to advertise for tenants. Unlike his rivals, he refused to invest in domestic and overseas cable services, where much of the industry growth was anticipated. "The whole place seems to be falling apart," remarked a media analyst for Merrill Lynch early in 1995. "The ratings are down, morale stinks, everybody seems to want out." A CBS-affiliated station manager complained, "Larry Tisch is going to be remembered as the gatekeeper who let the cows out of the gate."

Meanwhile, the wily Rupert Murdoch successfully dealt CBS two enormous defeats. In December 1993, Murdoch's Fox network outbid CBS for the TV rights to the NFL's National Football Conference, for four years beginning with the fall 1994 season; CBS had aired NFL contests since the 1950s. Affiliates subsequently saw their Sunday afternoon and early evening audiences shrink. "The absence of football has killed us," wailed a CBS executive. Yet an even bigger blow came in May 1994, when Murdoch took up a proposition originally made to Tisch. Fox would invest $500 million in New World Communications, which owned twelve TV stations, most in large markets. Ten New World stations—in Atlanta, Austin, Cleveland, Dallas, Detroit, Kansas City, Milwaukee, Phoenix, St. Louis, and Tampa—became Fox affiliates. Affiliate agreements that had originated with the start of telecasting in many markets ended. Tampa's WTVT cut a thirty-nine-year tie to CBS. "Fox knocked the stuffing out of the traditional network-affiliate relationship," *Electronic Media* reported. New World's alliance with Fox also upset agreements with ABC and NBC. By the time the dust cleared, seventy-two stations in thirty-four cities had switched network affiliation. Nevertheless, CBS was the most severely wounded. In many markets the network frequently had to sign affiliate deals with UHF stations, which disadvantaged viewers without cable in outlying areas; in Detroit, CBS had to settle for channel 62. The shifts most affected the audiences for programs aired before and after evening prime time, including "The CBS Evening News." CBS's David Letterman saw his strong ratings lead against NBC's "The Tonight Show" evaporate, in part because of his network's suddenly weak affiliate chain. CBS, Letterman joked, now stood for "Come Back Suckers."

Having all but gutted his network, ranked third in the ratings (and fourth in the 18-to-49 demographic group), Tisch sold CBS to Westinghouse for $5.4 billion in 1995. He had earned $2 billion on his investment. "Mr. Tisch did a masterful job of enriching CBS stockholders, himself included," Ron Arlidge of *Electronic Media* wrote, "but the company he leaves behind has paid a terrible price."

ABC, in contrast, had been a takeover success story and was, in the mid-1990s, a desirable property. Capital Cities had purchased ABC in 1986. As Ken Auletta thickly documented, Capital Cities ran ABC with skill while constantly participating in new investment opportunities. Capital Cities–ABC's strong performance attracted Disney, which bought the network in 1995. Michael Eisner had transformed Disney into one of the major entertainment industries of the 1980s. He had revived the company's film production unit while aggressively marketing Disney merchandise and successfully launching a pay channel. Disney even owned an Anaheim hockey team named for a Disney feature film, *The Mighty Ducks* (1992), as well as a portion of the California Angels baseball club. For Disney, purchasing a network was a logical step; there were only so many on-air channels. That scarcity restricted the number of potential non-cable networks, as Time-Warner and Paramount found when they too formed their own on-air networks in the early 1990s.

Although many missed the connection, a major incentive for the combination had come from the federal government. In 1995, the FCC abandoned its remaining restrictions on network ownership of and syndication rights to entertainment series. The networks could, for the first time since the 1960s, produce and hold the rights to evening prime-time entertainment. The original rule had come after a fifteen-year inquiry had strongly implied that networks usually scheduled series that they had produced or in which they had a financial stake, rather than others offered by non-network sources. This favoritism, the FCC had concluded, was not always based on the merits of a potential series but on the networks' proprietary interest. (This partly accounted for the unrelenting insipidity of most 1960s television.) Freed of this constraint in the late 1990s, would ABC turn down a more promising program from an outside producer in favor of a Disney-made series? In theory, the far more competitive environment would prevent such behavior.

But, Ron Arlidge warned, "in this Age of the Bean Counter, it is undoubtedly tempting to stock the shelves with house brands regardless of customer preference."

The government hardly cared any more. Thirty or forty years earlier, lawyers at the Justice Department, FTC, and FCC would have spent long nights writing briefs in opposition to such media conglomerates as Disney-ABC and Time-Warner. Anxieties over antitrust law, however, had been replaced by the mantra of the "global economy." American industry, including the mass media, had to compete in a new world economy and must not be impeded by earlier fears of gigantism.

The governing class did worry, as before, about indecency and violence in the mass media. Members of Congress and the Bush and Clinton administrations, as well as such self-appointed guardians as William Bennett, criticized the misogyny and violent hatred of police found in rap lyrics. (Bennett, who had once dated Janis Joplin, preferred classic rock 'n' roll.) President Clinton successfully persuaded the TV industry to adopt a program ratings system akin to the film industry's. And the 1996 Telecommunications Act required that all TV sets include a V-chip allowing parents to prevent the reception of channels that carried programs unsuitable for their children.

Individual TV stations had to reckon with many of the same competitive forces upsetting network television. As earlier, when not carrying network programming, stations ran syndicated material, including thirty-minute infomercials aired in time slots that drew only insomniacs. Early evening hours, which had once gone to locally produced children's or public affairs programs, were now dominated by nationally produced tabloid news shows. Some, like "Entertainment Tonight," cheerfully promoted the latest film or television show. Others, like "Hard Copy," were the video cousins of the supermarket scandal sheet, with decidedly frivolous news agendas. They were immensely popular. In the early 1990s, the Times Mirror Center estimated that one of five Americans regularly viewed programs like "A Current Affair"—far more than watched any of the networks' Sunday morning interview programs or PBS's nightly news hour. About 40 percent of all Americans regularly viewed "Entertainment Tonight."

Most stations carried another popular syndicated product: the daytime talk show. These programs were very inexpensive (costing less to telecast than popular recent TV series), and they could command good ratings. As a program type, the daytime talk show had begun innocently enough in the 1960s and had somewhat resembled NBC's "The Tonight Show." Hosts like Merv Griffin and Mike Douglas interviewed various show business celebrities who innocuously plugged their latest night club act, film, or TV series. Led by Phil Donahue, however, the daytime gabfest turned to serious topics in the 1970s and 1980s while inviting members of the audience to question the guests. Gradually, the format changed again, as the number of talk shows exploded in the early 1990s. Guests were (or in some instances pretended to be) dysfunctional ("men who dress as babies")—and throughout the show the audience taunted them, not unlike those patronizing the nineteenth-century freak show. One day in mid-September 1995, topics on different shows included prostitute patrons, runaway teens' mothers, bisexuals, and stale love lives. Early in 1996 some programs focused on the sexual proclivities of female teenagers and preadolescents (producers had the guests dress provocatively); columnist Bob Herbert compared the hosts to pornographers and pimps. They had "found a gold mine in the sexuality of troubled children." Poor Donahue, who bore some of the responsibility for the shift, found himself overwhelmed by competitors who shamelessly exploited the genre's possibilities. His show left the air in 1996. Donahue, Howard Kurtz remarked, "had been eclipsed by a younger brat pack that reveled in staged confrontation, in orchestrated humiliation, in screaming melees that seemed to soil everyone involved."

What few resources stations invested in their own programming went to TV news. They remained a key profit center (providing up to 60 percent of revenues), as well as the best means of distinguishing a broadcast channel from cable outlets. Despite claims to the contrary and large audiences, local news programs remained a journalistic embarrassment. Their news value was negligible. What appeared nightly was largely formula-driven, depending on the size of their markets. Larger ones deliberately exploited inner city crime ("if it bleeds, it leads"), even though most viewers lived in relatively safe suburbs. Cost-effectiveness partly explained this emphasis. A Nashville TV news director noted that one of his crews required only an hour or two to cover a murder scene or fire; reporting on the causes of crime or poor housing conditions might take weeks. "It's not that local newsrooms have a built-in predilection for violence," a former network executive wrote. "It's just that it's there—easy to get." After civil rights groups decried the barely concealed racism that often seeped into such coverage, some stations late in 1994 attempted to downplay urban crime in favor of "family-sensitive" news. Eight of the ten stations saw their ratings fall. Smaller market stations were merely superficial in their treatment of most stories. When they tried to match their big-city counterparts in blood and guts, the results could be pretty absurd. "Up here in the north woods," wrote a Traverse City, Michigan, man early in 1996, "we don't have the lovely array of murders, rapes, beatings, cop killings and cop killers. . . . [We] have to be satisfied with grisly auto and truck accidents, schoolyard fist fights, women in shelters with black eyes, stolen kiddy bicycles and lumberyard fires as nightly news items. It is worse than awful and less than meaningless."

Such lamentations were so many voices in the wilderness, literally or otherwise. Those polled in the March 1995 Times Mirror Center survey gave local TV news the highest grades of any news medium; 68 percent gave local TV newscasts an A or B. Timebuyers were even more enthusiastic. Advertisers, Phyllis Kaniss found, rewarded TV stations that delivered the largest possible audiences. Sponsors could care less about the serious reportage of public affairs. If anything, the vast majority of TV news producers felt that a local newscast should above all else be entertaining—like the big-city 1920s tabloid—and avoid complications. Such an attitude bespoke a contempt for viewers that only occasionally became public. Late in 1993, a Providence, Rhode Island, TV general manager declared that "90 percent [of the audience] is as dumb as shit and they're getting dumber." When all else failed, local news directors claimed that they had no choice. They had to compete with other local newscasts as well as cable outlets carrying non-news programming. "We have to be entertaining," a Miami general manager explained, "because we compete with entertainment options as well as other news outlets." Nevertheless, stations behind in the TV news ratings were not actually losing money; they simply were not earning as much as competitors. In producing local TV newscasts, Todd Gitlin observed "the point is not to make money but make more money—more than the other guy, more than you used to make, more than you feared you would make. And this is the real scandal: There are no sufficiently countervailing motives."

Yet the authority of local news increased. Until the late 1980s, the networks had controlled access to their stories. That is, viewers had to wait until the early evening network news to see footage that NBC, CBS or ABC crews had recorded that day. However, under pressure from affiliates who were now using CNN as an alternative, the networks began sharing their daily taping of stories and events. By 1990, Tom Rosenstiel reported, stations were receiving an average of eight hours of footage a day, and they were free to use any of it. Although the networks held back some stories for their nightly newscasts, a long-time monopoly on TV news images was broken. Viewers no longer had to wait for the network newscast for certain stories. The effect, to Rosenstiel, was to render the network news largely redundant for those viewers taking in the early evening local newscast and thus reduce the impact of the network news.

To many, the end of the network's domination was no loss. It was more democratic, more pluralist, to have the gate-keeping function shared by individual news directors across the land. But Rosenstiel cited one terrible instance in which stations did not exercise their new powers wisely. Early in 1992, stations had received footage of an ABC reporter questioning Bill Clinton about another sex scandal story in a supermarket tabloid. ABC had not planned to air the tape that night; the other networks were going to ignore the story. Local newscasts, however, ran the piece, and the networks—even PBS—had to follow their lead. "There were no gatekeepers anymore," Rosenstiel wrote. "Technology was democraticizing the political process but lowering journalistic standards."

Reader Best-Friendly

No other mass medium faced more challenges in the 1990s than did the American newspaper. Although TV gradually cut into circulations and forced the closing of many marginal big city dailies, the industry overall had been very profitable well into the 1980s. Some experts thought newspapers had finally crafted an effective response to television by making papers more attractive and more relevant to readers' lives. For many merchants, newspapers remained an effective advertising medium. A one-newspaper-town daily could make enormous amounts of money, year-in and year-out; it was "an unregulated tollbooth," observed investor Warren Buffett. Then came a succession of problems that went beyond redesigning the paper or making it more "reader-friendly." These included direct-mail advertising, in addition to a sharp decline in advertising sales due to the 1990–92 recession. Buffett, for one, ceased investing in newspapers. He had seen the future. Just as the industry began to recover from the recession, the cost of newsprint, which represented between 15 and 25 percent of a paper's total operating expenses, nearly doubled between 1994 and 1996. At the same time, circulation increases failed to keep pace with population growth. According to the Simmons Market Research Bureau, the percentage of adult weekday newspaper readers declined between 1981 and 1994, from 67.7 to 61.5 percent.

With demand from readers stagnant and operating costs soaring, more dailies combined—as in Milwaukee, Providence, and San Diego—or ceased operations. Houston, Little Rock, Pittsburgh, and Tulsa became one-newspaper towns. Many dailies froze or reduced their staff. In 1995, the *Miami Herald* cut 300 jobs; a buy-out plan at the *Hartford Courant* resulted in a 16 percent staff reduction. Some large papers eliminated their Sunday magazine supplements, which had afforded writing opportunities for regional talent and staff members, in favor of the very popular and very light nationally syndicated *Parade*.

Investors and owners spurred the drive to cut costs. By the 1990s most newspapers were part of publicly traded corporations, and the decline in profit margins upset the stock market. In the 1980s newspapers boasted 20 to 40 percent profit margins; they fell to half that or less in the mid-1990s. Such a deterioration should not have surprised anyone, given all of the problems besetting the industry. Yet as Philip Meyer observed, in the 1970s and 1980s the Gannett chain had masterfully set the quarterly profits expectation (with the help of inflation in the 1970s); Wall Street was not interested in excuses; it wanted a restoration. Family-owned newspapers faced a similar problem. The third or fourth generation lost patience when dividends failed to increase. In the early 1990s, a fourth estate "Family Feud" erupted among the Chandlers, who controlled Times Mirror, publisher of the *Los Angeles Times* and other dailies. Under family and investor pressure, Times Mirror in the early 1990s had cut the *Times*'s staff by one-third. Despite such moves, the company's 1994 profits were 9.4 percent, which was below those for any of the other nine largest newspaper groups. More surgery followed in 1995, when a former financial officer at General Mills, Mark H. Willes—a man with no newspaper experience—was named chief executive officer. Under Willes, Times Mirror closed the *Baltimore Evening Sun* and *New York Newsday*. Staffers began referring to Willes as the "cereal killer."

Amid such crises, newspapers strove to reinvent themselves again. Many editors sought more analytical reporting. The spread of TV and cable news services had been fostering such journalism; it was a logical way to distinguish a paper from broadcast or cable news. "Life unfolds today on television," the *New Yorker* observed in 1994, "and newspapers and magazines must play the role of the Greek chorus, commenting on the action." As the lines separating reporting and interpreting events continued to blur, even the *New York Times*, which had long prided itself on being the newspaper of record, began integrating more analysis and opinion into news stories. Comparing presidential coverage between 1977 and 1993, Stephen Klaidman found the number of subjective stories in the *Times*—that is, ones that willingly assessed individuals and issues without careful attribution—increased from near zero in 1977 to approximately 50 percent in 1993. Moreover, interpretation in stories was much less likely to include specific sources in 1993 than in 1977. It had become impossible, Klaidman found, to establish whether a reporter had based her analysis "on solid reporting, acute observation or educated guessing." No one exemplified this shift more smartly than Maureen Dowd. In her account of President Clinton's visit to Oxford, Dowd wrote that the president and former Rhodes Scholar "returned today for a sentimental journey to the university where he didn't inhale, didn't get drafted, and didn't get a degree."

While distinguishing newspapers from the headline readers on the local news and CNN, interpretive reporting could upset some readers, and create even more problems. Readers could not help but recognize the abandonment of an older standard of "objective" reporting. Former *Times* editor A. M. Rosenthal denounced "the increasing politicization of news by editorialization in the news columns." Newspapers risked "the three basic items that make up the stock in trade of a newspaper or magazine: trust, trust, trust." Many of Dowd's stories, for example, infuriated old hands. Adam Gopnik noted that her Oxford lead was not interpretive or analytical. "It just re-states the familiar with an edge of malice." Observed another, "everything she writes is hard-edged and opinionated." Reporters and editors might have shrugged off such criticism a decade earlier, but the economics of newspapering in the 1990s made everyone insecure. Morale among reporters, already low at the beginning of the decade, plummeted further. Editors were not much happier. "The business is scared, and the people running it, myself included, are confused about which way to point the papers and how to deal with the competition," admitted the editor of the *Philadelphia Daily News* late in 1995. "There's a real spiritual self-doubt that I don't remember experiencing before." Reporters and editors began wondering if they were too removed from their readers, too arrogant about defining the news for a community. "I knew guys at *Newsday* who could not care less what the reader wanted," one old-timer remarked. "If you win prizes for a 14-part series on nuclear non-proliferation and nobody can read it or understand it, no wonder your circulation is going down."

To combat the perception of being too detached from their public, many newspapers, in effect, handed their agenda-setting functions to readers—or a majority of readers. "News," a Wisconsin editor told his staff in 1991, "is what our readers say it is." If that consumer-driven approach meant less government or international reportage—and it almost always did—so be it. After an extensive study of reader preferences, the *Miami Herald* late in 1995 announced that the paper would start organizing its coverage around nine subject areas. Latin America made the list, but not the rest of the world. Nor did the upcoming presidential election. "When journalists begin acting like waiters and taking orders from the public and pollsters," one veteran reporter wrote in 1996, "the results are not pretty." In some cases, however, editing by reader surveys actually sharpened coverage. Focus group research caused Knight-Ridder's *Wichita Eagle* to rethink its 1990 campaign reporting. Issues became the centerpiece of stories; less space went to "horse race" items on who was ahead or who had attacked whom.

Focus group research also helped to foster "civic" or "public" journalism. Civic journalism represented a major initiative by some forty newspapers to reshape their communities' political cultures (while boosting flat circulations and staving off alternative media). In their mainly altruistic moments, proponents of civic journalism shared a common concern about declining citizen participation in politics and governing. Excessively critical or attack journalism, together with negative political advertising, may have had the unintended effect of deadening Americans' belief in the democratic process. To revive public interest in politics, newspapers invited readers to participate in candidate and issue forums. The papers sponsored such gatherings and then heavily covered them, as well as meetings that editors held with government and business leaders to respond to reader complaints. To detractors, civic journalism newspapers were manufacturing the news, and editors were becoming too close to the very officials whose performance they were supposed to monitor. Moreover, most civic journalism newspapers were not winning back readers; circulations remained flat.

All in all, newspapers in the 1990s endeavored to be more open, and less demanding. Editors sought shorter and shorter stories. The *Buffalo News*, which had long regarded itself as a hard-news paper, ran radio spots in 1995 declaring, "You can get the facts without straining your brain." For those whose brains were strained, papers began listing editors' phone numbers atop each page; some carried their internet addresses. Many dailies redesigned their editorial page to open up the section to more readers; several actually ceased carrying their own opinions, preferring instead to solicit the views of local residents.

Taken together, most of the changes at American newspapers, especially reductions in staff and size—and seriousness—threatened to marginalize the nation's dailies. They might earn more money, Meyer admitted late in 1995, yet in the process they would become less important. That year another former journalist wrote, "Newspapers will likely live on, but for now at least, as modest shops in gigantic corporatized information supermalls." Then, too, paying too much heed to readers' momentary preferences might ultimately invite only contempt. "Like it or not," David Remnick wrote, "part of the job of a great editor is to listen to public desires—and then, if necessary, act against them. The alternative is to scare oneself out of existence and accelerate the race to a no-newspaper town."

The Content Providers

Like the newspaper industry, moviemaking in America struggled in the 1990s. Revenues could not keep pace with production and promotional expenses; demand for films continued to be stagnant. Moreover, though moviemakers had more ancillary markets than ever—a larger foreign market, home video, television, and cable TV—the box-office success of a feature film remained the best predictor of its ultimate potential. In other words, Americans were much more likely to rent or buy a film like *Pocahontas* (1995), which had generated enthusiasm during its release in theaters. "It's still the box office performance," *Variety* observed in October 1995, "that substantially determines commercial life beyond movie screens."

Yet, investors in film companies could still be recruited—in Montreal, Paris, or New York. And they continued to be proven fools. Sony, which had purchased Columbia Pictures in 1989, discovered one American industry it could not master, and lost billions in the process. Matsushita's 1990 purchase of MCA-Universal similarly went sour, and was sold to Seagram's, the Canadian distillery company. Young Edgar Bronfman could have better invested his family's fortune, but he loved the glamor and had experienced the culture of filmmaking as a younger man. A French bank, Credit Lyonnais, assumed control of MGM-UA in 1992, after its previous owner had defaulted. Viacom purchased Paramount two years later.

Both new and old hands confronted the spiraling costs of manufacturing a movie. For more than a decade, industry leaders had complained about the great expense of filmmaking. As the major studios lost control over production deals in the early 1970s, talent agencies gradually gained the upper hand. The salaries for stars then rose, and rose again. Such expenses drove costs up, as did the higher production values necessary to distinguish a feature film from television programming. As the average cost of films increased, promotion became all the more important and expensive. Many studios tried to achieve efficiencies through tie-in deals with fast food companies like McDonald's and Burger King.

The larger film companies talked about containing expenses, but without much conviction. Although executives might be fired, nearly all had pricey buy-out deals or "golden parachutes," which greatly eased the trauma of dismissal. Until then, they could hide their spendthrift ways through unusually creative bookkeeping. And there was always the hope that overseas and video rental sales would compensate for a weak domestic box office. Impressive international grosses, for example, kept the extraordinarily expensive ($170 million) *Waterworld* (1995) from becoming a financial disaster for MCA.

If careless with money, filmmakers proved cautious with subject matter. In the mid-1990s, the average cost of a feature film was about $34 million; promotion might entail an additional $20 million or more. With expenses so high, studio officials regularly intervened in the scriptwriting and production process; thirty-five writers labored on the script of *The Flintstones* (1994). Such interference had the effect of killing many original ideas; once-promising first drafts became unrecognizable final cuts. One show business writer early in 1995 spoke of certain features "so tortured by executives in the production process that they ended up almost lifeless."

As earlier, the major film companies and producers held to a risk-averse strategy. Rigid screenwriting formulas became popular; these specified when "plot points" should occur and forbade ambiguous endings. They contributed, Phillip Lopate argued, to "the dumbing down of American movies." As before, the big studios sought to minimize their potential losses by banking on established, popular performers. The biggest beneficiaries included a few muscular male players—Arnold Schwarzenegger, Sylvester Stallone, Jean-Claude Van Damme, and Steven Segal. Forty years earlier, they would have been supporting players—or personal trainers. In the 1990s, they were stars. Their vehicles were cartoon-like action films that played well abroad even as their domestic box office sagged.

The international market had, in fact, become much more vital. In the mid-1990s it represented about half of the revenues from exhibition (compared to about 30 percent in 1980). *Die Hard with a Vengeance* (1995), with a total gross of $352 million, reportedly earned two-and-a-half times as much abroad as in the United States. The larger overseas audience not only encouraged action dramas like the *Die Hard* series but also stripped their screenplays bare. "In action movies," Lopate wrote, "one character may utter an expletive, the other say 'Duck!' and that is all the screenwriter wrote." Moreover, action films' many special effects and physical feats needed no translation. As a result, despite cries from the nation's political leadership, Hollywood continued to produce violent films. Mayhem was universally understood. "Violence travels well; violent movies do well in foreign markets," a producer admitted late in 1993. "Hence, the resistance to doing away with violence in movies."

As before, successful films meant sequels and still more sequels. They required less promotion. A variation on the sequel came into popularity the 1990s: feature films based on old TV shows. The success of *The Addams Family* in 1991 fostered a sequel—and more features based on old series. These included *The Beverly Hillbillies* (1993), *The Brady Bunch* (1995), *Car 54, Where Are You?* (1994), *The Flintstones, The Fugitive* (1993), *Maverick* (1994), *Mission: Impossible* (1996), and *Sergeant Bilko* (1996), with more on the way. To Hollywood's harsher critics, this trend revealed the cultural narrowness of producers, studio executives, and agents: women and men in their thirties and forties whose only cultural encounters had been with TV. They had, one producer complained, "no life experience other than television." But someone pitching a movie "concept" could logically argue that a film version of a popular television series from the 1960s and 1970s, which had been rerun on TV ever since, would be much less difficult to promote. Potential moviegoers already knew the characters.

Nevertheless, filmmaking continued to be a volatile venture, and most major film companies quietly shifted their place in the republic of mass culture. The larger ones began being defined as "content providers" for both broadcast and cable networks. (Largely for that reason, Ted Turner and Rupert Murdoch bought studios.) Then, too, the possibility of an international market for American-produced TV series loomed. Gradually, the biggest concerns—Paramount, Universal, Warner Brothers, and Disney—poured more of their resources into producing TV programs. Between 1969 and 1991, the percentage of network series produced by major studios increased from 43 to 63 percent. Most of this growth came at the expense of the smaller independent producers.

The more obvious approach involved entering telecasting. Both Paramount and Warner Brothers tried to create their own networks in the early 1990s. Disney demonstrated the greater wisdom by purchasing the well-established ABC. It was a late-nineteenth-century capitalist's dream, vertical integration carried to its logical extreme. A Disney feature film could be promoted on a network TV special, on network morning programs, and on prime-time "magazines." ABC, *Electronic Media* reported, "has the ability to cross-promote a project in different venues and potentially create big hits better than anybody." The network would gain, with Disney agreeing to produce Saturday morning children's programming, one prime-time series, and three one-hour specials. An excited Michael Eisner declared, "there are synergies under every rock we turn over." "The Disney-ABC deal would seem a perfect merger," *Electronic Media* contended. "Content provider meets first-class distributor."

Although ABC and Disney shareholders—as well as media analysts who used barren expressions like "content providers"—might have been ecstatic, the Disney-ABC combination signaled a dangerous trend. At the end of the twentieth century, Americans faced the prospect of a smaller number of companies controlling both the production and the distribution of mass entertainment. The virtual abandonment of broadcast regulation hurried the move to gigantism, as the FCC permitted fewer and fewer companies to own more and more TV and radio stations, even in the same community.

The fretful monitors of such trends had to remain calm—at least for the moment. For one thing (as the merger of Time Inc., and Warner Brothers proved, at least in its first years) not all mergers work. Distinct corporate cultures have to be able to mesh. In the case of Time-Warner, there were few if any synergies, only a lot of managerial and board room antagonisms, and huge shareholder debt. Even cohesive conglomerates did not become infallible merely by virtue of their bigness. A media giant might stumble. When Disney opened EuroDisney, a theme park near Paris, it proved to be Mickey's Maginot Line, *un désastre*. If Disney could fail, as Mickey sometimes did, then anyone could. Success at producing mass entertainment and mass information continued to be unpredictable, modern capitalism's alchemy. One Warner Brothers executive confessed, "You never know what's going to work."

Writing about the mass media in the United States fifty years earlier, the British political scientist Harold Laski hailed what he called the "self-correcting mechanism" of American democracy. Americans might put up with distorted news, bland or offensive entertainment, but not indefinitely. As long as consumers had some say in what they watched, read, or listened to, this mechanism would check the efforts of some to control the American mass media. Despite all of the merger activity in the 1990s, Americans had enough choices to favor, now and then, the modest-sized company. Independent TV production companies did not disappear. Carsey-Werner assembled some of the most successful series of the 1995–96 season. Despite all of the resources poured into feature films like *Waterworld* and *Batman Forever* (1995), small domestic and foreign companies put out features like *Babe* (1995) that did not require an ABC promotional special or Burger King tie-in in order to draw audiences. The system was not closed. The dividing of theaters into so many multiplexes, the flood of new cable channels and new cable service providers, combined with the possibilities of personal computers, have prevented any one corporation, or even a cluster of companies, from disproving Laski. As long as Americans make the effort, the "self-correcting mechanism" will continue to function.

The real problem was not how concentrated the system was becoming, but rather the nature of the system itself. The absence of countervailing pressures left everyone at the mercy of the marketplace. In some instances, to be sure, the marketplace might work. Americans watching television in the mid-1990s had more choices, notably in dramatic series, than at any time since the late 1950s, when network executives collectively began attending only to majority tastes. But other trends in radio and TV scheduling all but wrote off certain consumers because of their age, income, or race. For journalism, the advantages of competition were even harder to establish. Breaking stories reached Americans faster than ever. Yet it remains to be seen if the advent of the new news media, and the transformations of the old, are not simply creating a nation of headline-readers. Could American democracy survive that prospect?

Bibliographical Essay

The scholarly literature on the public arts since 1941 is ever expanding, and it is impossible to list all of the better work here. Nor can I present the great majority of contemporary commentaries I drew upon for this study. A good summary history is Robert C. Toll, *The Entertainment Machine: American Show Business in the Twentieth Century* (New York: Oxford UP, 1982). A more opinionated and contemporary analysis by a prominent writer on the mass media is Gilbert Seldes, *The Great Audience* (New York: Viking, 1950). David Halberstam's *The Powers That Be* (New York: Knopf, 1979), a history of *Time*, CBS, the *Washington Post*, and the *Los Angeles Times*, favors melodrama, relies too much on interviews, and should be used with caution. Christopher H. Sterling and Timothy R. Haight, eds., *The Mass Media: Aspen Guide to Communication Industry Trends* (New York: Praeger, 1977); Bruce M. Owen, *Economics and Freedom of Expression: Media Structure and the First Amendment* (Cambridge, Mass.: Ballinger, 1975); and U.S. Federal Trade Commission, Bureau of Competition, *Proceedings of the Symposium on Media Concentration*, 14 and 15 December 1978 (Washington, D.C., 1979), all include helpful information. On African Americans and mass culture, see Jannette L. Dates and William Barlow, eds., *Split Image: African Americans in the Mass Media* (Washington, D.C.: Howard UP, 1990).

On broadcasting, Erik Barnouw's three-volume *History of Broadcasting in the United States* (New York: Oxford UP, 1966–70), *Tube of Plenty: The Evolution of American Television* (New York: Oxford UP, 1975), and *The Sponsor: Notes on a Modern Potentate* (New York: Oxford UP, 1978), though episodic, should be consulted. David Marc has written two stimulating works, *Democratic Vistas: Television in American Culture* (Phil-

251

adelphia: U of Pennsylvania P, 1984) and *Comic Visions: Television Comedy and American Culture* (Boston: Unwin Hyman, 1989). Ron Powers, *Supertube: The Rise of Television Sports* (New York: Coward-McCann, 1984), is the best history of TV and sports. See also Benjamin G. Rader, *In Its Own Image: How Television Transformed Sports* (New York: Free Press, 1984), and Randy Roberts and James Olson, *Winning Is the Only Thing: Sports in America since 1945* (Baltimore: Johns Hopkins UP, 1989). Ella Taylor, *Prime-Time Families: Television Culture in Postwar America* (Berkeley and Los Angeles: U of California P, 1989), is most helpful for the 1970s and 1980s. Two textbooks provide valuable statistical compilations, Sidney W. Head and Christopher H. Sterling, *Broadcasting: A Survey of Television, Radio, and New Technologies*, 5th ed. (Boston: Houghton Mifflin, 1990), and Sterling and John M. Kittross, *Stay Tuned: A Concise History of American Broadcasting*, 2d ed. (Belmont, Calif.: Wadsworth, 1990). On TV and its complex relationship to the film industry since the late 1940s, see Tino Balio, ed., *Hollywood in the Age of Television* (Boston: Unwin Hyman, 1990).

The most helpful histories of the film industry for the postwar period are Garth Jowett, *Film: The Democratic Art* (Boston: Little, Brown, 1976), and Robert Sklar, *Movie-Made America: A Cultural History of American Movies* (New York: Random House, 1975). See also Tino Balio, ed., *The American Film Industry*, rev. ed. (Madison: U of Wisconsin P, 1985), an excellent collection of contemporary and historical analyses of Hollywood, as well as the second volume of Balio's history of United Artists, *United Artists: The Company That Changed the Film Industry* (Madison: U of Wisconsin P, 1987).

Introduction

Among the recent scholarship suggesting that the mass media have a significant influence are Shanto Iyengar and Donald R. Kinder, *News That Matters: Television and American Opinion* (Chicago: U of Chicago P, 1987), and Robert Kubey and Mihaly Csikszentmihalyi, *Television and the Quality of Life: How Viewing Shapes Everyday Experience* (Hillsdale, N.J.: Lawrence Erlbaum Associates, 1990). The older case for "limited effects" is eloquently stated in Raymond A. Bauer, "The Obstinate Audience: The Influence Process from the Point of View of Social Communication," *American Psychologist* 19 (May 1964): 319–28, and W. Phillips Davison, "On the Effects of Mass Communication," *Public Opinion Quarterly* 23 (Fall 1959): 343–60. In *The Urban Villagers: Group and Class in the Life of Italian-Americans* (New York: Free Press, 1962), Herbert J. Gans sensitively observed the consumption of the mass media in a

Boston neighborhood in the late fifties. On recent ethnographic analyses of the mass media and audiences, see John Fiske, *Television Culture* (London: Methuen, 1987).

Chapter 1. The Voluntary Propagandists

The press's relations with the federal government during World War II have commanded new attention among scholars. See especially Richard W. Steele, *Propaganda in an Open Society: The Roosevelt Administration and the Media, 1933–1941* (Westport, Conn.: Greenwood, 1985), and Patrick S. Washburn, *A Question of Sedition: The Federal Government's Investigation of the Black Press during World War II* (New York: Oxford UP, 1986). The most moving critique of the press's coverage of the war is Paul Fussell, *Wartime: Understanding and Behavior in the Second World War* (New York: Oxford UP, 1989). Maureen Honey, *Creating Rosie the Riveter: Class, Gender, and Propaganda during World War Two* (Amherst: U of Massachusetts P, 1984), is the best study of American women and the mass media during the war.

On radio during World War II, A. M. Sperber, *Murrow: His Life and Times* (New York: Freundlich, 1986), is the most detailed of several biographies of the CBS newscaster, while William Stott, *Documentary Expression and Thirties America* (New York: Oxford UP, 1973), includes a stimulating analysis of Murrow, radio news, and American culture. If hardly so daring, Mitchell V. Charnley, *News by Radio* (New York: Macmillan, 1948), is useful. Susan Hartmann, *The Home Front and Beyond: American Women in the 1940s* (Boston: Twayne, 1982), discusses the effects of the war on soap operas.

On Hollywood during the war, I borrowed heavily from Otto Friedrich's evocative *City of Nets: A Portrait of Hollywood in the 1940's* (New York: Harper & Row, 1986). Clayton R. Koppes and Gregory D. Black, *Hollywood Goes to War: How Politics, Profits, and Propaganda Shaped World War II Movies* (New York: Free Press, 1987), examines the film industry's relations with the federal government. See also Richard W. Steele, "'The Greatest Gangster Movie Ever Filmed': *Prelude to War*," *Prologue* 11 (Winter 1979): 220–35, and David Culbert, ed., *Mission to Moscow* (Madison: U of Wisconsin P, 1980). John W. Dower, *War Without Mercy: Race and Power in the Pacific War* (New York: Pantheon, 1986), compares racist imagery in American and Japanese propaganda.

My discussion of wartime consumption of news was informed by Bernard Berelson's famous survey of New Yorkers during a newspaper strike, "What 'Missing the Newspaper' Means," in *Communications Research, 1948–1949*, ed. Paul F. Lazarsfeld and Frank N. Stanton (New

York: Harper & Bros., 1949). Robert K. Merton's *Mass Persuasion: The Social Psychology of a War Bond Drive* (New York: Harper & Bros., 1946) suggests how radio could create a "pseudo-community" of listeners.

Chapter 2. Americans and Their Mass Media in 1945

Paul F. Lazarsfeld, Bernard Berelson, and Hazel Gaudet, *The People's Choice: How the Voter Makes Up His Mind in a Presidential Campaign* (New York: Duell, Sloan, & Pearce, 1944), is the classic study of opinion formation in a small town. Ralph B. Levering, *American Opinion and the Russian Alliance, 1939–1945* (Chapel Hill: U of North Carolina P, 1976), ably utilizes research by Merton and Lazarsfeld to describe the audiences for the American news media in the forties. "One-Newspaper Town," in *Fortune*, August 1947, 103–6, closely examines one community's news media consumption. Janice A. Radway's study of fans of the romance novel, *Reading the Romance: Women, Patriarchy, and Popular Literature* (Chapel Hill: U of North Carolina P, 1984), offers a compelling argument about women and reading.

On journalists, Leo Rosten's thick *The Washington Correspondents* (New York: Harcourt, Brace, 1937) is a pioneering and very long sociological study. See also Warren Breed, "Social Control in the Newsroom: A Functional Analysis," *Social Forces* 33 (May 1955): 326–35. Several autobiographies are especially useful: Russell Baker, *The Good Times* (New York: Morrow, 1989); Walter Trohan, *Political Animals* (Garden City, N.Y.: Doubleday, 1975); Theodore H. White, *In Search of History; A Personal Adventure* (New York: Harper & Row, 1978); and William L. White, *The Making of a Journalist* (Lexington: UP of Kentucky, 1986).

The entries of the *New Yorker* newspaper critic A. J. Liebling were published in *The Press* (New York: Ballantine, 1961). Frank Luther Mott, "Trends in Newspaper Content," *Annals of the American Academy of Political and Social Science* 219 (January 1942): 60–65, describes some dailies' increasing reliance on syndicated material, while Richard Kluger, *The Paper: The Life and Death of the New York Herald Tribune* (New York: Knopf, 1986), is a rich mine of information on a great metropolitan daily. Marshall Berges, *The Life and Times of Los Angeles* (New York: Atheneum, 1984), is one of several good histories of the *Los Angeles Times*. On the *Chicago Tribune*, Lloyd Wendt, *Chicago Tribune: The Rise of a Great American Newspaper* (Chicago: Rand McNally, 1979), is the most thorough study. William Randolph Hearst, America's most notorious publisher at the war's end, is skewered in W. A. Swanberg, *Citizen Hearst* (New York: Scribners, 1961). Two of the new, less intrusive chain newspaper owners are well profiled in Richard H. Meeker, *Newspaperman: S. I. Newhouse and the Business of News* (New Haven: Ticknor & Fields, 1983), and Charles Whited, *Knight: A Publisher in the Tumultuous Century* (New York: E. P. Dutton, 1988).

Henry R. Luce of Time Inc. has commanded the most interest among those writing on the postwar magazine. W. A. Swanberg, *Luce and His Empire* (New York: Scribners, 1972), is a well-researched exercise in demonology. In *Henry R. Luce and the Rise of the American News Media* (Boston: Twayne, 1987), I try to provide more perspective. The second volume of Robert T. Elson's authorized history of Time Inc., *The World of Time Inc.* (New York: Atheneum, 1973), is unusually balanced.

Erik Barnouw, *The Golden Web* (New York: Oxford UP, 1968), remains the best history of radio in the 1940s. Llewellyn White, *The American Radio* (Chicago: U of Chicago P, 1947), a staff report for the Commission on Freedom of the Press, is helpful on radio and its regulation. See also Judith S. Waller, *Radio: The Fifth Estate*, 2d ed. (Boston: Houghton Mifflin, 1950). John Crosby, *Out of the Blue* (New York: Simon & Schuster, 1952), is a collection of some of the late-forties criticism by the *Herald Tribune*'s lively radio columnist. On sponsor control over radio programming in the forties, see Frederic Wakeman's *The Hucksters* (New York: Rinehart, 1946), a novel by a former advertising agent. Radio's primacy to consumers was suggested in Paul F. Lazarsfeld and Harry Field, *The People Look at Radio* (Chapel Hill: U of North Carolina P, 1946). On radio news in the late forties, see Charnley's *News by Radio* and Paul W. White, *News on the Air* (New York: Harcourt, Brace, 1947).

On Hollywood at war's end, Friedrich's *City of Nets*, Sklar's *Movie-Made America*, and Jowett's *Film* are the most useful. Efforts at self-regulation are described in Leonard J. Leff and Jerold L. Simmons, *The Dame in the Kimono: Hollywood, Censorship, and the Production Code from the 1920's to the 1960's* (New York: Grove Wiedenfeld, 1990). Hortense Powdermaker's anthropological study, *Hollywood: The Dream Factory* (Boston: Little, Brown, 1950), is fascinating, as are the observations in *New Yorker* contributor Lillian Ross's *Picture* (New York: Rinehart, 1952). Garry Wills, *Reagan's America: Innocents at Home* (Garden City, N.Y.: Doubleday, 1987), discusses Hollywood and its labor troubles after the war, as does Friedrich. The significance of the Jewish background of some movie colony governors is explored in Sklar and more prominently in Neal Gabler, *An Empire of Their Own: How the Jews Invented Hollywood* (New York: Crown, 1988). The ticket-buyers are analyzed in Leo A. Handel, *Hollywood Looks at Its Audience: A Report of Film Audience Research* (Urbana: U of Illinois P, 1950).

Chapter 3. Test Patterns: Television Comes to America, 1945–1955

For newspapers, the report of the Commission on Freedom of the Press, *A Free and Responsible Press* (Chicago: U of Chicago P, 1947), tried without much success to set the industry tone. Several historians contend that journalists either encouraged a cold war with the Soviet Union or allowed themselves to be used by the government to foster Russophobia. See Les K. Adler and Thomas G. Paterson, "Red Fascism: The Merger of Nazi Germany and Soviet Russia in the American Image of Totalitarianism, 1930's–1950's," *American Historical Review* 75 (April 1970): 1046–64; Walter LaFeber, "American Policy-Makers, Public Opinion, and the Outbreak of the Cold War, 1945–50," in *The Origins of the Cold War in Asia*, ed. Yonosuke Nagai and Akira Iriye (Tokyo: U of Tokyo P, 1977), 43–65; and Thomas G. Paterson, *On Every Front: The Making of the Cold War* (New York: Norton, 1979). This is more stridently argued in James Aronson, *The Press and the Cold War*, rev. ed. (New York: Monthly Review, 1990). See also Louis Liebovich, *The Press and the Origins of the Cold War, 1944–1947* (New York: Praeger, 1988), and Richard H. Pells, *The Liberal Mind in a Conservative Age: American Intellectuals in the 1940s and 1950s*, 2d ed. (Middletown, Conn.: Wesleyan UP, 1989).

On radio's readjustment to peace, see Barnouw's *The Golden Web* and William S. Paley, *As It Happened: A Memoir* (Garden City, N.Y.: Doubleday, 1979). Paul W. White's *News on the Air* is telling regarding changes in radio news programming. See, too, the FCC's "Blue Book," *Public Service Responsibility of Broadcast Licenses* (Washington, D.C., 1946), and Charles A. Siepmann, *Radio's Second Chance* (Boston: Atlantic, Little, Brown, 1946).

Much of the research on postwar Hollywood has concentrated on the House Un-American Activities Committee's inquiry into the movie colony. The best study is Larry Ceplair and Steven Englund, *The Inquisition in Hollywood: Politics in the Film Community, 1930–1960* (Garden City, N.Y.: Doubleday, 1980). Victor Navasky's *Naming Names* (New York: Viking, 1980) defends the Hollywood Stalinists. Challenges to this revisionism include Richard Schickel, "Return of the Hollywood Ten," *Film Comment* 17 (March–April 1981): 11–17. A balanced analysis is Stephen J. Whitfield, *The Culture of the Cold War* (Baltimore: Johns Hopkins UP, 1991).

The effects of the Red Scare on Hollywood are especially well conveyed in Kenneth Hey, "Ambivalence as a Theme in *On the Waterfront*: An Interdisciplinary Approach to Film," *American Quarterly* 31 (Winter 1979): 666–96; Michael Rogin, "Kiss Me Deadly: Communism, Motherhood, and Cold War Movies," *Representations* 6 (Spring 1984): 1–36; Nora Sayre, *Running Time: Films of the Cold War* (New York: Dial Press, 1982); and Paul J. Vanderwood, "An American Cold Warrior: *Viva Zapata!*" in *American History / American Film*, ed. John E. O'Connor and Martin A. Jackson (New York: Ungar, 1979), 183–201.

On the coming of television, Leo Bogart, *The Age of Television*, 3d ed. (New York: Ungar, 1972), summarizes the first research on TV's influence, as does Thomas E. Coffin, "Television's Impact on Society," *American Psychologist* 10 (October 1955): 630–41. See also Cunningham & Walsh, Inc., *The First Decade of Television in Videotown, 1948–1957* (New York, 1957), a review of TV's effects in New Brunswick, New Jersey. Joseph Goulden, *The Best Years, 1945–1950* (New York: Atheneum, 1976), recalls the coming of television to a small Louisiana town. A stimulating study of early TV imagery in advertising and television programming is Lynn Spigel, "Installing the Television Set: Popular Discourses on Television and Domestic Space, 1948–1955," *Camera Obscura* 16 (1988): 11–47.

The diffusion of television and the station allocation problem are reviewed in Lawrence Lessing, "The Television Freeze," *Fortune*, November 1949, 123–27, and John M. Kittross, *Television Frequency Allocation Policy in the United States* (New York: Arno, 1979). Chicago's brief moment as a production center is summarized in Joel Sternberg, "Television Town," *Chicago History* 4 (Summer 1975): 108–17. See also Harriet Van Horne, "The Chicago Touch," *Theatre Arts* 35 (July 1951): 36–39.

Arthur Frank Wertheim, "The Rise and Fall of Milton Berle," in *American History / American Television*, ed. John E. O'Connor (New York: Ungar, 1983), 55–78, ably uses Berle's career to describe changes in the medium and its audience. Berle's celebrity at a Pacific Coast League game is recounted in Louis Cowan's 1967 memoir in the Oral History Collection of Columbia University, p. 209. Berle and his medium are frequently abused in Groucho Marx, *The Groucho Letters: Letters From and To Groucho Marx* (New York: Simon & Schuster, 1967), which includes the caustic assessments of Goodman Ace and Fred Allen.

On advertisers and the newest medium, Charles Winick, *Taste and the Censor in Television* (New York: Fund for the Republic, 1959), is the best source on sponsor interference in programming in the 1950s. Vance Packard's *The Hidden Persuaders* (New York: David McKay, 1957) is more hysterical.

Histories of television in the fifties, notably Erik Barnouw, *The Image Empire* (New York: Oxford UP, 1970), and Max Wilk, *The Golden Age of Television* (New York: Delta, 1976), bemoan the passing of a golden age. A thoughtful reconsideration is William Boddy, *Fifties Television: The*

Industry and Its Critics (Urbana: U of Illinois P, 1990). In "Television in the Golden Age: An Entrepreneurial Experiment," *Historian* 47 (February 1985): 175–95, I essentially accept the nostalgic view but suggest that economic circumstances, and not managerial high-mindedness, explained the medium's early programming. The best work on TV's first great innovator, Sylvester L. Weaver, Jr., of NBC, is Vance Kepley, Jr., "The Weaver Years at NBC," *Wide Angle* 12 (1990): 46–63. Weaver was profiled by Thomas Whiteside in the *New Yorker*, 16 and 23 October 1954.

Judy Fireman, ed., *TV Book: The Ultimate Television Book* (New York: Workman, 1977), contains the recollections of many survivors. See also John Crosby, "It Was New and We Were Very Innocent," *TV Guide*, 22 September 1973, 5–8. Kenneth Hey, "*Marty:* Aesthetics vs. Medium in Early Television Drama," in *American History / American Television*, ed. John E. O'Connor, 95–133, is outstanding on TV drama in the fifties.

Most of the work on TV news in the 1950s is of marginal value and has focused too exclusively on CBS and Murrow. The autobiography of his coproducer, Fred W. Friendly, *Due to Circumstances Beyond Our Control* (New York: Random House, 1967), is among the best of several by former CBS newspeople. See also Sperber, *Murrow;* Alexander Kendrick, *Prime Time: The Life of Edward R. Murrow* (Boston: Little, Brown, 1969); and Joseph E. Persico, *Edward R. Murrow: An American Original* (New York: McGraw-Hill, 1988). Although it generated much contemporary comment, the televising of the Kefauver and McCarthy hearings has yet to command a careful reexamination. Rod Steiger's remarks on McCarthy appear in his 1959 oral history, in the Popular Arts Project at Columbia University, p. 684. See also John Steinbeck, "How to Tell the Good Guys from the Bad Guys," *Reporter* 12 (10 March 1955): 42–44.

On political advertising the standard work is Kathleen Hall Jamieson's seed catalog, *Packaging the Presidency: A History and Criticism of Presidential Campaign Advertising* (New York: Oxford UP, 1984). See also Edwin Diamond and Stephen Bates, *The Spot—The Rise of Political Advertising on Television* (Cambridge, Mass.: MIT Press, 1984). Herbert A. Simon and Frederick Stern, "The Effect of Television upon Voting Behavior in Iowa in the 1952 Presidential Election," *American Political Science Review* 49 (June 1955): 470–77, suggested that television ads had no appreciable influence. Far more unsettling is a preliminary analysis of TV news coverage, Kurt Lang and Gladys Engel Lang, "The Unique Perspective of Television and Its Effect: A Pilot Study," *American Sociological Review* 18 (February 1953): 3–12.

Chapter 4. The War for Attention: Responding to Television, 1947–1958

The presentation of James N. Rosse and James Dertouzos in the Federal Trade Commission's 1978 symposium on the mass media includes data on newspapers' share of national advertising. Ben H. Bagdikian claims, in *The Effete Conspiracy and Other Crimes by the Press* (New York: Harper & Row, 1972), that advertising and not news consumed most of the pages added to dailies between 1940 and 1965. Harvey J. Levin, *Broadcast Regulation and Joint Ownership of Media* (New York: New York UP, 1960), describes newspapers' acquisition of TV properties.

In *The Information Empire: The Rise of the Los Angeles Times and the Times Mirror Corporation* (Washington, D.C.: UP of America, 1981), Jack Hart tells of Norman Chandler's costly gamble on the *Los Angeles Mirror*. The best history of the *Washington Post* is Chalmers M. Roberts, *In the Shadow of Power: The Story of the Washington Post* (Cabin John, Md.: Seven Locks Press, 1989). On John Knight and his papers in the 1950s, in addition to Charles Whited's biography, see Frank Angelo, *On Guard: A History of the Detroit Free Press* (Detroit: Free Press, 1981). Turner Catledge's autobiography, *My Life and the Times* (New York: Harper & Row, 1971), is very helpful.

On the press's generally deferential attitude toward government in the fifties, see James Boylan, "Declarations of Independence," *Columbia Journalism Review* 25 (November–December 1986): 30–45. Edwin R. Bayley, *Joe McCarthy and the Press* (Madison: U of Wisconsin P, 1981), the only book-length treatment of the senator's press, is uneven. More systematic is Gerald J. Baldasty and Betty Houchin Winfield, "Institutional Paralysis in the Press: The Cold War in Washington State," *Journalism Quarterly* 48 (Summer 1979): 273–78, 285. On the press and the Sputnik hysteria, see Walter A. McDougall, *The Heavens and the Earth: A Political History of the Space Age* (New York: Basic Books, 1985).

Changes in American popular music and the rise of rock 'n' roll have inspired an impressive literature. Among academics, it began with David Riesman's famous essay, "Listening to Popular Music," in *Individualism Reconsidered and Other Essays* (New York: Free Press, 1954), 183–93; see also his interview in *U.S. News & World Report*, 24 February 1964, 88. Two histories, Carl Belz, *The Story of Rock*, 2d ed. (New York: Oxford UP, 1972), and Charlie Gillett, *The Sound of the City: The Rise of Rock and Roll*, rev. ed. (New York: Pantheon, 1983), are also well worth examining, as are several excellent collections, including Jonathan Eisen, ed., *The Age of Rock: Sounds of the American Cultural Revolution*

(New York: Random House, 1969), and R. Serge Denisoff and Richard A. Peterson, eds., *The Sounds of Social Change: Studies in Popular Culture* (Chicago: Rand McNally, 1972). Much of this material is summarized in R. Serge Denisoff, *Solid Gold: The Popular Record Industry* (New Brunswick, N.J.: Transaction Books, 1975). An able sociological analysis is Simon Frith, *Sociology of Pop* (London: Constable, 1978). Richard A. Peterson and David G. Berger, "Three Eras in the Manufacture of Popular Music Lyrics," in Denisoff and Peterson, is especially helpful. See also James T. Carey, "Changing Courtship Patterns in Popular Song," *American Journal of Sociology* 6 (May 1969): 720–31.

Other important studies include S. I. Hayakawa, "Popular Song vs. the Facts of Life," *Etc.: A General Review of Semantics* 12 (Winter 1955): 83–95; Greil Marcus, *Mystery Train: The Image of America in Rock 'n' Roll Music* (New York: E. P. Dutton, 1975); and Richard A. Peterson and David G. Berger, "Cycles in Symbol Production: The Case of Popular Music," *American Sociological Review* 40 (April 1975): 158–73. The hit lists of different rock performers are compiled in Joel Whitburn, *The Billboard Book of Top 40 Hits, 1955 to Present* (New York: Billboard Publications, 1983).

Several semiautobiographical histories of the era, including Todd Gitlin, *The Sixties: Years of Hope, Days of Rage* (New York: Bantam Books, 1987), Jeffrey Hart, *When the Going Was Good! American Life in the Fifties* (New York: Crown, 1982), and Douglas T. Miller and Marion Nowak, *The Fifties: The Way We Really Were* (Garden City, N.Y.: Doubleday, 1977), discuss the advent of rock 'n' roll. On the new teenager of the fifties, see James S. Coleman, *The Adolescent Society: The Social Life of the Teenager and Its Impact on Education* (New York: Free Press, 1961); James Gilbert, *A Cycle of Outrage: America's Reaction to the Juvenile Delinquent in the 1950s* (New York: Oxford UP, 1986); and Dwight Macdonald, "Profiles: A Caste, A Culture, A Market," *New Yorker*, 24 and 29 November 1958.

On Hollywood's shrinking audience, see Frederic Stuart, "The Effects of Television on the Motion Picture Industry: 1945–1960," in *The American Movie Industry: The Business of Motion Pictures*, ed. Stuart Kindem (Carbondale: Southern Illinois UP, 1982), 257–407; and Douglas Gomery, "The Coming of Television and the 'Lost' Motion Picture Audience," *Journal of Film and Video* 38 (Summer 1985): 5–11. Sterling and Haight, *The Mass Media*, gives annual compilations of drive-ins and other exhibitors, while Jowett, *Film*, lists total annual weekly attendance.

On the effects of the Paramount case, see Michael Conant, *Antitrust Problems in the Motion Picture Industry* (Berkeley: U of California P, 1960).

Subsequent changes in structure and marketing are explored in Balio's *United Artists*, and Freeman Lincoln, "The Comeback of the Movies," *Fortune*, February 1955, 127–31, 155–56, 158.

Although they offer conflicting interpretations of the postwar film, both Seldes, *The Great Audience*, and Siegfried Kracauer, "Those Movies With a Message," *Harper's*, June 1948, 567–72, suggest that content discouraged some theater patrons. Michael Wood, *America in the Movies* (New York: Basic Books, 1975), and Benita Eisler, *Private Lives: Men and Women of the Fifties* (New York: Franklin Watts, 1986), comment on different aspects of the mid-fifties films. Gilbert, *Cycle of Outrage*, and Thomas Doherty, *Teenagers and Teenpics: The Juvenilization of American Movies in the 1950s* (Boston: Unwin Hyman, 1988), are excellent on the new adolescent film.

Hollywood's relations to television in the fifties are being reconsidered by historians. See especially Boddy, *Fifties Television*; a forthcoming study by R. Christopher Anderson; and Balio, *Hollywood in the Age of Television*. On "I Love Lucy," the first successful Hollywood-made series, see Bart Andrews, *The Story of "I Love Lucy"* (New York: Popular Library, 1976).

Chapter 5. Evenings of Avoidance: Television in the 1960s

On the size of the television audience and the number of hours Americans watched TV, see Robert T. Bower, *The Changing Television Audience in America* (New York: Columbia UP, 1985). See also George Comstock et al., *Television and Human Behavior* (New York: Columbia UP, 1978), and Gary A. Steiner, *The People Look at Television: A Study of Audience Attitudes* (New York: Knopf, 1963).

The American elite's frustration over television and its regulation is reviewed in my *Television's Guardians: The Federal Communications Commission and the Politics of Programming, 1958–1967* (Knoxville: U of Tennessee P, 1985). The best account of the quiz show scandals is Kent Anderson, *Television Fraud: The History and Implications of the Quiz Show Scandals* (Westport, Conn.: Greenwood, 1978). See also Richard S. Tedlow, "Intellect on Television: The Quiz Show Scandals of the 1950s," *American Quarterly* 28 (Fall 1976): 483–95. One concession to the critics, televising the 1960 presidential debates, is analyzed in Sidney Kraus, ed., *The Great Debates: Background—Perspective—Effects* (Bloomington: Indiana UP, 1962).

On TV news generally, Friendly, *Due to Circumstances Beyond Our Control*, and William Small, *To Kill a Messenger: Television News and the Real World* (New York: Hastings House, 1970), are helpful on CBS.

William Whitworth's profile of Huntley and Brinkley, "An Accident of Casting," *New Yorker*, 3 August 1968, 34–60, is invaluable. Robert E. Kintner's three-part *Harper's* series (April–June 1965) is useful, as is NBC newsman Ray Scherer's self-congratulatory "Television News in Washington," in *The Press in Washington*, ed. Ray Eldon Hiebert (New York: Dodd, Mead, & Co., 1966), 95–109. In one of several studies, John P. Robinson, "The Audience for National TV News Programs," *Public Opinion Quarterly* 35 (Autumn 1971): 403–5, suggests that the regular audiences for network newscasts were small. See also Comstock's discussion of TV news audiences in *Television and Human Behavior*.

The best scholarly review of TV news in the late sixties is Edward Jay Epstein's observational study of NBC News, *News from Nowhere: Television and the News* (New York: Random House, 1973). A frank insider's analysis is Robert MacNeil, *The People Machine: The Influence of Television on American Politics* (New York: Harper & Row, 1968). On TV news and the civil rights movement in the sixties consult *Race and the News Media*, ed. Paul L. Fisher and Ralph L. Lowenstein (New York: Praeger, 1967), especially "Television: The Chosen Instrument of the Revolution," by William B. Monroe, Jr.

Arthur Asa Berger, *The TV-Guided American* (New York: Walker & Co., 1976), is provocative on television in the sixties. Among the better works on the TV drama in the early 1960s are David Boroff, "Television and the Problem Play," in *TV as Art: Some Essays in Criticisms*, ed. Patrick D. Hazard (Champaign, Ill.: National Council of Teachers of English, 1966), 97–115; Harris Dienstfrey, "Doctors, Lawyers, & Other TV Heroes," *Commentary* 35 (June 1963): 519–24; Ida Jeter, "Politics in 'The Defenders,' " in *TV Book*, ed. Judy Fireman; and Joseph Turow, *Playing Doctor: Television, Storytelling, and Medical Power* (New York: Oxford UP, 1989).

The networks' growing power over advertisers and producers is documented in FCC, *Second Interim Report by the Office of Network Study: Television Network Program Procurement* (Washington, D.C., 1965), and more plainly in Robert Eck, "The Real Masters of Television," *Harper's*, March 1967, 45–52. On James T. Aubrey of CBS, see Merle Miller and Evan Rhodes, *Only You, Dick Darling! or How to Write One Television Script and Make $50,000,000* (New York: William Sloane Associates, 1964). David Levy's novel *The Chameleons* (New York: Dodd, Mead, 1964) is based on his work with NBC President Kintner and is suggestive on the Dodd hearings on TV violence. More evidence is provided in U.S. Senate, Judiciary Committee, *Investigation of Juvenile Delinquency in the United States: Hearings*, 87th Cong., 1st sess., pt. 10.

Television's tendency to avoid the great convulsions of the decade is observed in Muriel G. Cantor, *The Hollywood TV Producer: His Work and His Audience* (New York: Basic Books, 1971). In *Due to Circumstances Beyond Our Control*, Fred Friendly gives his side of the controversy over CBS's decision to cease airing the 1966 Senate hearings on Vietnam. Bert Spector, "A Clash of Cultures: The Smothers Brothers vs. CBS Television," in *American History / American Television*, ed. John E. O'Connor, 159–83, is a good review of the Smothers brothers' prime-time struggles.

On the TV coverage of the war itself, see Edward Jay Epstein, *Between Fact and Fiction: The Problem of Journalism* (New York: Vintage, 1975), 210–32, and Daniel Hallin, *The "Uncensored War": The Media in Vietnam* (New York: Oxford UP, 1986). Michael Arlen's criticisms of TV coverage are reprinted in *Living-Room War* (New York: Viking Press, 1969) and *The View from Highway 1* (New York: Farrar, Straus, & Giroux, 1976). Peter Braestrup, *Big Story*, abridged ed. (New Haven: Yale UP, 1983), bitterly contends that the Tet offensive was misreported. The possible influence of TV news on President Johnson is best described in Melvin Small, *Johnson, Nixon, and the Doves* (New Brunswick, N.J.: Rutgers UP, 1988).

Chapter 6. Competing for the Marginal: Television's Rivals, 1958–1970

On Vietnam and American newspapers, Peter Braestrup's *Big Story*, chap. 1, notes which dailies had Saigon bureaus. Also see Hallin, *The "Uncensored War"*; Henry Fairlie, "We Knew What We Were Doing When We Went Into Vietnam," *Washington Monthly* 5 (May 1973): 7–26; and Clarence R. Wyatt's extremely valuable study, "'At the Cannon's Mouth': The American Press and the Vietnam War," *Journalism History* 13 (Autumn–Winter 1986): 104–13. Montague Kern, Patricia W. Levering, and Ralph B. Levering, *The Kennedy Crises* (Chapel Hill: U of North Carolina P, 1983), attempts to calculate how different prominent dailies covered and affected the making of American foreign policy. David J. Garrow, *Protest at Selma: Martin Luther King, Jr., and the Voting Rights Act of 1965* (New Haven: Yale UP, 1978), chap. 5, similarly speculates on how coverage of a civil rights protest may have influenced members of Congress. Harrison Salisbury of the *New York Times* remembers his reportage in Birmingham and North Vietnam in *A Time of Change* (New York: Harper & Row, 1988). Hart's *Information Empire* is blunt about the *Los Angeles Times*'s shortcomings in the 1960s, while Bagdikian's *Effete Conspiracy* faults papers for failing to cover state government closely. In

"How Newspapers Use Columnists," *Columbia Journalism Review* 3 (Fall 1964): 20–24, Bagdikian also suggests that editors preferred more conservative seers.

The impact of *Times v. Sullivan* is discussed in Clark R. Mollenhoff, "25 Years of *Times v. Sullivan*," *Quill* 77 (March 1989): 27–31, and F. Dennis Hale, "Impact Analysis of the Law Concerning Freedom of Expression," *Communications and the Law* 8 (August 1986): 35–50.

Sterling and Haight, *The Mass Media*, provides statistics on the percentage of newspapers that were owned by groups. The effects of monopoly newspapers are analyzed in Gerald L. Grotta, "Consolidation of Newspapers: What Happens to the Consumer?" *Journalism Quarterly* 48 (Summer 1971): 245–52. On the effects of JOAs, see Robert C. Picard, "Pricing Behavior of Newspapers," in Picard et al., *Press Concentration and Monopoly: New Perspectives on Newspaper Ownership and Operation* (Norwood, N.J.: Ablex, 1988), 55–69. Jean-Louis Servan-Schreiber, *The Power to Inform: Media: The Information Business* (New York: McGraw-Hill, 1974), is the assessment of a French publisher.

On the "new journalism" of the sixties, Tom Wolfe, *The New Journalism* (New York: Harper & Row, 1973), is an instant and occasionally egoistic history. See also Michael Arlen, "Notes on the New Journalism," *Atlantic*, May 1972, 43–47; Kluger, *The Paper*; Jack Newfield, *Bread and Roses Too* (New York: E. P. Dutton, 1971), chap. 5; and Norman Sims, ed., *Literary Journalism in the Twentieth Century* (New York: Oxford UP, 1990).

Most studies of magazines in the 1960s focus on the crises facing the mass circulation periodicals such as *Life*. See, e.g., A. J. van Zuilen, *The Life Cycle of Magazines* (Uithoorn, Holland: Graduate Press, 1977). Chris Welles, "Can Mass Magazines Survive?" *Columbia Journalism Review* 10 (July–August 1971): 7–14, is an excellent summary. See also Stephen Holder, "The Death of *The Saturday Evening Post*, 1960–1969," in *New Dimensions in Popular Culture*, ed. Russell B. Nye (Bowling Green, Ohio: Bowling Green UP, 1969), 78–89. *Life*'s demise is analyzed in Magnus Linklater, "Death of *Life*," *London Sunday Times Magazine*, 11 February 1973, 39–46; Curtis Prendergast, *The World of Time Inc.* (New York: Atheneum, 1986); Loudon Wainwright, *The Great American Magazine: An Inside History of Life* (New York: Knopf, 1986); and Chris Welles, "Lessons from *Life*," *Saturday Review*, 13 February 1973, 20–23.

On radio in the sixties, Eugene S. Foster, *Understanding Broadcasting* (Reading, Mass.: Addison-Wesley, 1978), is a helpful text. See also Christopher H. Sterling, "Decade of Development: FM Radio in the 1960s," *Journalism Quarterly* 48 (Summer 1971): 222–30.

Most histories of rock 'n' roll in the sixties tie changes in the radio industry to the evolution of rock. See especially Belz, *The Story of Rock,* and Gillett, *The Sound of the City,* as well as James M. Curtis, "Toward a Sociotechnological Interpretation of Popular Music in the Electronic Age," *Technology and Culture* 25 (January 1984): 91–102. Analyses by Peterson and Berger and James T. Carey, cited for chapter 5, are also very helpful for the sixties, as is Ed Ward, Geoffrey Stokes, and Ken Tucker, *Rock of Ages: The Rolling Stone History of Rock & Roll* (Englewood Cliffs, N.J.: Prentice-Hall, 1986). See also David Manning White, ed., *Pop Culture in America* (Chicago: Quadrangle Books, 1970), pt. 4. John P. Robinson and Paul M. Hirsch, "Teenage Response to Rock and Roll Protest Songs," reprinted in *The Sounds of Social Change,* ed. Denisoff and Peterson, 222–31, and Paul M. Hirsch, "Sociological Approaches to the Pop Music Phenomenon," *American Behavioral Scientist* 14 (January–February 1971): 371–88, suggest that rock music had little influence on the adolescent audience. Denisoff, *Solid Gold,* offers the best summary of Top 40 radio's birth and impact. On country music and its audience see Richard A. Peterson and Paul DiMaggio, "From Region to Class, the Changing Locus of Country Music: A Test of the Massification Hypothesis," *Social Forces* 53 (March 1975): 497–506. James T. Carey also discusses country music.

The best treatment of the Beatles is Philip Norman, *Shout! The Beatles in Their Generation* (New York: Simon & Schuster, 1981). See also Pete Hamill, "The Death and Life of John Lennon," *New York Magazine,* 22 December 1980, 38–50, which stresses American influences on Lennon. Albert Goldman's hateful biography of Lennon, *The Lives of John Lennon* (New York: Morrow, 1988), unintentionally inspired some impressive commentaries on the Beatles, especially Louis Menand, "Lives of the Saints," *New Republic,* 31 October 1988, 30–35.

On Hollywood in the 1960s, Jowett, *Film,* and the essays by Robert Gustafson and David J. Londoner in Balio's *American Film Industry* are helpful, as is Charles Champlin, "Can TV Save the Films?" *Saturday Review,* 24 December 1966, 11–13. The changing film audience is reviewed in Leo Bogart, "The Return of Hollywood's Mass Audience: How a Social Institution Adapts to Technological Change," in *Surveying Social Life,* ed. Hubert J. O'Gorman (Middletown, Conn.: Wesleyan UP, 1988), and John Izod, *Hollywood and the Box Office* (New York: Columbia UP, 1988).

Chapter 7. Network Television Triumphant, 1970–1981

Les Brown, *Television: The Business behind the Box* (New York: Harcourt, Brace, Jovanovich, 1971), and Martin Mayer, *About Television* (New York:

Harper & Row, 1972), are valuable accounts of TV in the early 1970s. Sally Bedell wrote an excellent instant history, *Up the Tube: Prime-Time TV and the Silverman Years* (New York: Viking, 1981). See also Todd Gitlin, *Inside Prime Time* (New York: Pantheon, 1985); Horace Newcomb, *TV, the Most Popular Art* (Garden City, N.Y.: Anchor, 1974); and Robert Sklar, *Prime-Time America: Life on and behind the Television Screen* (New York: Oxford UP, 1980). Newcomb and Robert S. Alley conducted revealing interviews in *The Producer's Medium: Conversations with Creators of American TV* (New York: Oxford UP, 1983). *TV Guide* carried many useful features about television in the decade, some of which are reprinted in Barry Cole, ed., *Television Today: A Close-Up View* (New York: Oxford UP, 1981). On "All in the Family," Richard P. Adler edited an excellent collection of criticisms and research, *All in the Family: A Critical Appraisal* (New York: Praeger, 1979). Jane Feuer, Paul Kerr, and Tise Vahimagi, eds., *MTM: "Quality Television"* (London: British Film Institute, 1984), is a good history of a major program producer. Objections to TV's more explicit violence and sexuality are described in Geoffrey Cowan's superb *See No Evil: The Backstage Battle over Sex and Violence on Television* (New York: Simon & Schuster, 1979). See also Barry Cole and Mal Ottinger, *Reluctant Regulators: The FCC and the Broadcasting Audience* (Reading, Mass.: Addison-Wesley, 1978).

On TV evening news programs in the seventies, see Herbert S. Gans, *Deciding What's News: A Study of CBS Evening News, NBC Nightly News, Newsweek and Time* (New York: Pantheon, 1979), a critical observational study. Barbara Matusow, *The Evening Stars: The Making of Network News Anchors* (Boston: Houghton Mifflin, 1983), is the best history. Michael J. Robinson and Margaret A. Sheehan, *Over the Wire and On TV: CBS and UPI in Campaign '80* (New York: Russell Sage, 1983), is an intriguing comparative analysis. Dan Nimmo and James E. Combs, *Nightly Horrors: Crisis Coverage in Television Network News* (Knoxville: U of Tennessee P, 1985), contrasts the three network news divisions' handling of crises.

The relatively small congregations for the nightly network news programs are noted in Robert L. Stevenson and Kathryn P. White, "The Cumulative Audience of Network Evening News," *Journalism Quarterly* 57 (Autumn 1980): 477–81, and Lawrence W. Lichty, "Video versus Print," *Wilson Quarterly* 6 (Special issue, 1982): 49–57. Policymakers assumed the opposite. See, e.g., Lloyd Cutler, "Foreign Policy on Deadline," *Foreign Policy*, no. 56 (Fall 1984): 113–28. A clear review of research on citizens' use of the news media during campaigns, which also includes a survey of Alabama voters, is Margaret K. Latimer, "The

Floating Voter and the Media," *Journalism Quarterly* 64 (Winter 1987): 805–12, 819.

On TV and Watergate, see James A. Capo, "Network Watergate Coverage Patterns in Late 1972 and Early 1973," ibid., 60 (Winter 1983): 595–602; Gladys Engel Lang and Kurt Lang, *The Battle for Public Opinion: The President, the Press, and the Polls during Watergate* (New York: Columbia UP, 1983); and Lawrence W. Lichty, "Watergate, the Evening News, and the 1972 Election," in *American History / American Television*, ed. John O'Connor, 232–55.

On local TV news, Jeff Greenfield, "Making TV News Pay," *Gannett Center Journal* 1 (Spring 1987): 21–39, is a good overview. See also William T. Gormley, "Television Coverage of State Government," *Public Opinion Quarterly* 42 (Fall 1978): 354–59, and Mary Ellen Leary, "California 1974: The Browning of Campaign Coverage," *Columbia Journalism Review* 15 (July–August 1976): 18–21.

On TV news documentaries in the 1970s, see Charles Montgomery Hammond, Jr., *The Image Decade: Television Documentary, 1965–1975* (New York: Hastings, 1981). See also Garth S. Jowett, "*The Selling of the Pentagon:* Television Confronts the First Amendment," in *American History / American Television*, ed. John E. O'Connor, 256–78; Michael J. Robinson, "Public Affairs Television and the Growth of Political Malaise: The Case of 'The Selling of the Pentagon,'" *American Political Science Review* 70 (June 1976): 409–32; and Jimmie N. Rogers and Theodore Clevenger, Jr., "'The Selling of the Pentagon': Was CBS the Fulbright Propaganda Machine?" *Quarterly Journal of Speech* 57 (October 1971): 266–73.

In "Television and American Politics: 1956–1976," *The Public Interest*, no. 48 (Summer 1977): 3–39, and "The Impact of the Watergate Hearings," *Journal of Communication* 24 (Spring 1974): 17–30, and elsewhere, Michael J. Robinson accused network newscasters of fostering a "videomalaise." Other studies undermine this thesis, notably Jack M. McLeod et al., "Decline and Fall at the White House: A Longitudinal Analysis of Communication Effects," *Communication Research* 4 (January 1977): 3–22. See also David O. Sears and Steven H. Chaffee, "Uses and Effects of the 1976 Debates: An Overview of Empirical Studies," in *The Great Debates: Carter vs. Ford, 1976*, ed. Sidney Kraus (Bloomington: Indiana UP, 1979), 223–61. Alan Ware discounts the role of TV in *The Breakdown of Democratic Party Political Organization, 1940–1980* (Oxford: Clarendon, 1985), case studies of four party organizations in postwar America. Lessening partisanship and interest in voting, Michael E. McGerr, *The Decline of Popular Politics: The American North, 1865–1928*

(New York: Oxford UP, 1986), persuasively argues, came well before television.

Alternatives to television emerged in the late seventies. The condition of public broadcasting is diagnosed in Carnegie Commission on the Future of Public Broadcasting, *A Public Trust* (New York: Bantam Books, 1979); Stephen Chapman, "Down the Public Television," *Harper's*, August 1979, 77–80; Benjamin DeMott, "The Trouble with Public Television," *Atlantic*, February 1979, 42–47. On cable television, see Thomas Whiteside, "Cable," *New Yorker*, 20 May 1985, 27 May 1985, and 3 June 1985, and Don Le Duc, *Cable Television and the FCC: A Crisis in Media Control* (Philadelphia: Temple UP, 1973).

Chapter 8. The Babel Builders: Television's Rivals, 1970–1990

An early history of the fourth estate's duels with the Nixon administration is William E. Porter, *Assault on the Media* (Ann Arbor: U of Michigan P, 1976). Sanford J. Ungar, *The Papers and the Papers* (New York: Columbia UP, 1989), is the best account of the Pentagon Papers case. See also Harrison E. Salisbury, *Without Fear or Favor: The New York Times and Its Times* (New York: Times Books, 1980). Nixon's mastery of the White House press corps during his reelection campaign is told in Timothy Crouse, *The Boys on the Bus* (New York: Ballantine Books, 1973). See also Ben H. Bagdikian, "The Fruits of Agnewism," *Columbia Journalism Review* 11 (January–February 1973): 9–21.

On the reporting of the Watergate affair, Edward Jay Epstein's skeptical view, "Did the Press Uncover Watergate?" in *Between Fact and Fiction: The Problem of Journalism* (New York: Vintage Books, 1975), 19–32, should be consulted. Stanley I. Kutler, *The Wars of Watergate: The Last Crisis of Richard Nixon* (New York: Knopf, 1990), is the definitive account that, like Epstein's, gives the press little credit. Far more heroic assessments appeared in *Columbia Journalism Review* 12 (July–August 1973): 8–22 and 13 (July–August 1974): 10–15.

The best review of public opinion and Watergate is Lang and Lang, *The Battle for Public Opinion*. The extent to which the public initially ignored the story, despite heavy coverage in some dailies, is suggested in Jack M. McLeod, Lee B. Becker, and James E. Byrnes, "Another Look at the Agenda-Setting Function of the Press," *Communication Research* 1 (April 1974): 131–66. See also Steven H. Chaffee and Lee B. Becker, "Young Voters' Reactions to Early Watergate Issues," *American Politics Quarterly* 3 (October 1975): 360–85, and the special issue of *Communication Research* 1 (October 1974).

In the wake of Watergate, some political scientists worried that the press had acquired too much power and had made governing America a virtual impossibility. See Samuel P. Huntington, "The Democratic Distemper," *Public Interest*, no. 41 (Fall 1975): 9–38, and Paul H. Weaver, "The New Journalism and the Old—Thoughts after Watergate," ibid., no. 35 (Spring 1974): 67–88. Such analyses often borrowed from Daniel Patrick Moynihan, "The Presidency and the Press," *Commentary* 51 (March 1971): 41–52.

Other work dispelled the notion of the press as a truly independent or critical force in American politics. Michael Baruch Grossman and Martha Joynt Kumar, *Portraying the News Media* (Baltimore: Johns Hopkins UP, 1981), fails to find journalists becoming more critical of presidents. Nor does Mark Hertsgaard, *On Bended Knee: The Press and the Reagan Presidency* (New York: Farrar, Straus & Giroux, 1988). In "All the Congressmen's Men," *Harper's*, July 1989, 55–63, Walter Karp argued that correspondents had become the advance agents of congressional, rather than presidential, opinion. On journalists' heavy reliance on official sources generally, see Leon V. Sigal, *Reporters and Officials: The Organization and Politics of Newsmaking* (Lexington, Mass.: D. C. Heath, 1973). Thoughtful in-house criticisms include David Broder, *Behind the Front Page: A Candid Look at How the News Is Made* (New York: Simon & Schuster, 1987); Joseph Kraft, "The Imperial Media," *Commentary* 71 (May 1981): 36–47; and Tom Wicker, *On Press* (New York: Viking, 1978).

The background and ideology of American journalists were surveyed in two helpful studies, John W. C. Johnstone, Edward J. Slawski, and William W. Bowman, *The News People: A Sociological Portrait of American Journalists and Their Work* (Urbana: U of Illinois P, 1976), and David H. Weaver and G. Cleveland Wilhoit, *The American Journalist: A Portrait of U.S. News People and Their Work* (Bloomington: Indiana UP, 1986).

Less work is available on the smaller dailies of the seventies and eighties. Clarice N. Olien, George A. Donohue, and Phillip J. Tichenor have conducted numerous studies of the press in smaller towns, including "The Community Editor's Power and Reporting of Conflict," *Journalism Quarterly* 45 (Summer 1968): 243–52. Peter Clarke and Susan H. Evans review such papers' handling of the 1978 election in *Covering Campaigns: Journalism in Congressional Elections* (Stanford: Stanford UP, 1983).

On newspaper economics in the seventies, see James N. Rosse, "The Decline of Direct Newspaper Competition," *Journal of Communication* 30 (Spring 1980): 65–71. Helpful too are John C. Busterna, "Trends in Daily Newspaper Ownership," *Journalism Quarterly* 65 (Winter 1988): 831–88; and Stephen Lacy et al., "The Impact of Central City Newspaper Market Structure on Suburban Newspaper Existence and Circulation," ibid., 65 (Fall 1988): 726–32.

Several works suggest that those who lived in two-newspaper towns had a higher political awareness than those served by only one daily. TV news did not help. See Steven H. Chaffee and Donna G. Wilson, "Media Rich, Media Poor: Two Studies of Diversity in Agenda-Holding," *Journalism Quarterly* 54 (Autumn 1977): 466–76, and Peter Clarke and Eric Fredin, "Newspapers, Television, and Political Reasoning," *Public Opinion Quarterly* 42 (Summer 1978): 143–60.

The possible effects of absentee-ownership in different communities are skillfully tested in Theodore L. Glasser, David S. Allen, and S. Elizabeth Blanks, "The Influence of Chain Ownership on News Play: A Case Study," *Journalism Quarterly* 66 (Autumn 1989): 607–14. Kay Lazar, in "Provincial Profits," *News Inc.* 2 (March 1990): 20–25, assails the Thomson Group.

The best single study of recent circulation trends is Leo Bogart, *Press and Public: Who Reads What, When, Where, and Why in American Newspapers*, 2d ed. (Hillsdale, N.J.: Lawrence Erlbaum Associates, 1989). See also William B. Blankenburg, "Unbundling the Newspaper," in a collection to be edited by Lawrence W. Lichty; and the Times Mirror Center for the People and the Press, "The American Media: Who Reads, Who Watches, Who Cares" (Washington, D.C.: Times Mirror Center, 1990).

On the magazine industry, the expansion of special-interest publications is best summarized in Benjamin M. Compaine, "The Magazine Industry: Developing the Special Interest Audience," *Journal of Communication* 30 (Spring 1980): 98–103. Regarding the newsmagazines in the seventies and eighties, David Shaw's two-part *Los Angeles Times* feature, 1 and 3 May 1980, is a fine survey. See also Gans, *Deciding What's News*.

The best history of rock music in the seventies and early eighties is Ken Tucker's third of Ward et al., *Rock of Ages*. Richard A. Peterson, "Disco," *Chronicle of Higher Education*, 2 October 1978, R26–R27, overestimates disco's staying power but is otherwise a good summary of a controversial trend in popular music. MTV and music videos are harshly analyzed in Steven Levy, "Ad Nauseam," *Rolling Stone*, 8 December 1983, 30–31, 33–34. Rock's greater effects on young listeners is suggested in John P. Robinson, "Long-Term Information and Media Usage," in Robinson and Mark R. Levy, *The Main Source: Learning from Television News* (Beverly Hills: Sage, 1986), 57–85.

On the film industry generally, Timothy Noah, "Valley of the Duds," *Washington Monthly* 17 (October 1985): 13–21, 41, is unrelentingly critical. See also David Denby, "Can the Movies Be Saved?" *New York Magazine*, 21 July 1986, 24–35; Pauline Kael, "Why Are Movies So Bad? or, The Numbers," *New Yorker*, 23 June 1980, 82, 85–93. On TV movies in the seventies and eighties, Laurie Schultze, "The Made-for-TV Movie," in *Hollywood in the Age of Television*, ed. Tino Balio, 351–76, is the best single reference.

On the audience for films in the seventies and eighties, see Izod, *Hollywood and the Box Office*, and Leo Bogart, "The Return of Hollywood's Mass Audience," in *Surveying Social Life*, ed. Hubert J. O'Gorman, 487–501. Bogart also notes increases in the number of films having an R rating.

Harold Vogel, *Entertainment Industry Economics: A Guide for Financial Analysis*, 2d ed. (Cambridge: Cambridge UP, 1990), is the best economic guide to the colony. Helpful too is "A Survey of the Entertainment Industry," *The Economist*, 23 December 1989, while John Huey, "America's Hottest Export: Pop Culture," *Fortune*, 31 December 1990, notes foreign investors' sudden interest in the studios.

Chapter 9. The Shrinking Mass: Television and Mass Culture in the 1980s

In *Presidential Power: The Politics of Leadership with Reflections on Johnson and Nixon* (New York: John Wiley & Sons, 1976), Richard E. Neustadt notes how ineffectively postwar presidents utilized television. Many commented subsequently on Reagan's mastery of the home screen. For a differing view, see Elliot King and Michael Schudson, "The Myth of the Great Communicator," *Columbia Journalism Review* 26 (November–December 1987): 37–39. Joe S. Foote, "Ratings Decline of Presidential Television," *Journal of Broadcasting and Electronic Media* 32 (Spring 1988): 225–30, discusses cable's splintering of the national forum. VCR data are from Steve Sternberg, "VCRs: A New Medium, a New Message," *Marketing & Media Decisions* 24 (January 1989): 81–84.

For an excellent commentary on TV news in the 1980s, see Mark Crispin Miller, "Prime Time: Deride and Conquer," in *Watching Television*, ed. Todd Gitlin (New York: Pantheon, 1986), 183–228. Lawrence W. Lichty and Douglas Gomery, "Why More and More and More Is Less: The Future of Television News," in a forthcoming collection edited by Lichty, offers audience data on the networks and CNN.

Criticisms of the network news divisions were frequent by the 1980s. Ben H. Bagdikian, *The Media Monopoly*, 3d ed. (Boston: Beacon Press, 1990), and Edward S. Herman and Noam Chomsky, *Manufacturing Consent: The Political Economy of the Mass Media* (New York: Pantheon,

1988), include the broadcast chains in their indictment of the modern mass media.

On audiences' inattentiveness to TV news, see Robinson and Levy, *Main Source*, and Barrie Gunter, *Poor Reception: Misunderstanding and Forgetting Broadcast News* (Hillsdale, N.J.: Lawrence Erlbaum Associates, 1987). That Americans have less time to stay informed is disputed in John P. Robinson, "Time's Up," *American Demographics*, July 1989, 33–35.

Chapter 10. No Countervailing Motives, 1991–1996

Critiques of journalism in the 1990s have readily found publishers. Among the most prominent or simply insightful are James Fallows, *Breaking the News: How the Media Undermine American Democracy* (New York: Pantheon, 1996); Stephen Klaidman, "All the News That's Fit to Interpret," *Forbes Media Critic* 1 (Summer 1994): 56–63; Howard Kurtz, *Media Circus: The Trouble with America's Newspapers* (New York: Times Books, 1993); Philip Meyer, "Learning to Love Lower Profits," *American Journalism Review* 17 (December 1995): 40–44; Thomas E. Patterson, *Out of Order* (New York: Knopf, 1993); Larry Sabato, *Feeding Frenzy* (New York: Free Press, 1991); David Shaw, "Surrender of the Gatekeepers," *Nieman Reports* 48 (Spring 1994): 3–5; Steven Stark, "Where the Boys Are," *Atlantic* 274 (September 1994): 18, 20–21; Paul Starobin, "A Generation of Vipers," *Columbia Journalism Review* 33 (March–April 1995): 25–32. See also Adam Gopnik's brilliant review of much of this literature, "Read All About It," *New Yorker*, 12 December 1994, 84–90; David Remnick, "Scoop," ibid., 29 January 1996, 38–42; and Michael Schudson, *The Power of News* (Cambridge, Mass.: Harvard UP, 1995).

W. Russell Newman, *The Future of the Mass Audience* (New York: Cambridge UP, 1991), has informed many discussions; Newman believes fears of fragmentation are exaggerated. Ken Auletta, *Three Blind Mice: How the TV Networks Lost Their Way* (New York: Random House, 1991), is an exhaustive and thesis-barren recounting of the changes in the network ownership in the 1980s. Auletta, who has unrivaled access to the upper echelons of the entertainment industry, frequently contributes hyper-detailed updates in the *New Yorker*. For a rousing defense of the 1990s network TV drama, see Charles McGrath, "The Triumph of the Prime-Time Novel," *New York Times Magazine*, 22 October 1995, 52–59. On the feminization of the network television audience, see Paul Farhi, "In Prime Time, It's She-TV," *Washington Post National Weekly Edition*, 20 November, 1995, 11, and John Powers, "The Crying Games," *Boston Globe Magazine*, 30 January 1994, 8. Powers describes CBS's feminization of coverage of the Winter Olympics. On television news, see Daniel Hallin, *We're Keeping America on Top of the World: Television Journalism and the Public Sphere* (London: Routledge, 1994); Shanto Iyengar, *Is Anyone Responsible? How Television Frames Political Issues* (Chicago: U of Chicago P, 1991); Phyllis Kaniss, *Making Local News* (Chicago: U of Chicago P, 1991); W. Russell Neuman, Marion R. Just and Ann N. Crigler, *Common Knowledge: News and the Construction of Political Meaning* (Chicago: U of Chicago P, 1992).

Tom Rosenstiel of the *Los Angeles Times* has written the best lay examinations of television news, including *Strange Bedfellows: How Television and the Presidential Candidates Changed American Politics, 1992* (New York: Hyperion, 1993), and "The Myth of CNN," *New Republic* 22 and 29 August 1994, 27–28, 30, 32–33. The networks' use of experts during the Gulf War is carefully analyzed in Janet E. Steele, "Enlisting Experts: Objectivity and the Operational Bias in Television News Analysis of the Persian Gulf War," 1992, occasional paper of the Media Studies Project, Woodrow Wilson International Center for Scholars; the networks' 1992 political "ad-watch" series takes a beating in Stephen Ansolabehere and Shanto Iyengar, *Going Negative: How Attack Ads Shrink and Polarize the Electorate* (New York: Free Press, 1995). On the dismal science of the talking furniture, see Bruce M. Owen and Steven S. Wildman, *Video Economics* (Cambridge, Mass.: Harvard UP, 1992).

On the film industry, several recent essays informed my analysis, including Phillip Lopate's chapter in *Dumbing Down: The Strip-Mining of American Culture*, ed. Katharine Washburn and John Thornton (forthcoming), and John H. Richardson, "Dumb and Dumber," *New Republic*, 10 April 1995, 20–23, 26–29.

Significant New Scholarship Not Listed in First Edition

The number of important works on the American mass media since 1941 has expanded enormously since the first edition of this book was completed. These include James L. Aucoin, "The Re-emergence of American Investigative Journalism, 1960–1975," *Journalism History* 21 (Spring 1995): 3–15; David Abrahamson, *Magazine-Made America: The Cultural Transformation of the Postwar Periodical* (Cresskill, N.J.: Hampton, 1995); Joel E. Foreman, ed., *The Other Fifties: Interrogating Midcentury American Icons* (Urbana: U of Illinois P, 1996); Joshua Gamson, *Claims to Fame: Celebrity in Contemporary America* (Berkeley: U of California P, 1994); Carl F. Kaestle et al., *Literacy in the United States: Readers and Reading since 1880* (New Haven: Yale UP, 1991); and Wendy Kozol, *Life's America: Family and Nation in Postwar Photojournalism* (Philadelphia:

Temple UP, 1994). George H. Roeder Jr., *The Censored War: American Visual Experience during World War Two* (New Haven: Yale UP, 1993), is a thoughtful assessment of visual imagery, war, and public opinion. Three very fine studies in film history are Douglas Gomery, *Shared Pleasures: A History of Movie Presentation in the United States* (Madison: U of Wisconsin P, 1992); James M. Skinner, *The Cross and the Cinema: The Legion of Decency and the National Catholic Office for Motion Pictures, 1933–1970* (Westport, Conn.: Praeger, 1993); and Stephen Vaughn, *Ronald Reagan in Hollywood: Movies and Politics* (New York: Cambridge UP, 1994).

More disappointing are two general broadcast histories: Edward Bliss Jr., *Now the News: The Story of Broadcast Journalism* (New York: Columbia UP, 1991), and Robert J. Donovan and Ray Scherer, *Unsilent Revolution: Television News and American Public Life, 1948–1991* (New York: Cambridge UP, 1992). Two vital recent examinations of women and the postwar mass media are Susan J. Douglas, *Where the Girls Are: Growing Up Female with the Mass Media* (New York: Times Books, 1994), and Joanne Meyerowitz, "Beyond the Feminine Mystique: A Reassessment of Postwar Mass Culture," *Journal of American History* 79 (March 1993): 1455–482. Martha Bayles' attempt to transform the story of rock 'n' roll into intellectual history, *Hole in Our Soul: The Loss of Beauty and Meaning in American Popular Music* (New York: Free Press, 1994), is simply preposterous. Much more valuable is Paul D. Lopes, "Innovation and Diversity in the Popular Music Industry," *American Sociological Review* 57 (February 1992): 56–71. My comments, at the end of chapter nine, regarding Americans' spare time, would have benefitted from Juliet B. Schor, *The Overworked American: The Unexpected Decline of Leisure* (New York: Basic Books, 1991).

Work on 1950s television continues to grow. See especially Craig Allen, *Eisenhower and the Mass Media: Peace, Prosperity and Prime-Time TV* (Chapel Hill: U of North Carolina P, 1993); Christopher Anderson, *Hollywood TV: The Studio System in the Fifties* (Austin: U of Texas P, 1994); and Lynn Spigel, *Make Room for TV: Television and the Family Ideal in Postwar America* (Chicago: U of Chicago P, 1992). On the Vietnam war and the press, see Chester J. Pach Jr., "And That's the Way It Was: The Vietnam War on the Network Nightly News," in *The Sixties: From Memory to History*, ed. David Farber (Chapel Hill: U of North Carolina P, 1994), and Clarence Wyatt, *Paper Soldiers: The American Press and the Vietnam War* (New York: W. W. Norton, 1993).

Index

Baughman, James L. 1952–
   The republic of mass culture : journalism, filmmaking, and broadcasting in
America since 1941 / James L. Baughman.—2nd ed.
      p.   cm. — (The American moment)
   Includes bibliographical references and index.
   ISBN 0-8018-5520-9 (alk. paper). — ISBN 0-8018-5521-7 (pbk. : alk. paper)
   1. Mass media—United States—History.   I. Title.   II. Series.
P92.U5B345   1997
302.23'0973—dc20   96-26395
                                                                        CIP